INTERSTELLAR SCOUTS

BIKER DELTA SQUADRON 5-6-5

AND THE POLARIOUS SECTOR ASSAULT

Published in the UK in 2023 by Renegade Rock Star Publishing

Paperback ISBN 978-1-7394305-0-4
eBook ISBN 978-1-7394305-1-1

Edited by Sara Starbuck

Cover design and typeset by SpiffingCovers

INTERSTELLAR SCOUTS

BIKER DELTA SQUADRON 5-6-5

AND THE POLARIOUS SECTOR ASSAULT

MAX ANDERSON-HOPKINS

This book is dedicated to my Mum, Dad and brother who have watched me and this story grow together.

Also to my students, past and present, who have eagerly awaited this book for so long. I really hope you enjoy it as much as I have enjoyed writing it.

Max Anderson-Hopkins.

CHAPTER 1
OLI'S SACRIFICE

The gigantic moss-green and brown Flagship of the Interstellar Scouts' Intergalactic Emergency Response, Rescue and Strike Force; the I.S.S. Scout Hut, finally emerged from its lengthy, perilous passage through the dense fog and hyper-charged lightning storms of the Polarian Nebula, accompanied by a convoy of smaller cruisers and fighter escorts.

The flagship was named in commemoration of the Interstellar Scouts' Earth namesakes, with whom they had shared a common mission at the turn of the millennium alongside the Coastguards, Mountain Rescue and other heroic organisations.

The entire fleet was severely battle-damaged. Isolated parts of the cruisers still exploded with blue, fiery energy and sparks as they trailed wires and cables from the areas where huge chunks had been blasted away during their previous high priority mission just days ago. Their new mission was of equally high priority; to provide relief and recovery aid to the worlds located in the Polarious Sector while also rescuing any survivors of the brutal strikes that had taken place as the ruthless Deathstalker Squadron, led by The Knightfall, had torn through the system.

Unbeknownst to the I.S.S, the five giant, black, deadly ships of the Deathstalker Squadron were, in fact, sentient extensions of the evil, conquest-driven Astral Alias; Parathax, whose immense star cruiser; The Stealthy Intoxicator, was now silently closing in on their fleet as it too tore through the Polarian Nebula in pursuit of them.

The Deathstalkers had laid waste to many a populated world in recent weeks; stretching the fleets of the I.S.S. incredibly thin.

The final world to be struck by the Deathstalker Squadron, before the I.S.S. was able to intercept it, was the heavily-populated, glistening planet of Polarious, which had been reduced to an ocean world of molten silver within minutes. Following the catastrophic loss of life on Polarious, many sacrifices had been made, both by young Interstellar Scout Operatives and their Troop Leader superiors, to capture the Deathstalker Squadron. Anything that survived being melted or atomised in the strikes, now drifted; hauntingly, in the debris field above the planet's fifth moon; Polarious 5.

The Polarious Sector was isolated and hidden from a neighbouring system of planets by a stealth field, put in place by the Interstellar Scouts as a protective measure for the vulnerable populations that lived beyond it. One of the planets that rested, just beneath the stealth field, was Earth which, although hidden, was still frequently struck by stray wreckage, from Polarious 5's debris field as it slipped through and fell to the planet's surface. The most recent breach of the stealth field was by the Deathstalker Squadron itself.

One of the biggest and most heroic sacrifices made in the pursuit and capture of the Deathstalkers was made by Oli Robertson; a young, newly-appointed I.S.S. Patrol Leader who, after his fellow Operatives had driven the attackers away from Earth in a fierce stand-off, put a daring plan into action, superseding rank to capture the fierce ships; a plan that, despite working, ultimately backfired on him and his Patrol with terrible consequences.

Oli had known his luck would run out eventually. Despite his recent missions assisting Troop Leaders and other I.S.S. Operatives in providing food and medical aid to civilians caught in various galactic combat zones, Oli was the one who nearly always left with new signs of battle damage to his augmented cy-bionic suit or with a critical component destroyed on the vehicles that he rode into danger due to his bold attempts to uphold his Interstellar Scouting morals to do his best to help others; even in dangerous and, often, life-threatening situations. People frequently said he had too much heart for his own good. He was now starting to think they might be right; a realisation that might just have been too little, too late.

Still, many of the civilians now onboard The Scout Hut were

now safe from the horrors that plagued them on their home worlds and were on their way to start better, happier lives because of his own perseverance.

Although he was normally the admirable hero; flipping, back hand springing or rappelling into action, that everyone else wished they could be, Oli now lay, curled up on a sleeping-platform in his room onboard The Scout Hut, having anxiously wrestled with terror-stricken insomnia for almost two days as he awaited results on his potentially-fatal condition of what, he feared, could be Beconium Poisoning. This came after he and his Patrol, Biker Delta Squadron 5-6-5, had successfully secured the Deathstalker Squadron onboard The Scout Hut, only to be shot down by the Deathstalkers' accompanying ship; The Knightfall, which now sat in The Scout Hut's main hanger bay alongside the deadly squadron; discretely signalling the fleet's location to the inbound Stealthy Intoxicator while its pilot, a Reptilian from the planet Biolum by the name of Xzjytheous, now broke containment on the prison deck and charged through the cruiser; sabotaging it from within.

Oli and his Patrol had survived a crash-landing and endured a relentless sandstorm on the rusty, radioactive planet of Becon while awaiting evacuation. The rest of his patrol; Colin, Isaac, Nathan, Corey and Ethan had managed to take refuge within the crash-landed wreckage of their customised ground to air combat vehicle; the Rhinonoid, while Oli, dutifully, remained on watch for the extraction shuttle. It was during this time that one of the respiratory filters in his cy-bionic suit had taken a blaster bolt from an unseen assailant; exposing the young Patrol Leader to the rusty Beconium sediments that swept over him in the radioactive sandstorm.

Oli was dressed in a full black flight suit as he slept, and, while due to his young age, he wasn't particularly muscular by comparison to some of the adult Troop Leaders he worked with, his features were clearly defined due to the intense, military-like exercise programs that all Interstellar Scout Initiates and Operatives were put through daily. This disciplined lifestyle ensured that they were always prepared for whatever missions they and their Troop Leaders were called on to assist with in the vast galactic community;

whether combat, evacuation or post-disaster aid.

Despite their young age, preparedness, anticipation of worst-case scenarios and the ability to quickly determine how to resolve them to help those in need, were drilled into every Interstellar Scout from day one as an Initiate so, although they were children, they had the mentality, self-discipline and morals of their adult Commanders.

Mounted on the silver wall, at the foot of Oli's bed; alongside the protective metal shield that covered the room's large window, were various screens as well as a large, detailed blueprint of his Patrol's customised tank, the Rhinonoid, covered in annotations that offered interior and cross-section views of the customised vehicle and indicated its various capabilities including small vehicle deployment, its forward and rooftop pivoting blaster canons, ground to air thrusters and its remarkable Expansion Matrix.

Along the wall, opposite his bed, was a long, metal workbench above which was a shelf with a row of built-in hologram projectors into which were plugged a series of concept storage devices that held digital copies of Oli's ideas and displayed them in hologram form from the projectors.

Beneath the workbench were several large canvas rucksacks containing everything an Interstellar Scout could possibly need and more, including replacement flint cartridges, spare steel blades for striking the flint with to light fires while on missions, grappling hooks, harpoons, rappel lines, karabiners, flares and much more.

The top of the workbench was covered with a variety of projects-in-progress. These ranged from racks of tightly-sealed, standing glass test tubes that were labelled as containing bio-hazardous sample materials such as Beconium which were mixed with various substances to better understand the properties of the toxic sand; a project that Oli's former Troop Leader, Jason Campbell, never saw completed before being captured by a particularly persistent bounty hunter who was pursuing the Troop Leader for his unsanctioned recon and infiltration work on behalf of the Interstellar Scouts back when Oli was still just an Initiate. To say it was a baptism of fire would be a tremendous understatement as he had only been a few days into training, alongside the rest of his Patrol under Jason's guidance, when it happened.

Subtle signs of the escaped Reptilian's destruction throughout the cruiser were starting to take effect around the room as the power was drained from the flickering lights that hung over various soldering tools, wires and circuit-boards that littered the rest of the table next to various components from his personal range of customised armoured suits.

Oli often liked to make new modifications to anything he could get his hands on and then take experimental prototypes out on missions; transporting them in secret areas onboard the Rhinonoid. It was this attitude that had enabled him to help the I.S.S. capture the Deathstalker Squadron.

Recovery Kestrel Shuttles began to leave The Scout Hut's hanger bay as well as the other cruisers to begin their search and rescue mission. Little did the cruiser and shuttle crews know, they were now in the jaws of a deadly trap set by Parathax for the Interstellar Scouts and the attack on their fleet was now well underway; both from within, as the escaped prisoner killed the guards and cut power to the alarms down in Containment but now outside as well as the fleet fell within firing range of The Stealthy Intoxicator.

CHAPTER 2
ESCAPE THE REPTILIAN'S MASSACRE

A prickling layer of sweat soaked the young, blonde-haired Operative's face and darkened the naturally-occurring highlights of his fringe as the putrid stench invaded his nostrils; the scorching heat radiating from the wall, inches away from him. The wailing smoke alarm, triggered by the melting metal, sounded upon detecting the faintest wisp; blaring loudly throughout the room as the twelve-year old boy's bright blue eyes shot wide open.

Dazzled by the sparks that flashed and flared in front of his face from the window guard's damaged electrical systems, Oli instantly rolled away; reflex-like, from the fizzing metal; throwing himself to his bare feet in one fluid motion as the alarm and sizzling sound continued to permeate his ears. He staggered slightly; disorientated, as he tried to find his balance. The room seemed to spin around him from awaking and jumping to his feet too quickly.

Oli's blonde fringe, that he normally kept swept upwards so he could see his surroundings more clearly, was weighed down by the sweat that drenched it. Stunned, he slowly backed away as he watched on; trying to catch his breath from the shock. The sizzling, liquefied metal of the matt-grey, now-turned-red, window guard dripped onto his sleeping-platform faster and faster until it was so fluid that the entire shield came gushing over it like a waterfall; down onto the cold metal floor, solidifying instantly as, alarmed, the young Operative quickly stumbled backwards; away from it.

This was only the beginning of Oli's problems though. Looking up, through the exposed window, he was met with a daunting sight. The I.S.S. fleet, led by The Scout Hut, was now under fire from a fierce bombardment of plasma blasts that exploded around the convoy of ships from an unseen, pursuing enemy. Blaster bolt after enormous blaster bolt struck, amber, along the Port side of The Scout Hut, hitting the now-uncovered ballistic glass window as squadrons of hostile Black-Burn Fighters, piloted by the ruthless Con-Haarians in Quad-Con-Haara strike formation, now roared past the I.S.S. Flagship, right by the window; spraying the cruiser and the other ships in the fleet with additional blaster fire to weaken the shields for the approaching Stealthy Intoxicator to finish them off.

Although the debris field that the I.S.S. fleet was passing through did offer some cover from the attack by conducting the energy of many of the amber blaster bolts, it also absorbed the turquoise blasts of their own ships as they attempted to fire back.

The glass, while designed to withstand attacks, was quickly weakening as it began to crack and splinter under the bombardment. As he was in recovery, under alternative circumstances, Oli would have been able to use the room as an escape pod and jettison it away from the cruiser there and then but, with the structural integrity of the window rapidly failing, the outer clamps had locked; holding the room in place, as was indicated by the small, slow-flashing screen next to the door on the far side of the room.

Avoiding the solidified, yet still-very-hot, metal on the floor, Oli raced alongside his sleeping-platform to its head and urgently stepped up onto the round podium positioned against the wall next to it.

Upon the platform, stood a sleek, gleaming-emerald augmented cy-bionic exoskeleton with an opaque, shiny black visor built into the helmet. The exoskeleton served as both a uniform and a protective armoured suit for the wearer. It was illuminated by the bright, white light that radiated from within the opaque glass at the base of the podium.

The various pieces of armoured plating that formed the suit opened out on a variety of hinges, pivots and mechanical, bionic rods in response to his proximity; revealing a black-padded interior with grey lines splitting it into various sections, through which the bright blue lights of its sensory tracking system now darted back and forth.

Oli climbed inside and the armoured plating automatically closed itself back up again; the tracking system adapting the suit to his height and build. As the helmet closed up around his head and the visor covered his face, a second sensory system was activated. A green dot drew a diagonal downward line of emerald light on either side of the blacked-out visor followed by a parallel diagonal line moving upward on either side creating an almost double 'V' shape, one inside the other, before finally drawing a line across the top of the visor. These five lines served as sensors that transmitted information directly to the visor's internal heads-up display.

A variety of round, diamond and uniquely shaped ballistic glass badges illuminated on the suit's arms and chest. These multi-function badges were used by I.S.S. Operatives and Troop Leaders to aid them in their missions in an array of hostile situations, often in inhospitable environments. The higher the rank, the more demanding the missions; the more functions their badges could perform to assist both them and those in need of support from the Interstellar Scouts.

A large letter 'V' began to glow, gold, on the back of the armour between Oli's shoulder blades, reaching about a third of the way down his back; the space within the 'V' shape illuminating; royal-blue. This opaque, illuminated, ballistic glass embedded in the suit that indicated the suit's jet propulsion unit fuel reserves, reached over his shoulders and then, from his collar, down the centre of the suit's chest, illuminating two parallel, vertical bars constructed of the same glass and striped with the same gold and royal blue colours. Where the two bars angled into an intersection at his collar, a round, bright red button; the suit's jet propulsion unit and parachute ripcord deployment trigger, began to illuminate.

This wasn't Oli's usual cy-bionic exoskeleton; it was being used by him from surplus while his own suit was being inspected for damage and undergoing repairs following the blaster bolt that hit his respiratory filter on Becon.

On seeing that the suit's systems had been fully initialised on his visor display, Oli retracted his helmet into his suit as the illuminated, emerald lines on the visor disappeared in the opposite directions to when they were activated, leaving his head exposed and allowing him to see his surroundings more clearly. Unlike many in the Interstellar Scouts, Oli preferred to rely on his own eyes most of the time rather than the suit's built-in scanners.

He stepped down from the platform, aided by the interior sensory tracking system to move around in the heavy armour with ease. He then raced, as fast as he could, towards the door; the light of the podium slowly dimming behind him now that the suit had been removed from its charging station.

Oli had to get out of the room immediately before the, now-critically compromised glass of the window, exploded and he was dragged out into the deathly void of space.

Coming to an abrupt halt, Oli raised his hand to align a small, transparent, dewdrop crystal on his suit's wrist with the tri-laser code interface on the doorframe. Several narrow, scarlet lasers shot out into various angled parts of the tiny crystal and rapidly moved to various coded positions on it. Once the code had been cycled through, a black, rectangular strip was revealed beneath the emerald colour and it lit up gold with a diagonal black line further up onto his forearm. Oli scanned the strip on a receiver next to the laser emitter on the doorframe and, as the black line on the gold strip flashed off with a loud beeping sound and blink of a light from the scanner, indicating that the matt-grey door had been unlocked, it slid upwards, allowing him to exit the room.

Before Oli could leave and close the door behind him, a fierce jolt shook the entire room violently, throwing the twelve-year old forward, off his feet and out, amongst the chaos in the corridor. As the cruiser leaned to the side from the powerful blast, Oli rolled across the floor and crashed into the lights built into the wall opposite his sleeping quarters; causing them to flicker from the impact.

Quickly staggering back to his feet before someone tripped over him while placing his hand on the wall for support, Oli looked around, bewildered, at the pandemonium that surrounded him. A second wailing alarm that had been sounding the entire time from the corridor, was now deafening from outside the room.

Patrols of Operatives stampeded up and down the corridor in shiny, emerald suits identical to his, the badges being the only variations. The Operatives moved with great urgency and intent. Scattered amongst them were the fewer, higher-ranking Troop Leaders; adult Commanders, who were dressed in gold augmented cy-bionic suits, the strips of light on their visors, gold also. They shouted orders and responses to each other through microphones and speakers embedded in their helmets, straining to be heard over the wailing alarms. They moved into combat formations; crouching down while others took cover in the doorways of the rooms that lined the corridor, plasma blasters charged and at the ready.

With another powerful jolt, the entire ship shook again, causing Oli to stagger off balance. Had he not been leaning up against the wall of the corridor for support, he would have been aggressively thrown to the floor once more. Some of the other Operatives that had taken up their combat positions fell out of formation but quickly scrambled back into place with the aid of some of their comrades as the ship levelled back out.

The lights in the corridor, as well as the room Oli had fallen from, suddenly flickered and then lost power entirely, turning Oli's surroundings completely black but for the lights on the armoured suits and slow pulses of red that now flared and faded repeatedly overhead.

As the Operative's eyes darted around the corridor, there was an eerie stillness in the dark yet the environment seemed to change; morphing with every flash of red, the intervals drawn out as everyone regained their positions.

'AT ALERT! COMMISSIONER ON DECK!' shouted the voice of an adult Troop Leader as he and a number of others in gold-armoured suits, distinguishable against the rest by a bar of scarlet light across the front of each shoulder, moved around the corner at the far end and entered the corridor at a brisk pace. These were the Commissioner's Advisors. With a hurried stride, they escorted the Fleet Commander towards the hanger bay.

Commissioner John Hanson was an elderly man and slightly shorter than his Advisors. Also dressed in a gold armoured I.S.S. suit like the rest of the Troop Leaders, his position as the Commissioner was indicated by two thin, oval, scarlet lights embedded diagonally between the two royal-blue and gold striped bars that ran down the middle of his chest plate. With his helmet retracted, his extremely short, grey hair encircled a bald patch at the back of his head. He carried a strong, disciplined military presence about him as he strode, with purpose, down the corridor. His boldly expressive face was weathered by a lifetime of service to the Interstellar Scouts through many a dangerous operation; through the radiation sandstorms of Becon, the icy, blistering winds of Zonju, the relentless, bloodthirsty parasites of Felaloris and the list went on. His eyes were dated but strong and focussed with determination as he listened to the reports of the Advisors that escorted him towards the bridge.

'The pursuit from Earth to Becon was a trap to bait us. The Deathstalker Squadron and the Reptilian must have been planted to draw us out' insisted Commissioner Hanson; although why, he did not yet know.

Other I.S.S. fleets across the galaxy had reported increases in hostile activity recently but these brutal assaults of the past week or so were on a whole other level and escalating in aggression.

'The orbital stealth field density is becoming increasingly compromised by blaster fire from our attacker's weapons and our own ships. Meteorology reports are indicating that it's having drastic influence on Earth. There are indications of tidal swells and the crust of the planet is being ruptured and dragged up at various points as well' one of the Advisors informed the Commissioner while consulting a holographic display projected from one of the circular badges on the arm of his gold, armoured suit.

'How?' asked Hanson as he marched past the Patrols of Operatives and Troop Leaders.

'It's the magnetic field of Polarious Five. There are significant amounts of metal ore beneath the Earth's surface and, the more compromised the stealth field between Earth and Polarious Five, the worse the effects will become. We need to evacuate all cruisers under stealth and draw the attack away from this sector before it gets any worse' the Advisor warned.

'Break up the Scout Hut to draw the attack away and follow Contingency Protocol to evacuate all fleet personnel to the surface of Polarious Five' the Commissioner instructed.

'Yes sir' replied one of the Advisors, breaking away into one of the communication rooms to relay the message to the other cruisers in the fleet and to begin the process of the cruiser's breakup.

'Alert all Earth I.S.S. outposts as well as recruitment and training facilities. We need them on standby to provide aid in the aftermath if the stealth field is breeched. Then establish contact with all Earth Scout Campsites; have them liaise with our Consultant Patrols that they keep onsite. We need them to prepare for inbound ships carrying evacuated civilians; they may also need medical attention' Commissioner Hanson continued turning to another of his Advisors who immediately acknowledged the instruction and broke away into another room to establish contact with Earth.

As the Commissioner and his remaining Advisors passed the barricades of Operatives, blasters were pointed downwards to avoid accidentally discharging them at their superiors and then immediately raised back up in preparation for the enemy that they now knew had breached containment.

Looking about, Oli decided that the situation, whatever it was, posed a genuine threat and, with his own suit and weapons with a maintenance team to inspect the respiratory filters and clean out the toxic Beconium particulates blocking his weapons, all he could do was make for the hanger bay as quickly as possible to meet with the rest of Biker Delta Squadron 5-6-5.

Oli quickly activated one of the illuminated badges on his suit and, while repeatedly looking down at the end of the corridor, cycled through a variety of options; interacting directly with the projected hologram through a tiny, illuminated, emerald laser emitter on each of his black-padded fingertips, that lit up when he activated the badge.

Having cycled through the relevant options, a 3-D image of the cruiser rotated in front of him. Different parts of the cruiser were shown in different colours, indicating the structural integrity and allowing him to map out the safest and most direct route to the hanger bay.

More and more parts of the projection turned red at an alarming rate as it even showed large chunks of the ship falling away as the shields were breached; their generators destroyed beyond repair. Only a few green sections remained, indicating the safest parts of the ship as the rest of the hologram turned from critically-damaged-red to totally-destroyed-dark blue which was transparent and only showed the cruiser's outline.

The loud yells of a Troop Leader echoed down the corridor from the end; immediately followed by a loud explosion of smashed glass and a blinding flash, as the man smashed into one of the light panels on the wall, having been launched, through the air with immense force, by something from around the corner. A volley of grenades followed, clattering as they bounced and rolled across the floor.

'GRENADES!' yelled one of the Operatives before being quickly stunned into silenced as they detonated; deploying four tiny electrodes from each one.

The electrodes generated a circuit of surging, electric-blue energy between them; lighting up the darkness as they scattered through the air, dragging the Operative, along with several others, off their feet and pinning them up against the wall; alive but immobilised.

'VISUAL CONTACT! ON THE CEILING!' yelled an emerald-armoured Operative amongst a second group as they finished taking up the position of the first; now facing around the corner at the bottom of the corridor, roughly sixty feet away.

The Operatives began firing at the unknown assailant with the intent to wound only; upholding their morals to preserve the creature's life as they lit up the end of the corridor in a turquoise glow; the frantic, high-pitched sound of blaster fire overpowering the wailing alarms as it echoed down the hallway.

A loud, primal howl emanated from the end of the corridor. Oli's wide-eyes shot beyond the holographic projection as he slowly backed away from the sound. Suddenly, in the glow of turquoise blaster bolts and the slow-pulsing, red, overhead lights, he caught a glimpse of the enormous black shape. The escaped Reptilian had previously been hired by the I.S.S. to help locate and capture the Deathstalker Squadron but had betrayed them to aid Parathax.

With a silver cy-bionic helmet over its large head, intended to cover the creature's eyes and keep it docile, torn off lengths of hosing waved around violently like snakes, spilling various dense gasses from them into the corridor. Still connected to various devices and pieces of machinery that were designed to take readings of the creature's vital and bio-chemical levels, the Reptilian leapt out from around the corner.

It latched onto the far wall of the corridor where the first group was pinned up by the electrical containment field, and ran, with extreme speed on all-fours, down the passageway; straight at Oli while evading the blaster fire as it charged.

Leaving the door to his room open and abandoning his rucksacks full of survival equipment beneath his desk, Oli slammed his gloved hand against the badge on his arm; deactivating the holographic projection of the cruiser as he turned around and raced, as fast as he could, in the opposite direction. He ran down the corridor towards the hanger bay to meet with the rest of his Patrol, hoping desperately that he could outrun the escaped, attacking prisoner.

Moving through the blackness of the corridor was difficult as he had to memorise the obstacles in his path based on a brief flash of the red lights that occurred at slow intervals, map out his route and await the next flare while fighting to remain standing as the entire ship, now taking on a more permanent list, shook more frequently; the glass from the blackened lights in the walls and ceiling shattering; exploding around him, audible but entirely invisible in the deathly blinding darkness.

Oli held up his arm in front of his face, protecting his eyes from the projectile glass that exploded from the walls and ceiling, the blinding flares of light as they blew and showers of sparks that erupted in spontaneous blazing flashes from the exposed, damaged wiring as he ran past; skidding slightly, as he tried not to slip on the shattered glass covering the floor as it slid beneath his feet.

The Patrols of Operatives now positioned A.I. blaster turrets at strategic points in preparation for their attacker, overseen by the adult Troop Leaders.

There was now so much adrenaline surging through Oli's mind, he completely forgot that he was sleep-deprived from the horror of the past few days; the horror that had now come back to haunt him.

Resisting the temptation that urged him to jump dangerous distances down entire flights of stairs while his eyes tried to focus in the still-operational lights of the steel, spiral stairwell, Oli stumbled down several levels; trying to keep his footing as the ship rumbled, creaked and groaned around him.

The open stairwell was also much easier on his ringing ears than the deafening chaos of the corridor as his suit's communications system, a small speaker embedded in his collar, activated upon receiving multiple priority transmissions from the Gold Troop Leaders' suits.

'BARRICADE 'A' HAS BEEN BREACHED!'

'HOSTILE HAS BREACHED MAINTENANCE AND IS PROTECTED BY TROOP LEADER ARMOUR! CHECK YOUR TARGETS!'

'MULTIPLE TARGETS SIGHTED! BE ADVISED; MULTIPLE BIONICS ARE ACCOMPANYING THE PRISONER - ONE IN OPERATIVE GEAR!'

"B' AND 'C' ARE COMPROMISED!'

'IT'S THE TURRETS THEY'VE BEEN DISABLED!'

'TARGET HAS INITIATED A TROOP LEADEROVERRIDE! OPERATIVE SUITS AND BADGES ARE UNRESPONSIVE!'

'TARGET HAS BREACHED BARRICADES 'B' AND 'C''

'HOSTILE IS EXPOSED! I REPEAT, HOSTILE IS EXPOSED. THE BIONICS HAVE TAKEN BOTH CY-BIONIC SUITS AND SPLIT OFF.'

'HOSTILE IS ARMED AND APPROACHING THE STAIRWELL, ALL PATROLS, MAINTAIN SUPRESSING FIRE! TARGET MUST NOT REACH THE HANGER BAY!'

'HANGER BAY, INITIATE TOTAL LOCKDOWN ON ALL IMPOUNDED VESSELS; HOSTILE IS GOING FOR THE KNIGHTFALL!' screamed an array of Leader and Operative voices through the speaker built into the collar of Oli's suit.

Radio static and the background noise of alarms and blaster fire interfering with the transmissions only made the overlapping, frantic shouts of terror that much more frightening as a loud, primal screeching sound of the attacking creature, also emanated from the tiny speaker.

The anticipation lingered, threatening over his shoulder; like piercing eyes burning into the back of his head as an ever-present, yet invisible, danger. Based on these frantic transmissions, for all Oli knew, the enemy could be coming up right behind him in pursuit, about to pounce - RIGHT NOW!

A loud clattering sound echoed down the stairwell from behind him and, as he turned around, a gold-armoured Troop Leader tumbled down the stairs and came to a stop at Oli's feet. Oli quickly checked the Troop Leader for signs of life but he appeared to be unresponsive.

Flaming pieces of debris rained down through the stairwell from the floors above, crashing and clanging against the sides as they fell, while explosions erupted in balls of flame from various doorways. The escaped prisoner and its accompanying bionics had clearly been tearing their way through the ship and sabotaging it at strategic points; probably to prevent it from fleeing whatever was also attacking the ship from the outside, Oli rightly concluded.

The echo of a woman's desperate cries for help rang through the Operative's ears from nearby. Looking over the railings, at a doorway a few floors beneath him, Oli spotted an elderly female civilian with long, silver hair, who had been rescued and brought to The Scout Hut on a previous mission so she and the many other civilians onboard could be relocated to a new home world; away from the chaos and destruction that they had been caught up in.

Beyond the platform that the woman was standing on, near the bottom of the immense shaft, rotating reflectors cast an orange glow across the walls as groups of laser beams, emitted from several tri-laser code interfaces that were positioned on a huge, silver, cube-like chamber, moved around to various receivers on the sides of the shaft. Slowly, massive hydraulics extended from the chamber and began pushing out against the walls which, gradually, started to widen. The Scout Hut was formed of many separate components and, to avoid the entire Flagship being lost in combat, it had the ability to detach these components and send them adrift in different directions and then rebuild itself once the danger had passed.

The frail woman was cut off from the corridor by one of the many doors which had been closed to stop the Reptilian from reaching the hanger bay and to prevent anyone else from accessing the stairwell while the various large components of the cruiser were pushed out from one another by the enormous hydraulics. There was now very little time to rescue the woman and get off the stairwell before the section of the cruiser Oli was trying to get to was pushed away, leaving them both stranded on the stairwell until they were eventually exposed to the vacuum of space.

The blaster vibrated in Oli's tightening grasp and emitted a loud ringing sound that gradually increased in pitch as he charged it up. Once fully charged, Oli holstered the Troop Leader's blaster in the slot built into his suit's leg. Grasping at the handrail as he descended the final flights of stairs towards her, one of the falling pieces of metal struck Oli's hand-guard in passing, leaving a silver indentation where it scraped off the top emerald coating behind his knuckles. Stunned by the strike and, as the cruiser jolted again, Oli lost his grip on the rail and tumbled down the few remaining stairs.

A Troop Leader had positioned himself with a sniper blaster at one of the doorways to the stairwell, prepared to fire on the Reptilian if it made it past the many other defences positioned around the cruiser. He eyed Oli through the scope of his rifle and called out to him to get the woman and himself to safety. Oli looked up to the Troop Leader on the ledge and nodded in response.

A loud, clattering sound came from behind the Troop Leader who, stunned, slowly turned around to see the huge, furious Reptilian staring at him having dropped down from inside the ceiling further down the corridor. Slowly, the Troop Leader raised his arm to trigger the tri-laser code interface on the doorframe. Realising what he was doing Xzjytheous charged straight at him in a bid to stop his attempts to cut off another access point to the stairwell but it was too late, the door crashed down and sealed itself shut, trapping both Xzjytheous and himself in the corridor. The Troop Leader was only just able to barrel roll out of the way before he was slammed against the door by Xzjytheous' extreme momentum.

Revealing several deep dents, Xzjytheous pulled himself away from the door that he had collided into. The Troop Leader quickly removed the elongated barrel from the rifle, turning it into more of a hand blaster and fired a volley of blasts straight at the tri-laser code interface and accompanying scanner on the doorframe to prevent Xzjytheous from hacking it, should the creature get past him. Xzjytheous, having taken what he needed from his previous victims throughout the cruiser, generated a protective energy shield around the panels on the doorframe, causing the blaster bolts to backfire and fatally hit the Troop Leader while also striking the dewdrop crystal and scanner strip on his suit and on the suit Xzjytheous had stolen as they tried to shield themselves with their arms in the process, thus still preventing the Reptilian from getting through the door.

A fierce explosion erupted from a doorway five levels above Oli, where the Troop Leader had called out to him and, from the flames, leapt the giant, hulking Reptilian; launching itself through the air, almost in slow motion, as it hurtled across the wide shaft; hurling a volley of grenades straight at the young Operative.

Oli jumped in front of the woman, drew the plasma blaster from his holster and fired a volley of blaster bolts at the beast as the grenades clattered around the two of them.

The Reptilian kicked away from the wall, just three floors above, and launched itself straight at Oli and the frightened woman with immense power. Time seemed to slow down once again for Oli due to the shock that he now experienced.

Twisting through the air, a series of long, curved spikes thrust out from between the creature's now-black and dark red scales as its muscles enlarged and it hurled a pair of throwing knives straight at them.

Oli raised his arms to protect the pair of them from the blades, just as everything seemed to speed back up for him again. The

Reptilian's normally-amber eyes flashed, blazing-red, moments before it slammed down onto the platform where Oli and the woman were, shaking it beneath their feet; the huge beast's momentum dragging its long spikes across the chest plate of Oli's suit and leaving three long, deep gouges as they pulled the Operative against the railings; bending them outwards on impact and quickly snapping them. The Reptilian charged on; deterred but unscathed by the volley of blasts Oli had fired.

Oli clung on for dear life as he flinched and winced against the sparks that now violently flashed, spitting out in blinding flares from the gouges in his suit, a sharp pain shooting through his arms from the jolt as his tight grasp stopped him from falling. Looking to the wall next to him, he could see it now, slowly, moving further away from him as the hydraulics pushed the section of the cruiser that he was trying to reach, outwards, away from the rest of the cruiser.

The Reptilian had hit the platform with so much force that it had broken the extendable supports connecting it to the wall early, causing the stairs, that would normally be held in place at the top of the shaft and the hydraulic chamber near the bottom, after the walls had detached, to begin tearing away, in sequence, all the way down, in a rapid, spiralling motion as the woman began to fall.

Losing his grip, Oli fell down the shaft behind her, helplessly trying to throw himself into a head-first position to accelerate his pursuit of the falling woman. As he fell faster and faster, the bottom of the shaft growing ever-closer with each passing millisecond, he hurtled past the woman who, luckily, had been suspended in the air; pinned up against the outward-moving wall by the electrical field from one of the grenades that had been launched at them.

Oli used all of his strength to somersault in mid-air as he passed the immense hydraulics that dwarfed him in size. Once his head was pointing upwards, he quickly hammered the heel of his gloved hand against the round, red button in the centre of his collar. The cylindrical, royal-blue and gold striped bars sprung out, horizontal, from the suit and the ends of them locked down into a vertical position, revealing the squeeze triggers, much like the brakes on a bike's handlebars.

Squeezing the triggers hard, the ice-blue flames that exploded from his suit's jet propulsion unit's thrusters slowed his descent, allowing him to move towards the woman. He then quickly slapped one of the illuminated badges on his arm to allow him to hover in place without the need to squeeze the fuel-feed triggers. He grabbed the woman so he wouldn't have to keep readjusting his position to keep up with the wall pulling her away.

Reassuring the elderly woman as she was understandably terrified, Oli held out his other hand for her to hold onto and, while the streams of buzzing, crackling electricity from the containment field kept snapping out at him, Oli wasn't deterred. He kicked at one of the four electrodes with his heel, several times, until it came away from the wall and broke the circuit.

The woman wrapped her arms around Oli causing the two of them to slowly move further down the shaft but, driving some additional fuel into the thrusters to support the weight of two people, his jet propulsion unit rocketed them both back up, towards the entrance of the hanger bay corridor.

Oli helped the woman onto the narrow ledge next to the doorway. Looking over his shoulder at how far the wall had moved away from where the stairs had been, he knew that he now had just seconds before the section of the cruiser was fully pushed away and they were sucked out into space.

'Cover your eyes' he instructed, joining the woman on the ledge and locking the bars back into the suit's chest.

He drew his blaster and used the butt of it to smash a glass panel beneath the controls and pulled down a small handle to disable the locks. With a sudden jolt, the entire cruiser very nearly threw them both back off the ledge. Oli quickly grabbed the woman to stop her from falling but lost his grip on his blaster in the process and it joined the rest of the debris in falling to the bottom of the shaft.

Relying on the padded grip of his gloves, Oli used all of his strength to slide the door upwards, just enough for the woman to crawl under, feeling the strain in the biceps of his trembling arms as he lifted it higher still for him to also get through to the corridor.

'GO! FIND A SHUTTLE AND GET TO SAFETY!' Oli instructed, placing his gloved hand on the shaken-up but grateful woman's arm, reassuringly.

He was starting to feel a bit odd. It was almost like he was slipping into a trance-like state as he found himself fighting against a growing wooziness; trying to remain focussed.

Acknowledging that he was probably feeling this way due to the shock of everything that had just happened and pausing for a moment to wipe the beads of sweat from his face with the black, padded palm of his glove, Oli ran down the final corridor towards the hanger bay.

CHAPTER 3
POLARIOUS SECTOR PATROL: TERMINATED

A different siren was audible within the enormous hanger bay that contained a vast array of Viper Fighters, Funnel-Web Escorts, Operative and Vehicle Shuttles and other ground and aerial transports that were urgently evacuating both civilian passengers and I.S.S. crew from the ship. Also included amongst the vehicles, were the impounded Knightfall and the five, huge war machines of the vicious Deathstalker Squadron.

A huge, eight-legged tank, the Rhinonoid, was stomping its way past rows of other tanks and various ships towards the vacant deployment bay platform of a nearby I.S.S. Kestrel Shuttle, named for its unique capabilities which, unlike other shuttles, allowed it to remain stationary in flight and also go into a near-vertical dive from a prone position to evade hostile fire. The Kestrel was being closely guarded by a small group of Operatives as others rushed around, making preparations for the evacuation.

Once on the platform, the Rhinonoid came to a halt and slowly began to descend its main hull on its legs to make itself smaller and able to fit inside the Kestrel's deployment bay as powerful jets of white smoke blasted out diagonally from the vehicle with a loud hissing sound.

Having come to a resting position, just above the wide, sprawling feet of the tank, Nathan Lucas, one of the older Operatives of Biker Delta Squadron 5-6-5, just slightly younger than Oli, descended one of the four small staircases that folded out from their hatches in the side of the Rhinonoid. Nathan wore an emerald Interstellar Scouts cy-bionic suit, just like Oli's. He had hazel eyes; his hair a lighter shade of brown although darkened by a blended flare of dark red.

As the designated pilot of Biker Delta Squadron 5-6-5, following a series of successful aerial combat and extraction missions, Nathan was just about to head up to the Kestrel's cockpit to begin pre-flight checks when he caught sight of another group of Operatives nearby, their boots slamming to the floor of the hanger bay, having quickly and efficiently descended down the long silver poles that led down to the hanger bay from the deck above.

Sarah Easton, the girl with long, fiery hair and an equally fiery wit was the Patrol Leader of Biker Delta Squadron 5-6-5's newly appointed armed fighter escort; Viper Strike Squadron. She carried her emerald helmet under her arm and had a closed-pronged grappling hook holstered on her calf as, with a steady jog, she made her way towards one of the Viper Fighters accompanied by the other four pilots in her squadron but, suddenly, she began to slow down; pausing as she felt Nathan's eyes on her.

Nathan was the only boy, after her brother, Isaac, who was also an Operative with Biker Delta Squadron 5-6-5; that Sarah felt particularly close to. She looked back at Nathan and gave him a brave smile in acknowledgement of what she knew he would be thinking as the repeated announcements of smaller cruisers in the fleet being destroyed by the rapidly approaching ship, came through on the hanger bay speakers. All they could do was hope that the evacuation shuttles were launching fast enough to get everyone from the doomed ships, to safety in time.

Sarah, her eyes willing Nathan to just get to safety and to not worry about her, kept her own worries well-hidden despite the seriousness of the situation. She didn't even acknowledge the announcement that the Commissioner and his Advisors had entered the hanger bay; having left the bridge to evacuate, nor the tiny black dart that had just been stealthily fired into Commissioner Hanson's neck by one of the enormous, jet-black Deathstalkers that sat at the far end of the hanger bay.

Sarah knew the sacrifices made on Becon by Biker Delta Squadron 5-6-5, as well as the price paid above the planet while capturing the Deathstalker Squadron. The back of the hanger bay was littered with the battle-damaged Viper and Funnel-Web Fighters that told the entire, harrowing story and she didn't want to put her panic onto those she cared about after all they had already been through.

'Rhinonoid on board, I'm heading up to the cockpit!' yelled the urgent voice of Nathan. He shouted his update through his helmet's built in microphone as he made his way around the outside of the shuttle in the far right hand corner of the hanger.

Finally, after Sarah's subtle, silent urging at him, Nathan, who hadn't wanted to leave her unguarded, finally boarded the shuttle, after which she unveiled her feelings of fear and anxiety but only to herself; turning away and hurriedly moving towards her docked Viper.

Extremely versatile, Viper Fighters, with their striking orange colouration and tri royal-blue markings, were spared no capability, nor expense, in their construction and development. They were modelled on the known features of the ships piloted by the less than savoury inhabitants of the galaxy – Black-Burn Fighters, normally piloted by Con-Haarians. Viper fighters could match the high speed, rapid-spray firepower and shield density of Black-Burns and their various classes. The Interstellar Scouts were built on the principals of anticipation and preparation; a vital attitude to live by for anyone who found themselves on this side of the stealth field between Polarious and Earth, where galactic piracy and violent opportunists were rife.

It was for this reason that I.S.S. Viper Fighters had a key safety feature. Behind its curved cockpit and two angled Port and Starboard triangular stabiliser fins, was an under-curled, stumpy, scorpion-like tail that, while landed, served as a third leg alongside the stabiliser fins for the fighter to rest upon but, should the fighter be shot down and ejection systems be compromised, the fins could be jettisoned and the tail could deploy, extending beneath the ship's hull, while retracting its three-piece casing, and embedding the shiny, dark purple anchor spike with an emerald laser tip, contained within, into a surface; to prevent a crash-landing. In the event of a crash-landing, however, the tail, with the anchor spike covered, could also curl around the front of the cockpit; serving as protection for the pilot, as the fighter tumbled across the ground below; in a wheel-like fashion.

'Viper Fighter Escort standing by Five-Six-Five. Co-ordinates set for the surface of Polarious Five. I'll see you down there' Sarah announced into her helmet's built in microphone as she climbed across the uniquely-textured hull of her Viper that was customised specifically for her with an entire coating of tiny, raised dots for added grip and a number of eyelets at various locations on the hull for securing grappling hooks to, enabling rapid air to ground insertions, although, that wasn't the only thing Sarah used them for.

She settled into the cockpit and fastened her helmet strap; adjusting it beneath her chin, while still watching the rest of the activity outside the shuttle.

Two other Operatives; Isaac Easton and Corey Jones, rushed around making final preparations for the shuttle's launch under the instruction of a gold-armoured Troop Leader who had seen this as an opportunity to observe Isaac in his recently-appointed role as Assistant Patrol Leader in Oli's absence. His lack of experience at being in charge though, meant that he wasn't as confident as Oli or as commanding as he ought to be. The Troop Leader perceived him as taking too long as the Operative ensured that he had followed all of the instructions to the letter.

While Isaac and Corey rushed around, another two, younger Operatives; Colin Anderton and Ethan Stanley, were left to guard the ship with turrets mounted on tripods against anyone that tried to infiltrate the hanger bay.

At a passing glance, Isaac caught sight of the vast number of Kestrel Shuttles beyond the hanger bay. Some were evacuating the cruisers while others had already been out searching for survivors, two of which, he hoped, were his parents who had been on Polarious during the Deathstalkers' attack. While desperately trying to remain optimistic, he knew it was highly unlikely they had made it off-world in time.

'Pick up the pace Isaac, this isn't a drill; the enemy will be here shortly' instructed the Troop Leader, clapping his hands together in emphasis; encouraging Isaac to assign more of the tasks to Corey and to maintain communication with Nathan in the cockpit.

'Nathan, you're clear. Green light to retract deployment bay hydraulics' announced Isaac into the microphone built into his cybionic suit's helmet as he turned to see the Rhinonoid still waiting to be taken onboard the shuttle.

'Green light confirmed. Hydraulics retracting' replied Nathan's voice through the built-in speaker of Isaac's helmet.

A platform began to slowly rise up on the shuttle's huge, heavy-duty hydraulics, lifting the repaired but still-Beconium-stained Rhinonoid, into the inside of the shuttle. Sarah took this as a signal for her, and the rest of Viper Strike Squadron, to begin their Viper Fighters' launch sequence.

'Viper Escort, standby. Move into flank positions on Five-Six-Five on my mark' Sarah announced to the other four Viper pilots; Emma Longfield, Jessica Brophy, Timothy Boothe and Pete Davies, their ships docked behind her fighter. She and the other pilots pulled out their pilot controls on a long arm from in front of them and scanned their tri-laser code interfaces and access strips, causing two small screens to also deploy on diagonal, extendable arms; one on either side of them, which they used to initialise their Viper Fighters' flight and weapon systems, after which, as a loud, high-pitched humming sound came from outside in response, the screens returned to their original positions on either side of the hatch which, in the now-blacked-out cockpit, emitted a full emerald, holographic heads-up display across the ballistic glass.

'Affirmative, Vipers online and standing by for your mark Five-Six-Five Viper Alpha' replied Emma's voice through Sarah's suit's speaker as she continued to watch Isaac and Corey, now starting to board the shuttle.

'OLI!?' shouted Colin, one of the younger Operatives guarding the shuttle. He was stunned by the state of their normally-strong, charismatic Patrol Leader after initially shifting the mounted turret to aim at him as he entered the hanger bay. Equally shocked, were Isaac and Corey, who simultaneously reeled around at the top of the shuttle's loading ramp. Oli staggered into the hanger bay; now doubled over, coughing and spluttering. Something was very wrong.

Oli made his way towards the rest of his Patrol; sweat running down his face which now grew pale and grey; straining under the weight of his cy-bionic suit to look up at the group of Operatives through his stinging eyes.

'What!?' shouted Sarah; shocked and almost reflex-like from her cockpit. She raised the hatch back up and leaned out to look behind her ship as far as her safety restraints would allow.

On seeing the sudden deterioration in Oli's condition, Sarah hurriedly removed the crossed-over straps from over her chest, climbed back out and raced over towards the Operative.

The gold-armoured Troop Leader, who was preparing to board the shuttle along with Biker Delta Squadron 5-6-5, instructed Isaac to get Colin and Ethan onboard and to have Nathan begin the launch sequence as he rushed towards Oli but the Troop Leader was unable to reach him before the sickly Operative stumbled, leant forward and collapsed, unconscious, to the floor.

While Ethan boarded the shuttle, as Isaac had instructed him to, Colin was more reluctant. Colin was considered Oli's adoptive younger brother and refused to leave his station until he saw that Oli was safely moving towards the shuttle. Isaac felt the same way about Oli and the gold-armoured Troop Leader. He didn't want them to become separated in the heat of battle as that would mean he alone would be left in charge without guidance but things were increasingly getting worse. He'd been given an order and he was going to have to follow it to minimise the risk of further complications.

'Robertson! Robertson can you hear me?' The Troop Leader called out to Oli as he knelt down to inspect his vital signs but he was suddenly launched across the hanger bay by an unseen force. Tumbling across the floor, the Troop Leader slammed against a fuel canister and looked up at what now stood over Oli. Having powered down its stealth field generator, a tall, lethal bionic was revealed; a sentient, humanoid culmination of long metal rods and mechanics, dressed in an emerald I.S.S. exoskeleton. A second one raced by in a gold I.S.S. Troop Leader suit. The speed that it moved at as it rushed across the hanger bay made it obvious that it wasn't really a Troop Leader.

'GRENADES!' yelled Colin as he attempted to fire his turret on the rapidly-moving bionic. The grenades that had been thrown to different parts of the hanger bay distributed pressurised jets of rusty-coloured smog containing Beconium, forcing all I.S.S. forces to take cover and use their First Aid badges to deploy their respirator masks. Amongst the commotion, the fleeing Reptilian strode across the hanger bay, heading straight for his ship, The Knightfall.

Corey, who had a reputation for making snap-decisions in dangerous situations without thinking them through first; often in order to be viewed as the heroic member of the group, raced back down the loading ramp to engage the bionic and get Oli to safety.

'GO! BOARD THE SHUTTLE! NOW!' ordered Corey, rushing past Isaac and Colin as they watched on, astounded at the situation's sudden deterioration, from outside the shuttle.

'COLIN, GO!' Corey shouted again as he looked back at the young Operative who remained at the turret. As he shouted his orders, Corey gestured urgently at them all with his hand.

Racing as fast as he could to Oli's and the Troop Leader's aid, he was unaware that Sarah was also rushing past the docked ships to assist.

With everyone distracted by the bionic that had powered up its stealth field generator and vanished again, an enormous pulse of black energy exploded outwards from the Deathstalker Squadron; disrupting the operating systems of many of the I.S.S. fighters and corrupting their circuitry as strands of thorny, black energy wrapped and weaved their way around their hulls.

'Pilots, stand down and await your evac. designation!' ordered a woman's voice echoing loudly throughout the hanger bay. The roar of I.S.S. fighter engines filled the area as Sarah frowned and slowly came to a stop. That made sense. Why were fighter escorts already launching without clearance?

'Impounded vessel, stand down and disengage your launch sequence, launch authorisation is negative! I REPEAT, KNIGHTFALL, STAND DOWN!' ordered the female voice again.

Confused, Sarah slowly turned to look back over her shoulder; a look of unbridled terror now manifesting on her face as the enormous, growing shadow of The Knightfall engulfed her; the impounded ship rising into the air.

Amongst the chaos, nobody had noticed the further black streams of thorny energy that had spilled out of the five impounded Deathstalker Fighters and wrapped around several more I.S.S. Viper Fighters; animating them. The mechanical sound of blaster canons on the surrounding I.S.S. ships turned to acquire their targets. They weren't, however, hostile targets but strategic targets, intended to cripple the I.S.S; their own forces.

Just meters away from Sarah, the stabiliser thrusters of the impounded Knightfall pivoted the ship in mid-air as its pilot plotted new destination co-ordinates into the ship's galacta-nav. Moments later, The Knightfall vacated the hanger bay and vanished into the debris field beyond, en-route to Earth. Nobody had seen the Reptilian pilot nor the bionic that accompanied him as they boarded The Knightfall, which could mean only one thing; the escaped prisoner must also be in possession of stolen personal-use I.S.S. stealth field technology as well as the bionic. It couldn't possibly have been anything else as it would have shown up in the specially-designed lights positioned in the hanger bay that were built to reveal any cloaked, infiltrating craft. There was little time to contemplate this though as the blaster canons on the hovering Viper Fighters were now primed, their targets acquired.

Before Sarah was able to take cover, the entire room erupted in an inferno of fire and explosions around her, causing the huge ceiling to cave in as the I.S.S. Viper Fighters, animated by the Deathstalkers' black energy, began spraying the entire hanger bay with blaster fire, spitting fiercely like the venom of their namesake.

The woman's crackling, distorted voice now came through again, inside Sarah's helmet. The transmission was almost inaudible and was filled with gaps over the destruction that surrounded her but the gist of the announcement was to alert everyone to the unauthorised launch of The Knightfall and calling for the cruiser's main blaster canons to fire on it. However, it was too late. The Knightfall had skilfully navigated the debris field and vanished beneath the orbital stealth field to retrieve a high-value target from Earth for Parathax.

Corey, rushing to Oli's aid from the shuttle, used his momentum to slide across the floor of the hanger bay, towards his unconscious friend; rolling to the side twice in quick succession and taking cover from the falling debris within a hollow girder. The gold-armoured Troop Leader hadn't been as fortunate as his lifeless body now lay beneath the girder. Corey crawled through it, using it for protection as fuel tanks ruptured and ignited under simultaneous blaster fire from a variety of their own ships which continued to target strategic points around the hanger; destroying the vehicles before they could launch.

Other, more fortunate, pilots were able to launch and initiate emergency evacuation procedures; carelessly scraping their ships across the floor as sparks erupted into the air in their wake through their desperate, sometimes futile, attempts to guide the vehicles, filled with I.S.S. Initiates, Operatives, Troop Leaders and civilians, out of the line of fire. Some of the Viper Fighters were shot down before they escaped the hanger bay as they drew attention away from the shuttles while others were lucky enough to evacuate the cruiser before being targeted.

Corey safely made it to Oli who remained unresponsive but, as the flames and explosions erupted around them, he realised that he hadn't brought a means of quickly returning to the shuttle with Oli. There was too much falling debris for him to use his jet propulsion unit and Oli was too heavy for Corey to drag him to safety through the destruction.

At the bottom of the shuttle's loading ramp, Isaac had already noticed Corey's error as well as the unresponsive Troop Leader. Feeling extremely disorientated, he appeared to have slipped into a state of shock from the disastrous turn of events. Operatives and Troop Leaders rushed around the hanger bay; racing right by him, but all Isaac saw were blurs of emerald and gold as his eyes glazed over.

Coming back to reality, acknowledging that things were only going to continue getting worse and desperate to get himself and the rest of the Patrol out of the hanger bay as soon as possible, Isaac realised that he would first have to face his fears of taking control of the situation amongst the devastation.

Without thinking too much about the danger that surrounded him, Isaac did what he had to do. He turned and raced back up the loading ramp with Colin.

'Ethan, stand to the side' he instructed, urgently, as he quickly began reeling out a cable from a large spool inside the shuttle, his mind racing with so many frantic thoughts that just became lost, like the rest of the background noise, in the chaos.

'Colin, take over, keep feeding it out' he continued as he pulled a leaver on the wall to remove the ladder cover on the outside of the shuttle; parting it down the middle. Isaac then picked up the large, metal clip attached to the end of the cable and climbed the ladder on the outside of the shuttle to get on top of it; the dense smoke abrasive in his throat and stinging his eyes.

Colin used both hands and pulled as hard as he could at the metal cable to reel it out. Squinting through the smoke from the roof of the shuttle, Isaac could just about make out the shapes of Corey and Oli. He gathered up the slack and began slinging it around above his head; using the weight of the metal clip on the end to build up some momentum. He then launched the cable as hard as he could, through the air, in their general direction. It slammed against Corey's arm; getting his attention. Corey quickly clipped the end of the cable onto a metal ring on his suit's utility belt, grabbed hold of Oli as tight as he could and then tugged on the cable; indicating to Isaac that he was ready.

Nearby, Sarah removed her helmet to get a better view of her surroundings. She had found herself trapped from every direction as she looked around, desperately searching for a means of escape. It was hopeless. She noticed the hovering Vipers now pivoting, turning to open fire on her wingmen.

'FIVE-SIX-FIVE, FIGHTER ESCORT! EVAC! EVAC!' She yelled into her helmet's built-in microphone; her helmet held up to her mouth between her hands as she stumbled about; disorientated.

In the shuttle's cockpit, Nathan also received Sarah's distressed transmission. He began to close the shuttle's loading ramp but Isaac had seen his sister trapped halfway across the hanger bay. If he had truly lost his parents during the Deathstalker strike on Polarious, he wasn't going to risk losing his sister as well; there was simply no outcome where he would let that happen.

Having returned to the top of the ramp inside the shuttle, Isaac smashed a glass cover on the wall with his elbow and turned the crank handle behind it; locking off the loading ramp as the cable was rapidly reeled back in, dragging Corey and Oli across the floor of the hanger bay.

'Isaac! What are you doing? I need to launch!' shouted Nathan's frantic voice. Isaac activated one of the illuminated badges on his cy-bionic suit and, with the illuminated green dots on his fingertips, he interacted with the holographic projection that was emitted from it; accessing the Patrol's armoured suits using an Assistant Patrol Leader Override and activating their helmets and respirator masks which deployed from a compartment inside their suits; covering their noses and mouths and feeding them breathable air through tubes embedded in their collars. He didn't want to stop Nathan from launching if he absolutely had to but he was going to keep that hatch open for as long as he possibly could.

With his own helmet still open and feeling the blazing heat and prickling burn of the sparks spitting from the flames, against his face; a layer of sweat covering it, Isaac raced down the loading ramp, desperately trying to aid Sarah but he was immediately dragged back into the shuttle by Corey and Oli as they collided, with immense force.

'GREEN LIGHT! GO! GO! GO!' yelled Corey as he, Isaac and a still-unconscious Oli reached the top of the loading ramp. Corey cranked the handle back up and the loading ramp finished closing before Isaac could return to his feet.

Isaac quickly threw Corey and Oli off him and jumped up, racing to the closing loading ramp and yelling out for Sarah. He desperately hammered his fists, furiously, against the now-sealed hatch, hoping that, by some miracle, it would open back up but Nathan had already started the shuttle's launch sequence.

'I NEED EVERYONE IN THE COCKPIT, NOW!' Nathan announced through their suits' built in speakers.

'ISAAC! ISAAC! WE NEED TO GO! NOW!' yelled Corey, who was extremely shaken-up and eager to evacuate the cruiser as fast as possible.

Knowing that, even if he could leave the shuttle now, Isaac would be putting even more lives in danger, Sarah's included, he became furious at the situation and at himself for not being able to aid his sister. Feeling a sharp pain now shooting throughout his hands and wrists, which rested upon the closed hatch, Isaac and the others turned away and rushed through the shuttle, as his mind continued to race frantically.

'Where's our Designated Troop Leader?' asked Nathan, alarmed, as the group raced into the cockpit having left Oli secured to the cable inside the shuttle's closed entrance.

'He didn't make it. Stand-by to retract landing gear. Corey, raise the shields and monitor proximity alerts until we clear the debris field and land on Polarious Five; we don't want any collisions' announced Isaac, stammering slightly as he frantically tried to recall the process of previous evacuation drills while also fighting his worries about his stranded sister.

'THE VIPERS HAVE TARGETED US, WE'RE TAKING FIRE! CRITICAL DAMAGE!' yelled Nathan.

'COREY! GET THE SHIELDS RAISED, NOW!' Isaac shouted in a frantic outburst; turning back to Corey who was sat at a console behind them.

'SHIELDS HAVE BEEN DISABLED AND THE STEALTH FIELD GENERATOR IS UNRESPONSIVE!' replied Corey, a layer of sweat forming on his face.

Feeling a heavy frown coming over him as he focussed hard on remembering the different stages of the launch sequence, Nathan frantically hammered at the controls on the pilot's console.

Slowly, the shuttle lifted off the floor but, in his nervousness of piloting alone without a Troop Leader's assistance, he initiated some of the systems in the wrong order; causing the launch to be a lot more rough than it was supposed to be.

Debris rained down, clattering and clanging against the shuttle's hull as Nathan fired up the thrusters and the damaged ship soared out of The Scout Hut's main hanger bay.

The last thing Sarah saw from outside was Biker Delta Squadron 5-6-5's shuttle departing the hanger bay, accompanied by the remaining four escort fighters of Viper Strike Squadron; piloted by Emma, Jess, Timothy and Pete who, despite Sarah's order to evacuate, had remained to make sure that the shuttle launched safely. Sarah attempted to shelter within the wreckage of a Funnel-Web fighter that had already been blasted; hoping that her cy-bionic suit would protect her.

The part of the cruiser that she was inside began to list further as it sustained a critical hit that breached the hull. Sarah pulled her helmet back over her head for added protection as the wreckage she was sheltering inside began to slide and then tumble across the hanger bay, straight towards a pile-up of flaming wreckages and fuel canisters. On impact, the flames ignited the fuel, immediately engulfing the destroyed fighter that Sarah was sheltering inside and it collectively erupted into a powerful explosion.

Onboard the shuttle, Isaac, Nathan, Corey, Colin and Ethan stared, wide-eyed, into the Polarian Nebula, within which, a dark, blurred shadow of indescribable size was barrelling towards the fleet as its nose, that stretched ahead of the main cruiser, breached the shroud; enormous, amber blaster bolts exploding out from the clouds of gas and obliterating the smaller I.S.S. ships that made up the convoy, along with the shuttles that had gone out in search of survivors.

Nathan turned the shuttle away and vamped up the forward thrusters as high as they would go as blaster fire continued to bombard them from behind.

A pair of scarlet laser beams blazed past the shuttle from the attacking cruiser behind them; the blinding light temporarily dazzling Nathan as he swerved into a nosedive to manoeuvre away from both it and a small I.S.S. cruiser just ahead of them as it started the process of activating its stealth field generator, rendering it invisible to the naked eye.

'WE'RE NOT GOING TO MAKE IT!' yelled Corey as tiny fires began to burn around the inside of the cockpit.

'ISAAC! COLIN! ETHAN! GET THOSE FIRES OUT! I'M TEMPORARILY DISABLING FIRE-SUPPRESSION AND DIVERTING POWER TO INITIATE COUNTDOWN FOR AUGMENTED BURN!' shouted Nathan, now feeling way more out of his depth than he ever thought possible.

He could feel his heart pounding in his chest; the blood surging through his hands and behind his focussed eyes as he swayed and swerved the shuttle through the final stretch of the debris field; gripping the navigation controls much more firmly than was necessary and committing, entirely, to his decision of getting everyone to safety first and asking questions later.

Isaac and the two younger Operatives each grabbed a CO2 fire extinguisher, feeling themselves repeatedly fall off-balance, as they struggled to remain standing; the aggressive movements of the shuttle throwing them back and forth while they sprayed at the patches that had ignited; using all of their strength to keep their footing.

Isaac then caught onto what Nathan had just said as the fleet's contingency plan was to rendezvous on Polarious 5.

'NO! NATHAN, DISENGAGE AUGMENTED BURN! THE GALACTA-NAV HAS NO DESTINATION; WE'LL BE LOST!' Isaac yelled; turning back to the pilot but it was too late. In the blink of an eye, the shuttle was gone and Biker Delta Squadron 5-6-5 with it.

At the entrance to the shuttle, the high pitched ringing of alarms in Oli's ears faded as he succumbed to his ailment; leaving his life in the hands of his Patrol as he slipped away, into the darkness.

CHAPTER 4
THE INCANDESCENT CONTRIVANCE

Beyond the Polarian Stealth Field, the Earth trembled beneath the volatile waves. Huge rocks were torn up in fierce eruptions from beneath the sea bed; exploding from the swelling waters as each one cast a silhouette against an emerald aurora; mesmerising in its shimmer as it swept across the black, nighttime sky.

The towering waves crashed around the enormous, elongated rocks several hundred feet away from the shore, submerging them entirely in a spectacular, explosive display of shear power, testament to nature's rage as the lightning blazed from above; the result of stray blaster bolts from the fierce assault on the I.S.S. fleet above the stealth field, transforming the obliterated waves into fierce showers of sparks that erupted high into the air and rained back down to the swelling waters below.

The wooden rafters of the old stone house that perched, lonely, on the edge of the hill, creaked and trembled; standing strong against the battering of the wind and rain as it had for so many centuries previous; a fortress of defiance upon Scotland's North-East Coast for the terrified 11-year old boy who had taken refuge; hiding within its rugged, weathered walls.

In a small, dark room at the top of the house, Tino, dressed in a torn, black, I.S.S. flightsuit, had awoken, starving and dehydrated after two days of lying unconscious on the splintering wooden floorboards. On awaking to the ferocity of the storm outside, he had quickly found sanctuary beneath an old bed frame; his face dirty, eyes wide and heart racing through shear fear of the undeniable seismic power of the bellowing thunder that shook the entire house.

He repeatedly tried to muster the courage to move but every flash of lightning, every thunderous explosion of the stealth field being breached above the planet, paralyzed him with fright so beneath the bed frame he remained; petrified, as his fingernails dug into the splintering wood of the old, uneven floorboards, reddening the tips of his raw fingers. His only light, the blinding flashes through the slightly off-set window at the end of the room, were so bright that, for a fleeting moment, he could mistake it for the light of day before, once again, falling under a prevailing cloak of darkness.

For years, Tino had been close friends with Oli, the rest of Biker Delta Squadron 5-6-5 and Viper Strike Squadron. They had all been Initiates together when they were in their sapphire cy-bionic suits, back before any of them were invested as Operatives. Tino had, in fact, previously been Viper Strike Squadron's Patrol Leader before Sarah took over the role. Since then, however, Tino had lost all memory of his significance within the Interstellar Scouts.

In fact, being impaled in multiple parts of his body by a Deathstalker Fighter's bladed blaster canon during his final stand to protect the two nearby villages and draw the danger away from a nearby I.S.S. outpost had wiped his memory of the I.S.S. entirely. Not only that but it had wiped their memories of him too, resulting in his Patrol taking his emerald cy-bionic suit and leaving the supposed-dead young Patrol Leader in the abandoned house on Earth after falling from the Deathstalker's bladed blaster canon mid-flight and crashing down, through the roof of the building. With all memory of Tino erased, there had simply been no time to investigate who this child was and, if necessary, return to The Scout Hut with him as the enemy was fleeing and Oli's plan to capture them had been ready to implement.

Unbeknownst to Tino, a peculiar object ablaze in white flame, was tearing its way, at this very moment, across the ghostly night sky on the horizon; striking like a blade, wounding as it gashed, silver, and bled into the rain in the wake of its trajectory, on a direct collision course with the hill upon which the ancient house was perched.

The incandescent inferno smashed straight through the ancient stone ruins atop the old neighbouring graveyard as it came screaming by with a deafening roar; past the old house, dwarfing it in its inexplicable majesty.

The falling ship was sent spiralling off course by the collision and, instead of colliding into the beach at the foot of the hills, it swept in an arc, coming back on itself. With colossal force and, reflected in the depths, the immense contrivance, that was The Knightfall, smashed into the sea alongside the newly-emerged, elongated rocks; launching water and debris, in the form of large boulders, high into the air, before raining back down; striking the side of the hill, unabating in their frenzied bombardment.

Nothing was spared the brutal onslaught as the debris struck the nearby cliffs beneath the church of Gardenstown; the closest of the two nearby villages. Further victims of the bombardment were along the route to Crovie; the smaller, neighbouring village along the shoreline. The impact of the debris caused catastrophic landslides all along the narrow, winding path that joined the two communities. The rocks that struck near the house, rolled back down to the bottom of the hill; settling into the sand beneath it.

With the impact capturing Tino's attention even more prominently than the storm, his ears ringing in the aftermath of the object's near miss of the house, he found the courage within to start pulling himself out from beneath the wooden bed frame, his movements slow; his sweat-soaked hands closed tight into fists due to an intense pain that now surged through his shoulder, abdomen and thigh with every movement.

Hobbling on his pained leg, Tino approached the uneven, dirty window; the cracked, loosely-rattling panes of glass covered in mud, dust and sand.

Wincing at the sharp pain in his shoulder, Tino placed his hand, gently, against the glass; calming the shakiness and feeling the cold moisture against his palm as he wiped at the cumulated dirt that also covered the inside of the window; smearing it but making visibility slightly easier through the streaks. He could now see the dance of the haunting, green aurora in the sky much more clearly.

Although Tino couldn't see the impact zone itself from the bedroom window, he could see the boulders from the fallout, glowing with a radioactive-green hue at the bottom of the hill; reflected in the unyielding rain.

He wanted to get a closer look at the main object that had come down but, as he turned around, he felt the strange stabbing sensation in his abdomen, shoulder and thigh once again. He went to move forwards but the fierce pain worsened; aggressively surging through his body and causing him to stagger slightly. He turned back to face the window, using the explosions in the sky as a source of light so he could see what was causing him so much pain.

Slowly and carefully, Tino peeled back a piece of the torn, black fabric that was covering his abdomen to reveal a large, black stab wound with black lines splintering out from it, into the rest of his torso. Peeling back torn pieces of fabric covering his leg and shoulder, similar scars, with similar behaviours, were also visible.

Trembling and with hesitation, Tino slowly moved his hand towards the wound in his abdomen to inspect it more closely. With the slightest touch, a debilitating pain exploded through his body; triggering a series of terrifying memories held within the blackness that coursed through his veins as it influenced the neural pathways in his brain; almost like the substance that branched out through his body had an intelligence of its own.

In the vision, he felt like he was trapped in a dream while falling from a great height; through thick layers of white clouds. Suddenly, the vision cut short and jumped to another where he felt like he was tumbling down a hill at speed, unable to control or stop himself. Everything was spinning around him and all he could make out was what appeared to be the roof of a house that he was about to smash into. Once again, the vision cut short before he could see what happened next.

Although Tino could see, hear and feel everything going on in the visions, he had no memory of these experiences happening to him personally. Although he wasn't aware of it, the black toxins that worked their way from his wounds, through to his brain had insulated him from any trauma of the experience and, now that they had been stimulated, they could remove the painful sensation and quietly; unnoticed, do what they were created to do by the higher power that now awaited him beyond the Polarian Stealth Field;

Parathax, who had used the Deathstalker Squadron to create a sleeper agent in Tino intended to tear down the Interstellar Scouts.

With a sudden jolt, Tino now found himself collapsed on the wooden floor, slowly returning to consciousness as he tried to catch his breath. The room felt like it was spinning around him.

He frowned as he looked down, next to his hands, to find broken pieces of wood, stone and slate littering the floor around him. Picking up one of the pieces, he observed that, where the wood had broken, the inside wasn't as damp and rotting as the outside of it.

Tino looked about at the other pieces of wood that surrounded him, only to find that they had the same characteristics. Then, it caught his eye. The smashed rafters above him and the enormous, gaping hole over the bed, beneath which, he had previously been hiding. Whatever made the hole and the mess all over the floor had done so very recently.

The assault of bio-chemicals mixed with the black substance; all rushing through his brain, caused the room to take on a warped, sinister feeling; making Tino feel slightly disorientated as he closed his eyes and put his head in his hands. He immediately realised though, that cutting off his sight only enhanced his hearing and set him much more on edge.

Quickly pulling his hands away and looking about the room, extremely alert, Tino made his way back towards the bed. He searched the moist, old mattress; cold, damp and moulding from the leaking ceiling, with his hand and grabbed a torn, thin blanket that was bundled up on it against the wall. Glancing about himself, shivering, he wrapped himself up, using it as a protective cocoon.

He turned to look up at the door, at which point his eyes fell upon the chalky boot prints on the wooden planks, left, unbeknownst to him, by the I.S.S. Operatives that had left him there in the aftermath of the battle. His eyes widened as he contemplated them. The boot prints couldn't have come from him. After all, he wasn't wearing anything on his feet. Someone or something else had been there with him; perhaps they still were.

Unsure of whether he wanted to keep his arms under the blanket for what little warmth and security it provided or outside to be guarded against what he told himself was just in his imagination but, despite his best efforts, he couldn't help but doubt, Tino raised his hand out; penetrating the protective covering as he approached the door.

In furious defiance of his courage, a strong gust of wind rammed the door with all its might, throwing the battered gathering of wooden planks wide open. The explosive force was much too sudden for comfort as the door swung past him, slamming hard against the wall.

His eyes shot wider still, petrified; frozen in a moment of pure terror as his heart skipped a beat, having leapt straight to his mouth which hung agape; his jaw tense.

The door relaxed; the creaking, aching groan of the hinges slowly tailing off, accompanied by the moaning of the gale beyond the doorway that called out to him, daring him to approach the doorway. Tino remained frozen in place, his breathing shallow, as he stared; wide-eyed and alert, out into the blackness beyond the room. He was half expecting something unseen, malevolent, to be staring right back at him. His breathing shaky and with a tension in his shoulders, Tino cautiously edged closer, towards the doorway and continued out onto the landing.

Holding two corners of the torn blanket around his collar, the length of it traipsing along the floor behind him, the trembling boy was too scared to even realise what little warmth it was now providing. His eyes flicked back and forth, scanning his surroundings; his neck stiff, not daring to look back for fear of the footsteps creeping behind him as the floorboards creaked in his wake.

On reaching the rickety ladder at the end of the landing, he pulled the blanket over his shoulder and reached out, placing his hands on the sides; cautious of the rusty nails, now-toxic knives that stabbed at all they touched in betrayal of their purpose of making the ladder safe through its many repairs over the years of its long, tired life of rot and decay.

Tino placed his bare feet at the very ends of the ladder's rotting wooden steps, pressing them up against the sides and trying to avoid putting strain on the parts where they had split towards the middle as he felt for the next step and the next. Some of the horizontal wooden slats had been snapped away completely. He gingerly tapped the bottoms of his feet on the steps, knowing full well the splintered wood could pierce straight through his skin under his weight if he didn't take care.

When he reached the final step, Tino knelt on the ledge of splitting wood at the top and began crawling his way through the small, open space; feeling around for the holes that had been made in the planks beneath him and the nails that stuck out of the woodwork as he pushed aside the broken pieces of slate and stone from his path.

The rotting wood beneath him grew more and more damp as he moved along until it was saturated with water. When Tino finally reached the wall at the end, he leaned in close and peered out; squinting through the gaps in the stone. He tried to ignore the dark empty space behind him as he was repeatedly forced to back away from the cold spray of water, wiping it from his face and smearing the dirt that covered it before leaning forward to look outside again.

Although there was no glowing, silver object to be seen beneath the emerald sky, nor any fire or anything else resembling the massive machine that had fallen from above with so much power, there was now a much taller, broader rock in front of the longer ones that were tailing from behind. Little did Tino know, as he observed the enormous new rock, that the escaped Reptilian fugitive from the I.S.S. Scout Hut was eyeing the house from the crashed Knightfall; the ship disguised as the brown rock by stolen I.S.S. Assimilation Matrix technology.

The storm was intensifying and, while the lightning burned ablaze with white, Tino thought, for a second at least, that the initial flashes had mixtures of turquoise and amber colourations to them.

Blinking the relentless spray of water out of his eyes as he watched the waves crash down over the elongated rocks that they surrounded below, one of them reached up a little too high, catching a fierce bolt of lightning and casting it from wave to towering wave until, in a deafening explosion of dust and water, the blast struck the newly-introduced tallest of the long rocks.

Although the explosion was distant, the sheer force of the impact was still powerful enough to make Tino fall backwards with fright. He remained still for a moment, restrained by the sudden onset shock as he leaned back, propped up by his elbows, his hands clenched into fists.

Slowly recovering and leaning in towards the hole in the wall once more, Tino squinted harder through the rain, watching the smoke that now billowed from the rock; twirling and waltzing in the wind as it was carried away over the sea. He thought he could see a glowing scarlet shimmer where the rock had been hit.

Shifting his weight and moving into a more comfortable position, Tino observed, as the glow pulsed and then exploded into a blinding display of scarlet light. Blazing beams streamed out in all directions, sweeping over and obliterating everything in their path.

The initial shock caused Tino to move a little too quickly as he shuffled on his hands and knees, retreating away from the wall. He tumbled off one of the wooden planks and dropped through the floorboards to the hard, stone floor at the bottom of the house, tearing a new hole in the blanket, caught on the blades of splintered wood as he fell.

Teary-eyed, Tino's lips quivered; his nose bloodied from slamming into the ground; tiny drops of red, dripping down and being absorbed by the chalky dust as he slowly raised his head. Hyperventilating as he tried to keep from crying and with pained effort; Tino pulled his hands across the floor beneath him.

He began to stand back up, an aching pain moving through his legs from his now bruised knees. Wiping the dust from his grazed hands on his trousers, Tino felt a sudden sharp pain like he had sprained his wrist. He grasped at it with his other hand, gently moving it in a circular motion as he blinked back his tears, wiping at his eyes with the back of his hand. Although it got into his eyes slightly, the dust did help to dry the area around them. Tino could feel his frantic pulse pounding against his thumb as he squeezed at his injury.

His attention was quickly diverted away from the throbbing pain as he heard a distant rumbling sound from beyond the stone walls.

It was different to the wind and thunder that had been echoing through the house.

With a final loud exhale through his mouth, his breath wavering, he started to recompose himself. The sound was definitely lasting longer and appeared to be growing louder as he concentrated on it; followed it, listening closely; a frown growing in correlation.

Suddenly, the cumulating fear Tino had held at bay for so long, washed over him; overwhelming in one fell sweep and intensified by thunderous crashes from outside in quick succession as the lightning flashed; now blazing amber with rapid ferocity, bolts striking, cutting, tearing across the entire horizon as far as the eye could see at the exact same moment, without end.

Terrified, Tino raced towards the dusty wooden staircase, skidding slightly across the thin chalky layer that coated the floor as he reached the foot of it. The pain in his leg was numbed by the adrenaline that surged through his body. Tino quickly threw up his arms to hold himself up against the wall, wincing and crying out at the pain from his injured wrist and shoulder wound as the agonising sensation shot up and down, through his elbow.

With his breathing fast and heavy; his heart pounding frantically and almost exploding from his chest, he scrambled up the stairs on his hands and feet as he felt the ground begin to tremor, aggressively, beneath him; the entire house rumbling fiercely.

He ran straight back into the bedroom and slammed the door behind him. Pressing his weight up against it as hard as he could, he felt the wooden planks shaking violently beneath his palms. Whatever it was that demanded entry; rapping and howling from the shadows beyond; he couldn't hold it back any longer.

Tino threw himself to the floor and hastily began to crawl back under the bed frame when, suddenly, everything stopped.

A deathly silence fell; deafening, upon the instantly petrified room. Tino froze; his eyes glazed in reluctant submission as he awaited the harrowing inevitable. But it never came. Tense, he slowly moved back onto his hands and knees; alert in the torment of anticipation.

A burning sensation throbbed in his swelling wrist beneath his weight as he tried to ease himself off it, using it only for balance; coiling like a spring.

Laboured, the room began to re-awake, the ache of the wooden floorboards creaking; groaning around him. He could feel it intensifying beneath his raw-reddened fingertips, now more eerily, like they were slowly failing under growing strain.

The dart of the boy's eyes preceded the turn of his head; his neck and shoulders tense and his entire body poised to move for protection at any given moment.

Once more, the creaking slowly receded; a momentary lapse only, as a devastating seismic explosion, from one of The Knightfall's laser beams striking the hill beneath the house, obliterated its foundations.

The terrified boy was launched across the room with immense force; hurtling, screaming as he tumbled and smashed through the offset window frame. The entire house smashed to the ground beneath Tino as he fell through the wind and rain; ablaze with emerald and scarlet light, flooding his eyes and blinding his vision as he plummeted all the way down to the sharp, jagged rocks below.

CHAPTER 5
THE TESTIMONY OF BECON

The high-pitched, rhythmic sound of the visor's interior vitals monitor rang through Oli's ears as he regained consciousness; his eyes flicking back and forth before he even opened them. His eyelids gradually parted, just a bit at first and then a bit more until they were completely open, although they remained somewhat absent in his gaze. He flexed his aching fingers in tiny muscular twitches and slowly sat himself up.

Looking around, not much was visible beyond the variety of medical charts and displays on the inside of his helmet's visor, its built in respirator active; helping to clear his lungs of whatever had caused him to black out in the hanger bay. His mind was racing frantically. He couldn't fix on any single thought. There were too many questions, too many worries, too many changes of circumstance. Everything that had happened was a blur of chaotic recollection. What exactly had happened? How could he have possibly escaped the Scout Hut's hanger bay?

Placing the palms of his gloved hands on the sides of his emerald cy-bionic helmet, the various sections unlocked and split away from each other slightly while still roughly maintaining its shape, allowing Oli to slowly lift it off his head.

It took a moment for his eyes to adjust to the bright lights of the white rest and recuperation deck of the Interstellar Scouts evacuation shuttle that he now found himself in. The room was deserted and almost completely silent except for the quiet humming sound of medical equipment and the ships engines below which had an almost calming effect on him as he tried to get his bearings.

Oli reached for a metal canteen on the table next to him and took a drink of water from it as he searched for some sort of understanding of what he had just experienced on the cruiser. All he knew at this point, based on the fact that he could hear the engines running, was that the shuttle hadn't landed on Polarious 5 as originally planned. The shuttle would have only been in flight for a couple of minutes if they had landed. *Everyone else is probably in the cockpit*, he thought to himself; that's where he would find answers.

Taking a last drink of water from the canteen, he placed it back down and slowly rose to his feet. He suddenly began coughing; a sharp, stabbing pain shooting down the back of his neck and out, across his shoulders. Oli fell to his knees and strained to reach out for his helmet. He dragged it to the floor and, with strenuous effort, clumsily placed it back over his head, his face sweating. As the cy-bionics within the helmet closed the various pieces together again; locking them into place, an extremely uncomfortable sensation of pins and needles flared up all over his face; his cheeks, his forehead, beneath his eyes.

Gasping for breath from his respirator, he tapped an illuminated circle on the arm of his suit with a first aid cross on it. A holographic display was projected several centimetres away from the badge which, with a swipe of the green laser dot on his finger, he was able to use to cycle through the different options, interacting directly with the holographic projection as he strained to focus through his watering eyes; struggling to remain sat up. On locating the respirator mask icon, he selected it and then tapped a sensor on the side of his helmet. The helmet split into segments and retracted into the suit around his collar while leaving the respirator in place over his nose and mouth.

It hurt Oli's entire body to move, like the suspected Beconium contagion, from his crash-landing on Becon, had sunk its claws deep into all of his muscles but, slowly, Oli was able to pick himself up; returning to his feet and supporting himself with his hand on the platform he had awoken on.

Oli made his way across the well-lit room, dragging his feet as he moved past a series of tables designed for displaying medical readouts as holograms and for performing surgery on. His fingertips traced along the edge of one of them for support as he proceeded towards the doors.

On reaching the end of the room, he walked up a few long steps that were bunched tightly together, flicked a switch on the control panel to the side of the doors; causing them to separate and he entered the shuttle's dark deployment bay.

As Oli crossed the large room, his movements triggered a sensor, activating the long bar lights which illuminated the deployment bay entirely; forcing him to hold up his hand to shield his constantly readjusting eyes, squinting against the brightness. The strain of his eyes could be felt behind them, the sharp pain shooting across his forehead as he gently closed them for a moment, squeezing the bridge of his nose between his finger and thumb as he leaned against an angled pillar that reached out from the wall.

The large, black and grey room was not unlike a vehicle garage and there, in the middle, standing on the deployment bay platform was the pride of Biker Delta Squadron 5-6-5; the Rhinonoid, still dirty with rusty orange Beconium dust and battle-damaged from their crash-landing on Becon.

Oli slowly, wearily, made his way towards another door positioned behind the Rhinonoid; his arms swinging loose at his sides as he hung his head slightly to avoid relying on his aching neck. He flicked another switch on the wall panel and, carelessly, let his hand drop back to his side again; making his way through the doorway.

He slowly ascended up the steep staircase, his armoured boots heavy. Despite the aid of his suit's cy-bionics; they weighed down his feet with every step. His hand brushed across the wall for support as he moved into the softly lit cockpit where the rest of Biker Delta Squadron 5-6-5 sat around the room with their helmets removed. Some of them had their eyes closed, exhausted and in silent contemplation, others held their heads between their knees. The Rhinonoid's crash-landing on Becon a few days previous had been violent on impact and none of them had come away from it unscathed. It was understandable that, between their injuries and undoubtedly high blood-pressure from the dangers of the evacuation which surely gave them all a headache, they were now all in need of some time to recover.

Corey was sat on the floor; leaning back against the wall on the right-hand side of the room across from Isaac, next to the small console he had operated during the evacuation. He was holding his head in his hand; his brown hair hanging between his fingers. Turning, wearily, to look at Oli, Corey followed him with his eyes as he moved further into the cockpit.

While Corey appeared exhausted, from what Oli could make out, Isaac looked simply devastated as he hid his face but he couldn't make out why.

There was a calming ambience to the room, created by the various, quiet beeping sounds that came from the pilot's consoles and occasional flick of a switch as Nathan, the Patrol's pilot, operated the control panels. That was all that could be heard against the quiet humming of the engines, the sound of which had remained present throughout the entire ship.

Corey, while he had been watching Oli, had been sifting through a lot of mixed emotions. He had been terrified during the evacuation, driven to perform a heroic feat by being the one who rescued Oli and being humiliated by the fact that he had ran into the danger without preparing himself with an escape plan. However, now that he'd had time to process everything, the one thing that was eating away at him the most was that it was Isaac who ultimately had to step up and save both him and Oli. He had been relieved to escape the danger unharmed but the more he dwelled upon it, the more resentful he felt towards Isaac for showing him up as well as Nathan for stranding them away from the rest of the fleet.

Corey grabbed a chair that was facing the wall console and pulled himself to his feet as the chair compressed and swivelled slightly under his weight. He was in pain from holding onto the cable as it had dragged him and Oli across the hanger bay, causing him to wince as he placed his hand on his shoulder and across the bottom of his neck. Corey limped towards Oli but didn't stop as he reached him. Instead he silently gestured with a nudge of his head for Oli to follow him back out of the cockpit, into the deployment bay.

Oli knew things were bad as he watched Corey quietly make his way down the stairs. He paused for a moment longer in self-ridicule, taking a last glance at the exhausted group of Operatives that he had let down, now scattered around the cockpit. Oli was their Patrol Leader, he should have arrived at the hanger bay sooner and helped co-ordinate the evacuation. Finally, he turned and followed Corey back into the deployment bay.

'What happened? Where's our D.T.L?' Oli asked, dumbfounded; his voice muffled by his breathing apparatus as the doors to the cockpit closed behind him. D.T.L. was short for 'Designated Troop Leader' but the man in the gold cy-bionics, who was supposed to accompany them to safety on the shuttle, had given his life trying to get Oli to safety in The Scout Hut's hanger bay. It was this man's sacrifice that had distracted the hostile bionic from attacking Corey or Sarah and, instead, forced it to flee along with the escaped Reptilian as the two young Operatives had rushed to Oli's aid in the Troop Leader's place.

Oli repeated the process of cycling through the holograms projected from his suit's badge once more to collapse the breathing mask into its compartment within his suit as Corey obtained several items from a metal tool box that was magnetised to the floor of the deployment bay, next to the platform.

Oli observed that Corey was evidently still distressed as he had thrown open the wings of the tool box with force, rattling the tools inside rather than peeling the two sections apart. In an attempt to occupy both his agitated hands and mind, Corey turned to the Rhinonoid and began cleaning the Beconium off the hull with a worn wire brush that he clutched in his armoured-gloved hand for protection against the substance. He squeezed a small amount of white paste containing an abrasive grit compound from an old, worn tube that was curled upwards from the bottom, onto one of the vehicle's squatting legs. Beconium was only really fatal in the radioactive sandstorms on Becon but it was still harmful if it made contact with a person's skin wherever it was.

Although cleaning the hull of the Rhinonoid gave Corey something to occupy him as he spoke, in this moment, he was feeling anything but accommodating. 'Why has nobody cleaned the

Beconium off the tank yet? Are we waiting for the shuttle's hull to corrode before we do something about it?' he asked aggressively.

There was a long pause as Oli was caught off-guard by Corey's aggressive tone. 'Everyone's had a difficult time since the Deathstalker Squadron, the endless distress signals and mission briefings, the Reptilian double-crossing us. Viper Strike said they pursued the Deathstalkers to Polarious and the entire world had been liquidised to an ocean of molten silver. On top of all of that, we were shot down to the surface of Becon and stranded there. The entire Patrol will be in shock and exhausted at the moment. They can't be expected to be as sharp as normal until they've had time to process everything' explained Oli after a moment.

'It's not like it requires much thought' mumbled Corey, still not looking at Oli. Corey knew a lot more than Oli about what had happened on Becon, including what had attacked the Patrol Leader from the shroud of the sandstorm but didn't want to recap the trauma of the memories so he kept the knowledge to himself and continued to attack the rest of the Patrol instead. 'They're just neglecting any sort of maintenance and waiting for someone else to do it instead and, oh look, now I am' he continued with spiteful sarcasm.

'Corey. What happened?' Oli repeated his question.

'The tank shouldn't even have Beconium on it. If you had just listened to me while we were transporting the Deathstalkers onto the cruiser, we wouldn't have been shot down at all and we wouldn't have crashed down to the surface of Becon. I know you like to do everything your way, which usually involves putting Colin before the rest of us, but...' snarled Corey, causing Oli to grow defensive.

'Corey, where are you going with this? Colin's my brother' said Oli, a hint of warning in his voice for Corey to not step out of line.

'Adoptive brother' Corey corrected. 'I saw that attack coming. I warned you about it repeatedly. We were probably baited in the first place. The whole operation took way too long' he insisted turning to face Oli. Oli remembered hearing Commissioner Hanson say something similar back on the cruiser as he had walked down the corridor with his Advisors at the start of the attack, just hours ago.

'You made the decision to listen to Isaac, Colin and Nathan and look what happened as a result' Corey jabbed before turning back to resume cleaning the Beconium off the Rhinonoid.

'I think the Deathstalkers and the Reptilian were used to knock us onto our back foot and weaken us. There's a third, leading enemy of the I.S.S. out there looking to cripple us; maybe even destroy us. The Deathstalker Squadron and the Reptilian were accounted for onboard The Scout Hut during that assault, so who was attacking the fleet from outside with that much fire power when we reached the Polarious Sector? We were only on a simple patrol and rescue mission. They knew we would be there to lend assistance so they must be connected. Also, what happened to the fleet?' asked Oli, levelling with Corey before asking his question, now more forcefully, for the third time.

'Oli, you're just stabbing in the dark. You're a Patrol Leader, not a Troop Leader. If we had a Troop Leader onboard to tell us that then...' replied Corey but Oli cut him off.

'But we don't. Do we?' Oli interjected, realising that they really were alone.

'The entire Polarious Sector Patrol fleet is gone' Corey finally replied bluntly to Oli's question, his eyes still focussed on the work he was doing; haunted by what he and the rest of the group had just witnessed as he tried hard not to reflect too heavily on it.

From Corey's body language and sombre tone of voice, it wasn't difficult for Oli to gather that they hadn't simply evacuated the cruiser and lost track of the rest of the fleet.

Although this revelation hit hard and, undeniably, put him into a state of shock, Oli tried to remain composed as he searched for the right words, after all, Corey was right; he was the Patrol Leader of Biker Delta Squadron 5-6-5 albeit a newly appointed one. Whether he was prepared for it or not, this was now his responsibility merely by rank. Perhaps the responsibility was even more prominent with him though than he wanted to admit as he now had to make the calls that an experienced adult Troop Leader would normally make.

While he had assisted in many I.S.S. missions in the past, it had always been under the command of an overseeing Troop Leader. He had never headed a mission himself before except for those small, rare circumstances where he briefly went against his orders to serve the greater good and this was far more dangerous than any simple capture or rescue exercise where he knew the facts and the risks and he could be certain about his decisions. He was a child who needed to act as an adult immediately in this chaotic new situation. He needed to take command fast before whatever was hunting them could track them down. He confessed to himself though, he was entirely at a loss.

'Have we been able to reach any of the onboard Troop Leaders with the other evacuation shuttles? Send out a distress call?' Oli asked, hoping to still track down and get some adult advice or guidance from I.S.S. seniority so that he could just carry out the instructions and appoint the tasks to his Patrol to get them to safety, just as he normally would.

It was an awkward situation he found himself in as these Operatives, although experienced and familiar with each other, had only recently been grouped together as a Patrol and they normally looked to Oli for guidance, not the other way around. Corey remained silent as he continued scrubbing at the vehicle; the white, gritty substance now a mixture of orange and grey.

Oli silently looked from Corey to various points around the room as if searching for the right words, hoping they would materialise from thin air.

'The evacuation protocols will have been activated when the alarms were triggered which means the evacuation pods will have been standing by for launch and...' Oli started, looking down at the floor and trying to find reassurance that there would still be survivors out there.

'OUR OWN UNMANNED SHIPS TURNED ON US IN THE HANGER BAY OLI! THEY CREATED A DIVERSION FOR THE REPTILIAN TO FLEE IN THE KNIGHTFALL AND THEY DESTROYED THE OTHER I.S.S. SHIPS BEFORE THEY COULD LAUNCH!' Corey snapped furiously once more as he reeled around to face Oli; his voice growing more and more enraged. A metallic tool that he was also using to scrape at the vehicle let out a high pitched ring, as bright and sharp as an unsheathed sword, as he quickly pulled it away. The sound echoed through the metal room, cutting through the silence. Oli stood, frozen in place, stunned as he looked from the metal tool back to Corey who was seething with frustration.

After a few moments, Corey slowly relaxed his grip on the tool he'd been clenching tightly in his fist. He looked down at it as he gently tossed it aside; the tool clattering to the mesh of the metal, gridded floor.

After a moment of acknowledging his actions, although unable to muster an apology, Corey moved around to the side of the Rhinonoid, to one of the small, illuminated staircases that led up to the inside of the tank and sat on the second step up as he let out a loud, heavy sigh.

'We can't send out a distress signal. Nobody can know our location. If your theory is right and the Deathstalker attacks were intended to lead us to Polarious on a rescue mission so that this mystery enemy that was firing on the fleet could eliminate us, then that was a co-ordinated attack against the I.S.S; and, unless they got caught in the assault, there are mixtures of I.S.S. prisoners, civilians, Operatives, Initiates, Troop Leaders and extremely powerful enemies out there right now. Nearly all of them looking for survivors; looking for us' Corey pointed out.

As Oli contemplated what Corey was saying, he thought he saw the brief reflection of a small silver flash on the leg of his shiny, emerald exoskeleton; a reality check that he prayed were his tired eyes playing tricks on him and not the alert that his cy-bionic suit had detected something during an analysis of his potential sickness he feared he'd picked up from Becon.

Trembling slightly in acknowledgment of the small, blinking light, recurring on the inside of his suit's wrist-guard, Oli tensed his jaw, exhaling hard through his nose as a sudden feeling of anxiety struck through his body, creating a surge of panic.

Oli slowly turned away from the steps where Corey was sat and started making his way towards the doors leading to the rest and recuperation deck opposite. He deployed and removed his emerald helmet, placing it on the holo-bio projection table to auto-synchronise with it and transfer the analysed data. He then flicked a switch on the table, activating it.

'Where are we now? I'm guessing not Polarious Five?' asked Oli.

Corey gave Oli an exhausted look. 'Nathan put the shuttle into Augmented Burn as soon as we were clear of the debris field as we had sustained heavy damage during the evacuation. Navigation isn't providing us with much. Uncharted territory somewhere beyond the Polarious Sector, that's all we know. Since we left, Nathan's been scanning far and wide for I.S.S. signatures because Sarah and the rest of Viper Strike Squadron were supposed to evacuate with us as our fighter escort but there's no sign of them. Sarah, Emma, Jess, Pete, Timothy; they're all gone. Although it's hopefully not true, we're pretty sure that they either perished onboard the cruiser or were struck by passing debris above Polarious Five while evacuating. We've since had to stop putting out transmissions to avoid detection by anyone hunting for survivors. There were loads of I.S.S. signatures surrounding the fleet when we left but, one by one, they have vanished from the periphery of the scanners... All Interstellar Scouts, whether they are Operatives, Leaders or Initiates that evacuated safely from the fleet, are being hunted and shot down on sight' Corey replied regrettably as he paused halfway across the room and activated one of the badges on his armoured suit which projected a floating hologram of the shuttle's nullified navigation systems. Deactivating the badge once again, he joined Oli; leaning against the projection table.

'This enemy that attacked the fleet, whether it was tied to the Reptilian and the Deathstalkers or just pirates who had acquired a lot of firepower, when we were leaving The Scout Hut's hanger bay, we saw...something; some shapeless shadow emerging from within the Polarian Nebula. I don't know what it was but it was massive. It just kept getting bigger and bigger. It was moving fast for its size as well. Like a shark, swimming in the murky depths, coming right at us. The last thing we saw, before Nathan got us away from the attack, was the entire fleet being totally obliterated. Thousands upon thousands of amber blaster bolts raining down, endlessly, over the convoy, destroying cruisers in a matter of seconds' Corey explained; a distant look of horror on his face as he relived the ordeal of The Stealthy Intoxicator's assault. 'Nobody knows where we are now. Not even us' he finished wearily, coming back to his original reply only to find that he was repeating himself.

'Could work to our advantage' replied Oli. He had been unable to completely grasp the extent of the danger they had survived as he was so distracted with his current problem as he cycled through the holographic displays.

'There is no advantage to any of this' Corey dismissed, shaking his head.

'If we didn't plot any co-ordinates and nobody else knows our position then, if we can keep a low profile, it will give us the time we need to figure out our...next...move' Oli continued, his voice dull, dreary almost, his words slowly tailing off; now adopting a tone of dread.

Although trying to distract himself to soften the anticipated blow, not all of his attention was on what he was saying as he analysed the holographic bio charts and readouts which, to his horror, all showed signs of, what they referred to as 'Perpetual Biological Deterioration'.

'Beconium Poisoning?' asked Corey after a moment, removing his weight from the table and turning a sympathetic gaze away from the holographic charts to look at Oli. Oli hung his head with regret, nodding slowly and resting his entire weight on both hands which he himself now placed on the edge of the table. Although he had strongly suspected the problem to be Beconium Poisoning, he hadn't been prepared for the shock of confirmation from the holographic medical charts being projected from the table.

Oli suddenly felt very lightheaded from the shock and his breathing grew shaky; his heart racing with panic. As he started coughing again, his legs gave way beneath him and he collapsed to the floor. He tried to lift his heavy arm, reaching up to the surface of the table to try and pull himself back up but he was entirely incapacitated.

Corey had been protected from the Beconium by his suit's respiratory filters and the shelter of the Rhinonoid's wreckage while on Becon but Oli's filters had taken a blaster bolt directly to one of them while he was on watch for the extraction shuttle, exposing him to the radioactive substance. Oli hadn't been aware that the Reptilian had been on Becon with them, only that it had later been apprehended for assisting the Deathstalker Squadron. He was, therefore, unable to piece it all together.

Corey grabbed hold of Oli and pulled his arm over his shoulder, quickly helping him across the room to the sleeping platform before carefully placing Oli's helmet back over his head, allowing the pieces to close together and lock into place. As Oli grabbed at the Operative's arm. Corey retracted the helmet into the collar of his armoured suit and reactivated his respirator mask for him, using the illuminated circle on his arm.

Gasping at first, with the oxygen being fed to him being obstructed by his contracting windpipe, Oli finally took a few deep breaths, clutching desperately at the mask with his trembling hand. He felt like he was burning up, hemmed in by his armoured suit.

Frustrated, he twisted a ring on the cuffs of his suit and pulled off his gloves, dropping them to the floor at his side; his palms and forehead sweaty with fear, his symptoms worsening as his eyes darted around the room in frantic desperation, unsure where to look. Each time he exhaled, the shakiness in his breathing was very audible.

As he calmed back down and regained control of his breathing; his head bowed slightly, he slowly, gradually, flicked his eyes up to meet those of the concerned Operative crouched down in front of him. They both knew how lethal Beconium Poisoning was and it had now been days since they were on Becon.

'What do we do?' Corey asked, his hand on Oli's shoulder, helping him to remain sat up.

Just as both Operatives knew the severity of Beconium Poisoning, they also knew that both options and time were extremely limited and, in the heat of their missions, Oli often forgot that the Operatives in his charge were only kids. He himself was only a kid.

They weren't Troop Leaders. Their own Designated Troop Leader had been killed during the assault on the fleet. They couldn't even rely on reaching out to any other surviving Troop Leaders from the fleet now in case the transmissions were intercepted by the enemy. They were alone.

He slowly pulled the mask away from his face on a hinge positioned just above the rim of his collar. Although he knew that not only his days but, potentially, his hours were now numbered, he couldn't bring himself to accept it.

'We need to get to Crystalosis' Oli grunted, trembling through his heavy breaths.

Before Corey could respond, the room jolted violently. Both Operatives were thrown off balance and tumbled across the floor.

'WHAT WAS THAT!?' shouted Corey, stunned, over the now-wailing alarms but he was shouting to an empty room as Oli had once again, blacked out, and was lying on the floor, limp.

'VIPER FIGHTERS INBOUND! WE'RE TAKING FIRE!' announced Nathan's urgent voice through the speakers built into the collars of the Operatives' cy-bionic suits.

'Shuttle Assistant Patrol Leader calling all I.S.S. Viper Fighters, this is Kestrel Evacuation Shuttle designation: Biker Delta Squadron Five-Six-Five! I repeat, stand down, this shuttle is unarmed and requires urgent fighter escort to the nearest I.S.S. fleet!' announced Isaac's voice; taking over from Nathan's as he tried to make contact with the rogue I.S.S. fighters that were animated by the thorny, black energy which had pulsed and bled out of the Deathstalkers back onboard The Scout Hut.

Nathan used what experience he had to manoeuvre the shuttle, evading the incoming blaster bolts.

The shuttle continued to take hits as it swayed and swerved in response to Nathan's attempts to out-manoeuvre the attackers.

'Calm down Nathan, move the ship more smoothly' said Isaac cautiously as the shuttle jolted and juddered in response to Nathan's sharp, aggressive movements. The young pilot's hands were sweating as he struggled to direct the ship; panicking as the heels of his hands felt bruised from pressing them against the navigation grips with unconscious pressure for so long.

'I CAN'T DO IT! I CAN'T FOCUS PROPERLY ON MY OWN!' protested Nathan, growing increasingly frustrated with himself and ultimately resulting in him surrendering to his own self-doubt.

'ALL OPERATIVES TO THE RHINONOID, NOW! I WILL REMOTE PILOT FROM THERE!' ordered Nathan.

Corey dragged himself across the rest and recuperation deck to Oli who was being thrown about the room by the shuttle's drastic movements. He grabbed hold of the unconscious Patrol Leader's arm, threw it over his shoulder and hauled him through the doors and into the shuttle's deployment bay.

'Why are they still firing on us!?' yelled Ethan as the group ran out of the cockpit and into the deployment bay. He and Colin were thrown to the floor by a violent jolt along the way. Sparks exploded from the various electronic components around the deployment bay while extremely hot, pressurised jets of steam blasted out of the pipes on the wall as the two youngest Operatives stumbled, their helmets protecting them from the severe burns they would have otherwise got. Isaac helped Colin and Ethan to their feet, kicking aside the magnetised tool box in passing.

'They are unmanned fighters. Something else is controlling them!' shouted Nathan, wearing his helmet and interacting with a hologram projected from one of the illuminated badges on his armoured cy-bionic suit. He swiped through an array of vehicles until he reached the Rhinonoid image and then rapidly selected a series of drop-down options to start up the tank's systems as he raced past.

'Corey! Get Oli the medical help that he needs and then meet us in the cockpit!' shouted Nathan's voice in passing from behind his helmet as everyone ran up the steps and into the Rhinonoid. Everyone was moving so fast and Corey was under so much pressure that they just looked like green blurs as they raced by.

'Plot a course for Crystalosis, NOW!' Corey barked back at him, furiously, as he tried to haul Oli up the short staircase and into the Rhinonoid.

'Shielding and the stealth field generator are both compromised from The Scout Hut's hanger bay!' shouted Nathan as he took his seat in the Rhinonoid's cockpit, their movements triggering sensors that illuminated the cockpit and control centre with light and triggered the initialisation of all workstations in the control centre.

'Come on Isaac, I need you with me on this' Nathan continued as he looked over his shoulder to see the Assistant Patrol Leader, stunned; collapsing into his seat. Nathan then used the same badge on his suit again to select the specific class of shuttle that was carrying the Rhinonoid and it projected an intricate pilot's console in front of him.

Isaac climbed to his feet and leaned over Nathan's seat to inspect the remote holographic display for the shuttle.

'We're entirely vulnerable! They'll pulverise us in absolutely no time at this rate!' Nathan insisted through gritted teeth as he frantically interacted with the holographic console projection in front of him, tapping at different options and using his hands, in contact with the hologram, to guide the ship.

Looking out to the infinite expanse of space in front of them, Isaac recollected the events that took place onboard The Scout Hut which had been caused by the same ships that were now attacking them. He relived the traumatic experience of seeing their Designated Troop Leader's lifeless body beneath the girder, his sister trapped as she had searched for refuge and the immense destruction of the fleet.

While afraid of the very real danger they were all facing, he was also feeling immense resentment towards the situation and driven to save his friends from the same fate. Isaac retracted his helmet into the collar of his cy-bionic suit, revealing his fiery hair; his eyes determined and focussed beneath his quiff.

'NAVIGATIONAL SYSTEMS ARE FAILING!' yelled Nathan as he tried to use the automated stellar-mapping system to plot their course back into known territory and reach Crystalosis.

'I'm on it!' Isaac said, exhaling hard and letting his emotions get the better of him as he turned and raced towards the doors at the back of the control centre.

'ISAAC, THERE'S NO TIME!' Nathan protested, studying the holographic readings as he realised what Isaac planned on doing but the only response that came back was the cockpit doors closing behind the Assistant Patrol Leader as he quickly left the room.

Isaac raced back down the steps of the Rhinonoid, into the shuttle's deployment bay, grabbing a spool of soldering wire in passing from the toolbox Corey had been using earlier during his conversation with Oli. He stopped at the wall opposite the stairs, next to the doors that Corey and Oli had emerged from. Drawing a knife from a sheath on his utility belt, Isaac used the tip of it to hook under the edge of the panel cover, levering it away. Once the cover was removed and returning his knife to its sheath, he radioed through to Nathan.

'It looks like the circuit-breakers have been tripped to prevent a chain-reaction. I'm going up to the cockpit to check the extent of the damage and make the repairs!' he shouted over the alarms and violent rumbling of the shuttle.

He ran through the doors and up the staircase, to the cockpit; drawing his blaster as he went and twisting a small dial on the bottom of it, to the soldering setting. A red-hot metal rod sprung into position beneath the barrel of his blaster. He placed the blaster on the floor, threw himself down next to it and climbed beneath the shuttle's piloting consoles.

Squinting and closing his mouth tight, with a tension in his jaw, against the sparks that rained down over him from the console, Isaac yanked out the wires that controlled the positioning of the shields while trying not to get his hands tangled or snag at the other wires, used his knife to slice away some of the insulation, twisted all of the necessary wires together and reinserted them collectively into a different compartment; using the trigger on his blaster to intensify the temperature of the rod as he used the spool of soldering wire to solder the wires into place. It was both very makeshift and dangerous but it was all he had time to do.

'Shielding re-engaged, nice work Isaac!' announced Nathan, his voice audibly shaky.

'It's just generally evened out. It's thin but it should hold for a couple of minutes' replied Isaac as he pulled himself back out from under the console and retrieved his knife and blaster.

'It's good enough! Now get back to the Rhinonoid before we lose power again' Nathan instructed.

'I still need to reengage the stealth field' replied Isaac as he ran over to another separate console that Corey had been leaning against earlier and set about beginning repairs on those systems as well.

Suddenly, an unfortunately placed blast struck the shuttle; penetrating the shielding and causing the cockpit to catch fire. A second alarm began sounding as the CO2 fire-suppression systems, having been reengaged by Nathan since escaping the assault on the fleet, activated, flooding the cockpit with pressurised CO2.

'ISAAC! GET BACK HERE NOW! THE SHUTTLE HAS SECONDS LEFT AND THE COCKPIT DOORS ARE GOING TO ISOLATE THE FIRE!' Nathan shouted.

Agreeing with Nathan that this was now a lost cause, Isaac jumped to his feet, swept up his equipment and sprinted across the cockpit to the top of the staircase. He started running down the first few stairs and then leapt as far as he could, all the way to the bottom but he was unable to get through the doors in time before they closed and locked themselves.

'I'm locked in!' announced Isaac.

'Colin's on his way to override the door from the other side. The entire cockpit is flooding with CO2 so activate your respirator mask so you can breathe until the fire is out and the doors unlock. Then brace yourself, I'm going to pull some drastic evasive manoeuvres to shake the enemy off!' instructed Nathan.

Nathan's hope was that, should the shuttle be destroyed, they would all be able to safely escape onboard the Rhinonoid that the shuttle was carrying but, now that Isaac was trapped, the shuttle could no longer be treated as collateral damage. Nathan knew he would have to put all of his nerves and anxieties right to the back of his mind and focus. Blaming the absence of a Troop Leader to instruct him was no longer an option.

'There's no time and Colin can't put himself in danger to get me out' argued Isaac. Having activated his suit's respirator mask, he proceeded to use one of his other badges to access the Rhinonoid's systems. He then selected the option which read 'Assistant Patrol Leader Override' once again. As second in command of the group next to Oli, it was his responsibility to make sure that the group got away from this attack safely.

'Isaac, the steps have retracted into the tank and locked into place, what are you doing!?' shouted Nathan.

'Hold your position for as long as possible and, if I don't make it, make sure Oli does. Nathan, the Patrol will need a new Assistant Patrol Leader. I want you to take my place' instructed Isaac.

'Colin, don't worry, Oli's going to be fine, you all are; I'll make sure of it' he continued before Nathan could say anything.

'Isaac, I know you blame yourself for what happened to Sarah in the hanger bay. I blame myself too, we should have been able to help her but we couldn't; it just wasn't possible but she used her final transmission telling you, telling all of us, to get to safety. We owe her that after everything she has done for us. Now get up off the floor AND GET OUT OF THERE!' Nathan ordered as he watched the Operative through a camera in the cockpit, sitting on the floor and leaning into the corner next to the doors, accepting of his fate.

After a moment of remembering his sister, of whom Nathan spoke, Isaac looked down at his blaster and, nodding in agreement, adjusted the setting to retract the soldering iron and ignite a blowtorch flame in the hope of cutting through the locks. His helmet's visor deployed from his armoured suit's collar and suspended itself in place in front of his eyes, protecting them from the blinding light as sparks began flying from between the sealed doors.

As he cut through the metal, the flame quickly began to fade due to the oxygen being removed from the room by the fires and the suppression systems, leaving it with nothing to burn. Thinking fast, he removed his respirator mask and, holding his breath, he leaned in close while cupping it over his blaster; allowing the flame to feed off his suit's oxygen reserves.

'The clamps on the deployment bay hatch have released Isaac. I can't hold it back any longer, it's automated' announced Nathan's voice regrettably and with a slight catch but Isaac didn't reply. He just focussed on holding onto that deep breath he had taken from his mask and cutting through the final remaining lock.

Once he had cut through the last lock on the door, he pushed them apart and slipped through, allowing them to slam shut behind him. The fire-suppression systems were active in the deployment bay as well but Isaac wasted no time in his urgency getting back onto the Rhinonoid. He rushed through the clouded jets of pressurised CO2, used his badge to deploy the steps from the wall of the Rhinonoid and pushed both hands up from beneath the row of blue switches in the shuttle's wall, re-engaging the shuttle's stealth field generator.

The shuttle turned completely invisible to its attackers as Isaac ran back up the steps to the inside of the Rhinonoid's jet propulsion unit refuelling station, retracting and locking them back into place behind him. The sound of ceiling panels rising on their hinges to equalise the internal pressure and then, loudly, slamming back down in a wave, echoed throughout the room, as he breathlessly made his way back into the cockpit to join the others, returning his blaster and knife to their holster and sheath.

'We've hacked the Vipers' navigational systems and plotted a course back into known territory. Galacta-nav co-ordinates set for Crystalosis. Augmented Burn initiated' announced Nathan, clearly distressed; sweating and breathing heavily.

By the time Isaac was returning to the Rhinonoid's cockpit, Corey had gotten Oli into the medical bay and connected him to an array of life-support machinery. He had heard the commotion that had been going on as their voices had sounded through the tiny speaker in his collar. Of course he had been tending to Oli; nevertheless, he contemplated that, had he been in the cockpit, he could have been the one to save them all rather than Isaac. He wouldn't have been so careless in restoring the shields. Lost in his romanticised daydream that anybody else would have highly doubted if they knew, he considered how heroic he could have been as he rose to his feet.

Leaving the Patrol Leader to endure the remainder of the journey alone, Corey turned around and walked away, up the few narrow steps at the other end of the room, towards the doors. As the doors opened, Corey turned back to Oli, staring at him for several seconds before turning away once more; leaving the room and entering into the cold and damp of the dark refuelling station; a rekindled rage burning within having overheard Isaac appoint Nathan as next in command. He had been entirely overlooked.

CHAPTER 6
KNIGHTFALL ON THE AWAKING MOON

Tino awoke with a start, his eyes wide and alert, his hair cold, wet; clinging to his face and impairing his vision. The fall - What had happened? Shouldn't he have died when he fell out of the house and hit the rocks at the foot of the hill? That was the last thing he remembered...Where was he now?

Tino tried to turn his head onto its side to look around the cold, dark room but every part of his body appeared to be entirely paralyzed. His eyes strained as they flicked about, scanning what little of the environment he was able to, a frown of frustration growing heavier on his face; a frown that was accentuated as his desperation intensified, gritting his teeth.

Just slightly within his peripheral vision to his left, although very blurred, Tino could see multiple small, peculiar objects, each with a single red light being emitted from it. The objects appeared to be mounted on tripods and were slowly pivoting back and forth as if scanning the room. Although this was all he could see and despite being out of focus, he had a feeling there were more of these objects scattered about in the darkness around him.

Tino tried, repeatedly, to sit up, fighting, straining his mind to overcome his paralysis, just to move his arms and legs, his face growing red and contorted as he used all of his willpower but, despite his best efforts, nothing happened.

Realising that he was only tiring himself out, he decided that it would be best to save what little energy he had until he knew more about what was going on. He slowed his heavy breathing, closing his eyes so that he could listen more closely to his surroundings without distraction.

He could hear a low-pitched humming sound coming from the floor. The sound was faint but still audible. The metal mesh floor panels rattled with a gentle judder in recurring crescendos as if the entire room was shaking, as they trembled upon their supports.

The room suddenly jolted, quivering violently. Tino opened his eyes, darting them back and forth across the ceiling; silently interrogating his surroundings as a distant thudding of heavy footsteps now echoed from above. They appeared to be growing louder and louder, as if somebody was approaching.

Listening closely, with increasing intent, as he followed the footsteps, Tino flicked his eyes ahead of the impending sound, casting them down at his own feet in front of him. He could vaguely make out, amongst the shadows, the silhouette of a metal ladder that reached into the room from the illuminated floor above. The ladder, a taunt; mocking him with a means of escape, only reached about half way into the room and it definitely wasn't low enough for him to reach, even if he could regain the use of his arms and legs.

The heavy thud of the booted footsteps grew louder still as they neared the round hole in the ceiling through which the ladder protruded.

Staring helplessly at the hole and wishing the sound away, Tino felt his heart pounding; hammering within his chest, his raging pulse punching from inside his wrists as blood surged through his veins with every beat and a cold sweat covered his face. The thudding stopped. He could just about make out a shadow moving ever so slightly above the illuminated hole in the ceiling. It moved menacingly, a shapeless malice watching; observing its victim from a distance.

Suddenly, with a screeching crescendo of scraping metal and ending with a loud bang, the rubber feet at the bottom end of the ladder slammed into the floor; the powerful noise reverberating around the room. A long pause followed, drowning the room in silence once more.

Despite the stillness and deafening silence, the shadowy shape seemed intent on screaming terror into the frightened boy. The black silhouette of a large, leather boot slowly penetrated the light of the hole and stamped down, aggressively, onto the top rung of the ladder followed by the next boot on the second rung. The descent was deliberately drawn out and each footstep echoed loudly with a slow, rhythmic pulse around the metal walls of the entire room. It was as if the huge silhouette, now unveiled momentarily before becoming enshrouded in the darkness of the room once more, intended to instil dread and precede itself with the horrors that manifested within its victim's mind.

A small panicked sound slipped out of Tino's mouth as sheer uncontainable terror washed over him. Silence instantly fell as the final echo dissipated into the shadowy abyss. Not a breath could be heard. It was as if everything had frozen between one pound of his heart and the next.

Out of the corner of his eye, he could see the red lights of the pivoting objects, in ominous synchronisation, slowly, eerily, turning towards him as if the noise had captured their attention. Tino couldn't breathe. His chest had grown tight with fear. His face, no longer cold with anticipation of the unknown, now burned with panic.

A fierce bang on the metal floor panels penetrated the silence; enraged ferocity exploding from the shadows and shaking the already trembling floor panels of the entire room. Explosive sparks of electricity jolted up at the metal strap locks that ran across the boots that the dark shape wore; briefly illuminating the giant silhouette in blinding flashes that erupted at its feet. Although Tino didn't think it possible, his eyes strained wider still as the burning sensation was driven from his body. He grew cold, shivering in unbridled fear. He heard a single beeping sound from the shadows and the red lights on the objects around the room powered down.

Unsure of what was going on, Tino's eyes rapidly darted around the room as he began hyperventilating uncontrollably, his trembling breaths short and sharp with fright.

The heavy booted footsteps marched, quick and threatening, across the room as they waded through the furiously crackling flashes of bright, electric-blue sparks. The being's presence preceded itself much more prominently now as it strode towards Tino, echoing through the darkness to finally reveal the monstrous Reptilian, a large, lizard-like creature dressed in a sleeveless, torn, black flightsuit and a matching grazed, ankle-length, sleeveless trench coat.

The Reptilian appeared to have no tail and was walking on its hind legs as it charged right at Tino. The huge being towered over him as it came to an abrupt halt alongside the platform upon which he lay, slamming the panels down into their supports beneath its weight. The Reptilian hissed at him through its breaths, viciously baring its huge, razor-sharp teeth through which a long, forked tongue protruded. It stared down at Tino. The narrow, black pupils of its amber eyes, that reflected the raging sparks of electricity, were sunk deep within its scarred head which was patterned with a striking green and purple colouration; the ridged shape of its large skull clearly defined.

Tino's hyperventilation intensified as his mind raced frantically, his efforts desperate; increasingly erratic in trying to control his muscles to move away from the terrifying creature but alas, it was no use. He felt that, if he couldn't physically explode out of his own body, he would black out at any moment.

Extending a long, stained claw upwards, lines and marks of distress etched into it, the Reptilian slid a switch near the ceiling above Tino and the electrical current that ran through the floor panels, the walls and the slightly raised metal platform, upon which Tino lay, was instantly cut off, the snapping and crackling of the sparks ceasing.

The electrical current was used to disrupt the nervous system in the bodies of prisoners as, before serving Parathax, the Reptilian had previously been a bounty hunter and an assassin; driven by a vendetta to avenge the death of his family at the hands of the Biolum Military.

Moments later, as the creature watched on, Tino began to feel a surge of immense pain growing throughout his entire body from the fall, the discomfort in which his captor took great delight; sneering down at its prisoner. Tino started to feel the ache of his tired, battered muscles as they began to reawaken, allowing him to move and see his surroundings more clearly. Curiously though, the pain began to fade almost immediately until only his blackened wounds could feel it and, even then, the sensation was short-lived as his injuries became numb once more; the black substance resuming its job.

'The venom of the Deathstalker; that's the price you pay for your allegiances' the Reptilian hissed, peeling away the torn fabric that covered the black wound in Tino's abdomen.

The Reptilian knew that this child wouldn't understand his native language, Biolie, so reluctantly spoke in Com-Vox; the universally-recognised name for Earth-English. The boy looked from his wound and then back up at the Reptilian with dread as if he knew what was about to happen. To stimulate the muscles that were still slightly in spasm from the paralysing electrical current, the Reptilian pressed its razor sharp claw against the wound, causing Tino to scream out in agonising pain.

The pain triggered more visions as the sensation grew more and more excruciating, so much so, that it quickly became impossible to distinguish much from the images. The one thing that kept recurring was where he felt like he was hurtling through the air at extreme speed and, looking down, he could see a pair of emerald-armoured, gloved hands, as if they were his own, grasping at what looked like a long, black spear with four bladed prongs; a blaster canon of one of the Deathstalker Fighters that had hit him in mid-flight during Tino's attempts to fend off their strike on Earth.

Each of the giant, bladed prongs had four smaller blades that surrounded the barrel of the blaster canon, which had been used to inject the black substance into his body. Three of the four giant blades were impaled into his abdomen, shoulder and thigh; the same places where his blackened wounds were located. Tino thrashed and writhed, throwing his arms and kicking his legs as he cried out until the torture ceased, leaving him trembling, breathlessly.

Timid, as he turned his gaze away from the infected scar to look at the creature in front of him once again, he instead found himself staring down the barrel of a small blaster, clutched in the Reptilian's long, stained claws. This particular blaster was of specific significance to the Reptilian. It was the weapon that he had taken from the lifeless body of his military Commander, having killed him for the murder of his family. Using this particular weapon, the weapon of a murderer, heightened the Reptilian's hatred and drive to complete his missions...without mercy or compassion.

In apprehension, the boy slowly looked up, trembling from both the cold and immense fear that was impossible for him to hide behind the innocence of his young eyes, the palms of his hands soaked with sweat.

'Rise' the creature hissed fiercely, thrusting the weapon closer, threatening, until it almost struck the boy's bloodied forehead.

Although weakened and exhausted, Tino shuffled to the edge of the platform, gingerly feeling for the edge with his fingertips; unable to take his raised eyes off the weapon which was held so close to him, he was seeing double. He scarcely dared to breathe as his bare feet searched for the floor, leaning backwards as he tried, desperately, to avoid getting too close to the scaled creature who was already much too close for comfort.

Slowly and painfully, Tino rose to his feet, his sweaty handprint fading from the cold, metal slab seconds later as the Reptilian took a single step back but extended its scaled, muscular arm further towards him, ensuring that the terrified child remained so. It nudged to the side sharply with the blaster in its clawed hand before returning it to cover the petrified prisoner.

Tino cautiously sidestepped a couple of paces; slowly backing away from the creature who continued to advance towards him, forcing him to move towards the much darker centre of the room. Feeling around with his feet in case of any obstacles on the floor behind him and blocking out the growing pain of the metal mesh floor panels lining the bottoms of them with indentations, Tino's mind raced frantically; caught in an impossible fight or flight scenario. He saw a tiny red light illuminate to the side of him as the objects mounted on the tripods began to slowly re-animate, reacting to his proximity as they followed his slow, slightly wavering movements on their pivots.

Distracted by the intimidating ferocity of the creature, Tino was completely unaware of what had moved, unseen and unheard, into position and now awaited him, lurking in the shadows behind, now just a couple of paces away...another step closer... ...another... ...and another. The creature hissed with anticipation as it began to arch its back slightly, leaning down over him.

The back of Tino's heel felt something. He paused briefly, frowning as he turned and looked behind himself. He was startled by a series of bright blue lights that darted around in different directions against the blackness.

The Reptilian quickly re-captured his attention by exhaling, snarling loudly into his ear. Tino lost his balance as he reeled around, alert with fright and throwing his arms in front of his face to protect himself. Falling off balance, he stumbled against the stolen emerald Interstellar Scouts cy-bionic exoskeleton that awaited him in the darkness. He fell backwards, right into it.

The armoured suit swallowed up his entire body, encasing him inside and, before Tino was able to realise what was going on, looking about frantically and grasping at the armoured plating covering his forearms, a helmet closed up over his head. The various segments of it crawled over his face; quickly deploying from the collar before the blacked-out visor and green sensor lines on it slammed down. The floor opened up beneath Tino's feet and he fell through the opening, plummeting twenty feet, through the bottom of the ship, to the tangled metal ground of the moon below.

With a loud, metallic, grazing sound that rattled through the inside of his suit, Tino slammed down heavily. He gave himself a moment to recover from the fright, the sound of the suit's cy-bionics adjusting themselves to mould the various components to his height and build assaulting his ears, Tino slowly raised his head up to find a distorted display appearing on the inside of the visor that stretched across in front of his entire face.

After a couple of seconds of static, the fuzzy, strained words and numbers came into focus. Central across the top of the visor were the words

'I.S.S. Biker Delta Squadron 5-6-5'

and, beneath them,

'Patrol Leader – D-C-D-S-2-0-1-4 – Oli'

There were readouts to the left of the visor displaying charts that gave live indications of atmospheric readings, respirator function, armour integrity and, along the bottom, were percentages of breathable air and available fuel although, for what, Tino was uncertain. An objective marker lined the bottom of the visor that adjusted depending on what direction he was facing.

Tino reached out and grabbed hold of a long, silver pole that was protruding out of the tangled metal, pulling himself to his feet. Looking down at the shiny, emerald, armoured suit he was encased in, he could now see an array of lights on the arms and chest. Some were circular, others were diamond shaped and others had their own individual unique shapes but all appeared to have different images and words on them.

Turning his attention to his surroundings, all he could see was a vast, frozen wasteland of tangled scrap metal, crystallized in ice that stretched out, all the way to the horizon in every direction, an expanse, blazing; blindingly aglow with silver and white under the light of the distant sun which, surreally, only made his surroundings look colder.

The flickering atmospheric display on the inside of the visor was at 0%, confirmed only by the huge shadow that now slowly cast itself over Tino, darkness creeping, drifting in its wake, dulling all that shone around him as it crawled, dragging itself across the desolation. He turned his gaze upwards where, to his disbelief, he saw a vast debris field made up of millions upon millions of enormous chunks of metal that floated by in their own ghostly opera through the silent, deep blackness of space.

Overwhelmed by the spectacle, Tino found himself slowly stepping backwards, entirely struck with awe while also tainted with a poisoning angst.

Some of the debris radiated an amber glow, other pieces had a turquoise hue to them that were noticeable against the blackness of space however, they were not bright enough to illuminate the ground. As the boy watched, mesmerised, he noticed that, very slowly, the glowing chunks of metal were being attracted towards one another before he suddenly lost track of them.

The most imposing of the ghostly giants, he observed, must have been several miles across, like a bionic hand stretching, reaching out deep into the abyss, its crooked fingers touching the void beyond.

'What is this place?' Tino asked himself, exhaling quietly, his lips limp, barely touching as he looked about, gently brushing the dusting of ice off the palm of his glove.

'POLARIOUS FIVE!' a voice hissed loud and intrusive through a speaker inside his helmet. The sudden response surprised Tino, causing him to flinch, startled, as he threw his hand up in an attempt to cover his ear, forgetting that it was encased behind the helmet.

The metal on which Tino stood began to glow icy blue as the Reptilian, now encased in a stolen, gold I.S.S. cy-bionic exoskeleton, battle-damaged with silver scuffs, slowly descended towards the ground.

The creature deactivated the sapphire-blue flaming thrusters of the suit's jet propulsion unit, built into the back of it between the shoulder blades, and hit the ground heavily behind Tino with a loud clanging sound. It struck Tino as odd that the flames were able to burn without the need for an Oxygen-rich atmosphere. He didn't realise that an I.S.S. jet propulsion unit could rely on a reserve Oxygen supply from the suit's internal respiratory mask and other breathing aids which could automatically replenish their levels of breathable air as soon as it was available, ready for its next use.

'The fifth and largest moon of the molten metal ore planet, Polarious. The torment of the planet's fallen victims now embodies the entire moon' the creature continued, straightening up from its slightly crouched position, following the landing and drawing the blaster on Tino once more. Tino observed that his captor appeared to pull it from a built-in holster on the side of the armoured suit's thigh.

To prevent Tino from utilising the vast array of useful functions that the I.S.S. suit offered such as its jet propulsion unit, the Reptilian tapped one of the illuminated diamonds on its own chest which overrode all functions on the emerald suit that Tino wore, including the oxygen feed and compression / decompression of the suit.

All of the lights on the suit, that had strangely given Tino a sense of comfort, of security and safety, now dimmed until their glow faded entirely as the display at the top of the inner-visor now read

'Troop Leader Override'

in red letters contained inside a rectangular box. The words blinked in front of his eyes repeatedly.

'Walk or join in Polarious' fate' threatened the Reptilian, pushing the barrel of the blaster hard into the back of Tino's armoured suit with a fierce shove, making him stumble forward slightly as the emerald armoured plating intuitively adapted to the pressure of the push and angled itself to cover that part of the suit with a reinforced panel.

The Reptilian's statement made little sense to Tino. Nevertheless he complied as he was entirely at the creature's mercy.

As they crossed the vast metallic expanse, the boy discretely looked down at the armoured suit that he was encased in for a means of escape but the holster on his thigh and weapon slots on the suit's utility belt were all vacant. The suit had been entirely disarmed before he had been forced into it.

There was absolute silence as they walked along, except for the heavy breathing inside Tino's helmet, any one of which, the Reptilian made sure he knew, could be his last. He tripped on a protruding, arched length of cable as beads of condensation formed on the inside of his visor, a frustratingly thickening haze clinging to it, blurring his surroundings and blinding him to the dangers that lay right at his feet with every step - a troubling factor that was only worsened by the Reptilian's brute force as it grabbed hold of Tino every time he stumbled over the debris, shoving him forward aggressively.

With peculiar increasing effort, Tino lifted his weighted head, looking up at the Reptilian's imposing ship, The Knightfall. The black and silver vessel's name, having been identified by the suit, was displayed on the inside of his visor.

The Knightfall drifted above them, silently; as ghostly as the gravestones that floated, unwavering, beyond it; sailing on the shimmering, reflected light as it locked onto their objective.

It was peculiar, Tino thought; the ship had a striking resemblance to the rock that had been struck by the bolt of lightning during the storm back when he was in the house on the hill, although the surface of the ship was no longer encrusted in rock, it was silver and covered in imperfections. *Had this creature been there during the storm? Was it The Knightfall, under some sort of disguise that had fired the scarlet laser beam and destroyed the house's foundations? That might explain how I had fallen from the house and then awoken onboard the ship*, Tino contemplated.

He could see clearly that one of the larger external turrets had been badly damaged. It had a huge black scorch mark around it and a large chunk was missing. The blaster itself was dangling, unsupported, above their heads, revealing a large scarlet crystal within. This dangling turret appeared to confirm his theory.

After walking several exhausting miles, the weight of the armoured suit had continued to grow heavier and heavier, impressing an increasing toll on Tino's back and shoulders as each step he took became a conscious, demanding effort, unrelenting in every pull of his boots, blistering and increasingly leaded, away from the ground.

Eventually, after what seemed like hours of tedious searching, tireless in pursuit of its elusive prey, The Knightfall's scanners located the target and the ship automatically set down ahead of them next to a discarded double-barrelled turret protruding several feet out of the ground.

As the Reptilian, seemingly unhindered by the excursion, opened the cover to a small control panel beneath the cockpit on the side of the ship and flicked a variety of switches on it, the enormous blaster canons on the ship's hull came to life, automatically turning their barrels on their target, guarding the boy that stood beneath them.

Tino, out of breath and just thankful for the opportunity to rest his tired legs, sat down on a small, nearby mound of tightly tangled metal, the beads of condensation trickling down the inside of the visor, clearing narrow visible streaks through their trails and enabling Tino to see just how heavily guarded he really was.

As his captor worked on removing the old, damaged turret and replacing it with the much larger one that they had found, Tino silently contemplated how this unforgiving terrain had come to be. Huge, thick, elongated pieces of metal wrapped around each other and miles upon miles of thick wires and cables intertwined through the gaps. There was no atmosphere, no wind; no crashing waves, nothing to manipulate these objects into this state.

As the Reptilian started the intricate process of rewiring the turret to connect it to the ship's targeting systems, Tino, although doubting at first, thought he noticed something moving, only just in view, through one of the streaks at the bottom of his visor. Frowning, he looked down at his feet to investigate, leaning over to observe more closely. The holographic display inside his visor, displaying gradual inclines on many of its charts, flickered and strained; occasionally turning fuzzy with static interference as it had done previously. It lasted several seconds before the image cleared up again.

Although neither of them realised it, I.S.S. suits were extremely intuitive. After spending enough time within the vicinity of a vehicle, they could interact with it and remotely connect to its systems.

As the charts on the insides of their visors continued to spike higher and higher, showing increases in planetary mass density and magnetic field, a low groaning sound could be heard, ominously coming through the speakers inside their helmets. The sound slowly grew both in volume and pitch until it became a high screeching sound as the hull of the entire ship began to creak. They both looked up to see the ships external turrets pivoting, slowly and seemingly of their own accord, away from Tino and towards the Reptilian.

The Reptilian, although having never been to Polarious 5 before, had heard the stories of 'The Awaking Moon', the planetary body that was ever growing in mass, density and magnetisation caused by molecular alignment. It behaved in the same way as the oceanic tides did on many planets. The gravitational pull of the main planet, Polarious, pulled the metal of the moon tight together, aligning the molecular structure of all the scrap metal which then magnetised everything else to it. The Debris field above the moon was just metal that had drifted away whenever the magnetic field subsided. It was this intensifying magnetic field that now had the Reptilian staring down the barrel of the immensely large blaster canon.

Seeing that the Reptilian was distracted by the movement of the ship's huge turrets, Tino daringly eyed something that might help him escape or at least wound his captor enough to be able to steal his weapons and make him pilot the ship back to Earth, at blaster-point if necessary.

Cautiously sidestepping, casting his eyes back and forth from the Reptilian to the side and back again, anxiously, Tino bent his knees and leaned down, reaching out his hand and, gingerly, curling his fingers around a loose metal pole. This was really it - his chance to escape.

Slowly, with a slight effort under the seemingly growing weight of the suit, he rose back up to his feet and, warily, calculating, walked over towards the Reptilian, keeping out of its line of sight and trying not to draw its attention as it continued to observe the ship's peculiar behaviour, looking along the length of the hull towards where Tino had been sat, oblivious to his prisoner's intentions as Tino approached from behind.

The pole remained hidden behind one of Tino's legs until he got close enough to attack. Strangely, even his weapon felt like it was growing heavy, like there was an invisible force trying to pull it out of his hand.

He was within striking distance. HIS CHANCE WAS NOW! His muscles twitched around his elbow, adrenaline surging through his bicep, ricocheting back down to his wrist and almost paralyzing his fingers as they grew tense. He was determined yet terrified of making the blow to his captor.

Just as the enraged Reptilian reeled around to look at him, furiously drawing its blaster from the holster once more as it realised what the prisoner was doing, Tino swung at him but not before the creature could fire the shot. In a split second, the blast hit the pole and the captured energy surged its way down the piece of metal, narrowly missing Tino's hand as, suddenly, the pole was aggressively torn from his grasp by an unseen force. It thrust itself into the ground roughly twenty feet away and the blast of energy darted across the vast expanse of the moon's surface, channelling through the metal.

Tino, stunned, seeing his empty hands as the reality of the situation struck him, quickly turned to run but was instantly tripped over by the thick, metal cables that now wove their way down into the ground like snakes, slithering, swarming across the entire landscape as the ground came to life.

The images on the inside of his visor, once again, began to distort until the entire display was overcome with static. The boy was blinded and all he could feel in his frantic struggle were his feet being bound together by the cables that crawled their way over his entire body, growing tighter and tighter as they were dragged down into the creaking, mangled ground.

Tino began shouting and screaming as alarms began sounding inside his helmet, multiple red lights flashing as they flooded the space around his head, indicating the suit's compromised structural integrity.

As he fought and wrangled to get free, he felt the Reptilian grabbing hold of him and throwing him through the air. Tino slammed against a wall inside The Knightfall and hit the floor. As he heard the deployment bay doors slam shut and the ship's engines starting up, the pressurised seal of his helmet released, the various sections of it parting on the cy-bionics, and he pulled it off his head, throwing it across the floor.

Tino coughed and spluttered, shaking uncontrollably as he desperately gasped for breath. Crawling his way across the floor towards the ladder, it felt like his windpipe had contracted, restricting his breathing due to the panic.

There was a loud creaking, groaning sound as the entire hull of the ship was dragged down by the magnetic field, crushing its weight upon its landing gear; the legs buckling beneath the pressure.

Slowly, the ship lifted up off the ground and, fighting the pull on it, started to fly upwards, towards the debris field.

Loud explosions could be heard from outside as the ship navigated through the debris which was now also caught up in the intensifying magnetic pull of Polarious 5. Unable to escape the magnetisation that ensnared the ship, its thrusters burnt out and the ship began to fall back down towards the moon, along with entire hulls of star cruisers, shuttles, fighters and other space debris.

Unable to fire The Knightfall's thrusters back up, the Reptilian deployed a square panel from beneath the ship, activating its built-in laser wall emitter. A scarlet beam of laser energy exploded out, into the debris field, and began rotating to varying angles to destroy anything in the ship's path. Now spinning rapidly, the laser drilled a large crater into the surface of Polarious 5 which allowed the ship to fall further before impacting.

Suddenly the thrusters on The Knightfall fired back up as it sunk down, deep into the crater it had carved. The ship turned around and began flying back up, through the debris field; the constantly-adjusting laser wall tearing through the endless storm of falling scrap metal.

Small pieces of incoming debris struck the side of the ship, out of the laser wall emitter's range and it wasn't long until a stray piece of a destroyed fighter smashed straight into the square panel, destroying it and almost tearing it away from The Knightfall's hull entirely.

The Reptilian resorted to skilfully pulling off evasive manoeuvre after near-suicidal evasive manoeuvre as the ship resisted the pull of the moon, fighting fiercely at full thrust in desperation to achieve escape velocity; still restrained within the constantly increasing magnetic field.

In the deployment bay, Tino clung to one of the rungs of the lowered ladder for dear life, the light from the room above flickering on and off aggressively as the ship shook, juddering violently as it battled to hold up under the bombardment.

Eventually the ship's external blaster canons came back online and began tracking the projectiles, firing in all directions at the incoming debris and obliterating it before it could hit the ship.

Once they were clear of the debris field and the loud bangs had slowed, eventually stopping entirely, the ship began to settle. The Reptilian was relieved but still slightly stunned as, after a moment, it removed the gold helmet from its head using its built-in expansion matrix technology which had allowed the helmet to mould to the shape of the creature's skull when he had put it on. The helmet's cy-bionics now separated slightly into various sections so he could remove it.

The Reptilian plotted the co-ordinates into The Knightfall's galacta-nav for his rendezvous with Parathax on Zonju and engaged the ship's auto-navigational systems, allowing him the time to deal with the insolence of the prisoner that now lay, exhausted and on the brink of consciousness, down below in the ship's deployment bay.

In the urgency to escape Polarious 5 however, the Reptilian hadn't noticed the light on the ship's cockpit console indicating that the emerald I.S.S. suit had intuitively triggered The Knightfall's distress call under an I.S.S. signature and now the signal was out there. Unfortunately for Tino though, nobody was listening.

CHAPTER 7
I.S.S. BIKER DELTA SQUADRON 5-6-5

The huge deployment bay platform slowly descended towards the pearl-like crystalline surface of Crystalosis, the high-pitched hum of the ship's wide, heavy-duty hydraulics accompanying. The glaring sunlight, concentrated through the crystals, was a blinding assault on the squinting eyes of the I.S.S. Operatives, their emerald suits gleaming in the light as they emerged from the shadow of the ship's deployment bay.

The green lines on the Operatives' visors activated a thin, protective layer in front of their eyes which could adapt in accordance with the intensity of the light, allowing them to see more clearly without the need to squint or strain their eyes while operating in such a harsh environment.

The once- dark-green and brown, now battle-damaged to mostly silver, eight-legged customised juggernaut of Biker Delta Squadron 5-6-5, the Rhinonoid, now completely clean of the Beconium which had covered it earlier, stood proudly in the centre of the platform having risen up on its legs and locked its main body into position on top of them; a symbol of their pride and their independence, surrounded by the group of Operatives as they slowly approached the ground.

Oli, inside the medical bay of the Rhinonoid, was still connected to the vast array of respiratory and life-support equipment, all of which was monitoring and slowing the development of his deteriorating condition. The young Operative painfully drifted in and out of consciousness, his mind distant, disorientated and entirely compromised; leaving his life, unwittingly, in the hands of his Patrol of even younger Operatives who were now left to improvise the rescue mission without the guidance of an adult Troop

Leader or even a Patrol Leader to ensure the mission's success. By rank, it now fell to Isaac as the Assistant Patrol Leader to take the lead. However, Isaac was still in shock from the high-stakes, death-defying feat he had just performed to save the Patrol's shuttle from the Viper Fighter attack.

'He's in critical condition' announced Corey as he leaned against one of the metal poles of the extending hydraulics, grasping it with his gloved hand as he stood right on the edge of the platform, looking out at the landscape as they reached the planet's surface. He then turned and started walking across the platform towards the rest of the group who were now congregating at the front of the tank.

'Our objective is to reach these co-ordinates and we need to be there before sunset' he explained as the objective appeared on the insides of their visors.

'...Long before sunset. Timing is everything on this mission. The crystals aren't what we need. Oli needs exposure to a specific concentration of sunlight radiation created by a very particular crystalline structure. However, the light concentrated by the crystals becomes toxic if the sun begins to set so, not only do we need to heal Oli before then but we MUST be back here and off the planet by then as well' Isaac instructed, gathering his thoughts as he moved towards one of the small staircases built into the side of the Rhinonoid, closely followed by the others.

'No matter what' Corey continued, eager to have the last word in the briefing over Isaac and pausing as he placed his hand against the bottom of the Rhinonoid's hull, half turning his head to look back at the rest of the group following from behind him.

'Nathan will be monitoring everything to make sure that this all goes smoothly and will provide regular updates' Isaac reassured everyone.

'Standby for deployment' announced Nathan through the speakers in their helmets as he took his seat at the Rhinonoid's controls in the cockpit.

There was a loud, pressurised, hissing sound as the machinery came to life beneath their feet and the stairs retracted into the sides of the Rhinonoid. The rows of large, light-weight ceiling flaps raised up and then slammed back down on their hinges in a single large wave that swept across the room above their heads, allowing the tank's interior pressure to equalise. The jet propulsion unit refuelling station, inside which the group was now gathered, took on a different feel as the staircases secured themselves, locking into position within the empty spaces in the walls. The light that filled the room was now softer from the overhead lamps compared to the berating harshness of the sunlight outside.

'Go ahead Nathan, we're all onboard' replied Corey, casually, before Isaac could answer. Corey looked about at the group behind him and, just as he had hoped, nobody objected to him speaking on Isaac's behalf.

'Affirmative, all systems engaged. Rhinonoid deployed' Nathan's voice announced a few seconds later.

The Rhinonoid began to slowly march across the platform, stepping out onto the planet's surface. Nathan, while still extremely focussed on getting Oli the help he needed in time, felt much more at home operating the Rhinonoid without supervision than he did on the shuttle. He used the holographic projection from one of his badges to remotely engage the shuttle's stealth field generator along with the Rhinonoid's once they were off the platform, turning both vehicles completely invisible. He had had a lot more experience of operating the Rhinonoid and they were no longer under attack so he made himself comfortable in his seat and allowed himself the opportunity to have a bit of a breather.

The quiet, rhythmic thudding of the tank's footsteps could be heard stamping across the terrain beneath them as the Operatives, retracted their helmets into the collars of their armoured suits and made their way towards the cockpit.

On entering the cockpit's control centre, the group immediately dispersed in a casual manner, moving to their designated stations and setting about their tasks. Isaac collapsed, wearily, into his seat; still shaken up from his attempts to save the Patrol. Corey, however, noticing Isaac from the corner of his eye, once again saw an additional opportunity for himself in Oli's absence and was adamant that this was the best chance he would get to seize it while Isaac was still lagging from the Viper attack.

'Ethan, we still need to refuel the jet propulsion units. Can you go and prepare the station' instructed Corey, cutting off the youngest of the Operatives on his way to his console, his hand quickly intercepting and grasping at the headrest of Ethan's seat just as Ethan himself had reached out to it.

As Corey moved between the eye-length, brown-haired and slightly freckled Operative and his seat, Ethan turned to face him, looking up at the older Operative through the innocence of his bright, ice-blue eyes as he slowly retracted his hand and lowered his arm to his side.

There was a short pause as Ethan had assumed that, in Oli's absence, there would be more priority pinned on collective discussions about any extra tasks that needed completing. He thought there would be more communication of what the overall plan was in their mission to help Oli and a contingency plan. That's what he had learned when he was an Initiate but Corey seemed to be just jumping right in and taking control of everything himself right away while undercutting everyone else before the group could start debating the situation.

'...Yeah...sure' Ethan eventually replied as Corey's impatient facial expression pushed for a compliant response. There was another brief pause of reluctance from Ethan as he turned to look back at the console he had been about to sit at, his slightly-freckled face subtly betraying his feelings to Corey before quietly and, with an uneasy feeling, turning to leave the room.

Ethan already felt somewhat out of his depth working with an elite squadron of Operatives at his age as he hadn't long since traded in his sapphire armoured suit from his time training as an Initiate for his emerald suit to join Biker Delta Squadron 5-6-5 prematurely. His armour was still brand new without a single scratch and, whether or not anybody admitted it, everyone, except for Oli, would tend to avoid him as, next to Colin, who spent most of his time with Oli, Ethan was the youngest in the group and didn't quite fit in as much as the others.

Corey, having watched as Ethan left the room, now sat down and took over the young Operative's post at the illuminated wall-mounted control panel; swivelling in the seat to face it, his posture relaxed as he leaned back.

'Do you really think the entire fleet is gone?' asked Colin. This young Operative was slightly shorter than Corey. He was well kept with blonde hair which was parted neatly, hanging to the sides at his fringe. Colin always tried to keep his heart in the right place but often questioned his own judgement and turned to the other Operatives for confirmation and reassurance. All of these traits, he attributed to his strict, military-like upbringing before joining the I.S.S. He would always face what his farther referred to as 'disciplinary action' if he ever spoke out of turn or if his belongings or appearance were untidy.

'It's what the scanners are showing' sighed Corey, almost exasperated, as he exhaustedly leaned forward, burying his face in his hands; his elbows resting on his knees. He knew he was coming across a bit short with his response but he was feeling strained. 'Look, none of us have eaten or slept since the evacuation, our Designated Troop Leader was killed during our escape from the assault, our Patrol Leader is unconscious and in critical condition in the medical bay and we are stuck on our own with an extremely tight window in which to get Oli the medical attention that he needs' Corey continued before Colin could ask another irritating question.

Although he didn't admit it, Corey had serious doubts about this mission. There was absolutely no time to process the situation or plan their next move, everything needed to be an instant decision, done on impulse and without argument and without debate. Not only that, but while he had kept his cards close to his chest while accompanying Oli and observing his deteriorating condition, Corey had grown to resent being bossed around by other Operatives the same age as him and he was sick of his input being overruled by Oli and, even more so, Isaac. Corey wanted to prove himself as a Patrol Leader while he had this rare opportunity with Oli out of the picture and Isaac exhausted so there was a lot of responsibility weighing on his shoulders.

He knew from past missions though, that Isaac took the responsibilities given to him by the adult Troop Leaders very seriously and, now that his rank dictated that he was in charge in Oli's and the Designated Troop Leader's absence, he was going to cling tightly to that attitude once he caught up so Corey had decided quite early on that he would need to use a bit of brute force to take the lead on this mission and be viewed as better for the role than, at the very least, Isaac.

Corey was trying not to dwell on the fact that he had and was still manipulating the Patrol and the situation in order to benefit from Oli's potentially fatal misfortune. Of course he wanted to save Oli and didn't wish him any harm, they were friends but he too would be able to gain from this if Oli was saved and he was responsible for co-ordinating the rescue.

Colin exhaled through his nose as he contemplated the situation, leaning his elbow on the back of Corey's chair. Corey had remained quiet for a while now after snapping at him and had kept his face buried in his hands, his fingers pushing up beneath his eyebrows, hoping that Colin would take the hint that he just wanted to be left alone to monitor the readings in peace.

'I'm going to head up and mount the turret' Colin announced after a couple of seconds of waiting to see if the conversation was going to continue, gently slapping his gloved hand on top of the chair's headrest as he turned away.

He started to make his way towards the doors that Ethan had exited through when Corey spoke up.

'We're not anticipating any more combat on this mission now, take some of the weapons and armour from Becon up with you. The storm hit us hard. Try and clean them and see if you can salvage anything' Corey instructed, looking up from his hands, his vision slightly distorted at first; the area around his eyebrows reddened from the pressure of his fingers. He kept his eyes on the wall console straight ahead rather than looking at the Operative he was speaking to.

He wished that Colin would have taken the initiative himself to use this time more efficiently rather than avoiding his duties and hiding from work up on the turret deck. He was oblivious to the fact that Colin might need a bit more space than normal for the next couple of hours in light of Oli's imminent fate. That still didn't give him the right to dictate to Corey what he was going to do though. Corey, in his mind, was now the acting Patrol Leader and should be respected as such.

Pausing, Colin nodded in acknowledgment of Corey's orders, casting his eyes back over his shoulder at the dominating Operative before turning once again to leave the room as Corey finally looked over at him, sitting back in a slightly reclined position and watching as Colin exited through the door.

It seemed to Colin like he and Ethan were getting assigned all of the menial jobs that nobody else wanted to do. Despite being a team, Colin could see, quite clearly, that there was disharmony amongst them and he couldn't be sure but, since Oli became unwell, it was almost like Corey was trying to stand in for him. If there was one thing that Colin knew for certain from spending time with Oli, it was that, under these strained circumstances, the Operatives should be banding together as a Patrol, not competing for command over the rest of the group. The older Operatives should be leading, yes, but by example, not instruction. An Operative's life...no...Corey's friend's life was at risk and Colin strongly believed that, not only were Corey's priorities misplaced but the team's trust in him was extremely misguided as well. They had all seen, too many times, how incapable Corey was but nobody seemed to be stopping him.

Despite these feelings though, he couldn't help second guessing himself. Even if he disapproved of Corey's methods, perhaps it would be for the best to let him have his way and for the rest of them to just do as they were instructed just so that Oli could get the help he needed as soon as possible. Arguing and challenging Corey's methods would only hinder their progress and even risk compromising the entire mission.

'Hey' Colin greeted Ethan as he entered the dampness of the large, cold refuelling station. The row of enormous jet propulsion unit refuelling tanks spanned nearly the entire length of the space. Ethan turned and smiled at Colin, his eyebrows raised in acknowledgement as Colin walked towards him.

'Corey got you setting up the refuelling tanks?' Colin asked, trying to make small talk as he pressed a button on the wall, despite already overhearing and disapproving of Corey pushing authority on the younger Operative.

'Yeah' replied Ethan in an almost sombre tone.

'Yeah, he's got me cleaning Beconium off the contaminated weapons and armour in the Quarantine Wing' replied Colin as a long, zig-zagged corridor branched out from the side of the Rhinonoid and metal wheels descended to support the weight of it as the tank continued across the planet's surface.

Colin began to enter the corridor but then paused and placed his hand on the side of the doorway, gripping the frame of the opening as he leaned against it. He felt bad about the way Corey viewed Ethan and suspected that it was largely down to the fact that Ethan was also somewhat quieter than the rest of the Patrol and kept to himself a lot more than the others. Colin himself had once been where Ethan was - new to the ways that Biker Delta Squadron 5-6-5 did things, having to think fast under pressure to save the lives of those who were stranded during lethal natural disasters or aerial strikes on peaceful worlds from invading forces and, overall, often having to deal with situations that made him feel way out of his depth and that he would much rather have avoided. There was no denying though that these trials and tribulations had taught him a lot and enabled him to grow into the more skilled, competent Operative that he was now although, as Oli had always told him, he still had a lot of growing to do as he needed to have more faith in his own judgement. He was experienced but Colin had always been hesitant to draw conclusions based entirely on that alone.

Hanging his head slightly, he also felt guilty that he could have made more of an effort to include Ethan more himself. Tapping his index finger several times against the doorframe Colin quickly turned back to the younger Operative and walked over to him, his fingers swiftly brushing away from the wall. He leaned his arm against one of the huge refuelling tanks and offered the best advice he could think of while wearily rubbing the back of his finger between his raised eyebrows.

'With everything going on at the moment, there's no knowing whether we are on a combat mission or a rescue mission so there's no harm in being prepared just in case something does go wrong but believe me, missions change. Sometimes based on circumstance, other times based on agenda' he explained, turning to look back at the room they had both come from.

He knew that Ethan was feeling trapped and that he needed to follow Corey's instructions to the letter. It was just natural, Ethan was new to this and Corey was an experienced Operative but Colin felt bad for him regardless. He was doing well to hold up under the circumstances they all now found themselves in and nobody else seemed to be acknowledging it. He had seen the way the others avoided their newest member and, deep down, he didn't approve, regardless of how much younger Ethan was and he knew Oli never approved either. Ethan was unsure of how to respond so glanced at Colin briefly but remained quiet as he returned to completing his task.

Colin cast his eyes down at the console that Ethan was operating. He observed that Ethan's work was slow, careful and calculating as he thought each step through, dedicated to doing his task correctly. He then looked away from the console, back to Ethan again. He could see how lonely he was, regardless of whether he voiced it or not, yet he was still working hard and trying to help the team as much as he could despite the abuse he got from Corey.

'I'm going to mount the turret while I clean this equipment, do you want to give me a hand with it?' Colin offered after a moment as he observed Ethan finishing setting up the refuelling tanks.

'Yeah, sure!' replied Ethan after a brief moment of being caught slightly off-guard. He was thankful to have a task to do without Corey diminishing him and making him work alone. It was a nice gesture and it felt genuine. Despite putting him on the spot and making him feel slightly self-conscious as to why Colin wanted to spend time with him, he wanted to accept the offer. With a slight smile and a nudge of his head to the side, Colin led the way into the zig-zagged corridor of quarantined equipment, a chain of tiny white lights shooting along the sides of the floor and down the corridor, ahead of them, repeatedly.

'Isn't Beconium dangerous? I mean, that's how Oli got sick isn't it?' asked Ethan as he cautiously followed behind Colin, looking around at the vast array of compromised weapons and armour that lined the passageway. Some items he recognised, others were completely unfamiliar.

'Highly dangerous' replied Colin, looking back to Ethan as they moved from one angle of the corridor to the next. Colin indicated cautiously at a gap in the floor where one of the wheels had deployed as he stepped over the top. '...But only when inhaled in the radiation storms on Becon. These have all been in quarantine since we crashed there to allow the radiation to burn out but it's still best to make sure it doesn't make contact with your skin as some of the properties that make up Beconium can be absorbed into your body so, whatever you do, keep your gloves on and don't touch your face' Colin warned with a friendly smile as he began to take the contaminated equipment from the illuminated mounting racks on the wall, handing some of them to Ethan.

'Ok, let's head on up' said Colin after grabbing a few more items and a tool box of cleaning supplies. They turned and carefully made their way back along the corridor, trying not to drop any of the items that were stacked up in their arms.

Once they were back in the sub-zero temperatures of the refuelling station, Colin nudged a red button with his elbow. The slow-moving wheels retracted and the corridor drew its way back in towards the Rhinonoid's hull.

'How does that corridor even fit? Where does it go?' asked Ethan.

'Expansion Matrix Technology but, trust me, you have seen nothing yet' Colin replied, his eyes widening in exaggeration. 'Once we've cleaned this equipment, we'll get some food; we haven't even eaten since the evacuation' he continued as they both stepped onto the elevation platform that led up the short shaft to the turret controls mounted on top of the Rhinonoid.

'I'm not sure I could keep anything down after the day we've had' replied Ethan, casting his eyes down, doubtfully, as the platform began to automatically rise up towards the small, well-lit room.

'You'll need to keep your strength up for whatever needs to be done. Anything could happen before we rejoin the fleet' insisted Colin with a slight shake of his head, dismissing Ethan's doubts. 'I learned very early on as an Operative about the importance of nutrition. Especially because, with our Patrol, we sometimes get called on for missions that involve surviving in harsh environments, like Becon, for long periods of time which is all well and good when you have supplies with you but when those supplies run out and you can't obtain any more, which, believe me, can happen, your body needs to have the stamina and endurance to make it through the rest of the mission' he explained as he lifted the arm rest of the turret mount and sat on the edge of the slightly torn and insulation tape-patched leather seat, his legs hanging over the side. Ethan sat opposite, facing him on the edge of the square hole of the shaft, his feet dangling down into it as he kicked his heels gently against the side.

'Doesn't the Rhinonoid have supplies to last for long missions?' he asked. 'I mean, it's a one of a kind so won't blow an Operative's cover' he continued as Colin handed him a brush, scouring pad and a tube of the abrasive paste that Corey had used to clean the Rhinonoid while talking with Oli.

'Sure, but again, those supplies can still run out if you're on longer recon missions in baron terrain like this planet, where there are no I.S.S. outposts or safe houses to replenish those supplies. You have to be careful and always do your best to return to the fleet with some of your supplies which you can then use on your next mission. You can't get package drops either if you run out because that would blow our cover. Despite all of the amazing features, the Rhinonoid still draws attention, even from orbit. Because it's entirely customised, it doesn't blend in either' explained Colin as he started scrubbing at a gold Troop Leader wrist-guard.

'Although, Oli has been starting to look into more augmented adaptions of assimilation technology to mimic other vehicles in the vicinities we're operating in.'

Colin frowned to himself, pausing for a moment. Although the blueprints for the Rhinonoid were drawn up by Jason Campbell, 5-6-5's and Viper Strike Squadron's original Troop Leader, they had later been retrieved from his quarters by Oli before they could be secured in the I.S.S. archives. All of this had come about after the Troop Leader was captured by a bounty hunter for infiltration and intelligence gathering to aid the I.S.S long before Colin joined the I.S.S. but he had heard so many amazing stories from Oli's time as an Initiate under Jason's guidance.

Since taking possession of the Rhinonoid blueprints, which now hung on the wall of Oli's room onboard The Scout Hut, Oli had worked with the rest of Biker Delta Squadron 5-6-5 and Viper Strike Squadron to finish building the partially-constructed vehicle and he became the mind behind the Rhinonoid's additional modifications as Operatives were trained to improvise vehicles based on what they had available to them, to survive in dangerous situations and were all trained as engineers to repair damaged and crashed vehicles. Completing the Rhinonoid had been a relatively simple task as Jason had already done most of the hard work and they had access to the technology and machinery that drifted in the debris field of Polarious 5. Oli often came up with all kinds of crazy new concepts for the Rhinonoid along with his customised armoured suits which anyone else, including seasoned Troop Leaders, had thought were ridiculous ideas only for Oli to then actually build them, proving everybody wrong. He was stubborn like that. Colin exhaled through his nose, smiling to himself in amusement at his adoptive brother as he looked down, bringing himself back to reality and raising his eyebrows.

'Nope, when you're out there in a transport as unique as this, it's just the Patrol, a stealth field generator and your suit's Distress Signal Badge as an absolute last resort' he finished as he returned to cleaning the Beconium off the gold wrist-guard, the rusty dust falling into a small, slightly bent metal tray at his feet.

Ethan's eyes grew wide as he noticed that he had accidentally stained the jet-black, slightly padded palms of his gloves with faded orange streaks from the Beconium on the blaster that he was cleaning. The I.S.S. took immense pride in their armour and vehicles so he panicked at first but then noticed the state of Colin's more worn out gloves. He knew that Colin was very particular about the appearance of his armour so if his ever got dirty then anyone else could relax about the same thing happening to their suits. It made sense that a bit of wear and tear would be a factor for this particular Patrol as they were also skilled with vehicle mechanics and other jobs that were extremely hands-on so he remained quiet and continued cleaning the blaster, disregarding his initial worries.

Back in the control centre of the Rhinonoid, Nathan was scanning the environment all the way out to the edge of the planet's atmosphere to monitor any more potential threats coming their way.

'Looks like there's a hostile fighter squadron doing a sweep' he announced, tracking the blip on one of the screens and projecting it into a 3-D hologram of the entire planet with an altitude scale measuring how high up the squadron was.

'What class?' asked Corey, turning to him, again, before Isaac could speak up.

'Standard Black-Burns. Those Vipers must have relayed our co-ordinates back to whoever or whatever was controlling them and put a tracker on our shuttle designation' Nathan announced, continuing to track their signatures on the hologram. 'The Rhinonoid's stealth field generator is holding steady but, if their altitude decreases any further; I'm going to have to hold our position and wait for them to pass us by' he continued.

Corey turned to Isaac who was monitoring a variety of the vehicles systems from across the room. He wanted to gauge Isaac's mindset and get a feel for whether they would end up stepping on each other's toes.

'Hey Isaac, what do you make of this?' Corey asked.

Isaac spun around in his chair and looked across the room to Corey. 'What is it?' the fiery-haired Operative asked, frowning beneath his quiff. He stood up from his seat and made his way over to Corey's station.

'Looks like...maybe a landslide? In this trench up ahead' replied Corey, indicating at the screen as Isaac leaned forward, pushing his hair back away from his eyes and studying the displays.

'We could go around?' Corey suggested.

'There's not enough time, Oli wouldn't make it that far' replied Isaac, racking his brain to come up with a solution quickly as he tried to pull himself together. There was no time to accommodate any setbacks.

'He mentioned to me that he recently made some modifications just before the Deathstalker mission' Nathan interjected from the tank's main controls at the front of the room. '...Plasma disks that deploy at the front and sides of the tank to carve their way through obstacles. That could work' he suggested.

'I don't think so' replied Corey; Isaac shaking his head doubtfully behind him.

'The crystals could focus and concentrate the energy which could back-fire on us' Isaac continued.

'That rules out the Rhinonoid's thrusters as well then' sighed Corey, sitting back in his seat, wiping his hands down over his face and coming to a stop as he rested his chin on his fist.

'Personal jet propulsion units are an option' said Isaac thoughtfully. There was a long pause.

'How close are we to the objective now Nathan?' asked Corey after a moment of contemplation, both of Isaac's solution and his more focussed mindset.

Turning to face Nathan, Corey realised he had been pushing the bottoms of his toes hard against the wall in front of him under the pressure he was feeling as he pulled his feet away.

'Not close enough for jet propulsion units alone' replied Nathan.

'And those Black-Burns have descended below safety altitude as well so we need to hold our position here until they pass us. To be honest, we're pushing it a bit with the speed of the Rhinonoid as well, even without the delays. I've been picking up readings of additional fighter patrols above the planet for the past few minutes and it's only a matter of time before we are spotted by one of them, whether the stealth field is up or not. All they need to do is hit us with a sonar ping and they will come down on us. We simply aren't moving fast enough to get Oli there and back in time before sunset' Nathan warned, routinely referring to the hologram and displays on the tank's main consoles, adjusting the various controls to bring the Rhinonoid to a standstill, the tank emitting a loud hissing sound as it settled.

The roar of the Black-Burn Fighter engines could be heard in the distance, cutting through the silence and then, suddenly, there they were, flying close to the ground overhead. They were tangled within the same thorny, black energy that had animated the Viper Fighters. If it wasn't such a dangerous situation, the group would have been awe-struck by the impressive size of the enemy fighters but, for now, all they could do was watch and hope that they weren't detected.

The Black-Burn patrol set down on the ground ahead of the Rhinonoid and the group of Operatives began to panic that they may have shown up on the scanners or that they were investigating something else that could ultimately give away their position. They had just survived the Viper Fighter attack and they didn't want to face off against a squadron of Black-Burns as well.

'What's that black energy moving around them?' asked Corey.

'I don't know; the Vipers that attacked us were the same' replied Nathan.

'We don't have time for this' whispered Isaac, frustrated, as he and Corey joined Nathan at the front, watching through the window as the enemy Con-Haarian pilots vacated their fighters and assembled on the planet's surface. They were too far away to get a good look at what they were doing. From the Rhinonoid they just looked like wavy black blurs in the heat of the sun.

Normally they would turn to Oli, their Patrol leader, for a final decision on the best course of action and Oli would even turn to the Troop Leaders for guidance but the entire I.S.S. was now in complete disarray. As next in command, Isaac needed to make a decision and he needed to do it now. There was no ideal scenario available. Still, he didn't speak up, he was too indecisive and Corey noticed this.

'Refuel your jet propulsion unit and head down to the deployment bay' Corey instructed, turning back to Isaac. Although starting to catch on to what Corey was doing in trying to take charge of the group, Isaac nodded in concurrence and urgently made for the doors. There was no time to confront Corey about selfishly trying to take the lead right now. All that mattered at this point was saving Oli.

'Nathan, hold our position here. Set the Rhinonoid's stealth field generator to remain perpetual and engage the tracking beacon on a scrambled signature so we can find our way back without the enemy cutting off our escape then head on down to the deployment bay with Isaac. I'll get Ethan and Colin and we'll meet you down there with Oli' Corey continued.

'Right!' replied Nathan's distant voice over the sound of overhead switches being flicked by him as Corey quickly left the room.

Entering the refuelling station, Corey poked his head around the corner of the shaft that led up to the Rhinonoid's turret deck and slapped his hands several times on the wall to get Colin and Ethan's attention.

'We're on prep. for deployment! Get down here and refuel!' he shouted up to the two Operatives.

'On our way!' replied Colin's voice as he set down the equipment he and Ethan were cleaning and pressed a button on the wall next to the shaft, gently pushing aside the bent metal tray containing the removed Beconium to avoid kicking or stepping in it. The platform began to rise up as Ethan moved his feet, pulling himself up onto the narrow ledge he had been sat on, using the metal wire mesh fencing behind him. Colin smiled and rolled his eyes jokingly at Ethan in response to the self-importance that Corey must be feeling right now as he was the one leading the mission rather than Isaac and he was the one ordering everyone else around in preparation.

'We need to refuel our jet propulsion units before heading down to the deployment bay' Colin announced to Ethan as the platform lowered them back down.

Colin indicated towards an empty space at the base of the refuelling tanks for Ethan to refuel as he too quickly stepped into his cylindrical refuelling dock. The docks lit up as they entered and the cone shaped covers of the twin fuel canisters built into their armoured suits lifted up to expose the insides of them. Two refuelling pipes descended from above, interlocking with the tops of the canisters as the large, gold, outlines shaped like a letter 'V', began to glow brighter on the backs of their armoured suits between their shoulders. Slowly, the space within the 'V' began to light up from the bottom more and more, moving upwards with a royal-blue glow, indicating that the fuel levels were replenishing. The two blue and yellow striped bars also began to glow brighter in the fronts of their armoured suits from across their shoulders, meeting at the round illuminated red button at the centre of their collar and then reaching down to just below their chest.

These colours, identical to Oli's suit, indicated their jet propulsion unit fuel reserves and the cruiser that they were assigned to in the Interstellar Scouts. The brighter the lights, the more fuel they had available.

The two Operatives then activated their armoured helmets which deployed from their collars in separate segments and locked together, closing up around their heads.

'I'm heading down to initiate deployment procedures' announced Corey through the speakers in their helmets as he stepped out of his refuelling dock and ran past the two of them.

'Grab Oli and meet us down there' he instructed, indicating at the doors, behind which, Oli was now barely clinging to life. Nathan also entered the room to refuel his jet propulsion unit as Corey proceeded to the deployment bay.

'Can you give me a hand?' asked Colin, turning to Ethan and gesturing towards the room as he quickly made his way towards the doorway at the back of the refuelling station. Ethan rushed after him as the doors closed behind Corey at the opposite end, the self-appointed Leader stepping into the rubberised, black, ribbed tunnel that connected the front section of the Rhinonoid to the back section.

By the time Corey arrived in the deployment bay, quickly descending down a ladder, Isaac was already lowering the deployment ramp. The bright light from outside revealed 6 motorbikes lined up in uniformity at the top of the ramp as it slowly descended. Corey quickly strode across the deployment bay and set about releasing the straps that were holding the vehicles upright as extra support alongside their stands that were built into the floor.

These vehicles were more than simple motorbikes. Secondary dummy thrusters were built onto the twin exhausts with capabilities ranging from carrying replacement components to smokescreen jets. Adjustable and detachable triangular leg-guards ran almost the full length of the bikes to give extra protection to the Operatives and any cargo they were carrying such as various weaponry, ammunition packs and medical supplies. These were secured onto clips built into the bike, beneath the fuel tank, as a standard battle pack and were carried as a precaution in case a dangerous situation ever presented itself; one much like, the Operatives feared, they were about to ride into.

Once the ramp had been completely lowered, Isaac took up his position next to a wall panel, entering a code in preparation for Corey's signal.

Back in the Rhinonoid's medical bay, Colin and Ethan were urgently preparing Oli for transition down to the deployment bay.

'We need live readouts of his vitals while we are out there' said Colin, his tone both serious and determined, in deep concentration. There was nothing that could impede his focus as he worked. Although Ethan was right there beside him, Colin felt very much alone and entirely responsible for everything going on in that moment. It was like he had surrounded himself in an invisible, psychological force field that pushed aside the distractions of everything around him as well as all irrelevant thoughts and feelings, nothing could get near him.

Colin quickly started activating the unconscious Operative's portable respirator mask with the First Aid Badge on Oli's arm just as Corey had done for him earlier on board the shuttle. Oli groaned through the respirator mask in response to the disturbance, turning his head to the side. Colin silently cast his eyes up at the dying Operative like he was trying to convey reassurance and urging him to keep fighting through the power of his thoughts while not speaking a word.

As Ethan set about accessing Oli's vitals readings and distributing them to all of the Operatives' visors, he noticed that, peculiarly, a large assortment of badges was missing from the slots in the Patrol Leader's suit, including the rectangular Distress Signal Badge. Before he could say anything though, Colin had finished deploying Oli's respirator mask and was starting to sit him up.

'Ok, help me get him up' grunted Colin, through gritted teeth, as he struggled to get Oli into an upright position under the weight of him inside the emerald, cy-bionic suit of armour. Ethan quickly put one of Oli's arms over his shoulder and almost fell forward under the load but Colin quickly took the weight, putting Oli's other arm over his shoulder and allowing Ethan the time to get back into position.

'You good? You got him?' asked Colin urgently.

'Yeah...yeah, I'm good, let's go' replied Ethan, grabbing Oli's arm once again, throwing it over his shoulder and grasping at the unconscious Operatives wrist.

Oli let out a muffled groan behind his respirator mask once more as they started to stand him up, his head hanging loosely.

'Oh, shut up' whispered Colin through his still-gritted teeth, trying to maintain his composure and not be wavered by emotion as he and Ethan, despite their determination, struggled to move him across the room; walking slowly, one step at a time, the Patrol Leader's feet dragging behind him.

Despite the seriousness of the situation, Ethan found it difficult to contain his laughter at how ridiculous the entire scenario was when all Colin could do was tell their leader to shut up. This wasn't helped by the juddering sound that Oli's boots made as they moved him across the metal-grate floor panels of the refuelling station, his unconscious groaning continuing but now really shaky as he juddered across the room.

Ethan's eyes grew watery as he laughed harder and harder and he couldn't even do anything about it as his helmet was closed up. Colin tried to quieten him down. Even though he too could see the humour in the situation, it was still very serious and was more personal to Colin than he was letting on. With this in mind, he didn't take offence to Ethan's laughter but ensured that he was treating the mission with the discipline and seriousness that it warranted. He also knew that Corey wouldn't be amused and there was definitely no time for Corey's self-importance and authoritative talks right now. Ethan managed to compose himself, taking a couple of deep breaths and regressing as he apologised to Colin just as Nathan joined them and helped them the rest of the way through the doors and into the deployment bay with Oli. They descended on a loading platform as, with Oli in tow, the ladder wasn't an option for them.

'Ok, mount up!' shouted Corey, a hint of authority in his voice, gesturing at the motorbikes with his outstretched arm and walking quickly, with an air of control and self-importance about him, as the trio stepped off the platform with Oli.

As the group of Operatives mounted their motorbikes, Corey took over holding Oli up, dragging him with large, strong sidesteps over to a single quad-bike in the centre of the deployment bay.

He heaved Oli up onto the front of the quad-bike and attached 2 umbilical cables to the Patrol Leader's armoured suit; securing him to the vehicle at either side so he wouldn't fall off. He then mounted the vehicle on the seat behind him and they all started up their engines with a loud collective roar.

'We need the element of surprise. If we don't take out those pilots or disable their fighters in passing, they will pursue us and we won't stand a chance... Black-Burns are fast. VERY fast' announced Corey.

Corey then looked over at Isaac and, with a nod of his head towards the waiting Operative, Isaac adjusted the deployment speed setting and flicked a switch on the controls that he was standing next to. A door opened upwards in the left wall of the Rhinonoid and the row of motorbikes slowly moved out, sideways, on a black mechanical strip embedded in the floor.

The extended strip locked into position, causing the motorbikes to shake slightly with the harnesses removed and then, slowly, they were angled forwards so their front wheels were making contact with the ground. Isaac threw his leg over his bike, the nearest one to the inside of the deployment bay, and started its engine. He then looked along the row of Operatives to Nathan at the other end and with a clear hand signal, Nathan confirmed that they were ready to deploy.

'Biker Delta Squadron Five-Six-Five standing by' announced Nathan, his voice audible inside all of the Operatives' helmets.

'Copy' replied Corey's voice.

He paused for a moment and glanced at Oli's deteriorating vitals on the inside of his own visor. He then pushed aside any doubts he was having about their chances and turned his focus entirely to completing the mission successfully. He tightened his grasp on the rubberised handlebar grips and turned to face the opening at the bottom of the ramp. 'Five-Six-Five, deploy!' he continued.

Then, with a loud roar of engines and moving like powerful rockets, the four occupied motorbikes shot off the deployment strip and began tearing across the terrain, closely followed by the quad-bike which raced down the deployment bay ramp and moved into position behind them as they sped across the landscape, towards the horizon.

The Operatives drew their knives from the sheathes on their utility belts as the vehicles shot straight at the enemy fighters in the distance. Corey went to slash at one of the pilots in passing but the blade passed straight through the Con-Haarian without even making contact. Although the blade never physically struck the dark, ghostly figure, the black, thorny energy that appeared to form the creature's body transferred to the blade and began wrapping itself around it, working its way towards the hilt and Cory's hand. Panicking, Corey threw his knife away before the energy could reach him.

Isaac and Nathan, both of whom were much more calm and collected, thrust their blades up into the fuel tanks of two of the Black-Burn Fighters in passing; gripping the handle of their blades tightly as they ducked down beneath the wings. With the outside of the fighters still being red-hot from flight, the fuel ignited from the sparks that the blades generated and, in an inferno of flame and black, billowing smoke, they erupted in a fierce, fiery explosion from behind. Isaac and Nathan were also forced to discard their bladed weapons as the thorny, black energy began to make its way towards their gloved hands.

'Be advised, the pilots are decoys, they're not real' announced Corey, frustrated that he had failed where, once again, Isaac had succeeded. The remaining two Black-Burn Fighters slowly rose up from the smoke and gave chase to the five Operatives as they tore across the crystalline expanse. As they fired their lethal blaster canons at the group, Isaac turned to look back over his shoulder.

'Five-Six-Five, fall into cruise formation and initiate evasive manoeuvres' announced Isaac's voice; taking control of the situation before Corey could barge his way in again. On this instruction, the four Operatives riding the motorbikes formed an arc in front of the quad-bike, swerving sharply out of alignment with the pursuing fighters' targeting systems, explosions of crystal shards erupting fiercely all around them and grazing their armour as they escorted Corey and Oli towards their objective.

CHAPTER 8
COLLISION COURSE

Onboard The Knightfall, now en-route to Zonju, the furious Reptilian had returned to the ships deployment bay to deal with the prisoner's insolence back on Polarious 5. On reaching the bottom of the ladder, the creature looked down at the boy that lay at its feet. Using its foot, it rolled the prisoner over onto his back but he appeared to be limp and unresponsive.

Demonstrating its disgust, the Reptilian hissed aggressively, tearing its glare away and striding, heavy footed, across the deployment bay towards the control panel to electrify the room once again.

'Wait' whispered Tino's weak voice from behind as the creature extended its muscular arm towards the switch.

The weakened boy, his eyes only slightly open, distorting his vision, used all of his strength to sit himself up, shifting his weight little by little to lean himself back, propping his body up against the wall, his head leaning to the side.

The creature paused. Its clawed hand was now just an inch away from the switch. Slowly, it turned back to look at the wounded boy.

'Who...who are you?' Tino asked, his voice trembling as he found the courage to interact with his captor. He moved his head across the wall into a more upright position, his hair trailing behind. The creature let out a second sound of disgust, a growing rage burning within, flooding its mind and muscles with a fierce bio-chemical surge as it turned back to the switch.

'P-please' the boy quickly begged with a slight stammer. His eyes grew wide as he tried, desperately, to stop the creature from electrifying the room and shutting down his nervous system again. He threw himself forward slightly as, in a reflex motion, his foot jumped off the floor, landing back on its heel.

The creature paused again, its claw now touching the switch. In the shadows, with its back to the boy, its scales slowly darkened, turning dark-red and black. It could feel the enlarging of its muscles throughout its body, which parted its scales. A sharp, piercing pain grew as the large, curved spikes, tried to push their way out, from between the armoured scales, through the thin layer of skin as its amber eyes slowly turned to blazing-red.

Resisting the primal instincts that it was feeling and returning its size and colourations to normal, the Reptilian grunted and hissed aggressively as it turned to him once more, much more angry this time, pulling its hand away and quickly striding towards him. The gold I.S.S. Troop Leader suit that the creature had stolen while escaping The Scout Hut, opened up as the Reptilian moved across the room, allowing the creature to step out of it. The giant beast stormed, threateningly, right at him; dressed in its torn, black flight suit.

'MY NAME IS XZJYTHEOUS!' the creature hissed; growing more and more enraged as the Reptilian now towered over him. Tino kicked at the edges of the loose floor panels, trying to pull his feet closer to himself, hugging his knees to his chest as he pushed himself right back against the wall.

'YOU ARE TINO! VALENTINO PASYO - THE DESERTER, AND NOW TRAITOR, TO THE INTERSTELLAR SCOUTS! THE FINAL ACCESSORY TO THEIR DEMISE!' Xzjytheous continued, his voice growing louder and more driven, leaning in close to the frightened boy who was quickly starting to regret his act of bravery as he squeezed the sweat-soaked fingers of one hand together so tightly in the grasp of the other hand that he was cutting off his blood circulation to them as he wrapped his arms around his knees more tightly.

A couple of seconds passed as the Reptilian wrestled with his primal impulse, resisting the urge, that burning, instinctive drive, to eliminate his prisoner right there and then. That wasn't his assignment though and, despite how he felt and what had transpired, he knew that if anything happened to the prisoner, he would come off much, much worse at the hands of Parathax if he arrived on Zonju empty-handed or, worse still, with a corpse.

Xzjytheous straightened his back and turned to walk away again. Tino pulled himself to his feet and took a step forward

'I - I don't...' Tino started but Xzjytheous let out a deafening, primal howl and quickly slammed his fist against the control panel triggering a powerful jolt of electricity, against which, the Reptilian was insulated by the soles of the black boots he wore. The explosive blast of electricity struck Tino's emerald cy-bionic suit and launched him, with immense power, across the room, slamming him up against the electrified wall at the far end. The current held him up against the wall, several feet above the floor as sparks of electricity repeatedly snapped and bolted around his emerald suit. As soon as Tino was secured against the wall, Xzjytheous reeled around; blaster clutched in his claws and fired a single, powerful blast, narrowly but deliberately missing the boy's face, immediately silencing him.

The blast was so close that Tino could feel the heat of the burn mark on the electrified wall where it had hit, the putrid smell invading his nostrils through the wisps of smoke that rose from the scorch. He could hear the sizzle of the melting metal which trickled down, slowly ebbing towards him like molten, silver teardrops as they dripped onto the scuffed shoulder of his armoured suit, solidifying instantly.

With a wicked smile, satisfied that he had made his point and that the cy-bionic suit would take care of keeping him alive, Xzjytheous disabled the Troop Leader override that he had triggered back on the surface of Polarious 5 and turned away once more.

Tears, now filling Tino's eyes, slowly rolled down his cheeks, his lips quivering as he began to hyperventilate, crying helplessly as he, once again felt his muscles go numb, the electrical current disrupting his body's nervous system.

'I shall return for you when we reach Zonju' Xzjytheous hissed, amused, over the young boy's sobbing as Tino, now unable to turn his head due to the paralysis, went into uncontrollable spasm, forced to watch from the corner of his blurring eye, as the reptilian creature disappeared back up the ladder.

'Parathax awaits you and, there, you will die in agonising torture' Xzjytheous finished, slamming the access hatch behind him and sealing it tight shut with a loud screech.

Feeling his tears cumulating at his chin, all Tino could do now was hang there, held up against the wall by the electrical current as he cried, quietly, his tearful eyes glistening and his face red. He was helpless, lost and alone in the cold and dark as he awaited delivery to his imminent fate.

Xzjytheous stepped into the cockpit which was lined with an impressive assortment of weapons and trophies mounted along the walls which he had claimed from significant kills in his mission to avenge his family's deaths as well as his own Plasma Blaster Rifle complete with a retractable / detachable bayonet which he had owned during his time with the military on his home world of Biolum. It was this weapon that he had used to kill his Commander for murdering his family and was later used to kill many others that defied him, leading him to name the iconic weapon 'The Spitting Cobra' named after a deadly snake species found on Earth and Biolum.

Another unique trophy he had claimed and chosen to keep holstered for the time being, rather than return to its mount on the wall, was the small hand blaster he had threatened Tino with. It had once been owned and used by his Commander, accurately named 'The Poised Mamba' after another lethal snake species indigenous to both Earth and Biolum.

Various machines ran along the wall, out of the cockpit and into the cargo-hold where the round hatch was that led down to the deployment bay that Tino was being held in. These machines were used to customise specific weapons such as swords, throwing knives and grenades. These customisations were indicated by broken down samples that floated vertically in containment fields.

The current configuration for the customised knife on display was broken down into the separate pieces of the hilt at the top, the hand-guard beneath it, followed by the blade and the swirling, rusty Beconium that twisted in a DNA like pattern beneath the tip of the blade.

The grenade-customisation generator was similar but, in the containment field, was a disassembled grenade starting with the top of the casing, with the trigger beneath it, followed by the twisting, explosive contents of the grenade, including Beconium and shrapnel, and finally the bottom of the casing beneath it.

Xzjytheous cycled through a variety of combinations for the different components and set the customiser to generate a whole new batch of electro-containment grenades; the same type he had used onboard The Scout Hut.

He then climbed into the pilot's seat and pressed a button on the main control console, establishing contact with his employer, Parathax, on Zonju.

'Reptilian' came the static-filled voice.

'I have the bounty you requested, Parathax' he hissed, a tone of accomplishment in his voice.

'The I.S.S. will soon re-amass. Explain your impedance!' responded the irritated female's voice, without missing a beat.

'Repairs' Xzjytheous replied. 'My ship sustained heavy damage from the fleet's canons firing through the Polarian Stealth Field during the assault while I was recovering the target. I had to take a detour to Polarious Five...I trust I will be compensated for the inconvenience of imprisonment and modifications to my ship' he continued, the expectation clear in his voice.

'WHAT!?' the female's voice seethed.

'It came at great risk. The prisoner almost escaped when the magnetic field built up and my ship was almost buried on Polarious Five beneath the debris storm' Xzjytheous explained, lacking the restraint that he knew, even as he spoke, he should be exercising. Confident and fierce though he was, Parathax was one of the few beings that could and did intimidate him.

'Get that prisoner to me immediately. We shall then re-negotiate the terms of your commission. I trust that leaving Zonju with the scales on your back will be both payment and compensation enough for your insolence, Reptilian!' Parathax yelled in mockery of Xzjytheous' statement right down to his choice of words but before Xzjytheous could respond, the transmission was terminated by his enraged employer.

Back in the deployment bay, Tino was still crying, quietly, and unable to control himself, the tracks of his tears pulling his face tight. He knew he had to surrender to the drowsiness that was starting to grow over him, weighing heavier and heavier on his waning mind. As the electrical current continued to surge through his body, the emerald I.S.S. suit that he was wearing detected the dangerously escalating voltage.

Tino felt his head starting to tilt to the side as it slid against the wall behind him, his neck no longer able to support it. His jaw grew loose, his breathing turning from shallow defiance, to helplessly relaxed. He could feel the flow of air passing his lips as he began to slowly close his heavy, blurring eyes, unsure if he would ever open them again as he let go, drifting...drifting, he let the surging electricity carry him away.

He must have blacked out because the next thing Tino knew, his eyes began to slowly open, staring down through the gaps in the metal mesh floor panels, the varied colours of the insulated wiring blurring and blending into each other as his vision came back into focus, blinking his eyes slowly. He could feel the metal ridges of the floor panels digging into his forehead, creating painful, reddened, indented lines across it.

Gathering his thoughts, he realised that he was now lying down, sprawled out on his front across the floor rather than pinned up against the wall. But what was that? That pressure over his nose and cheeks. Breathing...LOUD BREATHING IN HIS EARS. SOMETHING WAS SMOTHERING HIS FACE. His eyes shot wide open and alert as he scrambled frantically to his feet, staggering as he threw himself backwards and slammed hard against the wall, looking about himself in frantic disorientation.

It took a moment for Tino to realise that he wasn't actually being attacked. He was inhaling breathable air and was now able to move as well. The intuitive cy-bionics of his armoured suit had generated an invisible, protective membrane around his body to protect him from the electricity that surged through the room. Tino's eyes darted about the deployment bay, his entire body still tense with fright; his fingers trying to cling to the smooth wall he was pressed up against. After several panicked moments, he slowly relaxed his strained calf muscles and gradually lowered himself down off his toes until his feet were flat on the floor.

Tino relaxed his fingers that were pressed up against the metal and peeled his hands away from the wall, although his fingertips took a bit more persuading. He slowly brought up his hand and gently grasped at the respirator mask which appeared to be connected to the collar in his suit.

As Tino calmed his racing mind and slowed his breathing, allowing his pounding heart time to recover, he gradually turned his head, looking around the room, surveying for something that could work to his advantage while, several times, back-tracking the flick of his eyes as he repeatedly thought he had seen something moving in the shadows. Noticing the helmet from his armoured suit on the floor, several feet away, he slowly, cautiously, glanced around the room once more for absolute assurance that he was alone and then looked up at the hatch to make sure Xzjytheous wasn't standing at the top of the ladder above him. The hatch was still sealed shut so Tino began to make his way, gingerly, with slow, small footsteps, across the deployment bay, as light-footed as possible.

The small pivoting turrets snapped into position, aiming at him as soon as he took his first larger step. Curiously though, they instantly powered down in response to an electro-magnetic pulse emitted from the armoured suit that Tino was wearing, almost as if it knew that he was in danger. The turrets all relaxed into a downward pointing position. Tino frowned, pausing as he looked around the room at them. He wondered if he could use them to help in his escape.

Slowly, and undeniably feeling the tension that was flooding his mind while keeping his eyes focussed on the turrets at all times, making sure they remained disabled, he began to bend his knees, moving into a more crouched position as he felt around on the floor with his hand.

On locating the helmet, he dragged it towards him, over the metal mesh floor panels, causing a metallic juddering sound which continued to ring out in the helmet's wake as he slowly picked it up.

What he hadn't realised, however, was that Xzjytheous had, in fact, been standing right behind him the whole time, once again wearing the gold armoured suit without the helmet and using a stealth field generator, hiding him from sight.

The electro-magnetic pulse that disabled the turrets had finally knocked out the reinforced stealth field generator and revealed the Reptilian, who now emerged from the gold armoured suit in his black, leather trench coat, as Tino reached down for the helmet.

As he slowly rose back up, he saw Xzjytheous' reflection in the shiny emerald helmet, his eyes blazing-scarlet with his pupils; a slither of black, slicing down the centre and illuminated, furiously, by sparks of electricity that erupted at his feet; jumping up at the metal strap locks on his boots.

Tino froze, right where he was, and his whole body tensed up as he unconsciously held his breath, unsure of what to do next, unable to even lock onto a single thought in his frantically racing mind. The prolonged exposure to the electrical current had temporarily blocked his hearing for the most part which meant that he hadn't heard the explosive snaps of electricity behind him. As he slowly turned around, considering hitting Xzjytheous across the jaw with the helmet, the Reptilian attacked without contemplation or hesitation.

With an animalistic roar of pure rage, he swung at Tino, aggressively, with his long claws, knocking the helmet out of his hands and sending it tumbling across to the other side of the room as bolts of electricity shot off in all directions, jumping up at the helmet from the floor and launching it back and forth across the room. Without stopping to think, Tino jumped aside, landing flat on the floor, just as the turrets rebooted and turned on him.

Still protected by the membrane generated by the suit and remembering how he had heard the metal floor panels rattling under the vibrations of the ship's engines earlier, Tino gripped at one of the electrified panels in the hope that it would serve as a weapon or at least part of a shield, despite the gaps in it. Although the panel was still secured to the floor, the broad screw was extremely loose.

A crescendoing, high-pitched ringing sound filled the deployment bay as Xzjytheous, slowly advancing, turned his charged blaster on Tino who was frantically yanking at the floor panel to try and tear it up as he repeatedly looked up at his captor, now his executioner, crying out with fright and desperation. He pulled and yanked at it as hard as he could, but the screw still wasn't completely loosened. He kicked at it repeatedly with the heel of his boot until, finally, he successfully snapped the screw.

Tino shook the panel loose, just as Xzjytheous began firing individual blaster bolts at him, now advancing with much more powerful, forceful strides. Tino, dazzled by the flashes of sparks that erupted at Xzjytheous' feet with every step, backed away at the same pace as his attacker's advances. He took cover behind his makeshift shield but, just like on Polarious 5, the mesh channelled the energy of the blaster bolts through the metal strips, shooting multiple smaller bursts out sideways from each of them, in a fierce volley of deadly blasts.

Tino finally lowered his shield to have his opponent in full view once again but, bizarrely, Xzjytheous had vanished. He couldn't have used the stealth field generator as it had been disabled. Suddenly a blaster bolt hit Tino in the arm, destroying one of the badges. Tino reeled around to see Xzjytheous, minus his boots, crawling on all-fours high up on the wall, grasping at the ceiling with the claws on his feet and protected from the electrical current by his scales, although it still snapped out at his metallic weapons.

The Reptilian moved, sideways, into the shadows in the corner of the room and ceased his attacks. Slowly, Tino moved towards the corner, in search of Xzjytheous, grasping his shield even more firmly, as he held it up, close to his exposed face.

With a deafening, primal howl, using the element of surprise and his immensely powerful leg muscles to his advantage, Xzjytheous leapt out of the shadows, straight at Tino, bearing his claws at the boy as the long, curved spikes thrust out from beneath its now-darkened scales which parted as the creature's muscles enlarged.

Tino stumbled backwards as the raging beast rammed into him with all of its power and, with no time to recover from the impact, Xzjytheous came at Tino again with a powerful onslaught of brute force, kicking and punching in various combinations until, with no restraint, he grabbed the boy, his claws wrapped entirely around his torso, piercing into the armour and launched him across the room like a ragdoll.

Xzjytheous continued to advance, grinning, toying with the terrified boy and firing his blaster as he went. Tino stumbled back to his feet, quickly staggering backwards as he struggled to keep his footing and maintain the space between them. All he could do was use the panel, which now had pieces sliced out of it by the creature's claws, to hold himself up between the attacks. The panel conducted the electricity from the floor through it and fired explosive bolts out around the room until he lifted it up again.

Tino could hear himself breathing very fast through the respirator mask as he struggled to block the constant blasts.

Suddenly, he had an idea. He turned the floor panel vertically and angled the bottom of it forwards. It caught the next blast and shot the multiple bursts upwards, towards the ceiling behind him as well as down at the floor, hitting Tino's target at Xzjytheous' feet. The exposed wiring, from beneath the floor panel he had removed, took the full power of the re-directed blasts, melting the wires and disabling the locks to the deployment bay hatch in the floor.

The doors in the floor slowly separated as Tino raced across the room towards the helmet on the other side of the deployment bay. A freezing cold, howling wind filled the room as the doors opened and everything that wasn't secure in the deployment bay flew out into the upper atmosphere of Zonju. Tino's respirator mask returned to the compartment inside the armoured suit as the room filled with breathable air.

The rims at the bottoms of Tino's boots lit up with round, white lights that flashed three times indicating that they had activated and then the lights repeatedly darted back and forth in a chain, indicating that they had magnetised as a safety measure. Being stopped in his tracks so suddenly caused him to jolt before he could reach the helmet which now slid and rolled across the floor, towards the gaping hole. Tino thrust his hand inside the helmet as it began to pick up speed, almost missing it. He had the helmet once again, however, with many of the floor panels not being secure; there was a whole new set of problems to take into consideration.

The Knightfall was now tearing through the atmosphere at extremely high speeds as flames roared, ablaze, engulfing the entire hull of the ship and flickering into the deployment bay. Tino had to think fast. Not only could he be sucked out of the ship at any moment but Xzjytheous was still firing at him. The boy, squinting, straining to keep his eyes open against the strong, cold wind, once again ducked for cover behind his protective shield and took advantage of the opportunity to secure the helmet over his head.

However, while Tino was distracted with the helmet, Xzjytheous saw a valuable opportunity to change tactics and, taking the chance, began firing at the floor panel, on which Tino stood. The rattling panel shook loose as the screw melted and both it and Tino hurtled through the air towards the open deployment bay hatch.

It was only sheer luck that the floor panel that was secured to Tino's magnetised boots wedged into the gap beneath another peeling floor panel, the impact of which removed the peeling panel entirely, flipping it into the air and striking Xzjytheous' across the head with immense force in a powerful, blinding explosion of electricity.

Tino immediately threw himself to the floor and gripped as hard as he could, forcing his gloved fingers into the gaps of two separate floor panels as Xzjytheous lost consciousness from the airborne projectile.

The Reptilian fell forward as the weight of his huge stature tore away the floor panels that he was gripping. He was dragged out, through the open deployment bay hatch, and sent plummeting down to the planet below along with the floor panel that was peeled away from Tino's magnetised boots. The boots let out a repeated buzzing sound and the lights on the rims of the soles turned red and repeatedly flashed on and off, indicating that they weren't magnetised to anything anymore.

Under the intense uncertainty of the situation and the sound of the howling wind and flames clearly audible, even behind the thick inner padding of the helmet and Tino's partial deafness from the electrical current, he hadn't even noticed the ship's wailing alarms and the slow, pulsing glow of the red lights illuminating the entire deployment bay.

Using all of the strength he could muster, Tino pulled himself across the floor of the deployment bay, hooking his fingers into the gaps in the panels and driving them right in as he desperately tried to avoid sharing Xzjytheous' fate. He had no idea what he was going to do but, for now, he just needed to get to that ladder and through the hatch in the ceiling which was now unlocked after Xzjytheous had entered through it.

Most of the debris, including the gold Troop Leader suit, had flown out of the deployment bay and now only what was strong and secure remained. Tino reached out for the bottom rung of the ladder but every attempt to move was countered by the strong force that pulled at him from outside. As soon as he let go of the panel, his tired arm was dragged away from the ladder and pinned to his side.

Now only holding onto a floor panel with one hand, he pulled himself as hard as he could, crying out in excruciating pain, but it was no use. He could feel the muscles in his arm starting to strain and grow more tired with each passing second. Every effort to pull himself against the powerful drag only made it worse. He closed his eyes and tried to rest for a moment as he relaxed every muscle in his body except for his fingers, the knuckles of which were aching more and more until the ache became a burning sensation.

Suddenly, he could feel his elbow starting to bend as he continued to cling to the floor panel. He slowly moved across the floor towards the foot of the ladder until he was able to reach it. He could still feel the wind pulling at everything around him but it felt like there was now no gravity. He began to climb the ladder effortlessly as he looked down at his armoured suit, all of the diamond, circular and various other badges were illuminated once more. The round hole in the ceiling glowed with an icy blue colour as Tino pushed against the heavy, round door and ascended through it. He hadn't realised it but the suit's jet propulsion systems had activated and were carrying him up to the cargo-hold above the deployment bay.

Tino grabbed the hatch cover and slammed it down over the hole, locking it shut. A high-pitched, oscillating siren emanated from his suit as the royal-blue and gold lights on his jet propulsion unit indicator and the bars in his chest plate went out and flashed with scarlet light in concert with the sound, indicating that the fuel reserves had been spent. The icy blue flames from the thrusters began sputtering as they grew weaker before fading entirely.

Tino removed the helmet and lay down on his back, sprawling himself out over the floor next to the hatch. He relaxed his arms and closed his tired eyes, giving himself a moment to recover as he slowly flexed the bruised joints in his fingers.

'IMPACT IMMINENT! IMPACT IMMINENT!' a female voice now announced, repeatedly, over the speaker from the nearby cockpit. Tino's eyes shot wide open and he quickly scrambled to his feet using his shaky arms to pick himself up from the floor as he tried to find his balance.

Using whatever was available to support himself against in passing, he stumbled his way into the cockpit and grabbed the headrest of one of the seats which pivoted slightly at first as he used it to hold himself up. Looking down at the vast array of flashing warning lights on the control console in front of him, he couldn't make sense of any of them as the interpretations were written in Biolie and the controls were far too technical for him to operate.

His eyes widened and his mouth fell slightly open as he looked up through the window at the spectacular black crystal clusters that reached high into the sky in front of him. All around, huge caves opened up in the sides of the immense, black mountains that dwarfed even the crystal clusters, thrusting up through a dense fog that settled about half way up, illuminated by the huge, silver moon.

Tino looked back at the controls, completely clueless. He couldn't even begin to figure out how to pilot this ship. He backed away a step. Then another. Then another. 'IMPACT! IMPACT! IMPACT!' announced the automated voice on the speaker with rapid urgency as Tino turned to run out of the cockpit. He leapt forwards and pulled the helmet back over his head as the cy-bionic components interlocked into position.

Not a moment later, the side of the ship struck, one of the enormous, black, crystal formations with immense force, sending the vessel spiralling, violently, out of control as it hurtled, at speed, down towards the ground, a trail of black smoke tainting the picturesque sky in its wake. Tino frantically reached about amongst fierce eruptions of flames and sparks for something to hold onto, almost blinded by the fog of pressurised CO2 now flooding the ship. It was no use; his hands found nothing in their desperate search as he aggressively tumbled from ceiling to floor to wall.

The ship smashed into one of the mountains, bringing it to an abrupt halt and throwing Tino, with uncontainable force, through the cockpit window in a shower of shattered glass. He hit the floor hard, scraping across it before being thrown into the air again, tumbling uncontrollably and with rapid speed, across the rocks and razor-sharp, black crystals of one of the caves.

It took a few seconds for Tino to stop hurtling across the cave floor, due to the sheer momentum that The Knightfall had hit the side of the mountain with. As he finally came to a stop, lying on his front, a sharp pain blazed across his lower lip where his tooth had cut deep into it during the tumble. He didn't dare move. Not even a thought entered his mind as he closed his eyes and just endured the pain, waiting for everything to stop spinning around him.

The alarm from his suit had stopped sounding sometime during the collision and now only the scarlet light flashed on and off until, it too, finally went out completely. Tino began to flex his fingers and bend at the elbows, slowly pulling his hands across the gritty, abrasive floor, a slight ache in his shoulder as he squeezed his eyes tight shut, breathing heavily. Every movement was slow and carefully precise to avoid the shock of a sudden pain from an injury that he might not have picked up on yet.

Feeling his lip swelling up already, he knew for certain that he wouldn't have survived the crash had it not been for the armoured suit, the padded gloves of which came out with just a few whitened scrapes and scuffs but, other than that, they were entirely intact. The rest of the suit had taken much more of a battering on impact.

Small shards of shattered glass spilled out of some of the illuminated, now-fuzzy, and flickering, badges on the arms and chest of the suit as Tino moved, clinking to the floor. Illuminated in the flicker of the lights, were flares of silver, brushed into a fade, over the emerald armour from grazing across the floor.

Painfully, as was reflected by his intense wincing, he eased himself to his feet and, trying hard to ignore the burning sensation that now intensified across his swelling lower lip, all Tino could think was whoever Oli was and whatever the I.S.S. was, their armour was built to withstand a lot.

On the inside of the flickering visor display, a white icon blinked repeatedly, with a slow pulse, at the side of the display which read

'O2'

indicating the presence of oxygen in the cave. After a couple of seconds, the blinking stopped and it remained on the display at the left-hand side.

The flickering lights from the various shaped badges on the armoured suit created a glow around Tino but the cave was so immense that he could see neither the walls, nor the ceiling. Only a small patch of the floor was visible at his feet.

Hoping that he would be able to find a way to descend down the side of the mountain, Tino turned to the cave's entrance. He jumped back with fright as his gaze fell onto a short, metal humanoid, one of Xzjytheous' bionics, that had aided in his escape from The Scout Hut. The bionic emerged from The Knightfall's flaming wreckage that blocked the exit and made its way towards a very wary Tino. Dust and black crystal shards fell over the ship from around the opening, tumbling off the hull, to the floor, but the bionic wasn't phased.

Coming to a stop in front of Tino, the bionic silently looked up at him, offering a rifle and a customised knife to him. Tino looked down at the bionic that was only slightly shorter than him. It was made of a culmination of silver, metal rods and looked like it had been poorly treated, which it had been. Xzjytheous often needed something to take his anger out on during his rampage across the galaxy to avenge his family. Xzjytheous had stolen the simple, sentient being from a junkyard on Polarious, long before its destruction, after assassinating its owner; an arms dealer who had provided the artillery to the Biolum military that was used to shoot his family's shuttle down. The bionic was the perfect emotional and physical punch bag for Xzjytheous; something he could make suffer without it ever retaliating.

The only option left was for Tino to accept the weapons and proceed into the cave in search of an alternative route accompanied by the bionic.

Also littered amongst the debris and the variety of peculiar weapons thrown from the ship, gently illuminated in the fiery glow of the flames, was a blaster and a knife. Tino looked down at the empty compartments on his armoured suit where Xzjytheous had previously disarmed it of its weapons. These must have been the items that had been removed. A spontaneous shower of sparks exploded out of the ship's cockpit as Tino reached down to retrieve the weapons, causing him to look up at the wreckage warily, his eyes strained wide and brows raised as, for a split second he paused, unconsciously holding his breath in response to the unpredictability of the wreckage. Looking down at the blaster and knife, he was surprised by their hefty weight and feel in his grasp, despite their relatively small size.

Unseen by Tino and the bionic, the bright flurry briefly revealed one of Parathax's giant, hulking spies, Anthony, who looked down on the crash site from above, hooded and dressed entirely in black. The mysterious silhouette stood in an opening that was carved into the wall of the cave, observing closely as Tino picked up the weapons, sheathing the knife, securing the blaster into its holster on his leg and slinging the rifle over his shoulder on its leather strap which had previously been shortened for him by the bionic. Anticipating danger ahead, Tino was taking no chances. He kept the customised knife, with a Beconium coated blade, clutched tight in his hand.

As Tino turned to begin venturing into the depths of the cave and tunnel system beyond, his new companion raced ahead to scout the network of passageways for potential threats and anything that could be of use.

'Hey! No, wait!' Tino called after the bionic in a loud, frustrated whisper to avoid giving himself away to any threats that might be nearby. The bionic, however, had already disappeared into the shadows, the frantic clattering sound of its feet fading into the distance.

Lowering his arm back down to his side, Tino looked around at his surroundings once more. A second shower of sparks flared up into the air, lighting up the ledge once more before quickly fizzling out as they rained back down to the ground but, by this time, Anthony had vanished back into the darkness.

CHAPTER 9
HUNTING BY MOONLIGHT

Triggered by close proximity between one another, the bionic now shared in the custom software that Oli had integrated into his emerald I.S.S. cy-bionic exoskeleton which Tino now wore. One of the many features that came with this access was the reception and transmission of crystalline harmonic resonance which meant that any sound that travelled between the black crystals of Zonju caused tiny vibrations in their structure and the bionic could now mimic those vibrations and transmit them to the suit that Tino was wearing so he could hear everything going on, wherever the bionic was.

As Tino walked along, one of the still-functioning, illuminated badges on his emerald suit activated in response to the bionic sending its readings back to it. A hologram was projected from the badge, floating in mid-air right in front of Tino who was slightly taken aback by it. He was now able to see everything that the bionic could see as well as written Voca-Com translations of the crystalline harmonic resonations, even though he could also hear it through the suit's built in speakers.

Proceeding down one of the cold, damp tunnels, Tino watched the projection as the bionic appeared to be crawling, slowly, down a wall from above into an enormous, round chamber. A large, black throne made up of tall, black crystals sat in the centre of the chamber, a flight of long, narrow steps leading up to the platform upon which the enormous structure sat.

'The Knightfall has arrived' echoed the deep male voice of Gala-Thius from within the shadows that skirted the well-lit chamber as Anthony delivered his report to him. The eerie glow spilled down in the descending fog, like a waterfall, through the vast hole in the top of the cave, bathing the chamber in silver from the enormous rising moon above Zonju. An unsettling chuckle of a female, low in pitch, built up, reverberating throughout the cave.

'The Reptilian succeeded' echoed Parathax's voice, slow, such that to hear it would make the listener hang onto every syllable. She continued to chuckle as she contemplated how to proceed. *They must be talking about Xzjytheous*, Tino thought as he watched and listened to the transmission from the bionic.

'Anthony' she said, speaking into the shadows. Parathax now spoke more quietly and with a lisp, as was the way Anthony spoke and insisted his name be pronounced. The figure dressed in black, who had observed Tino's arrival, stepped forward from the darkness.

'The Reptilian served his purpose well. Now kill him. Bring the prisoner to me' she continued with a ghastly echo to her voice as she rose up from her throne of blackened crystals, formed in a natural cluster with the room carved out into pillars, ledges and podiums around it. 'Kill only the Reptilian. Do not kill the boy' she instructed specifically, now more quickly and with certainty in her voice as she extended a single pale, icy finger from the darkness that enshrouded her.

'But...ensure that he comes to me of his own accord. He must not suspect.' she finished.

'THE LIZARD! KILL THE LIZARD!' yelled the insanity of Anthony's deep, abrasive voice from the shadows, echoing, as he ecstatically left the chamber to hunt down Xzjytheous and Tino.

The stealthily-observing bionic fired a laser beam, thinner than a strand of hair, down at Anthony's arm as he discarded his black cloak and ran out of the chamber beneath it. It then triggered an activation signal, transmitting back to The Knightfall. From the outer hull of The Knightfall's wreckage a long rack extended outwards, containing more bionics that stood in uniformity with various coloured markings on them. This augmented group of bionics was The Knightfall Guard; inspired by Xzjytheous' time studying Jason Campbell; 5-6-5's original Troop Leader when they first joined the I.S.S.

Xzjytheous had overheard Jason talking with another Troop Leader about an augmented group of purpose-built armoured suits that would be kept onboard the Rhinonoid once it was constructed to aid in missions when unforeseen problems occurred.

One of the bionics activated, leapt down from the rack and raced through the network of tunnels in pursuit of Anthony, homing in on the tracking signal that the laser beam had left on his arm.

Unaware of the new bionic in play, Tino felt the blood drain from his face with dread, knowing that this enormous madman was now hunting him through the tunnels. The weapons he carried would be of little use if Anthony found him. He was enormous, extremely muscular and, based on the transmissions coming from the bionic, would be impossible to reason with if their paths crossed.

'Gala-Thius' called the ghostly voice of Parathax, summoning the other of her followers as Tino, trembling and short of breath, continued to watch and listen to the bionic's transmissions, while repeatedly looking from the holographic projection coming from the illuminated badge, to the path in front of him.

An old, tall man, dark-grey-haired, bearded and also dressed in a long, black, hooded robe slowly emerged from the darkness. He appeared to carry a long, twisted, carved staff in his hand, forged out of the black crystals of Zonju with a core of rusty-orange Beconium, the same stuff that covered Tino's blade, embedded through the centre. Gala-Thius lay the staff down on the polished, black floor in front of Parathax as he knelt before her at the bottom of the steps and bowed his head.

'The Reptilian, Xzjytheous. He stole valuable Interstellar Scout hardware from their fleet before the assault at Polarious Five. His species is not one to form allegiances. However, the stolen technology could be acquired by another. Like he who put me in this eternal state' the echoing voice of Parathax explained.

'With respect...you must realise that the Founder of the Interstellar Scouts has been driven ever-further away by our allies. Sol is gone. He did not come to their aid at Polarious Five. The Knightfall didn't intercept or relay any responses to the I.S.S. distress calls during the assault' Gala-Thius replied, although hesitant at first.

There was a long pause, filled with anticipation and regret as the old man remained, his head bowed, awaiting a response, his eyes flicking about at the patch of ground in front of him, the few scattered, tiny, sprouting, crystals that his eyes darted between, like fangs in the chamber floor. His ears listened closely, the sharp grit of the floor digging into his knuckles as he wished desperately for the silence to end, wondering, with growing dread, whether he was speaking out of place.

'The Reptilian will die. Should your...pet fail, you will bring me the Reptilian's head and the stolen I.S.S. hardware yourself. I will then oversee Anthony's destruction personally' Parathax warned, returning to sit upon the black, crystal throne.

Parathax often referred to Anthony as Gala-Thius' pet as, despite his human appearance, his behaviour and intelligence were more beast-like. Gala-Thius also had a soft spot for Anthony so it was often Parathax's pleasure to exploit such feelings to torment the old man and remind him of his place of being in servitude to her.

'As you command' replied Gala-Thius before reaching for his staff once more and using it to aid him in rising to his feet.

Despite the fact that he was being hunted by Anthony, Tino was quickly realising that Parathax was the big threat in this situation, making everyone else do her dirty work while reminding them of the terrifying consequences of failure. She had sent Xzjytheous to capture him, sent Anthony to kill Xzjytheous and threatened Gala-Thius with killing Anthony if he failed. Tino didn't know anything about any of these people but, with Xzjytheous already gone and lying dead somewhere out there, he wanted to warn Anthony about Parathax's plans for him.

Survival came first though and Anthony was hunting him. Tino had a feeling that, if he was going to help Anthony and warn him about the danger that awaited him for not returning with Xzjytheous, he would first have to fight and wound him.

'Sol is not gone' announced Parathax, her rage apparent at the old man's remark while never raising her voice, as Gala-Thius turned and began to leave the chamber. He paused but didn't dare turn back to look at her. A silence fell heavily upon the chamber once more, the most sinister, malevolent silence as a deep, wailing wind slowly grew, howling in crescendo through the cold, damp tunnels beyond.

The old man gripped his staff gradually tighter in the sweating palm of his aged hand, his knuckles whitening, his thumb, cold, pressed hard into one of the grooves of the twisted crystal, slowly sliding up over one of the ridges as he raised his head within the oversized hood, just a little at first, then a bit more and then fully. His mind raced in frantic, uncertain anticipation of taking Parathax's wrath as his eyes darted about, glancing into the depths of the darkness before him as he shivered, his blood chilled, following her words. He had felt that slither of ice that pierced his ears once before, dripping down his neck and flowing beyond his shoulders, slowly melting through his spine. It was how he felt when he was charged with arranging for Xzjytheous to be delivered to Parathax so he could lead the Deathstalker Squadron. At last, the echo of Parathax's voice faded away.

Only after the silence had endured within the chamber for a few seconds, did he push his thumb, once more, over the ridge of his twisted staff in his search for courage. Gala-Thius then slowly continued out, through the archway, his eyes looking straight ahead the whole time, never deviating. The bionic, once again, fired the laser beam at Gala-Thius and another of The Knightfall Guard activated and raced into the tunnels to monitor the old man.

As soon as he was out of sight, Gala-Thius took a moment to compose himself, wiping the sweat from his eyebrows, the burning sensation around his face now prickling his wrinkled skin like electricity as the tension drained from his body.

Still gathering himself, he slowly turned his staff upside down and angled the jagged, black crystal top of it down, into the rocky ground of the tunnel. Placing his flat palm against the staff, he closed his eyes, slowed his still-pounding heart and his breathing, concentrating hard as he calmed his mind. The Beconium core, visible through the long, black crystal in his hand, slowly came to life, twisting its way through the staff and into the ground. The clusters of black crystals dotted around against the wall outside the chamber where Parathax resided now began to gradually emulate the staff with Beconium now silently materialising within all of them. More of the structures grew from the ground, walls and ceiling, developing into a deep, intricate web as they blocked off the remainder of the passageway that led to the chamber's entrance.

Slowly, as if emerging from a deep trance and unaware of the bionic from The Knightfall Guard now watching him and relaying the visual and audio signals back to Tino, Gala-Thius opened his eyes, looking about himself and listening closely for anything that might have followed him out of the chamber. He knew of the abominations that lurked in the shadows that did Parathax's bidding and he knew the horrors that they were capable of.

Gala-Thius was now satisfied that, if Tino was stealthy enough to steal past Anthony, he would never make it to Parathax's chamber. He pulled his hood further down over his face and exhaled heavily, releasing any residual tension before continuing on, into the darkness.

Years ago, Anthony had been a Troop Leader with the Interstellar Scouts but was forced to step down from his position after he suffered a trauma that had sent him insane while on a mission with Gala-Thius. Nobody except the old man knew the details of what had happened while they were away from the fleet and Gala-Thius never discussed it with anyone. Upon Anthony's leadership being revoked by the I.S.S, Gala-Thius, feeling responsible for the trauma Anthony had endured, chose to retire from active duty, stealing an I.S.S. shuttle and fleeing with Anthony to keep him safe as, due to his volatile nature and lack of understanding, the I.S.S. hadn't wanted Anthony to go free, they had wanted to put him in an asylum on Polarious where they could keep an eye on him. Their whereabouts remained unknown to the I.S.S. as they had deliberately crashed their shuttle upon arriving on Zonju. They had also ditched the remains of their gold armoured suits amongst the wreckage, preventing them from being tracked. Anthony was incapable of being left alone, that much was true. His behaviour, admittedly, often did become erratic but Gala-Thius had made it his responsibility to take care of him and keep him out of trouble.

Tino continued to observe the three holographic projections of Parathax, Gala-Thius and Anthony from their respective bionics as Anthony walked through the cold, moist tunnels, his dirty face, shaded with stubble, was occasionally illuminated as he walked by the cracks in the wall through which the silver, moonlit fog bled. The putrid smell of bacteria-infested slime and algae flooded his nostrils but he was used to it by now, he barely even noticed it. A scar cut across Anthony's face, slashing over his cloudy-white left eye which was blinded from a previous conflict with Xzjytheous. He was slightly hunched over, his arms hanging loose at his sides and his walk was almost animal-like. He grunted deeply as he moved through the caves and tunnels, the sound echoing loudly, reverberating off the walls.

Long, untidy, black dreadlocks with hints of grey mixed in hung past his shoulders, tied with bare wire twisted around each gathering of scraggly hair. The wire had been taken from the wreckage of the ship that he and Gala-Thius had stolen. Anthony was also a noticeably tall, muscular man, his clothing torn and old scars not only running across his weathered face, but his chest and arms too. Around his neck, hung a length of wire also taken from their ship which was threaded through a long talon-like claw which he had claimed from Xzjytheous after the injury to his eye. It dangling and scratched against his chest as he walked along.

A blue letter 'H' began blinking on the display on the inside of Tino's visor. The same icon appeared on the objective tracker at the bottom of it. Then, as he paused to look about himself, into the unrelenting darkness in every direction, he saw that, next to the 'O2' and the 'H' icons, now blinked a green indicator that read

'H2O'

also indicating it on the objective tracker where the blue 'H' had been. Tino, still frowning, unsure of what the letters and numbers were indicating, slowly removed his helmet from his suit to try and find another way to figure out what it was trying to tell him.

The cooling breeze that immediately swept over him felt amazing. He closed his eyes and simply enjoyed it for a moment, breathing in the fresh air, deeply. Then came the unmistakeable sound, like music to his ears as his hearing had fully restored. In the distance, he could hear what sounded like a waterfall. It was coming from the direction that the objective tracker had been pointing in.

The suit must have detected that he was dehydrated and this was the first source of water he had come across since he first awoke onboard The Knightfall.

Tino savoured the cooling breeze on his face and sweeping through his hair for a few more seconds and then put the helmet back over his head and, now moving more quickly until his fast walk became a steady jog, he followed the green objective marker displayed on his visor. It now became obvious to him that he was dehydrated. His mouth grew noticeably dry at the very thought of locating water and the running wasn't helping. He slowed back down but continued walking at a brisk pace, following the sound, now audible from inside his helmet. Tino hadn't even noticed Anthony lurking in the shadows, a long machete-like weapon clutched in his scarred hand. Stealthily, he followed behind his target, at a distance, as Tino moved in closer to the objective marker.

As he reached the top of a steep slope, Tino lowered himself to the floor and cautiously descended towards the bottom, moving over the loose shale which glided over the ground beneath him. Concentrating hard as he gradually walked his way down the small hill, his feet in front of him and using his gloved hands to control his descent; Tino's eyes fell away from the holographic projections. Anthony slowly and silently approached the top of the slope behind him, the large machete-like weapon hanging at his side, firmly in his grasp as he twisted the wooden handle in his fingers, occasionally tapping the blade against his leg.

As Tino reached the bottom of the hill, he walked through a jagged, black-crystal archway in the wall, removing his helmet and gloves as he went, perhaps a little too enthusiastically, then, stepping out into the opening at the end of the archway, he found what he was looking for, drinkable running water, at last.

Anthony took a couple of steps back and then ran forwards, leaping high into the air above the slope, the large blade raised high above his head as he came hurtling down, at colossal speed, towards the black crystal opening where Tino was now leaning down, over the edge of the drop-off, completely unaware.

CHAPTER 10
FATE DECIDED

'WE'RE APPROACHING THE TRENCH! announced Nathan's voice through the built-in speakers of the I.S.S. Operatives' helmets, as he repeatedly cast his eyes up, glancing at the sonar display on the inside of his visor, the ping being emitted from a small rectangular device that had deployed from the side of his helmet.

'THE FIGHTRS ARE STILL FIRING ON US!' shouted Colin, keeping his head as low as possible to avoid the debris that exploded into the air around the group with every blast.

The lead pilot of the Black-Burn Fighters detected the landslide in the trench that the Rhinonoid had detected earlier and, determining that the Operatives were too small to take out with blaster fire, gave the command for more drastic action. A loud alarm suddenly sounded inside the Operatives' helmets as a series of long humps on the wings of the Black-Burn Fighters folded out the flaps of their built in missile chambers and locked them into position to acquire their targets.

'MISSILES INCOMING!' yelled Nathan as he and everyone else frantically looked about for the incoming projectiles.

However, they weren't the targets of the Black-Burns' missiles. They looked up to see volleys of them soaring by, with a trail of red smoke, high above their heads.

'THE TRENCH! THEY'RE TARGETTING THE TRENCH!' yelled Corey. 'STANDBY TO ENGAGE JET PROPULSION UNITS!' he continued without giving it a second thought, carefully unclipping the cables that secured Oli to the vehicle they were riding on, as the huge, white crystal cliffs came into view ahead of them.

'Not yet! Five-Six-Five, move into arrow formation and increase velocity to max thrust' instructed Isaac.

The front of the arc formation opened up with two Operatives on one side and two on the other. Corey, letting out a sigh of uncertainty at Isaac's strategy, tightened his grasp on the rubberised grips of his handlebars, tucking his elbows in, tight, to support Oli between his arms as he accelerated through the gap, the roar of his quad-bike now growing much louder as his speed increased.

Once Corey was ahead of the other four Operatives, Colin and Ethan accelerated ahead, closely followed by Nathan and Isaac. The roar of their vehicles harmonised as they tore across the planet's surface.

The missiles struck their target, blasting away huge chunks of the cliffs and sending a second landslide of huge boulders and crystals that cut through the air like knives, straight towards the group.

The fighters continued to fire their blaster canons but now at the boulders rather than the Operatives in an attempt to create so much debris from them that they would be taken out by the obstacles in their path instead.

While the motorbikes continued to weave in and out, the Operatives, pressing their bodies as low as possible to their fuel tanks to make themselves smaller targets, Corey's quad bike was less capable of dodging the inbound debris due to its broad size and Corey had to concentrate hard on keeping control of the vehicle and keeping hold of Oli as the two wheels on his left-hand side were lifted up from the ground, the vehicle juddering as the handlebars wavered in his tense grasp before slamming back down, heavily, onto its suspension.

'Five-Six-Five, standby to engage jet propulsion units' instructed Isaac's voice having chosen a different timing for launch to what Corey had planned.

Just as they had rehearsed so many times previously in training, although still equally as daunting as the first time, they carefully lifted their feet off the black, rubberised foot pegs on the sides of their vehicles and moved into a crouched position on the seats, while still accelerating; fighting the urge to put their fingers over the brakes too soon.

'STANDBY, THIS IS GOING TO BE A BIG ONE!' shouted Corey over the still increasing roar of the vehicles' engines as their speed continued to increase.

Although he didn't admit it, he was growing increasingly nervous about pulling off such a daring stunt at these high speeds and having to carry Oli through the entire manoeuvre as well. The pursuing Black-Burn Fighters were carrying out Parathax's agenda to hunt down and destroy any I.S.S. presence to clear the path for her conquest but Biker Delta Squadron 5-6-5 had learnt by example from Oli as their Patrol Leader which had made them brave, daring and prepared to take risks that most wouldn't even dream of.

Isaac's plan was to draw the enemy Black-Burn Fighters in, as close as possible, to the trench to make the Operatives a more difficult target for both them and any more falling debris and then to use the jet propulsion units built into their cy-bionic suits to travel the rest of the way.

They each hit the glowing red button in the middle of their collars and the two illuminated, royal-blue and gold striped bars sprung up out of their chest plates, locking down into their right-angled positions and allowing access to the thrusters' trigger grips as well as their parachute ripcords.

Suddenly a volley of blazing blaster bolts exploded into the ground ahead of them as the Black-Burn Fighters attempted to cut the group off. While most of the group was able to veer around the obstacle, it was too late for Nathan. Making a split-second decision and feeling the wind resistance pushing against him, Nathan lowered his body back down so it was pressed up against the bike, tightened his grip on the bars of his bike as the vibration shook his hands through his gloves and his bike shot up a ramp that had been formed by the impact of the blaster bolts.

As he shot off the ramp and his motorbike roared through the air, another pair of blaster bolts surged right by him, narrowly missing his legs on either side as he felt the pressure of his legs squeezing, ever-tighter, close to the bike, keeping his head down as low as possible.

The blaster bolts impacted the ground in front of Nathan with such power that, as he came out of his dive, he vanished into a dense cloud of white dust, blind to any more obstacles that were in his path such as tufts of crystal shards or boulders. Finally, Nathan emerged from the shroud with just a few scuffs on his suit and visor as he returned to his crouched position, ready to fire up his jet propulsion unit.

Seeing that Nathan had made it, Isaac left his worries and anxieties about leading the group far behind as there was no longer any room for such feelings in this situation, he had to step up and get the job done, just as he would be expected to if they were accompanied by a Troop Leader. Isaac focussed hard on controlling his breathing as he and the others concentrated on hitting the precise mark with their timing. He then placed his gloved hands over the clutch and brake triggers of the handlebars, resting his fingers gently upon them. There were so many variables to factor in and, if a single one was misjudged or mistimed...well...now wasn't the time for such contemplation.

Isaac was about to give his next, carefully-timed instruction but Corey's panic and lack of faith in Isaac's leadership got the better of him. He cut Isaac's voice off, taking the Assistant Patrol Leader and the others by surprise as everyone had expected to hear Isaac's voice in their helmets.

'LAUNCH!' shouted Corey's voice, seconds before they collided with the cliffs.

Everything suddenly moved into slow motion for the Operatives due to their level of focus but, at that moment, it was like time had stopped altogether. At the exact same moment, they all squeezed hard on their clutch and brake grips, causing their vehicles to flip forwards.

As soon as the vehicles were at the peak of their arc, with huge blaster bolts from the enemy fighters tearing past them, missing by mere inches, Isaac's voice filled the silence.

'ENGAGE THRUSTERS!' he yelled, having adjusted his timing, within a split second, to accommodate Corey's out-of-line, premature command. Although Isaac had shouted it loud and urgently, it was like he had simply spoken it in an almost calm voice due to the level of concentration each Operative was applying to the manoeuvre.

The Operatives relaxed their grip on the handlebars and pushed hard with their feet, allowing the vehicles to catapult them high into the air, and, in a spectacular blue, fiery explosion, the jet propulsion units of their suits activated and they soared faster and faster through the air, higher and higher until, just when they were about to slam into the top of the cliff faces, they deactivated their thrusters and somersaulted in perfect synchronisation, clearing the ledge as they continued to gain altitude.

Unable to pull away in time, the two Black-Burn Fighters that had been pursuing the group clipped their wings on the edge of the cliff and spiralled out of control, exploding in a ball of flame, behind them.

Once the Operatives had successfully evaded the tops of the cliffs, everyone went into an angled dive, towards the ground to briefly accelerate their descent, evading the black, burning debris that rained down upon the cliffs.

The group of Operatives then quickly spread out their arms and legs to create as much wind resistance as possible, slowing down their descent except for Corey, who only spread out his legs as he was still holding on tightly to Oli. The force of the air beneath them pushed their arms and legs upwards as they pushed them back down against it.

Isaac, focussing hard to calm his racing mind, glided into position next to Corey. Each of the Operatives grabbed hold of the two extended handle bars which ran parallel to their bodies and pulled down hard on them, pulling the built in ripcords. Isaac pulled the ripcords on Corey's suit, immediately followed by his own so Corey could keep hold of Oli. Blue parachutes deployed from the backs of their armoured suits with a gold trim around the edges.

The hard part was done. They could now relax for a moment and allow their racing minds and trembling arms and legs to settle back down. Corey's eyes scanned the terrain beneath them while repeatedly consulting the objective indicator on his visor's display.

'That's it, there. Up ahead' announced Corey spotting a tall crystal pillar that had been toppled by seismic activity and was now leaning against another which was still upright and had a two-pronged fork shape, supporting the weight of the fallen one.

The Operatives landed back on the ground with their knees slightly bent to take the force of the impact.

'What's our time window for sunset Nathan?' asked Isaac, urgently, as they hurried to detach their parachutes from their suits.

'A little under an hour now' replied Nathan, referring to a holographic stopwatch projected from one of the illuminated badges on his suit with a variety of live readings displayed on it from the Rhinonoid's cockpit console. He and the other Operatives raced behind Corey as they approached the crystalline structure.

'We have just enough time. Get him into position' instructed Isaac as he and the others locked the ballistic glass bars back into the chest plates of their suits.

'He's still deteriorating' announced Corey, now laying a quivering Oli down on the floor and removing their Patrol Leader's helmet followed by his own as the sun wasn't as bright now as it was earlier. '...I don't know if he's going to make it...' he continued doubtfully, now reluctantly looking up at the other Operatives who were slowly removing their helmets too, placing them gently on the floor at their feet.

Everyone's eyes were fixed on Oli. The Patrol Leader's eyes were slightly open, looking up at them but they all knew he wasn't conscious. His breaths were audible, short and sharp as the Beconium viciously continued to attack his vital organs.

Unbeknownst to the group of Operatives, on top of the cliffs, the single physical Con-Haarian pilot, that had been co-ordinating the decoys, had pulled itself from the wreckage of its Black-Burn Fighter and sent out a transmission to all other Black-Burn and stolen Viper Fighter patrols in the vicinity, calling them to Crystalosis. While the pilot awaited reinforcements, it set about hotwiring the blaster canon of its fighter that was perched on the ledge, overlooking the group of I.S.S. Operatives below.

'What's happening?' asked Colin as a crust of rusty coloured Beconium formed over Oli's eyes; sealing them shut.

'DON'T TOUCH IT!' shouted Isaac as he grabbed Colin and moved him away.

A blinding beam of light shot down from the crystalline structure and streamed straight down into Oli's face. Everyone turned their backs away from the light to protect their eyes but, as they did, a powerful blaster bolt exploded to the ground next to them, followed by another, and another.

'WE'RE UNDER ATTACK!' shouted Corey.

'COVER OLI!' ordered Isaac, drawing his blaster from the holster in the leg of his emerald suit and firing back in the direction that the blaster bolts were coming from,

'THE RHINONOID IS DETECTING MORE SHIPS IN THE VICINITY! THEY'VE BREACHED THE ATMOSPHERE!' yelled Nathan as he looked at the holographic projection emanating from the badge on his suit, grabbing his helmet and taking cover behind the crystalline structure.

'I SEE THEM! THEY'RE COMING IN FAST!' replied Corey, looking up at the black dots in the sky behind them as he joined the others.

'HOLD ON! I'M ALSO GETTING I.S.S. SIGNATURES INCOMING!' Nathan continued.

'ROGUE VIPERS?' asked Isaac.

'THIS IS I.S.S. PILOT - NATHANIEL LUCAS OF BIKER DELTA SQUADRON FIVE-SIX-FIVE! PLEASE REPEAT!' shouted Nathan, over the sound of blaster fire from on top of the cliff, as he put his helmet on and established contact with the inbound I.S.S. ships. 'THEY'RE A TROOP LEADER RECON PATROL FROM THE LIBERA! THEY'RE RIGHT ABOVE THE PLANET! WE'RE SAVED!' Nathan shouted to the others.

Unable to contain their emotions, the rest of the group let out a heavy sigh of relief. They never thought they'd make it. Each and every one of them was overcome with emotion and immense gratitude to the pilots that had initiated a rescue mission for them.

'UNDERSTOOD! ACTIVATING TRACKING BEACON!' yelled Nathan, through his helmet's built in microphone as he pressed on an illuminated, rectangular badge on his suit for the rescue team to lock onto. 'I.S.S. RECON PATROL, PLEASE ACKNOWLEDGE BIKER DELTA SQUADRON FIVE-SIX-FIVE TRACKING SIGNAL!' shouted Nathan but no response came. 'I.S.S. RECON PATROL, PLEASE RESPOND!' he shouted again.

'SOMETHING IS BLOCKING THE TRANSMISSIONS! I'VE LOST CONTACT!' Nathan shouted, turning to Isaac.

Moments later, the incoming I.S.S. ships simultaneously exploded into balls of flame, raining debris over the crystalline expanse. Devastated, the group of Operatives watched on in absolute horror.

Suddenly, a thunderous sonic boom shook the ground beneath their feet; knocking the group to the ground as it cracked and ruptured around them.

'NO!' yelled Nathan, devastated by the loss of their only hope of rescue.

From the shroud of black smoke that spilled out of the falling, destroyed I.S.S. ships, came the enormous, jet-black, bladed silhouettes of the Deathstalker Squadron, surging towards them at such fierce velocity that they broke the sound barrier as they had breached the atmosphere.

The Beconium on Oli's eyes liquidised and started fizzing. His eyes shot wide open and he sat bolt-upright. Seeing the blaster fire raining down around them, he quickly moved to take cover with the other Operatives, behind the crystalline structure.

'IT'S THE DEATHSTALKER SQUADRON! THEY SURVIVED THE ASSAULT!' yelled Corey.

'GET BENEATH THE STRUCTURE NOW!' Oli ordered, urgently, as he grabbed Colin and Ethan, shoving them to a more safe position.

'WE HAVE TO DEAL WITH THE PILOT UP THERE!' shouted Isaac as blaster bolts continued to rain down around them, exploding dust and tiny shards of crystal up in their faces.

'What's that?' Oli said to himself as something, out on the horizon, caught his attention.

'What? What is it?'asked Corey, overhearing the Patrol Leader.

In the distance, Oli could see the true devastation of the Deathstalkers' seismic boom. The ground was falling away for as far as the eye could see and it was coming straight towards them at an increasingly rapid rate.

'HELMETS ON AND GET BACK TO THE SHIP, NOW! I'LL DEAL WITH THE PILOT AND DRAW THE DEATHSTALKERS AWAY!' ordered Oli.

There was a catch in his voice as he spoke as, despite being the charismatic, heroic Patrol Leader in the group, he understood just how dangerous this plan was now that the Deathstalkers were in play once again. A group of just five fighters that had the speed and destructive firepower to liquidise all of Polarious in a matter of minutes would strike fear into any Operative.

'GO! GO! GO!' Oli yelled as he began firing back at the pilot on top of the cliff. The sound of thrusters from the other five Operatives' jet propulsion units filled the air and, one by one, they rocketed off the ground and soared towards the cliffs.

Oli landed on top of the cliff, rolled out of the line of fire and smashed the glass visor of the Con-Haarian's helmet with the elbow of his emerald cy-bionic exoskeleton. He then flipped over his opponent as he pulled a short, thin blade of steel from the wrist-guard of his armoured suit, triggering a spring mechanism that locked a piece of flint roughly the thickness and half the size of a pencil, into position above his wrist. Striking the metal blade across the flint as he landed, Oli caused a flurry of bright sparks to erupt into the eyes of the Con-Haarian, blinding him. This was a trick that Oli had learned from Jason, his Troop Leader, back when he was an Initiate. With a powerful kick to its armour, Oli knocked the enemy pilot away from the blaster canon and over the edge of the cliff.

With the Deathstalker Squadron still swarming around, Oli quickly fired up his jet propulsion unit once again and set about catching up with the rest of his Patrol. It appeared that the Deathstalker Squadron had lost track of them as they swarmed above the wreckage of the I.S.S. fighters.

Oli felt a swell of adrenaline surging through his body as he saw their very brief opportunity to escape.

'We need to get out of here, NOW! I'm moving in on your position' announced Oli inside everyone's helmets as he locked onto Nathan's still-active tracking signal. The thunderous roar of one of the Deathstalkers grew in Oli's ears as he turned to look back, over his shoulder. One of the Deathstalkers had intercepted his transmission to the other Operatives and was now tearing across the sky in pursuit as the light of the sun blazed along its forward-stretching blades.

Oli squeezed the triggers of his thrusters as hard as possible, trying to inject more fuel into the burners with as much pressure as he could. Still, the bladed prongs of one of the ship's blaster canons moved ever-closer. There was no way he would be able to beat or even match the ship's growing speeds.

Colin looked back at Oli, just as the Patrol Leader cut off his fuel supply to his thrusters in an attempt to dodge a blaster bolt that erupted out of one of the bladed blaster canons.

The blaster bolt missed Oli and came surging by the rest of the group, narrowly missing Corey's chest plate. The heat from the blast, however, was still enough to slightly liquidise the chest plate of Corey's suit and create displacement around the bolt, forcing Corey to, inadvertently, fly higher.

Oli had been fortunate enough to not be vaporised by the Deathstalker's blaster bolt but the blades still carried indescribably fierce weaponry. Once the Deathstalker was close enough, it drew back the four short blades that surrounded one of its blaster canons and angled them in towards one another. A purple light began to glow on the tips of the four short blades and a bright, purple ball of energy began to materialise; contained within the lights. It grew as the blades drew back further and bolts of radioactive-green lightning darted around excitedly within the bubble. Once enough energy had been generated, the green lightning darkened until a pulse of black, thorny energy exploded out from it, just as it had done in The Scout Hut's hanger bay, engulfing Oli's cy-bionic suit and disabling his jet propulsion unit.

A high-pitched wailing alarm sounded throughout Oli's suit, indicating that there was no more fuel being injected into his thrusters. Oli tried desperately to re-engage his suit's jet propulsion unit but the harder he squeezed, the louder the sound of straining machinery flooding his helmet, along with the alarms, became.

As his forward momentum quickly depleted, angling him into a nosedive, Oli made a last ditch attempt at deploying his parachute but the ripcord bars had locked in place while he had been trying to fire the thrusters back up.

His face sweating with panic, Oli's visor began to steam up from within, blinding him. As the suit became more and more deactivated, the display on the inside of his helmet's visor strained and flickered in various distortions until, finally, it too shut off entirely and he plummeted into freefall, a trail of black smoke spilling out in his wake. Every illuminated badge and the lights in his jet propulsion unit indicator had dimmed entirely.

'OLI!' yelled Colin.

Isaac looked back in response to Colin's cries. 'Oli's down! Negative parachute! Adjust your course to intercept and initiate extraction' he instructed.

'Negative. We are running out of time and fuel. We'll never make it off-world if we stop now' Corey responded, sweating with fear behind his visor from the blaster bolt's near miss.

'COREY, THAT'S AN ORDER, ADJUST YOUR COURSE AND HELP US GET OLI TO SAFETY!' shouted Isaac but, in his fear of the Deathstalkers firing on them again, Corey ignored Isaac's instructions and continued on, towards the Rhinonoid, refraining from even looking back over his shoulder as everyone shouted after him.

In this moment, Isaac feared that if Corey went on alone, he may let his fear control his actions further, leading him to take the Rhinonoid himself, return to the shuttle and abandon the rest of the Patrol there in order to save himself.

Isaac was faced with an impossible decision, one that, in this moment, made him hate the fact that he was the Assistant Patrol Leader. He could either save Oli and risk them all being stranded on

Crystalosis beyond sunset or he could do what Oli would probably tell him to do and get everyone else to safety first and then attempt a rescue mission for him once the danger had passed.

With tears in his eyes, hidden by his helmet, Isaac initiated an Assistant Patrol Leader Override on Colin's suit, stopping Colin from using any of his suit's functions himself as Isaac had a feeling that Colin would go back for Oli no matter what anyone said.

With Colin's cries in his ears, he led the rest of the group back to the Rhinonoid, leaving the Deathstalker Squadron and Oli far behind.

CHAPTER 11
THE DESERTERS

The long, razor-sharp blade in Anthony's hand struck against the rocks sending a blinding flash of sparks into the air as Tino stumbled aside, losing his footing with the fright of the attack and falling over the edge of the waterfall. He cut the palm of his hand as he clung desperately to the sharp, jagged rocks and crystals. The sides of the waterfall were already wet but now his hands were covered in blood as well.

With his fingers still sore from the battle against Xzjytheous in The Knightfall's deployment bay, Tino could feel himself quickly losing his grip as he was dragged down under the weight of the suit he was wearing. A sharp pain burned once again in his knuckles as he looked up, desperately, at the man who stood over him, threateningly holding the long blade out at him.

Anthony was so focussed on Tino that he didn't notice a black crystalline structure with an orange-brown core running through it slowly flaring up out of the ground next to him.

Tino was now clinging with the very tips of his fingers as he dangled out from the ledge over the huge drop. The burn in his finger joints was now unbearable. The sharp pain flooded up into the joints beneath his fingernails simultaneously. Scraping his finger tips against the razor-sharp rocks, he let go.

In one fluid motion, within the blink of an eye, the crystals exploded outwards, elongating massively and disarming Anthony while a separate long, twisted crystal hit the man in the face knocking him backwards. The long, twisted crystal reached out to Tino who grasped at it with both hands, just as he began to fall.

It was still difficult to get a good grip on it due to the blood on his hands but the twisted structure of the crystal object helped with that. As he looked up, there appeared to be nobody holding onto the other end. The twisted, crystal staff was just floating there. Then, in a whirlwind of rusty dust, that almost looked like sand, a man dressed in a hooded, black robe materialised from the feet upwards holding the other end.

Gala-Thius placed the flat palm of his hand on his outstretched staff, just as he had outside Parathax's chamber and, slowly, individual black crystals grew outwards from behind the waterfall, creating a staircase, back up to the ledge.

Tino clambered onto the first outstretched crystal and paused for a moment to catch his breath. His hair had darkened from the splash of the waterfall and his hands and face were bloodied. Anthony ran back over to the ledge as Tino climbed his way back up but Gala-Thius blocked Anthony with his outstretched staff, now extending his other hand to help a breathless Tino back up onto the ledge.

Quickly retrieving his Beconium-coated knife from the floor, Tino looked at the cloaked, hooded figure, warily. The intimidating, aggressive man behind him looked uneasy, agitated even. The hooded figure pushed against the man with the outstretched staff with a small amount of force and he settled down, turning away and sitting on a nearby rock.

'Are you alright?' asked a deep, calming voice from beneath the hood. Tino stared for a moment before nodding in response.

'It's been many years since I last saw an Operative with the Interstellar Scouts' the voice announced, acknowledging the emerald, armoured suit as a pair of hands emerged from the sleeves of the black robe and pulled back the hood to reveal the old man's face. Tino frowned slightly. Despite the visual and audio transmissions of the bionics, who had now returned to The Knightfall, Tino was now getting a very contrasting impression of Gala-Thius and Anthony.

Anthony retrieved his weapon, which he found on the floor several feet away from the rock on which he sat. The ring of the blade scraping against the stone floor caught Gala-Thius' attention. Without turning or so much as batting an eyelid, the old man tapped the staff on the floor and, some thirty feet away, a black crystal shot up out of the ground, disarming Anthony once more in the blink of an eye and thrusting the blade into the ceiling, embedding it in the rock, high above him.

'AWW!' echoed Anthony's deep voice from across the cave, like a disappointed child.

The old man smiled down at Tino as he heard Anthony repeatedly jumping up into the air behind him, trying to reach the weapon which was clearly way out of his reach.

'He doesn't understand' the old man explained, simply. He then gestured at a nearby rock, inviting Tino to sit.

Tino, with slight hesitation at first, walked over and sat down on the rock as the old man used his outstretched staff, pointing it into the ground, to create a chair out of the crystals that grew from the cave floor next to the boy.

'Valentino Pasyo, My name is Gala-Thius' he said as he casually took his seat. Tino cast his eyes down, unsure how to respond. He couldn't recall his name, only the name Xzjytheous and now this man claimed it was.

'Are your wounds painful?' asked Gala-Thius who could see the impalements of the Deathstalker's bladed prongs in Tino's body despite the emerald suit of armour concealing them.

'How do you know about that?' asked Tino, keeping both of them in his field of vision and discretely tightening his grip on the Beconium-coated knife in his hand, still unsure of whether they could be trusted after what he had heard and seen through the bionics' transmissions.

'You are one of a very few fortunate survivors of an apocalyptic battle between The Deathstalkers Squadron and the rest of the galaxy' replied Gala-Thius. Tino remembered Xzjytheous also mentioning the Deathstalker Squadron back when they first met on The Knightfall.

'The Deathstalkers are a sentient group of five aerial war machines created and used by a being known as Parathax who keeps us trapped here in servitude to its dark bidding. It was Parathax's sentience that launched the Deathstalker Squadron from this mountain and was the guiding hand that rained their destruction across so many worlds, causing mass genocide. Through the Deathstalkers, we saw everything' Gala-Thius continued.

'What do you mean; everything and what does any of it have to do with me?' asked Tino.

'After you were impaled by a Deathstalker's bladed blaster canon, giving your life on Earth to protect your Patrol from their invasion force, a lethal black toxin entered your body through those wounds and you lost all recollection of your life as a Patrol Leader with the Interstellar Scouts. I fear that you may have gained something else in its place' Gala-Thius explained, leaning forwards, towards Tino. There was no easy way to tell Tino these things and he could see, quite clearly, how wary and untrusting Tino was. Gala-Thius couldn't afford to sugar-coat it as he needed Tino to trust him.

'Gained what?' asked Tino, terrified by these revelations.

Gala-Thius paused and then, rising to his feet, he turned his back on Tino. 'You have joined the Astral Alias' he replied with a heavy sigh.

Tino's face grew pale. He didn't know what this meant but the solemn tone that Gala-Thius spoke in and his body language suggested that it was something tragic.

'The Astral Alias?' asked Tino. Gala-Thius turned back to the boy and sat back down.

'Millennia ago, long, long before the Interstellar Scouts, there was another intergalactic defence organisation created by those who foresaw the events that would lead up to the coming conflict. This future catastrophe was referred to as The Apocalyptic Genesis. Among the Founders of this organisation were beings that had the capability to regress to a younger stage when they reached the end of their lives and Anthony and I were among them. Also among them were a brilliant scientist by the name of Sol, a Reptilian by the name of Xzjytheous and a peculiar young woman by the name of Parathax.

While Xzjytheous was aiding in peacefully resolving galactic conflicts, Anthony and I studied the mystical conjurations of the universe and Sol advanced our technological capabilities, creating, alongside many other brilliant scientists, a fleet of ships that would patrol the star systems and serve the intergalactic community. However, Parathax, unbeknownst to the rest of us, was also studying the mystical conjurations of the universe and performing cruel experiments on small creatures that she captured on various worlds in an attempt to learn new powers to overthrow us, take the fleet for herself and rule the galaxy in her own dominion. When the rest of us learned what had happened, a fierce battle broke out in an attempt to stop what we viewed as the start of The Apocalyptic Genesis.

Parathax murdered everyone except us, the founding members. Xzjytheous fled to the planet of Biolum. Sol held Parathax back while Anthony and I took a cruiser that was still under construction but functional and we went into hiding to form a retaliatory strike force in secret. We named the ship The Solar Flare in honour of Sol, the scientist who had built it and allowed us to use it to evacuate.

We landed the cruiser on a world of old, retiring shipyards to finish The Solar Flare's construction but, during that time, a meteorite containing a radioactive substance known as Beconium, struck the planet and reduced it to a rusty desert world in a matter of hours.

Eventually, we were rescued by Sol who had a plan to rebuild the organisation from scratch himself, codenamed The Inter-Solar Scouts. It wasn't long before Parathax began tearing her way across the galaxy in her new dark, ghostly form as an Astral Alias, caused by a series of critical overloads in her lab during her battle with Sol but now she was also guarded by the abominations she had created from her experiments, Polarian Beconi' which contained the tormented souls of her victims, including our friends who fell in the battle. Since we had fled, she had stripped down the cruisers we had been using to aid the galactic community and formed them into one enormous war machine, The Stealthy Intoxicator.

Many years later, she used her dark conjuring capabilities to create more machines of war and conquest which were just extensions of her in alternative forms including The Deathstalker Squadron that, just days ago, you sacrificed yourself to' explained Gala-Thius.

Tino was overwhelmed.

'The house...If I sacrificed myself to the Deathstalker Squadron, how did I wake up in that house?' he asked as he tried to piece everything together.

'I'm given to understand that you fell through the roof of the house when you slid off the bladed prongs of the Deathstalker's blaster canon once it had transferred the black substance into your body but just as you remember nothing about the Interstellar Scouts, they also remember nothing about you. That is why you were left there at the end of the battle but you are now in the one place that the I.S.S. would have tried to protect you from' A howling wind blew through the archway, hitting them hard in the face. 'It knows you are here...and they are coming for you' he continued.

'What knows I'm here? Who's coming?' asked Tino, alarmed as he jumped to his feet. If the Interstellar Scouts had forgotten that he existed, Tino thought, then it must be...

'PARATHAX!' Gala-Thius replied, his eyes wide, staring hard at the boy.

Back inside the chamber, Parathax had grown impatient and was beginning to suspect that something had gone wrong. The prisoner should have been there by now. Scratching her sharpened nail along the white lines within her black crystal throne, she contemplated both the competence and allegiance that Gala-Thius and Anthony had pledged to her.

'SEND OUT THE POLARIAN BECONI'!' Parathax commanded, angrily, her face contorted as she rose to her feet, quickly striding forwards to the top of the steps that led to her throne. From high above, three of her lethal sentient guards glided down from the cavities carved out in the walls, emerging from the shadows and hovering menacingly before her.

The Polarian Beconi' were constructed of two rotating dishes salvaged from the Polarious Sector. They contained a miniature Beconium storm, trapped between them, held in place by the energy field generated by the metal of Polarious 5. The two dishes rotated in opposite directions maintaining the containment field at the correct balance to also contain their fallen victims within the storms.

'Hunt the old man, his pet, the boy and the Reptilian. Bring them all here and the I.S.S. will come to us, bringing aid to their fallen' she commanded. Silently and ghostlike, the Polarian Beconi' drifted out of the room, effortlessly obliterating the crystal barrier that Gala-Thius had conjured and absorbing the Beconium from the crystals upon leaving the chamber. Parathax had anticipated treachery long before Gala-Thius had even been summoned. She smiled, cunningly, as she watched the Polarian Beconi' begin their hunt.

'Sentiment' she laughed wickedly to herself in distasteful contemplation of her enemy's morals, slowly shaking her head.

Back at the waterfall, the clock was now ticking. 'Polarian Beconi' are lethal hybrid abominations' Gala-Thius explained, standing up and approaching the edge of the waterfall, closely followed by Tino who was determined to get answers from the old man.

'You've told me that but what should I do?' asked Tino, nervously, hoping that he had finally gained an ally and he wouldn't have to figure everything out for himself. He occasionally looked over his shoulder and out, over the ledge, for those that hunted him.

'Parathax does not determine between the living, the dead and the inanimate' Gala-Thius continued, shaking his head urgently, looking down at Tino, directly in the eye.

'You are a resource. As much so as the scrap metal of Polarious Five that now lingers in those shadows and the toxic sentience of Parathax's victims that hunts you within them.' Gala-Thius didn't hold back in his explanations. The boy needed to understand the imminent danger he was in if he was going to survive it.

'I can help you escape this cave but we can't come with you now. It's too late. Once you are out there, you're going to be on your own. Stick to the land as much as possible. The waters here are treacherous and filled with giant, fierce monsters of the deep. You must take shelter as far away from here as you can get, for the entirety of the daytime. Only venture on at night, until you reunite with the Interstellar Scouts and, when you do, alert them to The Apocalyptic Genesis' instructed Gala-Thius.

Tino opened his mouth to argue, hoping to persuade the two of them to come with him but Gala-Thius cut him off.

'Anthony and I have betrayed Parathax in assisting you. If we come with you, we will be endangering both yourself and the I.S.S. when they get here. Your suit has sent out a distress signal so they shouldn't be long but execution is all that awaits us now. Should you be located in time by the I.S.S, have them initiate an extraction for Anthony and myself, we'll hold out as long as possible' he said, the realisation of the true weight of his actions now dawning on him.

'Come' said Gala-Thius after a moment, returning to the very urgent matter at hand as he led Tino to the edge of the waterfall and assisted him down onto the first step of the black horizontal crystals that had previously led Tino to safety. Tino looked up helplessly at the man, the splash of the waterfall hitting his face as he squinted. Gala-Thius handed him the emerald I.S.S. helmet and the gloves Tino had been wearing. He looked back at the boy, reassuringly in response, hiding his loss of hope behind a gentle smile, although his eyes betrayed him as he rested his full weight on his staff with both hands, watching the fleeing boy descend.

Once Tino reached the bottom step, placed his helmet over his head and pulled his gloves over his still-bleeding hands, Gala-Thius pressed the jagged crystal flare at the end of his staff into the ground once more and, just as they had done previously, giant, black crystals began to emerge from the wall behind the waterfall and out along the long, deep trench as they began to create a path to safety above the swelling currents and crashing waves below. As more crystals created a path ahead of him, Gala-Thius made it so the old ones broke away, preventing Tino from being followed.

Tino climbed up onto the first crystal, using all of the strength he could muster, his boots scrambling against the wet side of it as he pulled himself up. He then paused for a moment as he waited for the next one to grow out further as it was just slightly out of reach.

'THEY'RE HERE, HURRY!' Gala-Thius called out to Tino as two of the Polarian Beconi' entered through the archway. The sentient Beconium storms swirled and raged around between the hovering dishes. The tormented screams of those they had claimed previously could be heard as they approached. Gala-Thius could make out the contorted, pained faces of the victims amongst the swirling clouds of smog and Beconium sediments, crying out, trapped in eternal anguish. He identified many of them as those who faced Parathax when her evil intentions were first discovered.

The third of the Polarian Beconi' now entered the cave. Gala-Thius quickly returned to creating Tino's escape route as much as he possibly could before Anthony and he were claimed by the merciless hunters which now surrounded their prey. Tino bounced at his knees a couple of times as he prepared to jump, concentrating on timing it just right so he and the crystal would meet as they approached each other. He then took a leap of faith, his arms outstretched towards the next step. He only just caught it but his fingers were slipping as his gloves were wet from traversing the wall behind the waterfall. There was still a long way to go yet to reach the end of the trench-like cave.

Suddenly the entire cave echoed with agonising cries of pain from Anthony. Gala-Thius, alarmed, turned to see his friend reeling, his long machete-like weapon embedded in his shoulder. Horrified, he watched on helplessly until Anthony fell to the cave floor, quivering. Gala-Thius slowly backed away as the Polarian Beconi' converged on him until he was pressed right up against the edge of the waterfall. He turned to look down at the enormous drop-off behind him. There was nowhere left to go without putting Tino at risk.

Taking one last look at his dear friend, lying down on the floor near the cave's archway, Gala-Thius accepted his fate and gently closed his eyes, slowly tilting his head backwards as he did. The two rotating dishes of each of the Polarian Beconi' began to rotate rapidly; separating further to thin out their containment fields and allowing the storms to breach them. The miniature Beconium storms danced and swirled through the air towards him as the tormented cries of the dead within the shroud rang through his ears.

At that moment, Gala-Thius cried out in pain, quickly followed by a loud, primal howl that echoed throughout the cave and down the trench as the old man's eyes shot open, his entire face tense. He looked down and saw five long claws protruding through his torso, visible through the orange-brown clouds of smog.

'NO!' Tino screamed in despair, through his struggle to climb the outstretched crystal.

The boy watched as the stealth field generator powered down, revealing Xzjytheous dressed in his torn black clothing and clinging to the side of the waterfall where Tino had been just minutes ago.

Xzjytheous snarled and hissed, his eyes, blazing scarlet, as he looked up at the old man who quickly went limp. The Reptilian's forked tongue shot out, wrapping around the man's neck and throwing him out of the smog clouds and down, into the crashing waves at the bottom of the trench.

Noticing Tino, the creature grinned menacingly at him, as the Beconium storms returned to containment within their energy fields, between the rotating dishes.

The Polarian Beconi' hovered in place but didn't attack. It was almost like they were studying Xzjytheous and observing his actions, his behaviours, as he climbed up onto the ledge. It was as if the entities trapped within the Beconium Storms still recognised him from all those thousands of years ago before Parathax had killed them.

Xzjytheous walked right between two of the hovering hunters, disregarding any threat they posed and approached Anthony, his eyes still ablaze with red, his colouration, darkened, and muscles enlarged, allowing the curved spikes to slowly protrude from between his scales, thrusting out through the holes torn in his long, black coat.

'Didn't see it coming this time' he taunted, hissing down at Anthony as he reached down for the weapon that he had embedded deep in the man's shoulder while invisible. Placing one clawed foot on the wounded man's chest, he grasped the weapon's handle and tore it out aggressively. Anthony watched, his vision going in and out of focus as Xzjytheous twirled the long blade around in his hand, his foot crushing down, heavier and heavier on Anthony's chest. He placed the cold metal of the blade against the wounded man's throat and paused, letting the tension escalate, letting the dying man's weakening heart race through its final beats. He then raised the weapon high into the air and slashed at the length of wire around Anthony's neck, removing the decorative claw that rested on his chest, the trophy that he had taken following their previous encounter.

Only when Anthony's chest stopped rising and falling beneath his foot, did Xzjytheous step away from him, throwing down the bladed weapon and turning to face the Polarian Beconi'. His spikes slowly retracted beneath his scales once more and his eyes returned to amber, making his black-slit pupils more prominent.

There was a moment of silence as Xzjytheous watched the Polarian Beconi' closely. In the blink of an eye, he drew his blaster from his holster and fired a single blast straight past them which struck the crystal Tino was dangling from, right between the boy's hands.

Xzjytheous charged on all-fours, leaping right over the edge of the waterfall. As his momentum carried him through the air, he grasped at a pair of grenades in each hand and launched them, with all his strength, straight at Tino. He then, quickly, grasped at the wall of the trench with his claws, watching on, in a horizontal position.

The crystal had exploded on impact from the blaster bolt and, as the boy plummeted towards the crashing waves of the water below, the grenades detonated, deploying four electrodes from each one which scattered and secured themselves to the wall of the trench in a bid to re-capture Tino.

The last of the grenade contents landed right alongside Tino as he fell but he was just inches outside the containment field so, rather than pinning him up against the wall, the electric-blue energy lashed out at him, leaving a scorch mark on his cy-bionic suit as he was cast away, hurtling away, down the long trench.

Xzjytheous was mortified. He had failed to bring the boy to Parathax and had even aided in his escape.

The Polarian Beconi' viewed Xzjytheous' behaviour as a threat. The dishes span rapidly in opposite directions, just as they had done while attacking Gala-Thius and they hurtled through the air, all around Xzjytheous as the Beconium storms remained in place at the top of the waterfall, blocking his retreat back to the ledge.

The spinning dishes glowed with scarlet lasers at the edges as they surrounded him, smashing into the wall of the trench around him, as a sign of aggression. The Reptilian returned his blaster to its holster and the clouds of Beconium began to slowly part, allowing him to be escorted, under armed guard by the dishes, back onto the ledge. The fog then drifted towards him, forcing him to walk very slowly and carefully through the archway as the dishes continued to encircle him, escorting their objective to Parathax, minus Gala-Thius, Anthony and Tino.

In the stillness of the cave, through the echoing of the crashing waves far below, the thin wisp of a twisting Beconium vortex rose up from the destroyed crystals that Gala-Thius had created and slipped between Anthony's dried, cracked lips.

Moments later, Anthony's eyes shot wide open, bloodshot and alert.

CHAPTER 12
RETURN TO THE RHINONOID

There was silence but for the sound of jet propulsion unit thrusters powering down. Nobody spoke a word as the members of Biker Delta Squadron 5-6-5, minus their Patrol Leader, stepped over the cracks and ruptures in the crystalline ground, caused by the seismic boom of the Deathstalkers' atmospheric breach.

The group walked back up the deployment bay ramp, past the vehicles they had ridden to the trench which had automatically homed in on the Rhinonoid and returned to their docks. The sound of helmets decompressing and detaching their separate pieces from one another as the Operatives removed them from their armoured suits could be heard as they entered through the doorway and moved down the passageway towards the cold, sub-zero temperatures of the refuelling station.

Colin opened up his armoured suit and stepped out of it, dressed in his black flight suit. He left his cy-bionic armour standing in the middle of the room, with the bright blue tracking dots aimlessly darting about the grey lines inside it, as he split off from the rest of the group, striding over to the elevation platform that led to the Rhinonoid's rooftop turret where he and Ethan had been cleaning the armour and weapons earlier.

Ethan went to follow him but Isaac placed his hand on his shoulder, holding him back. Colin needed time alone to grieve for his adoptive brother as the platform began to rise up, his back still turned to the rest of them, hiding his face. They all needed to take some time to grieve and mourn the loss of their friend for that matter but there was important work that needed to be done and they needed to continue on while Colin took the time that he needed more than anyone else.

The silence continued as they moved into the control centre and cockpit of the Rhinonoid, still teary-eyed. Some silently felt bad for Colin after Corey's lack of sensitivity to the situation. Others, although they didn't want to consider the future in that moment, even questioned whether Corey was a suitable leader for them now that Oli wasn't there anymore and Isaac was struggling to fill the role.

The fact of the matter was that Corey could act on making the hard call when it mattered whereas the rest of them couldn't. They would hesitate. While questionable, this made Corey the most suitable candidate for leadership at the moment as they were way out of their depth now. Still, nobody said anything. Not a word. They simply obtained new weapons to replace the ones that had been abandoned during the attack on the Black-Burn pilots and collapsed into the seats at their workstations.

At the top of the shaft, everything was just how Colin and Ethan had left it, back when there was hope of him getting his brother back. Although they weren't actually related, Colin disregarded it. From the moment they first met, Oli had been an older brother to him in every way he possibly could be. Colin's eyes welled up once more as he sat up against the black leather chair and picked up the wrist-guard he had been cleaning before they left.

A single tear silently rolled gently down his cheek as he stared at his reflection in the metal, reminiscing about everything the two of them had been through together since that first night on Earth in the courtyard. At the turn of the millennium when explosions had erupted all around him, those terrifying creatures had killed his parents along with everyone else and that firework that had been knocked over and pointed straight at him. He thought in that moment he was going to die as a blazing fireball had exploded towards him. He had tried to jump out of the way but jumping had put him in the line of fire of one of the creatures' blaster bolts which had just been fired. In that moment a powerful force had collided with him, tackling him at the waist and driving him down into the ground as it took the full force of the blast in his place.

His helmet had split into multiple separate sections and retracted into his shiny emerald suit of armour to reveal a blonde-haired boy with bright blue eyes leaning down over him. Oli had told him to stay down on the floor until extraction arrived while he continued to fire his blaster at the invaders. He had then taken it upon himself to get Colin to safety onboard the Rhinonoid before mounting the rooftop turret to fire on the attackers as the entire tank had slowly risen up, high into the night sky and returned to the shuttle in a nearby field where Colin's Earth Scout Group was putting on their own fireworks display. With no time to say goodbye, Colin left the planet. He hadn't returned to Earth since that night – He'd had no reason to.

He exhaled a heavy sigh as he heard the opening and closing of the ceiling panels equalising the interior pressure as the staircases retracted and locked into place within the walls of the refuelling station below. Moments later, the Rhinonoid's engines started up. Although it was risky, it appeared the rest of the group had made the decision to use the Rhinonoid's thrusters embedded in its feet to fly them back to the shuttle due to how little time they had left.

Watching out of the window as the Rhinonoid lifted up into the air, just as it had done that fateful night he had first come into contact with the Interstellar Scouts, Colin tapped on a black sensor that was a part of his flightsuit, activating its Assimilation Matrix. Interacting with the projected hologram, he selected a bottle green sweatshirt and navy blue trousers; emulating the uniform of a Cub Scout from Earth. Right now he wished that was what he still was. No space battles and weapons and visiting hostile planets, just a simple Scouting lifestyle of exploration where nobody suffered. Perhaps that would have remained his childhood instead if he had never met Oli and joined the I.S.S.

There was a deep roar of the thrusters which shook the Rhinonoid slightly as it rose higher up into the air, more powerfully now, and turned away from the direction they had travelled in. The slightly reddened eyes and tear streaks on Colin's face shone brightly, glistening in the light of the sun as it swept over him through the window. He turned the turret back to face the direction where Oli had been left, although he was much too far away to see, Colin just watched, helpless and alone, as the tank carried him away.

Down in the Rhinonoid's control centre, Isaac, Corey and Nathan were silently keeping their distance from one another. Each of them had thought that they were finally safe when the Troop Leader Recon Patrol was moving in to extract them and they had successfully saved Oli as well. Now things were a whole lot worse. Oli was lost, the extraction had failed and now the Deathstalker Squadron, that so many had given their lives to secure, was once again raining destruction across the galaxy.

'We'll be arriving at the shuttle in about two minutes' announced Nathan, not even turning to look back at the others, his eyes remaining fixed on the expanse in front of him as he used his fingers to hold his head up, pushing just above his eyebrow and resting his elbow on his seat's arm-rest. Ethan looked around the room from one Operative to the next, unsure of what to say or do. Isaac turned to him and nodded.

He could tell that Ethan had formed something of a friendship with Colin and that he wanted to be there for him. Although Colin needed time to grieve, perhaps having someone there to sit with him quietly would be a bit of a comfort to him. Also, there were words that needed to be exchanged in the control centre and it was for the best that Ethan wasn't involved.

Ethan stepped out of his armoured suit, wearing the same standard issue black flightsuit that Colin had been wearing and returned to the refuelling station, leaving Isaac, Nathan and Corey alone.

Isaac watched Corey out of the corner of his eye. It was the loud, aggressive switch flicks that drew his attention. Nathan swivelled around in the pilot's seat, also noticing how loud Corey was being with the controls. He looked from Corey to Isaac who met his glance and then back to Corey again.

Letting out a loud, heavy sigh and feeling the two of them watching him despite having his back to them both, Corey pulled off the headset that he was wearing and tossed it onto the console.

'There was nothing I could do! I tried!' he shouted as he stood up, feeling like the rest of the group blamed him for what had happened to Oli.

'Of course you did' replied Isaac, trying really hard to bite his tongue. 'You also forced me to drag a crying kid away from his brother who, for all we know, might still be alive out there!' he continued stepping towards Corey and gesturing with his hand.

'His 'adoptive' brother and I had no choice!' Corey exclaimed defensively. He knew there was a possibility they could have gone back for Oli but it was a massive risk. A risk he hadn't been prepared to take, especially after the near miss of the Deathstalker's blaster bolt. Instead he chose to hide behind the urgency of the situation and the pressure they were under to get back. Both Operatives were disgusted by Corey's use of the technicality, insinuating that Oli was JUST Colin's adoptive brother and not his real brother.

'We should have brought him back with us. We would have still had time to get off-world' said Nathan, slightly calmer than Isaac.

'There was a chance we wouldn't have made it back at all under the extra weight with the Deathstalkers chasing us! I did what I thought was best in that moment! For all of us! You can't blame me for that!' argued Corey, trying hard to emphasise his point and justify his reasoning.

'Apart from anything else, you don't get a say in this. You're not a Patrol Leader or an Assistant Patrol Leader are you? Isaac saved the shuttle and made it back before you got that chance' he continued as he turned to attack Nathan, hoping to push him out of the argument but Nathan didn't care that Isaac's survival on the shuttle meant not getting the role Isaac originally transferred to him.

'He's more a leader than you're proving yourself to be' argued Isaac.

'Is that why you chose him over me?' asked Corey without skipping a beat. He'd been waiting, filled with jealousy, to get the question out in the open ever since Isaac asked Nathan to take his place while he was trapped in the shuttle's cockpit during the Viper Fighter attack.

'What?' asked Isaac, so astounded that he was almost laughing in disbelief.

'Did you offer the rank promotion to Nathan instead of me because he's a better leader than I am?' Corey repeated.

'It wasn't a promotion. It was a life or death situation and Isaac had a responsibility to keep us all safe if he didn't make it back to the Rhinonoid' explained Nathan.

'Right. So I'm the more likely one to put everyone in danger then?' concluded Corey.

'Corey, give it a rest. You're just being dramatic now' insisted Isaac. Corey turned back to Isaac to argue with him.

'Yes you are. Your love of drama rivals Timothy's, rest his soul' Isaac continued, cutting him off.

'I'm an Operative in this Patrol just like the rest of you; Timothy was just a Viper pilot' replied Corey.

'A Viper pilot who has saved your life more than once, show some respect' Isaac shot at him. 'When you're a Patrol Leader or Assistant Patrol Leader, you don't just go blundering in and do everything that you think is right without thinking it all the way through. You should have learned that lesson on Becon because, honestly, you were extremely lucky to have survived that radiation storm without being affected and I don't think you appreciate just how lucky you were. Oli wasn't so fortunate and that's part of the job when you're a Patrol Leader or Assistant Patrol Leader! Leading the group, taking control of the situation and taking responsibility for the consequences of your decisions! If you'd like I can pull up the mission debrief archives right now and list the consequences of all your decisions' shouted Isaac as he went to activate one of his badges to pull up the previous mission records but Corey smacked Isaac's hand away from the badge before he could activate it, glaring at him fiercely. Nathan was waiting to see if he needed to stop the two of them from fighting but Isaac, by nature, wasn't a confrontational person and would know to de-escalate the situation before it got to that point.

There was a long pause. Corey didn't know whether he was going to escalate the situation further. He knew that Isaac was right but he didn't want to give him or Nathan the satisfaction of hearing him admit it. It was how Oli had lived his whole life with the I.S.S, leading by example, even before he became the group's Patrol Leader.

‘You wanted this position, well these are the consequences of your decisions’ Isaac eventually said quietly as he turned and walked out of the room.

Corey turned to look at Nathan but he had already returned to piloting the Rhinonoid. He wasn’t prepared to continue the discussion with Corey who was coming across as being in denial. It worried Nathan that their lives were now, apparently, in Corey’s hands. He could only hope that, when Isaac calmed down, he would take control of the situation again.

Back on the turret deck, as Colin heard the elevation platform rising up through the shaft, he turned his head away and closed his eyes. He didn’t want to talk to anyone or for anyone to see him like this; he just wanted to be left alone. He felt something land in his lap. He opened his eyes and slowly turned his head to see what it was. It was a packet of freeze-dried food. Looking over his shoulder to see who was standing there, it was Ethan who was now holding out a bottle of water to him. Colin could feel his eyes starting to well up again, now with gratitude at the kind gesture. He couldn’t control his emotions at all right now.

Sniffing as he tried to compose himself, he smiled at Ethan and took the bottle from him. Ethan also put a packet of decontamination wipes down on the floor as well, remembering what Colin had told him earlier about the skin being able to absorb some of the chemical properties of Beconium, which currently surrounded them from earlier in the day.

‘You told me earlier that sometimes missions change based on circumstance’ said Ethan, pushing aside the items that he had been cleaning earlier. Colin nodded as he pulled a decontamination wipe from the packet.

‘Yeah. I also said they sometimes change based on agenda’ he whispered, wiping at his fingers. Colin understandably seemed somewhat distant, but not so much that he couldn’t make his accusation about Corey.

‘I never really got to know Oli properly’ said Ethan after a brief pause as he too pulled a wipe from the packet.

'What was he like? As a brother I mean?' he asked, smiling as Colin forced himself to eat something despite his lack of appetite. Colin smiled back, shaking his head as he went back to remembering his brother but couldn't bring himself to talk about him, it hurt too much.

'We were adoptive brothers' were the only words he could get out.

'The Kestrel's landing zone has sustained heavy damage from the Deathstalkers' seismic boom. Standby for Rhinonoid docking and prepare for a quick launch. We have no time to lose in getting the shuttle off the ground' Nathan's voice came through on a speaker in the wall as Colin took a drink from the bottle of water. This meant that they all needed to make their way back to the control centre and cockpit.

Colin and Ethan looked out of the window and were faced with a sheer drop-off where their landing zone had been. Clearly the shuttle was still there, just invisible under its stealth field. Nathan would be able to see it on the cockpit displays but Ethan, despite his lack of experience compared to the rest of the Patrol, had a feeling that landing the Rhinonoid with all of its weight on such fragile ground and boarding it onto the shuttle would be extremely risky.

Ethan activated the elevation platform, calling it up to them.

'We're not leaving' Colin muttered.

'What?' asked Ethan, not catching what Colin had said over the noise of the rising elevation platform.

'We're not leaving' Colin repeated, louder this time.

He stood up and threw himself into the torn leather seat and grasped tightly at the blaster canon controls, disengaging the handbrake that stopped the canon from pivoting loosely and stamped his foot down, hard onto the pedal to disengage the remaining turret locks and help guide the huge blaster. Normally, with the handbrake and pedal taken into consideration, Colin would still struggle to guide the huge blaster canon but, with the rage and determination he was feeling in this moment, there was nothing that could hold him back. Ethan watched on, nervously, unsure of what to do. Colin kept the pedal pressed as he directed the barrel of the blaster canon down towards the landing zone.

Although the shuttle's stealth field generator was still active and Colin couldn't see it, he began frantically firing blaster bolt after powerful blaster bolt down at the ground to try and disable the ship, covering the ground around the shuttle's landing zone in huge craters.

'WE'RE NOT LEAVING! I'M NOT LEAVING HIM!' Colin screamed, his face red and tears streaming down his cheeks as he gritted his teeth, resisting Ethan's attempts to drag him out of the seat.

'You did this' accused Isaac, having rushed into the control centre behind the cockpit as he shot a furious look over at Corey.

'I'll stop him' insisted Corey as he began striding his way across the control centre towards the doors.

'You've done enough damage' Isaac interjected, stepping in front of Corey and grabbing him by the shoulder of his armoured suit, cutting him off.

'HE'S GOING TO EITHER DESTROY THE SHUTTLE, THE LANDING ZONE OR GIVE AWAY OUR POSITION!' Corey shouted, the rage evident in his voice. He couldn't do right for doing wrong. Meanwhile, more and more chunks were being blasted away from the drop-off and falling into the darkness below.

'I'll sort it out, just get to your station' Isaac ordered, doing his best to regain his composure. He needed to remain calm and level-headed right now.

Infuriated, Corey shot Isaac a fierce look of confrontation and, for a moment at least, both Isaac and Nathan thought Corey was going to punch Isaac after all.

'I could have stopped him by now. Now who's the one putting us all in danger? Again' insisted Corey, looking Isaac straight in the eye.

After a moment had passed, he aggressively shrugged Isaac's hand off his shoulder and walked over to the wall mounted console he had been operating earlier, throwing himself down into the chair.

Isaac used the badge on his arm once again to initiate an Assistant Patrol Leader Override, just as he had done while trapped on the shuttle, disabling the tank's rooftop blaster canon. In this moment, he felt like this made him no different to Corey, just like when he dragged Colin back to the Rhinonoid after losing Oli but Colin wasn't thinking straight and was endangering them all. Isaac knew that Corey would be viewing him as a hypocrite and he may have had a point but Oli would have wanted Isaac to take control of the situation.

Colin, having ceased hammering at the disabled controls on the turret deck, bruising his arms in frustration, silently rose up from the seat, hanging his head as Ethan silently watched his broken friend. Colin knew he wouldn't even be able to look at Corey in the cockpit right now which meant that he would probably end up coming across a bit cold towards everyone for the time being, as was evidenced, he realised, by the way he was treating Ethan right now.

'I'm sorry' said Colin, looking at Ethan from the corner of his teary eyes.

He did genuinely appreciate Ethan making the effort for him, even if it wasn't what he was dwelling on at the moment. Colin activated the platform which rose up once again to meet them as Ethan stepped aside, smiling at Colin with caution but soft understanding.

Once at the bottom of the shaft and Colin had retrieved his armoured suit, the two Operatives walked through the doors, into the control centre and cockpit. As they entered the room, Isaac moved past them swiftly from behind and walked over to join Nathan, not even acknowledging Corey in passing.

Corey silently deactivated the relevant controls, his back turned to everyone else. It was very clear to both Colin and Ethan that there was a lot more tension in the room than there was when they first arrived back at the tank. Deciding that it was best not to say anything, Ethan made his way to the near left hand corner of the long room and climbed back into his armoured suit.

'Alright, we're setting down. Get ready to move and fast' said Nathan as Colin and Ethan joined him and Isaac at the front of the room.

The thrusters in the bottoms of the Rhinonoid's feet began to slowly decrease in power, setting them down gently amongst the craters caused by Colin's outburst. Once the tank's hull settled above its legs, Nathan began walking it onto the shuttle's deployment bay platform. Corey still didn't join the rest of the group at the front, deciding that if they weren't talking to him right now, he would just keep his distance.

'Ok, we're docked' Nathan announced as he began powering down all of the Rhinonoid's systems. 'We have minutes until sunset, let's get moving' he continued as he flipped a switch to deploy the staircases in the sides of the Rhinonoid. The Operatives began making their way out of the room and down the short staircase onto the shuttle's deployment bay platform.

Nathan thought he was the last of the Patrol to leave but, standing up from his seat, he saw that Corey was still sat at his console.

'Corey, come on, we need to get on board' Nathan instructed urgently.

'Yeah, I'll be along in a moment' replied Corey as if talking to a bossy parent, resting his chin on his hand, his elbow leaning on the edge of the console in front of him.

Suddenly the Rhinonoid and the shuttle jolted as one. The ground was starting to give way beneath the forward leg of the shuttle's landing gear. In a matter of seconds, the shuttle, the Rhinonoid and the group could be plummeting down to the bottom of the deep, dark chasm.

'There's no time, we have to go. NOW!' Nathan insisted.

Corey turned to him, paused for a moment, staring at him and then nodded. As he began to stand up, Nathan rushed out of the room to join the others. Corey slowly followed with minimal urgency.

On his way to the staircase that led out to the shuttle's deployment bay platform, he stopped for a moment next to it and then continued across the room, also passing a second staircase that led down onto the platform. He came to a stop outside the open doorway to the medical bay and gazed into it from just outside, without entering.

The furious voices of the rest of the group shouting at him to get outside barely even penetrated his ears. He hadn't slept for days and the room projected a haunting feeling of eeriness, almost like Oli was still in there staring right back at him. He stood for a moment, just staring at the platform where Oli had been and the vast array of life-support equipment that surrounded it.

Inhaling deeply through his nose, he flicked a switch on the wall panel, closing the door to the room, without even looking at the controls. He then peeled his hand away from the wall and descended the nearby staircase, down to the deployment bay platform.

Another jolt shook the shuttle as it continued to lose stability and leaned further forwards. Corey stumbled and rolled across the deployment bay platform towards the edge.

Colin tried to grab Corey as he tumbled by but he was moving too quickly as the deployment bay platform was now gradually tilting downwards as the hydraulics began to retract, raising the platform into the ship's underbelly. Simultaneously, the Rhinonoid began to descend on its legs to fit into the shuttle's deployment bay as powerful jets of white smoke surged out, diagonally, at the platform, the loud hissing sound making everything else around them inaudible.

'NATHAN! GRAB HIM!' Isaac shouted across the platform over Corey's yelling.

Nathan only just heard Isaac but couldn't make out what he had said over the noise. He suddenly eyed Corey moving towards him faster and faster as he tumbled out from amongst one of the dense, white smoke jets. Nathan tried to grab Corey's arm but the cy-bionic suit Corey was wearing was too smooth and slipped straight back out of Nathan's grasp.

As Corey tumbled over the edge, Isaac, without giving it a second thought, sprinted across the platform after him, hitting the illuminated, scarlet button in the middle of his collar to deploy the royal-blue and gold striped bars from his suit's chest plate as he went. Without hesitation or showing signs of slowing down, Isaac threw himself into a somersault as he jumped over the edge after him.

'ISAAC!' yelled Nathan as he reached out to the Assistant Patrol Leader but it was too late.

Corey had gained a lot of speed as he had tumbled across the platform which meant that he was now falling even faster than Isaac could pursue him. Once in an upside down position Isaac fired up his jet propulsion unit for a brief burst to shoot himself down into the blackness after Corey.

All Nathan, Colin and Ethan could do now was stare, panicking, into the darkness, hoping to see some sign that the two Operatives were ok. There was no knowing how deep the long canyon was but it was deep enough for the bottom to not be visible. With Nathan unable to stop the emergency evacuation procedures that had been implemented, the platform continued to rise up towards the bottom of the shuttle, moving them further and further away from the other two Operatives.

'I did this' Colin said to himself, horrified by the fact that he alone was responsible for the damage to the landing zone by firing the Rhinonoid's blaster canon. He didn't even stop to consider that the Deathstalkers had created the giant rupture in the ground in the first place. First he had left Oli behind and now Nathan and Corey were gone as well.

Ethan tried to comfort Colin but Colin had already spiralled into devastation and resentment for himself as he turned his back on his friend.

Looking up at Nathan, Colin was hoping that he would reassure him but Nathan appeared to be in total shock and completely lost as he remembered Isaac had said he was to be next in command if anything went wrong back onboard the shuttle. It was starting to look like that now might actually be the case.

Suddenly Nathan eyed a tiny flicker of blue light far below, in the darkness. He leaned over the edge as Colin and Ethan also spotted it. Everyone held their breath in anticipation as the light grew bigger and brighter.

'Come on. Come on, please' Nathan whispered to himself, his heavy breaths trembling.

'They're not going to make it' announced Colin as he looked at how close the rising platform was to the bottom of the shuttle.

Colin rushed to the edge, closely followed by Ethan and reached out his hand towards the approaching, flickering light.

'Back...GET BACK!' yelled Nathan as he grabbed Colin and Ethan, urgently dragging them away from the edge and throwing them towards the middle of the platform before launching himself away from the edge also.

Both Isaac and Corey squeezed their jet propulsion unit thrusters' triggers as hard as they could, releasing their grip only just as they were about to pass the platform so their momentum would carry them the rest of the way.

They landed heavily right where Nathan, Colin and Ethan had just been standing. Isaac immediately scrambled up onto his hands and knees and positioned himself between the ledge and Corey, who was frantically kicking his feet to get them clear of the edge before the platform locked into place.

'MOVE! GET TO THE COCKPIT, NOW!' shouted Isaac.

WE'RE CUTTING IT SHORT!' yelled Nathan as, wasting no time, he rushed past Corey, making his way to the ship's cockpit, closely followed by the others.

There was a lot of urgent shouting between Nathan and Isaac as they prepared the ship for takeoff.

In their rush to get off the ground, they had to neglect some of the less important steps which made the ship's departure very rough but that was the least of their worries right now.

'Keep the levels stable and account for wind resistance, we're not at the correct angle for exiting the atmosphere' instructed Nathan as he nervously worked his way through the shuttle's launch sequence.

'Stay calm Nathan, we'll make the corrections as we go' replied Isaac; focussing hard on making the adjustments that Nathan was being forced to skip.

Several squadrons of Black-Burn fighters descended beneath the clouds on the horizon as the shuttle lifted off, a huge chunk of the ground falling away into the blackness of the canyon mere moments after they were safely clear of it.

'Ok, here we go' announced Nathan as the shuttle shot up into the sky and out, beyond the atmosphere, safely undetected.

Down below, the crystalline surface of the planet burned orange and black as the crystals began to cast long, dark shadows like cold, crooked fingers stretching out across what had been a beautiful expanse of pearl mixed with a whole spectrum of shimmering colours, now poisoning all that they touched.

'We're clear of the atmosphere. Toxic photon emissions are minimal' announced Nathan.

This would normally have been a cause for celebration but everyone was exhausted and grieving. Having been really tense and breathing shallowly for the entire time they were leaving the planet, they just let out a sigh of relief as they turned away from the cockpit window to go about their jobs.

'We're still being hunted and now the Deathstalkers are searching for us as well. We should find somewhere secluded on a planet where we can set up camp and recover. I don't want to make the same mistakes Jason made when that bounty hunter was looking for him. So, where are we going now?' asked Nathan.

'I don't know' replied Isaac, turning to Corey after a moment of silence. 'Where are we going?' Isaac parroted Nathan's question in his direction, putting him on the spot. After all, it was Corey who so desperately wanted to be the heroic leader in the group. Corey looked back at him, clearly irritated. He could see what Isaac was doing.

'Who's Jason?' asked Ethan, turning to Colin.

'Jason was their Troop Leader when they all first became Initiates, before I even joined the I.S.S. They were out on a training camp on Felaloris. Turns out he was a wanted man for his work within the I.S.S. When a bounty hunter and a Reptilian turned up on the planet...' explained Colin.

'There was nothing to be done' interjected Isaac with a cold tone.

This was quickly becoming a recurring theme where things went wrong and the group took action, which ultimately paid off but always came at a price.

'Where are we going Corey?' Isaac asked again, pressing for a response.

'Wait! Wait!' shouted Ethan before Corey could respond. Everyone fell silent, staring at him with surprise. It wasn't like

Ethan to speak up like this. 'What's that noise?' he asked after a moment.

The Operatives listened closely to the high pitched beeping sound coming from the console. The sound had been audible throughout the entire launch but nobody had even noticed it amongst the chaos.

'It's a distress signal' Isaac announced, frowning as he looked down at the blinking red light on the control console, which flashed in time with the sound.

'Does it have a signature?' asked Nathan flicking a switch next to it, turning on a small screen. There was a brief pause as they watched; waiting for the details to appear on the screen.

'It's an I.S.S. Patrol Leader' replied Isaac. 'I'm going to track the signals co-ordinates' he continued as he activated a variety of switches and buttons on the console.

'It's best to ignore it' announced Corey from behind them, reflecting on his last conversation with Oli. The Operatives turned and looked at him disapprovingly. They were disgusted that an I.S.S. Operative, one that considered themselves the leader of their group, would just turn his back on a call for help without looking into the legitimacy of the transmission.

Disregarding Corey's thoughts on the matter, Isaac turned back to the screen.

'Polarious Five. No, wait...Zonju' he announced, pulling away from the screen as he straightened his back.

'It's a trap. We were attacked at Polarious Five and the entire sector is a debris field. Whatever attacked the I.S.S. fleet could have easily boarded a disabled I.S.S. ship and sent the signal from there. There would be an ambush waiting for us as soon as we arrived and probably the Deathstalker Squadron as well' insisted Corey.

'Except the signal isn't coming from Polarious Five anymore, it's coming from Zonju' argued Isaac, subtly indicating that Corey wasn't paying attention to what he'd said.

'Where's Zonju?' asked Ethan.

'It's in this system' replied Nathan. 'It's also known as the twin planet of Crystalosis although it's much larger and much closer to the sun so the crystals have been permanently poisoned by the light to the extent that they are dead unless in contact with the light of the sun' he continued.

'Isn't that the same as Crystalosis?' asked Ethan.

'As Nathan said, they're twin worlds but Crystalosis is a benign world except during sunset, Zonju is lethal any time except through the night. Crystalosis will be the same one day but it will be a long time before that happens. Zonju can work to our advantage though. Because it's much larger than Crystalosis, the nights are much longer on Zonju so we are in less danger from the environment' explained Isaac before turning to Nathan.

'What are the chances of us getting there to locate the signal and set up camp?' he asked.

'It depends on where about on the planet the signal is coming from. Like you said, due to the large size of the planet, night time lasts a lot longer which means that the crystals won't harm us with there being no sunlight to concentrate its deadly properties but, if the signal is coming from the light side of the planet, we'll need to wait it out until nightfall at those co-ordinates before we can land' Nathan replied.

'I recognise that Operative number' announced Colin as he leaned in close to the screen.

'D-C-D-S-Two-Zero-One-Four. That's Oli's suit sending the distress signal' he continued, looking up at Isaac.

Standing next to them, Ethan frowned, confused. This didn't make any sense. Although everyone else was unaware, Ethan had noticed that the distress signal beacon on Oli's suit was missing as it was just a temporary one he had been wearing. Ethan anticipated Oli potentially sending out a distress signal if, by some miracle, he survived which is why he had thrown his own distress beacon badge from his armoured suit amongst one of the discarded parachutes while everyone was distracted and trying to escape from the pursuing Deathstalkers. But why would the signal's signature be coming from a different planet and be identifying itself as Oli's rather than his?

'Except Oli's on Crystalosis' Corey pointed out, feeling the need to remind everyone of what they had just been through seeing as, as usual, they weren't taking what he was saying onboard.

'SHUT UP!' shouted Isaac, angrily turning to Corey.

He was becoming really annoyed with Corey's lack of sensitivity. Colin was standing right there. Why would he just point that out like it was nothing? The two Operatives locked eyes furiously. Normally Isaac would be uncomfortable with this level of confrontation but he was starting to discover a side to himself that felt very unfamiliar as Corey continued to push him.

After a couple of seconds had passed and Isaac felt like he had made his point, he turned back to the screen.

'Oli wasn't wearing his own suit when we evacuated the cruiser, it was being treated for Beconium Contamination and having the respiratory filters inspected after we crashed down to Becon' Colin pointed out.

'So, somewhere out there somebody is posing as an I.S.S. Operative in Oli's suit' said Isaac thoughtfully. 'It's been boosted by quite a powerful transmitter. Is there any indication of what the signal was relayed through?' he asked.

Nathan was already a step ahead of him though and, just moments later, The Knightfall appeared on the screen along with all of its statistics. 'It's The Knightfall' replied Nathan. 'The same ship that the I.S.S. impounded and then fled The Scout Hut's hanger bay during the Polarious Sector Assault.'

Behind the group, Corey rolled his eyes, shaking his head in exasperation. 'What can that be other than a trap?' he asked, throwing his hand out, gesturing at the screen. The Reptilian even stole an Operative suit during his escape. What if it was Oli's suit that he stole?'

Admittedly, Corey did have a point. It almost certainly was a trap but it might also be a surviving Operative from their fleet who only had Oli's suit to hand during the attack, perhaps a member of the maintenance team that had been working on it. Corey had made it perfectly clear that he had too much of an ego to lead and believed that the rest of the Operatives should blindly follow his instructions. He hadn't, however, told the rest of the group what he knew about The Knightfall and its pilot. Isaac disagreed with Corey's beliefs and, as it turned out, so did Nathan.

'Set a course for Zonju. Lock onto the source of the distress signal' Isaac instructed.

Nathan went to enter the co-ordinates into the shuttle's Galacta-Nav but was suddenly interrupted by Corey.

'No, hang on a minute. I thought we were keeping a low profile and finding somewhere safe to set up camp to recover. You're all idiots if you're going to go after The Knightfall alone. I don't know about the rest of you but I plan to survive until we re-group with the I.S.S. You can all fly around being the Super Boys saving the galaxy as much as you want then' Corey protested.

'Corey, we're not re-grouping with the fleet. They're gone. You watched it happen. We can't go in search of another fleet because the Deathstalkers will be tracking us now and we would be putting any other I.S.S. forces we come across in danger' replied Isaac, finding it painful to admit as he turned away. 'We might re-group with another fleet at some point if we survive long enough for the danger to pass but that distress signal is coming from this system. The enemy might already be intercepting it and I'm not prepared to just ignore it. We can't do that, we still have responsibilities, even if we're on our own' he insisted, looking back to Corey but addressing the entire group. 'Nathan, set a course for Zonju and lock onto The Knightfall' he repeated after a moment.

'Already locked in' replied Nathan. Isaac was met by the harsh glare of an annoyed Corey as he turned around.

CHAPTER 13
IMPROVISATION

Oli awoke in the night, far beneath the surface of Crystalosis, at the bottom of a deep ravine created by the Deathstalker Squadron's seismic boom when they had breached the atmosphere. Although long gone, the devastation that they had caused remained as a stark reminder of their attack.

His attention was caught by the sound of falling debris nearby as huge chunks of the crystalline ground gave way and tumbled into the ravine from above. Unable to see much more beyond the visor of his scuffed, emerald helmet, he retracted it into his collar and clambered to his feet, looking about at his surroundings. The impact from his long fall had mostly been taken by his armoured cy-bionic exoskeleton but he was still sore from hitting the ground with so much force.

The suit, with all of its power leeched from it by the Deathstalkers, was incredibly difficult to move in as the bright blue sensory tracking dots had also been disabled inside his suit meaning that its assisted mobilisation function was inactive. Sooner or later, its backup power would kick in as the inner-lining of an I.S.S. cy-bionic suit was an Operative's last line of defence against any hostile situation including adverse environmental conditions. For now though, the heavy components of the suit would only move if he had the strength to move them.

Oli knew that he needed to escape the ravine quickly and establish contact with Biker Delta Squadron 5-6-5 before they moved out of range...If they weren't already. Stumped once more by the fact that he wasn't in possession of his own armoured suit, a distress signal beacon nor any of his climbing equipment as he had left it onboard The Scout Hut during the evacuation, he looked about for a means of climbing the side of the trench with just his hands and feet. With the exception of areas where large chunks of debris had fallen away though, the sides of the ravine were relatively smooth and didn't offer much in the way of hand or footholds.

Some distance down the trench, Oli could see the badly-damaged, almost-unrecognisable wreckage of one of the I.S.S. ships that had been taken out by the Deathstalker Squadron. Pained, he tried to run down the trench to get to the wreckage in the hope that it would contain some climbing equipment and emergency supplies. There was an ominous, ghostly, lunar-like glow coming from beyond the wreckage, creating a silhouette against it.

When he finally reached the blackened, tangled metal of the ship's wreckage, Oli climbed up on top of it and finally saw what was causing the silver hue in the distance. The bottom of the deep chasm had become a riverbed for the liquidised, molten crystal that spilled over the edge from above in a viscous, waterfall-like fashion. The river of molten crystal, caused by the immensely destructive temperatures of the Deathstalker Squadron's blaster bolts, was ebbing down the channel, straight towards the shuttle. Oli knew he had mere minutes in which to do a lot of work because as soon as that slow-moving substance made contact with the wreckage, it would slowly begin to melt and its contents would be lost forever.

It crossed his mind that he could escape by using his jet propulsion unit if he found a way to restore power to his suit but he had serious reservations about using up his fuel reserves in case he needed it later.

Crouching down to the centre of the cockpit hatch where the bottom of it met the hull, the dewdrop crystal on his suit that was supposed to interface with the tri-laser code scanner on the middle of the hinge also appeared to be disabled along with everything else and, in any case, the laser emitter on the destroyed Kestrel Shuttle appeared damaged beyond repair from the crash.

With several kicks of his boot as he stood back up, Oli smashed the glass of the cockpit window, making sure that it shattered away from the pilot's face. He quickly leaned forward, twisted a textured ring on the cuff of his glove that secured it to the rest of his suit and removed it to check the gold-armoured Troop Leader for signs of life.

With the black inner-lining of his suit now finally starting to run on its backup power source, a bright, oscillating blue glow radiated from the inner cuff of Oli's suit as the tracking dots moved around in his sleeve, illuminating the pilot's face. It didn't take long at all for Oli to realise that he was long gone. Another Troop Leader that had given their life for him, the third one since the attack on the fleet. Oli's head dropped and he let out a heavy sigh as, for the first time, he started to feel like he was truly on his own.

Returning his glove to his hand and securing it to the rest of his suit with the cuff ring again, he found one of the ship's exposed power cells. Pulling out the wires from the components that it was connected to, he improvised a rapid recharge for his suit, feeding the wires into the armour's interior where his cy-bionic suit's power core was located. His suit quickly came back to life, the badges, bars and fuel reserves indicator illuminated with blindingly-bright light and mobility became much easier as well as the interior sensory tracking lights powered back up.

Wasting no time, Oli climbed inside the ship and retrieved the emergency climbing equipment from behind the Troop Leader's seat as well as any emergency rations he could find, just as a sizzling sound emanated from beneath the wreckage. Oli looked down at the ground, beneath the ship, to see it disappearing beneath the molten crystal river. He had to work faster.

Being careful not to fall off the ship, Oli clipped a karabiner onto his armoured suit, ran a cable through it and secured the other end of the cable to an eyelet on the hull of the ship. He then activated one of the badges on his suit and interacted with the hologram projected from it to access the ship's weapon systems. Because the blaster canon on the ship was a turret on a pivot, Oli had to put absolute faith in his equipment that tethered him to the ship. He gave the cable a few hard tugs to ensure that it wasn't going to detach and then walked backwards until he was in a lying-down position with his feet pressed against the side of the ship. He then interacted with the holographic projection to position the blaster canon and began firing blaster bolts in a tight, zig-zag pattern, all the way up the side of the ravine.

He then climbed back up on top of the ship and, quickly realised that, despite the training and past missions he had been a part of to become Biker Delta Squadron 5-6-5's Patrol Leader, stunts like this still got his heart racing and flooded him with adrenaline. He deactivated the badge on his suit and carefully detached the cable clip from the eyelet on the ship's hull. The molten crystal was rising beneath him and making the wreckage less stable as it began to lift off the ground.

Oli closed up his helmet and quickly picked up a harpoon gun, that he'd found amongst the climbing equipment behind the pilot's seat. He primed it and aimed at the area of the wall he had blasted. As he squeezed the trigger, the weapon recoiled. Normally this wouldn't be a problem but the wreckage was now extremely uneven beneath his feet and, as it listed in response to his sudden shift in weight. Oli fell backwards once again and quickly slammed the heel of his hand against the cable lock of the gun.

He swayed from side to side aggressively as he tried to balance himself against the wreckage but, as it continued to move beneath him, he lost his footing. Stumbling towards the molten crystal beneath the wreckage, he quickly kicked his legs out into a horizontal position, hit the illuminated scarlet button at the middle of his collar and the two royal-blue and gold striped bars sprung up from the chest of his armoured suit. He squeezed at one of the jet propulsion unit thrusters' trigger grips with his one free hand and, as soon as he was in the air and off the wreckage, he powered down the thrusters, disengaged the cable lock on the harpoon gun and squeezed the trigger to begin reeling in the cable as he swung over the molten ground.

His face grew contorted as he squeezed as hard as possible at the harpoon gun's trigger, hoping that, by the time he reached the wall, he would have wound it in enough and he wouldn't just slam into it and drop into the molten crystal. The next thing Oli knew, the bottoms of his boots kicked up, hard, against the wall and he frantically scrambled to move his feet into the nearest footholds as pieces of debris fell away beneath his feet, into the deadly substance just a few feet beneath him.

Despite how reliable he knew they were, much like the heads-up display on his visor, Oli didn't like entrusting his life in a single harpoon cable. He activated a sensor on the side of his helmet which slid open three vents, one on either side of his jaw and one in the top of his helmet to allow it to ventilate as he climbed so his visor wouldn't steam up. A blue glow radiated through the three open vents from the suit's interior tracking dots and he quickly set about climbing the wall, kicking his boots into the makeshift footholds as he continued to reel in the cable.

When he finally reached the ledge, he threw his leg over as hard as he could and wasted no time in rolling the rest of his body up and over onto the ledge behind it. Trembling from the dangerous climb, Oli took a moment to catch his breath and regain his composure before closing up his helmet and trying to reach out to Biker Delta Squadron 5-6-5.

'Calling all Interstellar Scout Patrols in the vicinity, this is I.S.S. Patrol Leader – Oliver Robertson, signature designation: D-C-D-S-Two-Zero-One-Four. Requesting extraction.' No response came, only static across all channels.

'Calling I.S.S. Biker Delta Squadron Five-Six-Five, is anyone there? Requesting extraction' he radioed through his helmet once again. He listened in silence for a few more moments but no response came back.

He looked down at the bottom of the ravine and saw the shuttle being carried far away, almost engulfed in the liquidised crystal now. He felt a tear roll down his cheek as he paid his respects to the pilot.

Slowly, Oli sat himself up and looked around at the destruction that had been caused by the Deathstalker Squadron as they had taken out the I.S.S. reinforcements and pursued Biker Delta Squadron 5-6-5. He could only hope that his Patrol managed to make it off-world in time, leading him, for the first time, to ask the question, how did he survive the toxicity of the planet's sunset? The depth of the ravine must have shielded him from the photonic radiation.

Glancing around as he locked the spring-loaded bars back into the chest of his armoured suit, Oli's visor detected movement on the horizon. He couldn't see it properly against the night sky so he activated another of his badges and selected the sonar ping option from the projected hologram. A small, rectangular device sprung out from the side of his helmet and it began firing the rhythmic pings in the direction of the detected movement. Gradually the information came back and the statistical analysis started to appear on the inside of Oli's visor.

Spectral wave lengths that indicated the royal-blue and gold colours of the object appeared on various charts alongside density readings and a diagram of what was causing the movement based on the sonar signals that bounced back to the cy-bionic exoskeleton's built-in receiver.

Combined with the chart readings that depicted the colours, the extremely low density readings and the scrambled image, Oli concluded that it was almost certainly one of Biker Delta Squadron 5-6-5's parachutes that had been carried away in the wind. It struck him as odd though that the other parachutes were nowhere to be seen, they weren't even detectable by his visor.

Believing that it was possibly caught on something, it occurred to Oli that the fabric would serve him well for building a shelter. Relieved that he hadn't used up his jet propulsion unit's fuel reserves to escape the ravine, he deployed the ballistic glass bars from his emerald, armoured suit once again, gripped the triggers and launched himself high into the air, towards the parachute in the distance.

When he finally arrived, landing on the ground with his knees bent, Oli quickly gathered up the fabric while noticing that it wasn't caught on anything as he had originally suspected. He then realised why the parachute had been carried away so slowly. A rectangular I.S.S. Distress Signal Badge fell from the bundled up fabric and clattered to the ground at his feet. Frowning as he crouched down to retrieve it, he identified it as Ethan's.

What he couldn't understand though was why he would have removed it from his suit and left it behind. Then he realised, Ethan must have seen that he wasn't currently wearing his own armoured suit and, as a result, the distress signal badge was missing from the one he was borrowing.

Oli smiled to himself as he suddenly didn't feel quite so alone. Ethan, despite being the youngest and least experienced Operative of Biker Delta Squadron 5-6-5, was extremely observant of things that a lot of other Operatives would likely miss while dealing with the more demanding tasks.

Oli inserted the badge into the empty, rectangular slot in the chest of his armoured suit and activated it, sending out a signal to the I.S.S. to come and rescue him. In the meantime, he decided to take advantage of the parachute, and the small tufts of variously coloured crystal shards that surrounded him, to build his shelter utilising the parachute cords to secure the shelter to the crystal tufts.

He then opened out his armoured suit and emerged from it. Immediately feeling the cold, Crystalosis wind through his flightsuit, he quickly detached the black, thermal lining from the inside of his suit which doubled as a sleeping bag and adapted to the varying harsh conditions that Operatives often found themselves in. He tried to swipe away at the abrasive, white dust that covered the ground where he was hoping to sleep to avoid getting it on the lining of his suit which would be really bad for his suit when he climbed back into it but no matter how hard he tried, he simply couldn't get rid of it all as the faintest breeze would carry more dust and grit beneath his shelter from outside, replenishing it.

Frowning, Oli reluctantly accepted that he would never get it perfect and at least the ground was a lot better now than it had been.

He then pulled out the food and water rations from the backpack that he had retrieved from the shuttle wreckage and settled down for his meal and a night of much needed rest, the first he'd truly had in days.

CHAPTER 14
THE EMPTY-HANDED BOUNTY HUNTER

Moving through the archway, the cave opened up into a circular chamber. Enormous black crystal pillars reached high up into the darkness. The floor glowed silver in the light of the huge moon above. Parathax chuckled to herself, the sound reverberating around the room in a deep echo as Xzjytheous stepped out of the shadows and into the light, guarded closely by the Polarian Beconi'.

'Reptilian. You have failed' she said simply and calmly. There was no longer a need for her to show any sign of rage or displeasure in his results. What was done was done. Tino, Gala-Thius and Anthony had all been lost due to Xzjytheous and her mind was already made up. Xzjytheous was now only there, kneeling before her, for her own amusement before she had him executed for his failings. There was nothing that Xzjytheous could say or do to convince her to show him mercy.

A slight smile came over Parathax's face as she feigned interest in the Reptilian's pleas for her to spare him, her eyebrows raised. There was little else she enjoyed more than making others suffer hopelessly. Gone was the fierce creature that had aggressively attacked Tino, Gala-Thius and Anthony back in the cave. All that remained now was a grovelling, cowering creature, begging desperately for its life. His words continued to fall on deaf ears as Parathax rose up from her throne and gave a wave of her hand.

The Polarian Beconi' moved in for the kill as Xzjytheous began crying out, trembling. Parathax's laughs grew louder as she watched how the hunters toyed with their prey. The clouds of smog and Beconium flooded the area of the room where the creature stood, now coughing and gasping for breath as he tried desperately to flee. The razor-sharp dishes swept through the air and came about to intercept their target. Suddenly, all six dishes of the three Polarian Beconi' clattered to the floor.

A confused frown now came over Parathax's face as the realisation dawned on her. She stopped laughing and leaned forward slightly, her eyes narrowing as she looked down into the shroud. Suddenly, Anthony came charging out of the toxic clouds, running right at her, his long bladed weapon raised above his head and screaming with rage. Driven by the Beconium that had possessed him – a phenomenon Parathax had never encountered before, he was so furious at the death of Gala-Thius that the wound in his shoulder no longer held him back. He unleashed himself at Parathax with everything he had.

Seeing an opportunity to regain Parathax's favour, Xzjytheous drew his blaster and took a single shot at Anthony's wounded shoulder.

Anthony fell to his knees half way up the steps leading up to the throne. There was a pause as, weakened and breathing heavily through the pain and exhaustion, he raised his bowed head to look up at Parathax, who now smiled down at him, wickedly.

With an outstretched hand, the Beconium was leached from Anthony's body as a powerful blast of black energy surged from the cloak of darkness that enshrouded Parathax, upper-cutting like a powerful, clenched fist beneath his chin. Anthony was thrown from the steps, high into the air, over Xzjytheous' head, before landing heavily on the ground, tumbling at speed towards the archway and into the shadows at the edge of the chamber.

CHAPTER 15
THE TRUTH COMES OUT

The I.S.S. shuttle had set down on the flat rocks at the foot of the enormous mountains that reached high into the Zonju night sky. The Operatives looked up in awe as they descended down the loading ramp onto the wet rocks. The waves crashed over them, battering the ship as they exploded around it. Isaac unravelled a long, thick, metal cable with karabiners connected to it every few feet.

'Secure yourselves' he instructed through their helmets as he clipped it onto a loop on his utility belt and passed it along to the other Operatives who did the same. Nathan activated one of the badges on his armoured suit and studied the holographic projection that was showing the same image as the one they had been following on the ship.

'The tracking signal was last registered at the top of that drop off' announced Nathan pointing down the long trench towards the waterfall at the end.

'It's going to take a while to get up there' announced Corey from the back of the line.

'We'd better start climbing then' replied Isaac, countering the Operative's negative attitude as he started to lead the group, tethered to him, towards the rocky cliff face.

'Keep your jet propulsion units inactive, the flames will ignite the cable and we'll fall to our deaths if we're not careful' Nathan pointed out, ensuring everyone heard him, as he followed behind Isaac, Ethan and Colin.

Making sure that his gloves were tightly fitted and deploying the spikes from the fronts of his boots as the others did the same, Isaac placed his hands on the razor-sharp rocks in front of him and began to climb. Ethan followed behind him, closely followed by Colin, then Nathan and finally Corey.

The ascension was slow as they had to proceed, both vertically and horizontally down the trench and every hand and foothold was tested carefully by each Operative before committing any weight to it. This was nothing new to most of the Operatives as they were required to do strength training and obstacle courses that consisted of hostile environments plus many of their previous missions, especially infiltration and rescue operations, involved climbs like this, however, Ethan was new to these sorts of missions and had only recently traded his sapphire-blue Initiate armoured suit for his emerald Operative one. Had the I.S.S. been intact, he would never be sent out on a mission like this until he was more experienced. That being said, none of them had a choice.

Ethan was growing weak as he tried desperately to grab at the rocks and, even though he tried as hard as he could to hold on and convince himself that it was mind over matter, his muscles didn't agree. His grip grew weaker until he couldn't hold on any longer. His fingers slipped off one of the rocks and, because he was only standing on a protruding rock at the time, rather than kicking his spikes into the wall, he also lost his footing and fell.

Fortunately, Ethan was directly behind Isaac so he only had to deal with the weight of one person dragging at him rather than him pulling the other Operatives away from the side of the trench as well with the sudden jolt.

As Ethan cried out, Isaac looked over his shoulder at the shouting Operatives beneath him while Colin tried desperately to help Ethan to sit back up and grab at the rocks again.

'Nathan! Get him back up!' Isaac shouted urgently, gripping as hard as he could and pressing his head against the rocks as he tried to just concentrate on supporting Ethan's weight while the others helped him up.

'I can't reach!' Ethan cried.

'You've got to!' Isaac shouted back to him. Every time Ethan tried to sit up, his lack of muscle and his fatigue caused him to fall backwards once more, jolting on the cable and Isaac's armoured suit. Although nobody could see Isaac's face for his helmet, he was struggling desperately to keep hold, gritting his teeth and squeezing his eyes tight shut.

'I need to use my jet propulsion unit!' shouted Ethan.

'No! Ethan! Your thrusters are in direct contact with the cable! If the flames hit it we'll fall!' Nathan shouted.

'Colin, grab hold of him! Corey, get up here and help!' he continued but Corey had frozen in place, choosing to, instead, conserve his energy for the rest of the climb.

'Corey! He's going to fall! Help me push him back up!' shouted Colin.

'COREY!' yelled Nathan once more. Ethan began kicking his legs frantically, unable to control his fear as he cried out.

Tears came streaming down his face behind his helmet as he dangled hundreds of feet above the rocks, crystals and crashing waves. All Isaac could do was cling to the wall of the trench as he listened to Ethan's desperate sobbing through the speaker in his helmet.

'Ethan, Ethan! Calm down' Isaac instructed through his helmet's built-in radio.

Isaac knew he couldn't hold on any longer with Ethan's continued flailing. 'Colin, help him kick his spikes into the wall and then push him up' he continued, now struggling to breathe under the stress his body was under.

It was too late. Amongst the panic and frantic attempts to get Ethan sat back up, nobody had noticed the small, silver device embedded in the rock of the wall, one of the electrodes from Xzjytheous' grenades that he had launched at Tino during his escape.

Ethan's armoured suit had moved close to it several times as he had struggled, causing tiny, blue, electrical fingers to reach out to his suit from it. The electrode was mostly burnt-out at this point but, now, Ethan's panic got the better of him. He moved too drastically and the thrusters on his jet propulsion unit were suddenly triggered by the few remaining sparks from the electrode, the flames, inadvertently, burning through the cable.

The Operatives all shouted out simultaneously as the blast also pushed them all away from the wall. Suddenly, there was a massive explosion of dust, rock and crystal shards from the wall, just above Isaac's head.

A gloved hand reached down from the cloud of dust and grabbed Isaac's wrist, pulling him up into the hole in the wall. There was no time to question what was going on. Isaac dug his heels into the ground and used all of his strength to pull Ethan inside, causing the others to slam into the side of the trench once more. Ethan powered down his jet propulsion unit and helped Isaac and Gala-Thius, now dressed in a gold armoured Interstellar Scout Troop Leader suit, to pull the rest of the Operatives up.

Once everyone was safely inside the cave, they removed their helmets and fell to the floor exhausted and entirely out of breath as they detached their karabiners. Corey was furious with Ethan. He climbed to his feet, not even caring how tired he was and strode across the cave shouting angrily at the youngest of the group. Gala-Thius came between them as the others tried to pull Corey away.

'This is why everyone avoids you, you're a danger to us all! Why were you even assigned to us anyway? What do you bring to our Patrol that is actually helpful?' Corey shouted angrily, throwing his helmet aggressively to the floor, his voice echoing around the cave. The other Operatives struggled to pull him away as he kept trying to throw himself at a terrified Ethan.

'HEY!' Isaac yelled as he grabbed Corey by the collar and threw him aside, causing him to stumble.

'HE ALMOST KILLED US!' Corey shouted angrily. Although his words were directed at the rest of the group, his eyes remained on Ethan. Nathan walked over to Corey to try to calm him down. Tensions were running high from the confrontation on board the shuttle but they also hadn't slept for days and, although some of them had managed to have a small amount to eat and drink on the flight to Zonju, it wasn't enough to give them the energy they had needed for the climb, nor the energy they needed now.

Shaken up, Isaac watched as Nathan walked Corey away.

'Are you with the Interstellar Scouts?' Isaac asked, looking up at the figure in the gold armoured suit as he continued to try and get his breath back while pushing himself to take charge and assess the situation.

'No' the figure replied.

'You're wearing an I.S.S. Troop Leader Suit' said Colin, frowning and also out of breath from everything that had just happened.

'A memento' replied the figure after a moment.

'A memento of what?' asked Nathan seriously as he approached the rest of the group from behind the mysterious man, leaving Corey at the edge of the cave to compose himself.

Isaac cast his eyes past their rescuer, directing them at Nathan whose hand now rested over his blaster in its holster. Nathan was on high alert, still on edge from piloting the shuttle and the climb. He immediately suspected that this was the potential trap they had anticipated on receiving the distress signal and was taking no chances.

'The Apocalyptic Genesis.' the man replied

'The what?' asked Colin but Isaac sharply held out his hand as a signal to Colin to stay out of it so he could take control of the situation.

'The fall of the I.S.S. followed by conquest of the entire galaxy. It's already begun' the muffled voice replied from behind the gold helmet.

In the blink of an eye that even took Colin by surprise, Nathan and Isaac both whipped out their blasters from their holsters and a ringing sound emanated from them, the weapons vibrating in their grasp as the sound quickly increased in pitch and volume, charging up.

'WHAT DO YOU KNOW ABOUT THE ATTACK ON OUR FLEET?' demanded Isaac, his voice reverberating around the cave as he fiercely trained his blaster on the man's helmet. Corey looked over at the commotion from the other side of the cave and, also reaching for his blaster, began racing over to investigate.

The man remained silent. 'On your knees. Now' ordered Nathan as, despite feeling very uneasy, he tried to keep a cool head about him. Nathan came around the side of the man and joined Isaac in front, also keeping his blaster held out at him.

'Colin, remove his helmet' instructed Isaac as he called back to the younger Operative while keeping his eyes firmly on the prisoner.

Suddenly, as Colin approached, a long, twisted crystal staff materialised in the man's grasp which he used to strike out in a powerful swing to quickly knock Colin off his feet before he could remove the helmet. Yelling to one another, the Operatives moved into a combat formation and began firing their blasters at the man but not before he was able to thrust the staff into the ground. Black crystals immediately exploded upwards in every direction, knocking each of the Operatives to the ground as the structures formed a complex network around the cave. A rusty-coloured mist began to seep out of the cracks in the crystals as they splintered from crashing into the walls and ceiling around them.

'BECONIUM!' yelled Colin.

'HELMETS! NOW!' ordered Isaac, sharply, a great deal of urgency in his voice.

'GET DOWN ON THE GROUND, AS LOW AS YOU CAN AND ACTIVATE YOUR RESPIRATOR MASKS!' Nathan yelled. The Operatives all threw themselves to the ground and lay as flat as possible to try and get beneath the rising toxic fumes as they interacted with their First Aid Badge holograms to activate their respirator masks. They then retrieved their helmets, quickly placing them over their heads.

There was a distant cry for help that Ethan could only just hear from across the cave. It was Corey. He was struggling to activate his respirator mask and had left his helmet behind, having thrown it at Ethan's feet in his rage before Nathan had walked him away.

Corey's helmet was just about within Ethan's reach. As he grabbed hold of the helmet and dragged it beneath the toxic crystals that had shot out of the floor, he threw himself down to the ground. Due to his small size, he was able to army-crawl his way across the floor of the cave, something none of the other Operatives would have been able to do. Once he was close enough, he pushed it as hard as he could; rolling the helmet across the floor, over to Corey.

Corey, now holding his breath, scooped it up along with the karabiner cable that lay on the floor next to it. He quickly secured his helmet to his armoured suit and charged towards the hole that had been made in the wall of the cave. The other Operatives shouted out to him but there was no time, he leapt out into the trench and, with one end of the cable in each hand, he hooked it over a rock beneath the hole in the wall.

There was a strong jolt as the rock took his weight and he slammed against the wall but there was no time to ponder the situation. He quickly grabbed both ends of the cable in one hand and deactivated his helmet which retracted into the collar of his emerald, armoured suit. With the trench acting as a wind tunnel, it carried the Beconium mist that had been contained in his helmet away from him and he finally exhaled, gasping for breath.

'Corey? Corey, are you there?' asked Isaac's voice through a small speaker on his suit's collar.

'Yeah. I'm fine' replied Corey using the microphone built in next to the speaker.

'I don't think I can get back to you though. I'm going to use my jet propulsion unit to get back to the ship' he continued.

'Alright. Run a diagnostics check on the ship's systems, make sure nothing has been damaged by the waves and do a vitals check on yourself to make sure the Beconium hasn't infected your system' instructed Nathan, overhearing the interaction between Corey and Isaac.

'Alright' replied Corey. He then deployed his helmet over his head once more and, kicking away from the wall, he did a back flip and fired up his suit's thrusters, soaring down the long trench, back to the ship's landing zone.

Back inside the cave, the remaining Operatives were checking their vitals scanners on the insides of their visors for traces of Beconium Poisoning.

'All clean' announced Isaac, relieved but guarded, after a few seconds of having pulled up everyone else's displays on his visor.

'He's gone. Who was that guy?' asked Colin as they made their way out of the clouds of Beconium and into a narrow passageway beyond the cave.

'I'm not sure' replied Isaac, retracting his helmet into the collar of his armoured suit as the others copied. Isaac was confident, certain even, that their disguised assailant was still somewhere in the network of tunnels.

'Be on your guard. Nathan, watch our six' he instructed.

As the Operatives proceeded down the passageway, they could hear the echo of shouting and a blaster shot nearby. Isaac stopped suddenly and held out his arm; blocking the others off and shushing them. Silence fell. Not even the echoes could be heard now. Isaac drew his blaster and silently indicated to the other Operatives to follow him. As they rushed down the tunnel, the other Operatives drew their blasters.

As they came around a bend and approached an archway, they came to a stop, pressing themselves up against the wall and listening closely. There was a sudden thud followed by a long rumbling sound which moved straight towards them. Isaac held out his blaster, clutched in both hands, as Anthony came to a stop in the archway.

The untidy man with long dreadlocks appeared unresponsive so Isaac cautiously lowered his blaster and, slowly, crouched down towards him, removing one of his gloves. A powerful stench permeated Isaac's nose as he leaned over the man, feeling beneath his chin with two fingers in search of a pulse.

'He's alive' whispered Isaac. 'Give me a hand' he continued turning to the others. Grabbing the man's arms, they dragged him around the corner, into the passageway.

A howling wind came from the chamber and rushed out, straight past them. Then, once again, everything fell completely silent. Feeling on edge, Isaac slowly turned to the others.

'Nathan. Investigate the source of that noise' he instructed.

He was sure it was just the wind moving through the network of tunnels but there was something about the spontaneity of it that just didn't sit right with him.

'Con-Haarian transport shuttles. Looks like a small convoy of four moving in to land' announced Nathan as he squinted through a crack in the wall.

'Are there any Black-Burns, stolen I.S.S. Vipers or Funnel-Webs?' asked Isaac who hadn't noticed the dark shroud of Parathax quickly and stealthily vacating the huge cave through the nearby archway, abandoning her plan to capture Tino in a bid to evade a confrontation that she was not yet ready for.

'No, there's no escort at all' replied Nathan who, as a shuttle pilot for the Interstellar Scouts, viewed this as extremely odd. Transport shuttles, even armed ones, always travelled with a fighter escort as shuttles were more vulnerable due to their lack of manoeuvrability, Kestrels aside but even they had escorts.

'The Con-Haarians seem to be playing a prominent role in whatever has been going on recently. What did that guy call it? The Apocalyptic Genesis?' Isaac consulted with Nathan.

'We need to find out what's going on. If there is a plot to destroy the I.S.S. like he said, we need to try and get a transmission out to any survivors and warn them' insisted Colin.

Isaac wrestled with his thoughts. He was extremely tired and unsure of whether his judgement could be relied upon.

'We can't give away our position, it wouldn't help anyone. Nathan and I will investigate the convoy and gather what intelligence we can. You and Ethan get somewhere safe and let us know if he wakes up' instructed Isaac, indicating at Anthony who lay unconscious at their feet.

Nathan looked at Isaac with uncertainty as he thought it through. Unlike Corey, Nathan was one of Isaac's closest friends and he had faith in Isaac as the group's Assistant Patrol Leader but there was no denying that, if they found the Con-Haarian shuttles, the two of them would be immensely outnumbered and, not only that, but there was a chance that they could be transporting dangerous cargo.

They needed to put a stop to the enemy steamrolling across the galaxy though and, if they could remain covert, maybe they could find a way to stop the downfall of the I.S.S. Finally, Nathan committed to the plan. The two Operatives quickly proceeded down the tunnel in the direction of the Con-Haarian shuttles' landing zone.

'How far away from the landing zone are we?' asked Isaac.

'It's quite close. It looked like they were moving to set down within a nearby cliff. We will need to climb to get to them though' replied Nathan. Isaac looked down at a variety of tools clipped into place on his armoured suit's utility belt which he had brought from the shuttle to aid in climbing along the trench. He was trying to decide on whether he could make use of what he had.

'I am worried though' Nathan confessed after a moment, confiding in Isaac as both his friend and Assistant Patrol Leader.

'About what?' asked Isaac.

'I'm a pilot. I don't have as much experience as you or Corey in combat situations' Nathan explained.

'Don't worry about being skilful with a blade or a blaster with the Con-Haarians. They're Methane-breathers so just damage their breathing apparatus and, whatever you do, don't use your blaster or your flint and steel or we'll all go up in flames' replied Isaac.

'How are you feeling about all of this?' asked Nathan who was still shaken up from the repeated close calls that the group had faced. He had been wanting to test the waters for a while now to see if Isaac was comfortable with being in charge despite the dangers they had faced and Corey's behaviour. He wanted to be sure that he could comfortably leave his life in Isaac's hands the same way he would always confidently do with Oli.

Nathan's question had awoken the fearful side of Isaac again and made him actually think about the true gravity of the situation.

'Honestly?' asked Isaac, slightly hesitant. Nathan nodded in response, equally hesitant. 'I wish we had Oli with us. We've been knocked from pillar to post ever since The Scout Hut's hanger bay and I feel like we have only made it this far because of your piloting. You really should give yourself more credit, none of us could pilot that shuttle under fire the way you did. That's why I handed my position over to you when I got trapped on the shuttle. You don't just have skills that the rest of us don't, you also have the heart and indomitable spirit of a leader' replied Isaac. 'I can't talk like this in front of Corey but I'm exhausted. I've hardly slept since Becon, I'm totally broken over my parents on Polarious and really, I'm not cut out for the full leadership role regardless of what anyone else thinks' he explained.

This wasn't the answer that Nathan had wanted to hear. He was hoping that Isaac would say that he was starting to settle into the role now which, after all, is the impression he gave off while standing up to Corey and interrogating the man in the gold armoured suit.

'I can't stop thinking about Sarah either' Isaac said simply, turning to Nathan to reveal his teary eyes. He had pushed himself so hard and for so long to stay strong that, now that everything was a bit calmer, his emotions had caught up with him.

Nathan turned to Isaac with a sympathetic smile and placed his hand on his shoulder. 'Me too' he replied.

'If Corey hadn't been so stupid and careless in rescuing Oli, I could have reached Sarah and brought her onboard with us. I...I really could have...' said Isaac, struggling more and more to hold himself together.

'She would be really proud of her older brother to see him now though, doing shuttle repairs mid-flight while under fire, facing off against the Deathstalker Squadron, putting Corey in his place and interrogating the enemy. It's not easy and I don't think anyone has really slept much since Becon. Between the injuries we suffered and the things we saw, the whole thing was a nightmare. I can't even imagine what Sarah saw on Earth after the stories of the Deathstalker strikes on Polarious and Fulgon' Nathan continued.

Despite what he said about not believing what anyone else said about his leadership skills, right now, for the first time, Isaac actually thought to himself that perhaps he was actually doing a good job as the Acting Patrol Leader.

'She would have punched me for going back to the shuttle while we were under fire, screamed insults at me while trying to work on the repairs...and I think I would have actually felt bad for Corey if Sarah was here as well' Isaac laughed.

It was the first time he had laughed in a long time but, when Nathan also started laughing, as they both imagined Corey facing

Sarah's wrath, they found themselves unable to stop, laughing to the point that they were crying for a totally different reason and almost falling to the floor in hysterics.

'I'm sure she's out there with the rest of Viper Strike right now trying to track us' said Nathan as he composed himself and diminished any worries that either of them had that she hadn't survived the assault. Isaac smiled back at him as they approached a hole in the side of the mountain.

'She has struggled over the past few days though. I don't know if she's said anything to you but she came back from Earth with her injuries, especially that nasty one to her head and she was talking about an Operative that was left behind but everyone was accounted for after that mission and then when I talked to her about it later, she had no idea who I was talking about. I just worry that she has suffered some sort of trauma. I mean we've all heard the stories of Captains Tony and Thius and even Squadron Commander Noel Jenson' Nathan explained.

'I'm sure it's just a bit of confusion following the battle. It was a lot worse down there than anyone could have anticipated but I will check in with her when I see her' replied Isaac before stumbling over his words. He had talked about Sarah surviving so much that he had genuinely believed it. 'Can I ask you a question though?' he asked as he looked down at the tools clipped onto his utility belt once again and detached a small harpoon and cable spool from it.

'Sure' replied Nathan as he too began detaching his harpoon and cable spool.

'Is it true that you've had a crush on Sarah since we were all Initiates?' asked Isaac.

Nathan suddenly became very defensive and made numerous attempts to deflect the question but Isaac simply stood there staring at the awkward pilot with a grin.

'Has she said anything to you?' Nathan stammered.

Isaac gave him a pitiful look and then locked the cable spool and harpoon onto his blaster. Using an invisible laser emitter function on his blaster, Isaac locked a small scope onto the weapon and pointed it out at the cliffs opposite. Looking down the scope it showed the invisible laser up in colour. To his disappointment though, the laser was showing up as red rather than green.

'It looks like our cable spools are going to be too short to get us up there. We'll need to cover part of the distance with our jet propulsion units and then ascend up the side of the cliff with our harpoons once we're within range' announced Isaac, removing the scope and returning it to his utility belt.

'Any idea what we're going to run into when we get to the top?' asked Nathan.

'That depends. How many shuttles did you see?' asked Isaac, pressing the glowing red button in the middle of his armoured suit's collar.

'Four' recalled Nathan as he did the same.

'Probably...four Quad-Con-Haara' in that case, so sixteen soldiers in total' replied Isaac.

'SIXTEEN!?' repeated Nathan, his eyes wide, mouth hanging agape as Isaac deployed his helmet from his armoured suit.

Isaac then squeezed the trigger grips on the deployed royal-blue and gold-striped ballistic glass bars and he shot off the ledge, towards the cliff face opposite. Nathan stepped up to the ledge and deployed his own helmet. He was starting to miss piloting the shuttle that he had held so much resentment for earlier. He too then fired up his jet propulsion unit and soared through the air, towards the cliff face.

The two Operatives released their grip on their thrusters' triggers and fired their harpoons next to a nearby rupture in the cliff face as their momentum carried them forwards. They then swung on their cables, high above the crashing waves beneath them and their feet met the cliff face beneath bent knees.

'Are you locked?' asked Isaac through his helmet's built-in microphone.

'Cable locked' confirmed Nathan's voice as he double-checked to make sure that the spool of cable wouldn't start unravelling again during the climb.

The climb towards the rupture in the cliff face was short.

‘We need to gain some altitude so we can gather the intelligence and also have the element of surprise’ said Isaac’s voice through the speaker inside Nathan’s helmet.

‘We can climb up this shaft and use our stealth field generators’ suggested Nathan. Isaac paused for a moment, looking about and considering different possibilities.

‘Hold off on the stealth field generator. We really need to conserve our suits’ power and if any dust or water makes contact with the stealth field, the enemy will see and hear us as well but have it on standby as a last resort. We’ll initiate Blackout Protocol and use the shadows to stay hidden’ Isaac replied, noticing the shadows cast by the moonlight bleeding through the rupture behind them. The two Operatives deactivated all light sources within their suits to make themselves harder to see.

Isaac was now starting to realise the broader extent of his responsibilities. Of course he had to ensure the safety and efficient teamwork of his Patrol but, if their armoured suits’ power was spent, they had no access to the round podium charging docks onboard The Scout Hut anymore. He had to start being smart in his leadership decisions as, when he thought about it, he was really racing against a ticking clock.

Making sure that their gloves were comfortably fitted over their hands and their cuff rings that secured their gloves to the rest of the suit were properly tightened, the two Operatives began ascending up between the walls of the narrow shaft.

Once they reached a natural ledge about three quarters of the way up, they stood up on it, hugging the wall tightly and began slowly side-stepping their way out of the passageway and into the cave where four large shuttles had docked, the sound of their engines cooling still audible.

The two Operatives were stunned by what they saw outside the shuttles below. As Isaac had predicted, exactly four Quad-Con-Haara’, totalling sixteen soldiers, were assembled in the cave beneath them but they weren’t alone. In the centre of the chamber, the creatures surrounded a large crowd of prisoners. It was impossible to get an idea of how many there were. Fifty? Sixty?

Maybe even seventy civilians were herded into the middle of the cave in a huddled group, held in reluctant compliance, at gunpoint.

'What are they doing?' asked Nathan, unable to hear what was going on but not daring to lean away from the wall to listen more closely for fear of falling from such a great height. 'We have to save them' he continued.

'Wait' instructed Isaac. 'There has to be a reason for all of this. There's no point in gathering all of these prisoners and bringing them all here just to kill them. They're waiting for something' he deducted.

'I see what you mean about them being Methane-breathers, I can smell them from up here' said Nathan as he tried to refrain from gagging and retching from the stench that surrounded the creatures. Suddenly, Nathan lost his footing on the ledge as the rocks broke away beneath his boot.

The Quad-Con-Haara', on high alert, looked about as they heard the distant tumble of the small rocks. A dense cloud of dust flew up into the air, enshrouding the area where the rocks had landed. The creatures, seeing a silhouette amongst the dust, discharged their blasters at it. The prisoners cowered in response to the show of aggression as the Methane ignited and sent beams of blazing flames across the chamber. As the dust settled however, the silhouette was revealed to be a cluster of thin rocks and black crystals, parts of them now blown away by the blasts.

The Con-Haarians turned back to the terrified prisoners and started aggressively ushering the strays back into the centre of the cave.

With the Con-Haarians, once again, focussing on their prisoners, Isaac and Nathan deactivated their stealth field generators to reveal them dangling from a cable that was attached to a grappling hook. Isaac had had just enough time to throw it to a nearby cluster of black crystals, that jolted out from the wall nearby and they had swung away from the enemy's line of sight. Nathan, dangling from Isaac's feet, slowly positioned his hands and feet back onto the rocky wall and moved alongside him, taking the weight off the cable that Isaac had cast out.

Straining to look over their shoulders, below, the two Operatives saw what the Con-Haarians had been waiting for. Peculiar, seemingly-sentient machines constructed of two ancient-looking metal dishes turned inwards on one another hovered into the cave from various entrance points, followed by more of them that trailed in from behind, like snakes, twisting and winding around the chamber. The ones that were at the front of the long chains seemed to have an orange hue about them. They were also quite small, heavily damaged and appeared to be contaminated with Beconium but it was difficult to make out much more from Isaac and Nathan's less-than-convenient vantage point. The prisoners grew agitated and cried out in terror as they became surrounded.

'This just got a lot harder' sighed Isaac.

'Alright, forget gathering intelligence. We're going in now. Remember, no sparks or blasters' he continued.

Isaac then let the gathered up cable drop to the floor of the cave, behind a gathering of boulders, and the two Operatives descended, rapidly, down the cable, in a swift tactical insertion.

The chamber immediately erupted into chaos as the two Operatives launched a surprise attack on the Quad-Con-Haara' and the machines that swarmed around the chamber. The two dishes on each of the leading machines that twisted through the chamber began rotating rapidly above one another in opposite directions and began to separate. Dense clouds of Beconium flooded the chamber as the prisoners cried out in horror.

'BECONIUM! NATHAN, RESPIRATOR MASKS, NOW!' Isaac yelled. 'GET THEM OUT OF HERE!' he continued, grabbing the arms of the prisoners and hauling them down to the ground beneath the rusty-orange shroud as they coughed and spluttered.

Isaac knew there was a good chance many of them would be infected with Beconium Poisoning by now but he still had a duty to help them. Nathan guided the prisoners out of the chamber and into the breathable air of the tunnel system.

Once Isaac heard the cave fall quiet, he slowly rose to his feet, protected by his suit's respiratory filters, mask and helmet. He climbed up onto a tall boulder to assess the situation but was interrupted by a retching, grunting sound amongst the shroud and, as it faded, a single surviving Con-Haarian emerged. It had taken one of the prisoners hostage and was slowly approaching Isaac. The sound, Isaac now realised, was the creature making demands in exchange for the prisoner's life. The only problem was that the Con-Haarian was speaking Haarish, its native language, a language that Isaac didn't understand.

He knew that Con-Haarians mostly kept to themselves and, therefore, wouldn't understand Voca-Com which was an abbreviation of 'Vocalised Transmission Communication', the galactic military name for Earth English as opposed to the standard term, Com-Vox.

All Isaac could do was try to calm and reassure the distressed man that had been taken hostage while he desperately tried to think of a solution. Isaac was at a loss and knew that, if he didn't do something immediately, the creature would act on its threat, which didn't require translation.

Suddenly, a flaming blaster bolt struck the creature in the back and, igniting the Methane in its respiratory tank, sent it rocketing across the cave at speed, straight past Isaac, until it smashed into the wall behind him.

As the Beconium particles in the air dissipated and the dangerous indicators disappeared from the inside of his visor, Isaac retracted his helmet into the collar of his suit and he squinted into the shadows at the figure that now approached, surrounded by a glowing silver aura. Stepping out into a ray of moonlight that shone down through the ceiling, they revealed themselves to be an I.S.S. Operative.

Isaac frowned as the Operative went to retract their own helmet. The helmet split into various sections and retracted into the Operative's own cy-bionic exoskeleton revealing a dark-skinned, black-haired girl of a similar age to Isaac, maybe slightly older.

'Are you done starin'?' the girl asked in a thick, Earth-Zimbabwean accent after a moment as she continued across the cave towards Isaac with an intimidating presence. 'You think you can just come in here and terminate my mission early huh?'

Isaac could only frown in bewilderment, his jaw slightly dropped.

'You...you're part of Polarious Sector Patrol' said Isaac, acknowledging the illuminated scarlet and gold striped bars on the front of her suit and the upside down scarlet triangle with gold trim on her back. '...You were onboard one of the escort cruisers' he continued.

'Nice work statin' the obvious, genius' the girl replied in a loud, sarcastic tone as she moved past Isaac.

'Your mission? Wait...What?' asked Isaac trying to catch up on what the girl had said.

'So, come on Mister Save-The-Day, you killed all of the pilots. How are you going to get all of these prisoners and me off-world huh?' she confronted him.

'Well...technically...you killed the last one' mumbled Isaac, hiding his face slightly.

'What was that?' she snapped, leaning in close to Isaac and forcing him to flinch and retreat slightly.

'I killed the last one? WHAT ABOUT THE OTHER FIFTEEN!? WHAT ABOUT THAT, HUH!?' she shouted waving her hand, furiously, in front of Isaac's face as he leaned away, a look of panic and uncertainty in his eyes.

Isaac looked over his shoulder, hoping that Nathan would have rejoined him by now but there was no sign.

'Lookin' for your friend to back you up?' the fierce girl asked.

'He's a pilot' replied Isaac, slightly sheepish.

'Oh! Oh I see! Fantastic' the girl replied, sarcastically, encouraging a half-smile from Isaac before shooting him back down. 'And the other three pilots that I need?' she asked bluntly, her facial expression hard and intimidating.

While the girl was berating Isaac, Nathan had escorted all of the rescued prisoners out of the Beconium-covered cave and into the rupture that ran all the way through the wall.

'Don't worry, you're all safe now. My name is Nathaniel Lucas and that's Isaac back there. We're with the Interstellar Scouts and we are going to organise an extraction for you all. Just take this time to rest up for a minute and get your breath back' Nathan announced.

There was no danger in letting the survivors know who he was because. Once extraction had been arranged, they would all remain in the care of the I.S.S. until the crisis they were facing had passed. He wasn't, however, sure of how the extraction would work.

Alongside some of the more able survivors, he helped the injured ones that were unable to move on their own and started tending to the wounds that he was able to using his First Aid Badge to access his cy-bionic suit's various medical devices.

As he worked, he noticed a young boy and girl watching him from nearby with their terrified, trembling mother. Smiling softly, Nathan returned to his feet and approached them.

'Alright, which of you two is responsible for this smell?' he asked as the Methane from the Con-Haarians wafted down the passageway.

The two children looked up at the Operative, unsure of what to make of him.

'Was it you?' he asked the boy who shook his head, slowly, in response.

'Was it you?' he asked turning to the girl who mimicked the boy's reaction.

Nathan then had an idea and leaned in close to the two frightened children. 'Is this your mum?' he asked, pointing up at the woman standing between the two young children who nodded simultaneously.

'It's ok, it will be our secret...I think it was maybe your mum that made those smells wasn't it and she is keeping quiet about it. She's waiting for you two to take the blame isn't she' he whispered mischievously, with a playful smile.

The two children smiled at one another as Nathan began to joke around with them.

'UGH! IT WAS YOUR MUM! SHE'S JUST DONE IT AGAIN!' Nathan cried out dramatically as he jumped to his feet and wafted his hand in front of his nose, much to the amusement of the two children as they started laughing hysterically while the visual displeasure of the woman standing over them was clear.

'I can't...I just can't take this anymore' Nathan continued, triggering his First Aid Badge once again and deploying his respirator mask over his nose and mouth.

'No. No, keep back please. This is now a bio-hazard quarantine zone' he said in a muffled voice as he grasped at his mask, pressed it closer to his face and held out his hand to the woman, who was also starting to see the humorous side to Nathan.

With the two children much more at ease after the ordeal they had been through, Nathan returned his mask into his suit and addressed the woman. While the rescued prisoners seemed more at ease; Nathan realised that he had inadvertently also made himself feel more at ease as well.

'Don't worry, you're safe now. My name is Nathan. I'm an Operative with the Interstellar Scouts. Those creatures can't hurt you anymore' Nathan explained, trying to reassure the woman as he had done with the entire group collectively but he wanted to personally make sure that the woman felt safe.

He felt a nudge on his arm and, as he looked down, he saw the boy and girl poking at his badges.

'Nice try. You need these cool gloves with green lights on the fingers to use these badges' he announced as he disengaged the suit's Blackout Protocol, illuminating it and activated one of his badges. He showed off the emerald lasers dots on his black fingertips and then opened out his suit to step out of it.

He removed two pens that were clipped onto a pocket on his flight suit's thigh. 'Here, see if you can draw this blue and gold triangle on the back of my suit onto the back of each other's shirts. Then you will be a secret Interstellar Scouts Operative' he instructed.

'I'm going to speak with the other Operative back there and make a plan to get you all to safety' Nathan announced to the group of survivors.

Finally, much to Isaac's relief, Nathan rejoined him, only to find he was now also accompanied by the girl back inside the cave.

'Here he is. The one out of four pilots' the girl attacked, stopping Nathan in his tracks. Nathan looked to Isaac, his facial expressions asking a variety of questions ranging from 'Who is this?' to 'Why is this girl yelling at me?' Isaac just shook his head, exhausted.

'The prisoners are at the end of the rupture but many of them are badly injured. We need a way to get them to safety so their wounds can be tended to' announced Nathan.

'Can we use one of the Con-Haarian shuttles?' asked Isaac.

'It will be difficult for me to operate it in such a tight space. I recommend bringing our shuttle up from outside and using the Rhinonoid as a backup' replied Nathan.

'The Rhinonoid? You're with Biker Delta Squadron Five-Six-Five of The Scout Hut' the girl interjected, knowing the Patrol by reputation.

'Nice work stating the obvious, genius' Isaac threw back at her under his breath.

'HUH!?' asked the girl but Isaac just shook his head again, immediately regretting his decision, resulting in the girl punching him hard in the arm with her gloved hand, although the armour cushioned the blow.

'Activate your distress signal badge and establish contact with Corey. Ask him to lock onto the signal and bring the shuttle up for the extraction' Isaac instructed, turning to Nathan but repeatedly turning to look back at the girl in case she tried to hit him again. He hadn't realised in the moment but he was actually shuffling sideways, in tiny steps, away from her to create some distance.

'Corey? NOT COREY JONES!?' the girl laughed hysterically at how ridiculous the situation was becoming.

'You've heard of us then?' asked Isaac.

'I've heard stories. As Initiates, you commandeered The Scout Hut's primary blaster canons to fend off an attack from two bounty hunters, the time Oliver was stranded and set adrift in the Polarian Nebula, the time you captured the Deathstalker Squadron, the crash landing on Becon' the girl listed.

'I'm afraid...the story of the Deathstalker Squadron is only partly true. There were a lot of Operatives and Troop Leaders involved in that mission and we were betrayed by a Reptilian spy who had been hired to lead the mission. Our fighter escort – Viper Strike

Squadron was called in to assist the battle on Earth, we just came in at the very end to capture and secure the ships as they bypassed Becon. They escaped during the attack on our fleet and are now back out there' Isaac explained.

'You've seen them?' the girl asked, suddenly turning serious. Isaac nodded regrettably.

'We were attacked on Crystalosis while we were trying to save our Patrol Leader, Oli...He didn't make it back to our ship. They took out an entire convoy of Kestrel Shuttles, our extraction, with some sort of seismic boom when they breached the atmosphere' he explained.

'I was on Earth with my Patrol, Daniel, Megan, Stephen and Mark during the battle with the Deathstalker Squadron. I remember, right at the very end, there was an Operative that drew one of the Deathstalkers away from the small outpost that my Patrol and I were relaying information back to the fleet from. He gave his life for us when he was impaled and dropped, hundreds of feet through the air, before crashing into our nearby safe house' the girl recalled. 'Good people gave their lives that day. We need to locate an I.S.S. fleet to alert them and put a stop to it' she insisted.

'Not only that but we need to have rescue ships on standby as well but we have been tracking I.S.S. signatures from our shuttle and the enemy has been picking them off very quickly' replied Isaac. 'So who are you and how did you and all of these people end up here?' he continued.

'My name's Tamatha. Tamatha N'Ocea. I was onboard one of the Kestrel Shuttles dispatched from The Libera that was searching the Polarian Debris Field for survivors from the Deathstalker attack on Polarious. When our fleet came under attack, the enemy was also gathering survivors, or rather, harvesting them. To try and find out what was going on and to give the other survivors a fighting chance, I used an Assimilation Matrix to disguise myself and left the rest of my Patrol on the shuttle to flee the attack while I allowed myself to be captured' the girl replied, becoming more co-operative but clearly feeling on edge as she relived the experience.

Isaac was starting to understand Tamatha's furious attitude

towards the two of them. Much like Sarah and many other Operatives that had been on Earth to fend off the Deathstalker strike, she had seen and been through things that no Operative of her rank should ever have to endure. She was clearly shook up and tense from remaining under cover onboard the Con-Haarian shuttle and probably believed that nothing could be done when the peculiar metal dishes entered the cave. This was just an outburst of cumulated nervous energy. She would be fine shortly, or at least that's what Isaac was hoping.

'I'm Isaac Easton and this is Nathan Lucas. We're the Assistant Patrol Leader and pilot of Biker Delta Squadron Five-Six-Five, stationed onboard The Scout Hut' replied Isaac.

'There's no response from Corey' Nathan announced, having rejoined Isaac and Tamatha from the rupture and waited for Isaac to turn to him for an update.

'The signal probably can't get through the mountain' replied Isaac, frustrated, realising the flaw in his plan.

'I know I can't pilot these shuttles in such an enclosed space the way the Con-Haarian pilots did but they do appear to be armed' announced Nathan studying the docked ships. 'If I can access the weapon systems on one of them, I might be able to create some space for me to guide them out' he announced.

'We still need to rendezvous with Colin and Ethan and find out who that guy is that they are guarding' replied Isaac.

'That's the only thing, once the shuttles have been boarded and we have them outside, we need to try and make our way back to the rest of our Patrol and you'll be on your own' said Nathan, turning to Tamatha.

'Will you be able to get the survivors somewhere safe and arrange medical treatment for them? There are Black-Burn Fighters, stolen I.S.S. Vipers, possibly I.S.S. Funnel-webs as well and, of course, the Deathstalker Squadron, all out there hunting and eliminating anyone who has ties to the Interstellar Scouts' Isaac explained.

Although hesitant, as she realised what she was going to be up against, Tamatha nodded. With everyone in agreement, Nathan boarded one of the Con-Haarian shuttles and set to work while Isaac and Tamatha informed the survivors of the plan.

With an enormous hole blasted in the wall, Nathan created an exit that was large enough for him and three other slightly experienced pilots among the survivors, to guide the shuttles out, into the open.

'Remember, the I.S.S. is being hunted. Keep communication as limited as possible to avoid being intercepted. If you come across any I.S.S. survivors, inform them of the danger and try to track down a fleet to pursue the Deathstalker Squadron. Hopefully, when this is all over, we'll see each other again' said Isaac through the speaker built into Tamatha's helmet.

With that, Nathan handed control of the shuttle he was piloting over to Tamatha and turned to the mother with her two children. 'Remember, you are secret Operatives with the Interstellar Scouts now' he announced, looking down at the makeshift jet propulsion unit indicators the two children had drawn on each other and taking the pens back. 'That means you always do your best to help anyone who needs it and care for all creatures. Take care of each other' he instructed.

Nathan then hopped off the loading ramp and back into the cave where Isaac was waiting. The four shuttles then pulled away and disappeared into the night sky as the two Operatives watched on.

'What were those things?' asked Nathan, looking down at the metal dishes that now lay, inanimate, all over the cave floor, coated in a light dusting of Beconium.

'I don't know but I'm worried there are more here and we can't get through to the rest of our Patrol. We should get back to Colin and Ethan as quickly as possible' replied Isaac, a tone of worry in his voice. The whole plan in coming to Zonju was to keep a low profile and rest up but it seemed like more and more hostiles were coming into play.

'Are you ok?' asked Nathan. He felt like Isaac had suddenly closed himself off since getting the survivors onboard the shuttles and seeing them off safely.

'I'm fine...It's just...Tamatha was onboard one of the shuttles that was sent out to look for survivors from Polarious. Those people were all that were located to be brought here' explained Isaac.

'...But they're safe now. We rescued them' replied Nathan, confused.

'My parents were on Polarious. They were transferred there from Earth by the I.S.S. for their protection back when I was just an Initiate...but they weren't here with the other survivors. They never made it off-world when the Deathstalkers attacked' Isaac concluded before falling quiet once again.

On meeting back up with Colin and Ethan, Isaac and Nathan found them both holding the now-awake, scruffy, smelly man at blaster-point while hiding behind a cluster of black crystals. They had retreated into a small cave, just a bit down the passage way from where Isaac and Nathan left them. Colin informed the two older Operatives that they had heard sounds coming from within the large chamber shortly after they had left to investigate the shuttles. Isaac looked across the passageway to the enormous chamber's entrance.

He didn't need to say anything. They all knew how he was feeling, they felt the same way. It was as if something was watching them, toying with them, lingering, invisible in the shadows as it waited to pounce.

Isaac, once again, composed himself and raised his blaster. He had been lulled into a feeling of security by not being the only one in charge and being on more of a level mindset with Nathan and Tamatha. He was now starting to understand why Oli always preferred the Patrol to work as a team rather than him dictating everything but now Isaac alone found himself in charge once again.

He took a couple of deep breaths, searching for his courage, looked to the others to make sure that they were ready and that the prisoner remained covered and then charged into the huge, moonlit chamber, determined to put a stop to whatever was happening before it even started.

'Get down on your...' Isaac started in a loud, commanding voice that he forced on but he was instantly rendered speechless as Xzjytheous reeled around to face the Operatives, hissing aggressively.

'You?' Isaac said, stunned, as he unconsciously lowered his blaster. It was like he had slipped into a trance.

The other Operatives were confused by Isaac lowering his blaster and, while normally they would be expected to follow his lead, they kept their weapons trained on the Reptilian in front of them as a precaution as they could see the look of horror on the Assistant Patrol Leader's face. Nathan looked up at the round ceiling to see an enormous hole blown out in it. It was like they were standing inside a volcano that was long-dead.

'You were there...on Becon. I saw you when the extraction team captured you and took you onboard the shuttle for delivery to The Scout Hut' said Isaac. 'You're the one who betrayed us to aid the Deathstalker Squadron, leading the strikes on all of those peaceful worlds...The strike on Polarious. You're the one who shot the Rhinonoid down above Becon and then sniped at us when we crashed to the surface' he painfully recalled.

'He's more than that' announced Nathan as he stared at the Reptilian. 'Don't you recognise him? It's the same Reptilian that helped that bounty hunter track down and capture Jason' he continued.

'You survived' Xzjytheous hissed, relishing in Isaac and Nathan's torment as he relived the experiences.

'MY FAMILY WAS ON POLARIOUS!' shouted Isaac as he felt the red mist descending, his rage growing. Isaac raised his blaster back up, aiming directly for the creature's head, his jaw growing tight.

'Isaac' said Nathan, afraid that the Assistant Patrol Leader was about to do something they would all regret. Isaac's hands shook violently as he held the blaster in place, a single tear rolling down his cheek as his lower lip began to quiver. This wasn't him. He was an I.S.S. Operative. He had more control, pride and respect than this. Shaking his head in horror, Isaac slowly backed away from the situation and Nathan stepped in to take the lead until he calmed down.

Back at the I.S.S. shuttle, Corey made his way down to the rest and recuperation deck to run the medical tests, checking for traces of Beconium Poisoning in his body. Just like on the Rhinonoid, the silence and stillness of the room where he and Oli had conversed, following their escape from the attack on the fleet, now created an eerie feeling. Once again, it felt like Oli was right there, haunting him, blaming him for abandoning him when the Deathstalkers prevented his escape.

Corey tried desperately to push the unsettling thoughts, born of a guilty conscience, to the back of his mind as he set about powering up the nearby holographic projection table. The more he tried to distract himself though, the more it felt like Oli was right there, shouting in his ear. Agitated, Corey quickly walked around the table but the feeling followed him.

'Stop' he said out loud looking desperately around the room. 'Where are you?' he whispered, feeling a layer of sweat coating his face. 'Where are you!?' he shouted louder in contest with his intensifying guilt as he reeled around, growing disorientated.

Up until now, Corey had been shielded from it by the presence of the other Operatives, the operation of the ship and the mission's priorities but now that he was isolated from all of that, his senses suddenly deprived, his overactive imagination continued to manifest these thoughts that plagued him. 'STOP!' he shouted at the top of his voice as he stumbled backwards, drawing his blaster as he fell to the floor. He fired a volley of blaster bolts from his blaster, across the room, shattering a variety of glass screens mounted on the far wall, one of which shared the electrical systems with the door, causing it to unlock.

The unlocked door slid open behind him without the need for direct interaction, the motion sensor being triggered in response to his presence and causing him to jump with fright as he turned around aggressively, his breathing fast and heavy. Then, just like that, the room returned to normal, like whatever he thought had been there, had left through the open door.

Corey's eyes darted cautiously around the room, wide and alert. Slowly, he began to calm down but he remained sat on the steps that he had tripped on, which led from the operating floor to the door. Emotional and in torment, he buried his face in his hands and sat there in silence as he tried to get his mind back on the task at hand while praying that whatever had been there moments ago, if indeed there was something, would now leave him alone and just wander the rest of the ship.

He looked up at the holographic projection from the lit up table in front of him and, to his relief, it showed no indication of Beconium Poisoning. Still, it had all become too much for Corey. Feeling plagued with guilt for abandoning Oli, the disrespect he had shown to both Isaac and Nathan and having no Troop Leader to talk with about it all, he buried his head in his arms and immediately started to cry.

Regaining his composure after several seconds, Corey exhaled a heavy, trembling sigh. He looked around the room once more through his slightly-blurred eyes before pulling himself to his feet and marching, quickly, towards the table, turning it off and then rushing out of the ominous room, not daring to look back for fear of what might have returned, what might have been watching him from behind.

CHAPTER 16
OPERATIVE IN DISTRESS

Corey made his way up to the ship's cockpit and began running the checks to make sure that the craft was flight-ready for when the rest of the group returned. The huge, powerful waves battered the thick glass of the cockpit window, blurring everything outside as the water ran down it, only for another wave to hit as soon as it cleared up. The cockpit created a feeling of safety and security, separate from the rest of the ship. It was silent except for the almost soothing sound of the waves crashing about outside and the occasional sound from the console as it began running through its diagnostics.

Suddenly, an alarm started wailing throughout the ship, making Corey, who was already paranoid and very much on edge, jump with fright. This particular alarm didn't just indicate a distress signal; it indicated that an Operative in the vicinity was in mortal peril.

A holographic projection covered the entirety of the long cockpit window and a box began moving around it, showing a zoomed-in image of something that it was tracking amongst the waves. Corey watched closely, frowning and then, there he saw it, a sudden glint of green. He leaned in closer, concentrating hard as he waited for the waves to reveal it again. Not a moment later, it was confirmed. There was somebody in the water wearing an emerald Interstellar Scouts Operative suit.

Hardly believing what he was seeing, Corey knew he had to take action now and there was no time to reach out to Isaac and the others. There was only one course of action that he could take. He backed away from the console and rushed out of the room as fast as he could. He raced down to the deployment bay and ran up the steps in the side of the Rhinonoid.

Just as he arrived in the cockpit, he remembered that the shuttle was flat on the ground, as the waves would have toppled it and swept it away if the landing gear had been deployed. This meant that the deployment bay platform couldn't be lowered. He slammed his fist against one of the seats in frustration and raced back out to the elevation platform in the Rhinonoid's refuelling station.

As the platform slowly reached the top of the shaft that led to the rooftop turret, Corey kicked aside the equipment that Colin and Ethan had been cleaning, knocking some of the items back down the shaft onto the platform below. He then mounted the turret, climbing into the leather seat and pulling down the arm rests. Reaching down, he pulled out a leaver beneath the seat to disengage its lock and took hold of the two triggered joy sticks on the arm rests. Placing his foot on the pedal he disengaged the handbrake and sat back in the seat, reclining it into a lying down position and pointing the turret upwards, towards the ceiling of the shuttle's deployment bay.

'Corey. It's Isaac. Have the ship ready for immediate launch. We're on our way back to you now' announced Isaac's voice over the speaker in his collar. Corey paused to let out an exasperated sigh as he rolled his eyes. He had the opportunity to redeem himself in this moment. The rest of the group would just have to accept the reality of the situation; they would still have the Rhinonoid.

He then squeezed the two triggers on the controls, completely obliterating the ceiling and upper decks of the shuttle. As the blaster canon pivoted on its axis, chunks of metal fell on top of the Rhinonoid from above until it finally penetrated the ship's hull.

Corey then pushed back the armrests and jumped up from the seat. He didn't have time to wait for the elevation platform to come up and take him back down so he just jumped. As he landed, he found a blaster with a grappling hook loaded into it. He had knocked it down from the ledge where Ethan had been sat when he and Colin were cleaning the equipment. Sweeping it up in passing, he rushed back into the cockpit.

Remembering what Nathan had said back on Crystalosis about Oli's laser modifications on the front and sides of the Rhinonoid, he started activating various controls which closed up the tunnel between the two sections of the Rhinonoid, forming it into one large tank and then began activating all of the tank's drilling equipment.

The plasma beams angled at the front and sides of the tank as well as enormous, hooked scarlet spikes and horns that sprung out on the roof.

He then retracted the staircases into the sides of the Rhinonoid, initialised the tank's systems to raise its main body up on its legs and activated the thrusters in its feet. The enormous tank began to slowly rise up through the ship, the beams of scarlet energy cutting away at any obstructions as it ascended, it's main hull pushing aside any other obstacles in its path.

As soon as he had breached the ship's hull and the Rhinonoid was outside, Corey flipped a switch, projecting the tracking screen in the shuttle's cockpit which, remarkably, was still operational, to the Rhinonoid's cockpit window. Once the shuttle and the Rhinonoid had synchronised with locating the target, he flipped another switch to transfer the signal to the Rhinonoid's scanners alone.

As the box darted around the cockpit window, indicating the Operative's position as he was thrown around by the waves, Corey guided the Rhinonoid towards him, lowering the airborne tank down towards the water.

The closer he got to the fierce waves below, the more dangerous it seemed, the fewer opportunities became available. There was only one possible scenario that could work and it was extremely dangerous but time was running out. He had to act now.

He set the Rhinonoid to hover above the water and quickly made his way down towards the tank's deployment bay. On arriving, he activated the same controls as Isaac had back on Crystalosis. The panel in the side of the Rhinonoid opened up and the strip in the floor extended out over the enormous crashing waves below, angling the six motorbikes downwards. As Corey approached the opening in the wall, the sheer power of the water below, now also much louder, made him very uneasy, causing him to question whether the Operative was still alive and whether he himself would still be alive after attempting his plan. He owed it to Oli to try to save them though.

He squinted through the spray of the waves that immediately soaked his face as he placed his hand on the wall. Stepping out onto the strip, it was already soaking wet beneath his feet and the wind was strong enough to make the Rhinonoid sway slightly as it hovered. Corey deployed his helmet around his head, pressed the illuminated red button on the collar of his emerald, armoured suit to deploy the royal-blue and gold bars from his chest and activated his jet propulsion unit. He had to move with extreme precision, working with the wind rather than against it as he flew towards the motorbike at the end so that he was as far away from the Rhinonoid's powerful thrusters as possible.

Corey deactivated his jet propulsion unit and landed on the wet seat of his motorbike, returning the bars to his armoured suit. He quickly activated one of the badges on his suit and interacted with the projected hologram to activate the Rhinonoid's Expansion Matrix.

Slowly, using the same intuitive technology that was contained inside the I.S.S. suits combined with Oli's innovation, compartments began opening up all around the Rhinonoid's hull.

A network of metal catwalks began extending, endlessly, in all directions with various shaped holes at the sides and large rows of lights in varying colourations that ran in short chains along the road, like on an aeroplane runway. The centre of the roads was marked with two rows of green lights, the edges, before the trims with the holes in them, were indicated with two rows of red lights and the area between the middle and the edge were indicated with two rows of amber lights which enabled Corey to see where he was going in the low visibility and treacherous conditions.

Corey started the engine of his motorbike and placed the blaster, containing the grappling hook, into the holster on the side of it, beneath one of the leg-guards. He then interacted with one of his other badges which transferred the tracking signal from the Rhinonoid to the display on the inside of his visor.

As soon as one of the extending catwalks moved past him, Corey deployed his motorbike and rocketed down, towards the fierce, swelling waters below. The road unfolded in front of him as he scanned around for the Operative.

Diving down, deep into the water, it formed a protective, illuminated, square tunnel around Corey, pushing the water back with the walls that developed ahead of him, leaving the tunnel in its wake. Corey skidded his bike across the metal floor as the tunnel turned a corner. Referring once again to the scanner, it indicated that the Operative was close by outside the walls. Corey revved the engine, accelerating his motorbike which, in turn, accelerated the development of the tunnel in front of him.

This was taking far too long. There was no way the drowning Operative would be alive by now. Suddenly, the tunnel opened out once more to a flat, open road that stretched out across the surface of the water. A powerful backwash flew into the air behind Corey's motorbike as he tore across the surface. He could feel the severe lack of grip between the tread on his tyres and the road beneath them, there was absolutely no resistance as he turned the handlebars, the wheel smoothly gliding across the surface.

Enormous waves crashed down over the road all around him and he needed to time his acceleration bursts just right to avoid being hit by them.

The scanner indicated that the stranded Operative was to the left of him and fast-approaching. As Corey looked to the side, he could see the emerald suit being carried along in a towering wave that was headed straight for the hovering Rhinonoid. Corey revved his motorbike's engine as hard as he could as he activated one of his badges, selecting the Rhinonoid's Expansion Matrix function again which, interacting with a different function, allowed him to dictate the route that the Rhinonoid created with a directional swipe of his finger on the holographic projection cast by the badge.

Racing the incoming wave, Corey began his ascent as the road continued to open out in front of him, rising higher and higher. Visibility worsened the closer he got. He wiped the padded palm of his gloved hand over his visor but it simply smeared the water and distorted everything even more. This made it impossible for Corey to judge his distance from the Operative, his timing to collision with the wave and his target and, therefore, his required speed.

There was no avoiding this now. Whether he was in position in time to grab the Operative or not, he was going to get hit by that wave. The best he could do now was swallow his pride and make the same sacrifice that any of the other Operatives would in a heartbeat.

Corey retracted his helmet into his armoured suit and the deafening sound of the furiously-crashing waves flooded his ears. He squinted hard and closed his mouth with a tight jaw against the spray, focussing on timing it right. He hit the glowing red button on his collar again, priming his jet propulsion unit once more and drew the blaster with the grappling hook from the holster on the side of the bike.

Pulling his knees up towards his chest in preparation for his jump to grab the Operative, Corey's foot got stuck between the body of the bike and the leg-guard. Corey hadn't realised but the leg-guard on his right-hand side had been slightly dented by the debris on Crystalosis as Nathan had avoided the attacks of the pursuing Black-Burn Fighters. Corey tried to shake his foot loose but it was no use.

He jettisoned the triangular leg-guards off the sides of his bike, lightening its load and allowing him to rocket, increasingly faster, towards his target. With his trapped foot now released, he slowly brought his feet up onto his seat, preparing to jump. Looking from the wave to the Rhinonoid and back to the wave again, calculating his timing, he held out the blaster towards the airborne tank. Corey then deployed his helmet once more, pushed with his feet and fired up the thrusters on his jet propulsion unit.

He fired the grappling hook up at the Rhinonoid moments before the wave smashed into him. The strong wind, however, carried the hook away from the tank but, to Corey's relief, it caught onto a rectangular hole in the trim at the side of the road, created by the Expansion Matrix. Tucking the blaster under his arm, he held out both hands and caught the armoured figure.

The two of them swung violently from the force of the impact but, as the wave broke and fell back down to the water below, Corey used the karabiner cable on his utility belt to tether the Operative's armoured suit to his own. With his hands now free, he could retract his helmet into his collar and breathe a huge sigh of relief as he took a moment to just dangle from the cable.

He then grabbed the blaster from under his arm and, with his arms outstretched above his head, he triggered the blaster to begin reeling the cable in. As the two of them ascended, Corey took a moment to think that, if Colin and Ethan hadn't been taking their responsibilities seriously while cleaning the equipment, there would have been no chance that the extraction would have been a success.

His consideration was suddenly cut short as a powerful blast surged right at the two of them, narrowly missing them as they swayed in the strong winds.

Corey immediately stopped the ascension as he looked up, sharply, squinting through the spray of the crashing waves. The blast had come from the Rhinonoid.

He deployed his helmet back over his head and drew his own blaster from its holster. Watching closely, he could see the enormous turret on top of the Rhinonoid pivoting around freely. He had forgotten to re-engage the locks after blasting through the shuttle's hull.

As he watched, it suddenly stopped pivoting randomly in the wind and appeared to now move with intent. As it began to turn towards the two Operatives, Corey could swear he saw a black, ghost-like shroud standing on the roof next to it, guiding it towards its target.

Once trained on him, the turret stopped pivoting. A look of terror came over Corey's face as he stared at the enormous blaster canon through his visor. The turret, operated by Parathax, began firing blast after blast after blast in their direction. He tried to return fire from his blaster but he didn't even know what he was firing at and his remaining arm was feeling more and more strained by the second.

Eventually, the inevitable happened. A blast from the canon struck the cord that the two Operatives were dangling from and they both plummeted down to the water below. It was just sheer luck that they landed, heavily, on a part of the Rhinonoid's expansion just beyond the tunnel that Corey had raced through while pursuing the drowning Operative, where his motorbike had also skidded off and slammed against the wall.

The water washed over the makeshift road, almost sweeping them both off the edge and, even with the edges of his boots magnetising to the metal surface, they were no match for the battering the two Operatives were taking. Corey threw himself on top of the Operative and kicked the spikes in the fronts of his boots into the holes at the edge of the road as hard as he could, holding strong against the water as another wave slammed down on top of them.

The turret continued to fire at the two of them from above so Corey grabbed the other Operative and dragged him, with all of his strength, out of the line of fire and into the safety of the tunnel, the rubberised soles of his boots squeaking against the wet metal floor. Corey, very cautiously, peered around the corner at the Rhinonoid as the blasts continued to explode around them, smashing into the water outside.

As the bombardment pummelled at the side of the tunnel, echoing loudly, its structural integrity failed and large chunks of the wall and ceiling were blasted away. Corey pushed the Operative right up against the destroyed wall to hide him from view. He too then lay down, flat on the floor behind what remained of the wall and discretely opened up his cy-bionic suit.

Using only his arms, he dragged himself along, crawling with all of his strength, his black flight suit soaking up the water and weighing him down further. Allowing the Rhinonoid to continue firing at the spot where he had been positioned, he took cover further along and then fired a volley of blasts back up towards his attacker. He remained behind his cover until the blaster fire from the Rhinonoid ceased.

Shortly after, he heard the loud roar of thrusters coming from the Rhinonoid above. With a feeling of sheer dread, he looked out from behind his cover and, sure enough, his invisible attacker had boarded the tank and it was now detaching from the expansions as it pulled away.

Corey desperately blasted up at the armoured plating of the Rhinonoid but it was no use. The tank continued to shrink as it vanished, high into the sky, abandoning the Operatives on Zonju as it left the atmosphere.

Corey stared, dumbfounded, at the empty space where the Rhinonoid had been. He removed his helmet as he slowly turned away, unsure of the best course of action. Throwing his helmet to the floor in exhaustion, he approached the Operative who lay on the wet tunnel floor, illuminated by the bar lights that the Rhinonoid's Expansion Matrix had also generated above them.

Crouching down, he carefully removed the helmet from the rest of the suit to reveal a boy that he didn't recognise, lying in front of him, completely unresponsive. The circular, diamond and other variously-shaped badges on the emerald suit were all completely smashed; the suit grazed and dented having been thrown, repeatedly, against the rocks by the waves.

Corey began checking for signs of life from the unconscious boy. There was no indication that he was still alive so Corey set about trying to resuscitate him. Suddenly the boy sat bolt upright, accidentally head-butting Corey in the face as he gasped for breath, his hands pressed against the floor at his sides. He kicked with his feet, pushing himself backwards, against the wall of the tunnel.

'It's ok, I'm here to help' Corey said reassuringly, as he brought his hand away from his bloodied nose, holding it up to show that he wasn't a threat. The boy stared at him, wide-eyed, in disbelief.

'I'm Corey. What's your name?' Corey asked, after a couple of seconds, his voice calm to help the boy feel at ease.

'Tino' the boy stammered.

'You're safe now Tino' Corey smiled at him, reassuringly.

Tino began to slide against the wall as he blacked out once more. Corey caught him before he hit his head on the floor and lay him back down gently. He then retrieved his armoured suit and climbed back into it, thankful for the warmth it provided before lying down on the floor also, the explosive sound of the waves echoing down the tunnel as they pummelled the sides.

'Isaac, we need a change of plan' announced Corey into the microphone built into his collar, taking a moment to wipe at his nose, close his eyes and catch his breath.

CHAPTER 17
COMMANDEERED

A cold, wailing wind swirled through the Rhinonoid as Parathax wandered the shadows and sub-zero temperatures of the refuelling station, grinning to herself. It had been so long since she had been onboard an Interstellar Scouts vessel and now that the Operatives in the caves were distracted by her Polarian Beconi' and the Quad-Con-Haara, she'd had the opportunity to not only take over an I.S.S. vehicle but actually take over Sol's famous I.S.S. Rhinonoid, a concept merely stolen by Biker Delta Squadron 5-6-5. She could now advance her conquest, hunt down the surviving members of the I.S.S. and eliminate them. At long last she and her Polarian Beconi' would finally track Sol down and he would serve a new purpose under her own agenda or suffer the same fate as the rest of his precious organisation.

Before she could launch her final assault, she first needed an army and a fleet large enough to eclipse any sun that gave life to the worlds beneath it. With the Rhinonoid now in her possession, she had a cargo-hold of infinite size to gather resources from the Polarious Sector. She would then go to Becon and create an entire galaxy-destroying force of Polarian Beconi'. She stroked her icy-white, clawed fingers along the wall as she slowly stepped across the room towards the control panel that activated the Rhinonoid's expansion in the refuelling station. She stopped as her finger landed on a switch, flipping it as she slowly turned to face the opening in the wall.

With a deranged look on her face, she let out a low, wicked chuckle and stepped into the Quarantine Wing filled with equipment contaminated with Beconium. As she slowly moved along the passageway, she knocked many of the items down, clattering to the metal floor while she took others and concealed them within the black spectre-like shroud that billowed and flared from her body.

On reaching the end of the zig-zag corridor, she discovered another two doors opposite her in the hexagonal area she now stood in. She flicked the switch to open the door on her left-hand side and stepped through it, as the room, behaving as if it had a life of its own, unfolded and expanded before her. The white room glowed brightly, illuminated by the lights embedded in the walls, floor and ceiling.

Stood in uniformity, lining the walls of the long room was a vast array of armoured suits. Some were simple and elegant and others were constructed with much more ambition but each was designed to fit a specific purpose.

'Sol's prototype suit collection' echoed Parathax's ghostly voice as she looked around the room. She glanced down at the bright white floor, studying a long, broad, winding 'S' shape, running across the room, illuminated scarlet with tiny, sparkling, white lights floating around in it, as if contained in a liquid.

An alarm began to sound in the room - The same alarm that had been activated when the shuttle detected Tino's mortal peril distress signal. Parathax, her pale, deathly face now visible in the light, snarled up at the flashing red light. She then faded away on the spot.

Once again, the icy wind twisted through the passageways of the Rhinonoid, all the way through to the cockpit, where Parathax slowly reappeared, standing at the control console.

The screen indicated an I.S.S. Operative was in mortal peril, based on the distress signal coming from the nearby planet of Crystalosis. An icy-white hand, once again, reached out of the black, smoky shroud of Parathax's cloak and her claw-like finger nail of her finger slowly scratched across the edge of the console causing various switches and buttons to activate the tank's systems to home in on the signal as the finger moved past the controls while never touching them.

The Rhinonoid adjusted its course, intercepting the signal while, from the billowing blackness that enshrouded Parathax, drifted the variety of golden armoured pieces, contaminated with Beconium, that she had taken from the Quarantine Wing. They drifted into their relevant places where they would normally have fitted if she had a physical body and, as they positioned themselves, the remaining shininess dulled, the armour becoming blotched and pitted with even more Beconium. It was time to hunt down and kill the first I.S.S. Operative of her grand conquest, paving the way for her Deathstalker Squadron to wreak havoc across the galaxy and draw Sol out.

CHAPTER 18
THE STOWAWAY

The distant sound of thrusters approaching awoke Oli as he lay beneath the canvass of his improvised shelter made from the recovered I.S.S. parachute. The air was stagnant and droplets of moisture had cumulated on the inside of the shelter as the fabric didn't breathe too well. This didn't bother Oli at all though as it appeared that Ethan leaving him the Distress Signal Badge had paid off.

He stood up and quickly set about brushing away the white specks of crystalline dust that had stuck to the lining of his suit. He didn't want to risk it getting into the cy-bionic components of the suit or obstructing the blue tracking lights in the black, interior lining.

As he and Corey had both concurred previously, putting out a distress signal could also attract unwanted attention, so Oli was quick to climb inside his emerald cy-bionic suit and close it up around him, the black lining returning to the inner suit and its blue interior tracking lights darting around, positioning the various armoured components around his body. He then quickly turned off the tracking beacon and activated his suit's stealth field generator, making him entirely invisible and affording him the opportunity to assess the situation before letting his guard down.

It was still quite dark as dawn was just starting to break outside. Oli slowly emerged from beneath the parachute and, looking up to the sky, he was relieved to see the Rhinonoid coming into view overhead, its thrusters roaring loudly beneath it. As relieved as he was that his Patrol had returned for him, to Oli, the landing approach was an extremely dangerous risk that the pilot was taking and made him question whether it was, indeed, Nathan operating the vehicle as it should be. Nathan would know that the flames from the thrusters could be concentrated into lethal beams of energy by the crystals and such unpredictable circumstances could kill both him and everyone onboard if they became unstable. It also seemed odd that they weren't arriving on the shuttle.

Oli's worries worsened as the tank set down on the ground with thorny, black energy twisting and wrapping around the hull.

Oli swiftly moved beneath the tank's underbelly and around to the side, being careful not to touch any of the hot machinery. He quickly climbed up one of the legs to reach a ladder further up the tank's body so that he could reach the roof and get a better look at what was going on without being spotted. He knew that his stealth field generator would probably keep him hidden but, as a Patrol Leader, Oli was always thinking ahead and planning for something going wrong. At least on the roof, he was out of sight no matter what.

He lay down on his front, as flat as possible, on top of the tank to avoid touching the mysterious claw-like thorns that protruded from the tangled black vines of energy and watched, waiting for, hopefully, the Operatives of Biker Delta Squadron 5-6-5 to emerge but they never did. Nobody emerged at all.

As he continued to watch closely, Oli started to notice a black shroud forming around his encampment, concentrated mainly on the parachute. In a sudden, fierce demonstration of pure rage, the parachute flared up into the air and shredded, seemingly either of its own accord or maybe it was that of the black, shapeless entity that surrounded it. The pieces of fabric drifted to the floor in flames.

Monitoring the black spectral creature's behaviour with extreme caution, Oli silently climbed back down the side of the Rhinonoid and was able to stow aboard without giving himself away.

As he watched from the doorway, the black shroud faded away once more, leaving no trace but the remains of shredded burning fabric. Oli knew that this was going to be a very difficult situation to navigate as there was no telling where the mysterious entity would show up. As a precaution, Oli also initiated the Blackout Protocol which, like with Isaac and Nathan, deactivated any source of light within his cy-bionic suit.

As Oli crept through the massive refuelling station, the ceiling flaps repeatedly opened and slammed shut in peculiar, rapid sequences, making him jump with fright each time as the energy that surrounded Parathax surged through the inside of the Rhinonoid. Despite using his stealth field generator, he was quickly realising that he couldn't rely on it to keep him hidden as it appeared to be faulty, probably damaged either by Xzjytheous on The Scout Hut when he made the huge gouges in his suit or during his encounter with the Deathstalker that disabled his suit during the Patrol's escape from Crystalosis. The stealth field flickered repeatedly as he moved through the dark room.

Oli ducked and dodged as he quietly ran from cover to cover, hiding amongst the enormous fuel tanks and waiting for a sign that he wasn't going to run into whatever had stolen his tank which, by the way, he wanted back.

Oli crouched down behind a stack of supply boxes in a shadowy corner as the dark entity revealed itself at the doors to the cockpit and control centre. He crouched down as low as he could, and listened for the sound of the doors opening and then closing again.

The sound, however, never came. Oli frowned to himself, trying to find the courage within himself to stick his head up, above the boxes and investigate.

Finally, he confirmed that the intruder had moved through the doorway, by some other means as the Rhinonoid's security was of the same standard as other I.S.S. vehicles, consisting of a tri-laser code interface and scanner strip, identical to the one in Oli's room onboard The Scout Hut.

Oli waited a couple more seconds to allow time for both the spectral being to create some distance between them but also for him to get a handle on his nerves before following. He slowly rose to his feet, placing his hand on the top box for support as he cautiously gazed around, ready to throw himself to the ground at a moment's notice.

Slowly, he approached the doorway and raised his hand to align the dewdrop crystal on the sleeve of his suit with the tri-laser code interface on the doorframe. The three narrow lasers moved around into their different positions until the black strip lit up with a gold glow on his forearm. He scanned the strip and the black, diagonal line running through it disappeared, indicating that the doors had unlocked. The doors were relatively quiet as they opened which meant that he could sneak in quite easily without being detected.

Oli stepped through the doorway where, to his horror, all of the lights in the command centre and cockpit suddenly turned on simultaneously and the various computer systems in the command centre activated with a variety of loud beeping sounds.

Oli jumped with fright, his eyes wide. He threw himself against the wall and crouched down, retreating as fast as he could but he was unable to make it through the doors before they closed in front of him and locked, as indicated by the black line that now re-appeared on the gold strip on his forearm which was accompanied by a loud buzzing sound as he frantically tried to re-scan the strip.

Looking back over his shoulder for signs of the black-shrouded figure, Oli quickly raised his wrist up to the tri-laser code interface and used his other hand to steady it as he trembled with terror, almost to the point where the dewdrop crystal fell out of alignment with the lasers. The doors slid open as he swiped the gold strip against the scanner and he stumbled back out of the room.

Oli looked about himself desperately and quickly slid himself between a broad, arched pipe and one of the refuelling tanks.

Once again, the panels that formed the ceiling lifted and all slammed down heavily as the dark being appeared at the doorway. Remaining as still as possible, Oli followed the dark shroud with his eyes as it drifted by. He felt uncharacteristically claustrophobic in the confined space he had hidden within.

As he waited and tried to calm his racing mind along with his frantic-beating pulse, the open doorway to the Quarantine Wing caught his eye.

The small staircases retracted back into the sides of the Rhinonoid as the sound of the tank's thrusters could now be heard beneath him. The ceiling flaps opened and closed in their usual single wave sequence as the pressure equalised but, as familiar as this function was to Oli, this time it felt like something was riding that wave and charging right at him. Several moments passed and nothing happened, other than the ceiling flaps continuing to open and close in spontaneous sequences.

The tank began to rise back up off the ground, confirming to Oli that the coast was clear for him to make a dash for the door, hopefully undetected this time. Whatever else was on board was, right now at least, inside the cockpit. He quickly and quietly made a run for the open doorway, dashing through, into the Quarantine Wing.

He turned sideways-on and looked back repeatedly as he swiftly made his way down the zig-zagging corridor, being careful not to touch the contaminated equipment with his still-flickering suit. This was particularly difficult now, given the mess of Beconium-stained cy-bionic components and weapons that the intruder had littered the floor with.

Knowing exactly where he was going, he quickly stepped out of the corridor, into the hexagon-shaped area with two doorways in front of him. He quickly moved through the narrow doorway to a room that angled off on the right-hand side. This was where he kept all of his specialised tools, fuel canisters and weapons for his customised suits as well as spare standard equipment.

Not wasting any time or being picky about what to take, Oli picked up a knife and a blaster and inserted them into the vacant slots of his temporary armoured suit, arming himself, at last.

He then returned to the corridor and immediately moved into the adjoining, brilliantly-lit, white room which angled off to the left-hand side. This room contained all of his personal, customised cy-bionic suits. While this was extremely fortuitous, it also raised concerns about the fact that an intruder had accessed the room previously and, not only that, but contaminated it with Beconium as evidenced by the very light coating of orange-brown dust on the floor.

Oli approached the various armoured suits, each very different in its aesthetic, assessing which would be best to help him overcome the situation. The Pyrotech Suit was no use unless he wanted to blow the entire Rhinonoid into oblivion with him still onboard, nor was the Inferno Suit as he wasn't looking to suffer a fiery death or create a raging tornado of flame.

He turned to look at some of the suits on the other side of the room but was met by the piercing eyes of the pale, seething, now-humanoid spectre that towered over him, so close that the black billowing smoke of its body flared over him. Oli froze in place, petrified, his entire body tense and eyes wide, holding his breath as he slowly leaned backwards away from it. After several seconds, it slowly faded away on the spot again.

It took Oli a moment to get over the fright and to relax and actually release the breath that he had clung to so tightly. Had it even seen him? Or was the stealth field keeping him hidden, allowing the creature to look straight through him at the armoured suit standing behind, unaware that he was even there? He didn't care, he just wanted one of them to be off this flight of terror NOW.

Oli cautiously made his way back towards the door when his glove suddenly slipped off his hand and dropped to the floor. He frowned as he crouched down to retrieve it, feeling a tingling sensation in his hand. As he reached out, he fell backwards with fright as he saw his hand. It wasn't a human hand of skin, flesh and bone. Although it still resembled a human hand, it was made entirely of Beconium particles that swirled and twisted around the shape in a malleable manner.

'What the...?' Oli whispered as he turned his hand to look at the back and then the palm again, flexing his fingers. He tried to put his weight on it to return to his feet but there was nothing to support him anymore, it just piled up on the floor in a heap of orange-brown grains that resembled sand.

He had been so distracted by what was happening to him that he never even realised what this also meant. This had been one of the causes of his flickering stealth field generator from moving loosely within the suit. When the glove fell off his hand, his stealth field generator had deactivated fully, unveiling him.

Retrieving his glove with his other, still-gloved hand, Oli looked up and found himself locking eyes with the black, ghostly entity, making him jump with fright. A powerful blast of black energy smashed straight into the chest of his emerald suit with immense force, punching his body through the wall of the tank and creating a massive hole in the side. The vacuum dragged him out into the deathly-cold abyss of space.

CHAPTER 19
SETTING UP CAMP

'What happened?' asked Isaac, a look of despair on his face as he stepped out of a small gap in the foot of the mountain and onto the rocks where Corey and an unconscious Tino awaited the rest of the group along with some supplies gathered from the smoking shuttle wreckage which was sat some distance behind them. The other Operatives mirrored Isaac's devastated facial expression as they too emerged, holding a disarmed Xzjytheous at blaster point along with Anthony, who followed behind the rest of the group, guarded by Colin and Ethan.

'Where's the Rhinonoid?' asked Nathan, looking past their prisoner to Corey.

There was nothing Corey could say or do now to make this right.

'We need to get inside' he said quietly, finally swallowing his pride.

'What?' asked Isaac, who was now preparing to rip into Corey once again.

'I need help to get him inside' replied Corey more specifically, as he looked down at Tino, disarmed entirely by the death stares that the group of Operatives were shooting at him for stranding them.

Xzjytheous hissed in amusement at the level of disarray that the group was in. All he needed to do was wait for the right moment to flee his captors.

'It's almost daytime' announced Ethan, looking up at the sky and recalling the group's discussion back onboard the shuttle.

Colin stepped forward to offer his assistance to Corey as the others watched on.

'Keep the prisoners covered' Isaac instructed, turning to Nathan as he followed Colin across the rocks to also offer his help.

Once they got Tino safely inside the cave and lay him down on the floor. Isaac turned to Corey for an explanation.

'This is the suit that sent out the distress signal' Corey said.

'Is he alive?' asked Isaac, leaning down over Tino.

'Surprisingly, yes' replied Corey as Isaac did his own checks, removing a glove to feel for the boy's pulse and check if he was breathing.

'Look at the state of the suit' Colin pointed out, acknowledging the smashed badges, huge, silver scuffs and rows of holes where it appeared that...something...had pierced the armour; multiple times.

There also appeared to be something broad, long and white embedded, deep in the metal. Isaac knelt down and grasped at it, tugging with all of his strength and moving it from side to side to try and loosen it, so that it could be removed. When it finally came out, leaving a large hole in the metal, Isaac held the object up, for everyone to see. It was a huge serrated tooth. Fortunately, it didn't appear to have any blood on it, which meant that the armour had done its job.

Looking out at the huge waves crashing and exploding over the rocks and shuttle wreckage, they realised that the tide would soon sweep into the cave and there was no telling what monstrous creatures of the deep were out there, beyond those walls.

'Do we know who he is? Is he an Operative?' asked Nathan, helping to move Tino deeper into the cave.

'I don't know' replied Corey, rubbing at his tired eyes.

'We have a long climb yet. You destroyed the ship and lost the Rhinonoid. The only way we are getting out of here now is if we repair another ship. We saw a few crashed about half way up the mountain as we were making our way back. Maybe we can repair one of those' said Isaac, not showing any sympathy towards Corey for his tiredness.

Corey knew that he was responsible for stranding them all there but the only choices he'd had were bad ones so he did what he thought was best, much like he did on Crystalosis, although, he had come to seriously regret that decision. He was done arguing though.

If they were going to survive this and leave the planet safely with their prisoners, they really did need to come together as a team, not as one Operative ordering the others around or creating segregation. Although it seemed like that's what Isaac was doing to him right now, singling him out, there was a job that needed to be done and Corey knew Isaac, he would come around eventually, he hoped.

As the group finally reached the crashed wreckage of The Knightfall, Isaac and Colin climbed inside through the smashed cockpit window to assess the damage while the others waited outside with Xzjytheous, Anthony and Tino.

Ethan and Corey began retrieving the variety of unique weapons that littered the cave floor, having been thrown from the ship along with Tino when it had crash-landed.

Corey retrieved a plasma blaster rifle with a long bayonet fitted on the end of it and studied it, admiringly, in his hands, unaware of Xzjytheous watching on. The Reptilian was fascinated that Corey had picked up the weapon that had committed more dark deeds than any other that surrounded them.

Although he was a prisoner, Xzjytheous was badly wounded from falling from The Knightfall when he had fought Tino and all members of the Interstellar Scouts, whatever their rank, had a duty to care for all creatures in need, regardless of what they had done. Upholding these morals, Nathan set to work on cleaning and patching up the Reptilian's wounds with the medical supplies they had brought from the Kestrel Shuttle's wreckage.

Isaac paused as he and Colin crossed the cockpit, noticing the wall mounts that still had a couple of trophy weapons sat upon them. He looked down at the small hand blaster he had taken from Xzjytheous and returned it to one of the smaller mounts before moving on.

'It's admirable...What you did back there' Isaac said, turning to Colin inside The Knightfall's cargo-hold. 'Helping Corey to get that kid to safety, regardless of what he has put us through' he continued.

'Well. We're all in the I.S.S. We do our best to help others...Even if our best isn't enough' replied Colin as they both crouched down around the closed hatch that led down to the ship's deployment bay.

Isaac knew Colin was very mature for his age and, although there was no doubt that Colin was very upset, he was handling Corey's behaviour really well. Maybe Corey had been doing his best but his fear was just too much for him to control. Isaac wasn't prepared to forgive him yet though, not after what happened between them on the Rhinonoid and the shuttle flight to Zonju. He was sure he would eventually but it would take time and Corey would need to change his attitude.

Although it was Colin that was with Isaac, the words he spoke resonated with him as they had been very much in the style of Oli's leadership. As Colin tried to heave the hatch open, Isaac paused and placed his hand on Colin's shoulder.

'Oli would have been so proud of you' he said, trying to do for Colin as Nathan had done for him on their way to save Tamatha and the prisoners. Colin looked up at him smiling in an attempt to hide his real feelings.

'I'm...I'm sorry for getting angry and firing the Rhinonoid's canon on Crystalosis...I just really wanted to go back for him. He's the only family I've had since I left Earth' explained Colin.

'Hey, don't worry about it. Honestly, given the chance, I would have gone back for Oli myself. We just ran out of time. I'm sorry too, that I was forced to disable the blaster canon...I didn't want to hurt you any more than you already were...I had to do it for your own good and, truthfully, I think Corey had the same intentions... really, REALLY deep down, he just went about it all wrong' replied Isaac, regrettably.

'I know' said Colin, looking back down to hide his quickly-saddening face.

'And, although it might not feel like it at the moment, you do have family in all of us...even Corey' Isaac continued, still keeping his consoling hand on Colin's shoulder.

Slightly teary eyed, Colin smiled back up at Isaac and then returned to working on the hatch as Isaac joined him. The hatch's bulky metal hinge screeched as they pulled it open.

'Watch your step' warned Isaac as Colin lowered himself down, through the round open hatch and onto the ladder which led down into the pitch-black deployment bay.

'I can't see a thing' said Isaac as they both reached the bottom of the ladder and looked around. Several tiny, red lights began to appear, dotted all around the floor and the mechanical sound of turrets pivoting and locking into position followed shortly after.

'CONTACT! GET DOWN!' yelled Isaac, grabbing Colin and throwing him to the floor before quickly drawing his blaster from its holster.

In that moment, the room was illuminated with a bright light that streamed upwards towards a single point from each of the weapons. Every single turret simultaneously powered down and went limp as a glowing ball of bright, white energy, formed by the power that had been drained from them, moved slowly towards Isaac and Colin, drifting across the deployment bay as Isaac looked up at it. He slowly climbed back to his feet helping Colin up behind him but remained ready to throw him aside, for protection, at a moment's notice.

'What is it?' asked Colin, squinting his eyes from the brightness.

Isaac shook his head, clueless. As it drifted through the air, shards of black crystals could be seen littering the floor of the deployment bay amongst the small turrets.

The bright ball of light stopped in front of them and, as Isaac leaned in to examine it more closely, an outstretched hand appeared beneath it. Immediately after, the light illuminated another hand, clutching the twisted black crystal staff in it, that they had been attacked with earlier. Isaac tightened his grip on his blaster and poised himself for attack, backing Colin away.

Finally, the elderly face of the man in the gold I.S.S. armoured suit, who had attacked them with the Beconium crystals, was revealed. Isaac took two quick strides backwards, training his blaster on the old man as Colin copied.

'WHO ARE YOU!?' shouted Isaac.

'My name is Gala-Thius. I'm here to apologise. And to thank you' the man replied.

Isaac recognised the name immediately. He had heard many stories of Captain Thius from his time as an I.S.S. Troop Leader, they all had except for Colin and Ethan. For the time being though, Isaac chose to remain quiet about it.

'Thank us? For what?' asked Colin.

There was a long pause. 'Come. Let's step outside' said Gala-Thius, moving towards the ladder.

'I'm the one in command here' said Isaac, a serious look on his face as he moved in front of the old man to block his path, his blaster still trained on him, charging up as it let out a high pitched ringing sound and vibrated in his grasp.

Gala-Thius stopped, not through intimidation of the Operative's ferocity but out of respect and understanding for the boy who stood in front of him, trying to control the situation.

'Up the ladder. Move.' Isaac ordered as he allowed the old man to walk past. 'Colin, you go up ahead of him' he continued.

Colin moved past Gala-Thius and climbed up the ladder, through the hatch in the ceiling. Gala-Thius then, effortlessly, levitated up off the ground and rose through the hatch as the two Operatives watched on in disbelief; following his ascension with their blasters. The man then landed softly on the floor of the cargo-hold as Isaac climbed up the ladder behind him.

The three of them carefully climbed back out through the cockpit window and, as soon as he saw his friend, Anthony let out a shriek of sheer joy and excitement and ran over to hug the old man. Gala-Thius smiled as he placed a reassuring hand on Anthony's back.

'You almost killed us back in that cave' Isaac told the old man, a hint of restrained anger in his voice as he returned his blaster to its holster. The pieces were falling more into place for Isaac now, based on the man's reaction to Gala-Thius, surely that made him Captain Tony, the one who went insane while they were out on a mission together.

'I apologise for that' replied Gala-Thius, trying to peel Anthony away from himself.

'My intentions were merely to delay you as I fled. The crystals can become...volatile, if fractured. I was careless in my haste' he explained.

'You survived!?' seethed Xzjytheous.

'If you are going to steal and then discard an Interstellar Scouts suit, Reptilian, be sure to destroy it afterwards' Gala-Thius replied. 'The scars will remain but the interior tissue damaged was repaired immediately by the internal cy-bionics' he continued. The Operatives looked to one another, surprised at how much more technical the Troop Leader suit was than their emerald ones.

Xzjytheous, hissed with disappointment in his failure.

'You're all weary. You need rest and sustenance' announced Gala-Thius, turning to the Operatives. 'We haven't got any food. Most of our supplies were onboard the Rhinonoid' replied Colin.

'FISH!' Anthony shouted excitedly at the top of his booming voice, which echoed all around the cave as he listened in on the conversation. The Operatives turned to look at the ragged, smelly man, frowning at him.

'Do you want fish?' asked Gala-Thius as he looked Anthony in his single working eye as if speaking to a young child or an excited pet.

'FISH! FISH!' shouted Anthony, bouncing excitedly at the knees.

'Ok, you go and get us some fish then' replied Gala-Thius.

Anthony turned to the other Operatives, grinning from ear to ear with excitement, his teeth black and rotting. Feeling extremely uneasy, the Operatives forced a slight smile in response as the man continued to stare them out.

'Anthony? Fish' Gala-Thius reminded him.

'FISH!' Anthony bellowed repeatedly, his voice echoing once again as he turned and excitedly gallivanted into the cave and tunnel systems, still audible long after he was out of sight.

'It's not looking too damaged in there. Some missing floor panels, a bit of damage to the wiring beneath them and the deployment bay hatch is open in the ship's underbelly which might have some debris wedged into it but Corey, Colin and I will take a look at that with Gala-Thius and the prisoner. Nathan, can you find out what repairs need to be made to the ship's navigation and flight systems?' said Isaac as he turned to the group of Operatives.

'What about me?' asked Ethan.

'Check the structural integrity of the ship's hull. Make sure there are no holes torn in the roof...and keep an eye on him' instructed

Isaac, looking down at Tino who was still unresponsive on the medical mobilisation platform from the shuttle that Oli had been placed on earlier.

Ethan nodded in response and then stepped onto a nearby rock to help him climb onto the side of the ship.

'Move, stay in front' ordered Isaac, drawing his blaster on Xzjytheous while the others followed suit. Gala-Thius joined them, accompanied by the glowing ball of white light to illuminate the deployment bay as Xzjytheous approached the wreckage, carefully stepping through the smashed glass of the window and into the cockpit.

The shards of glass slid across the floor beneath his clawed foot and he slipped, falling to the floor. The Operatives gathered around, training their blasters more aggressively on him in response to the sudden movement. Xzjytheous slowly returned to his feet. Although he made it look like an accidental fall, he had done it deliberately, affording him the opportunity to discretely conceal a shard of broken glass in a hidden knife sheath wrapped around his leg under his long, black coat and accessed through a hole torn in his flightsuit.

'Keep him covered' instructed Isaac as they proceeded into the ship.

Nathan stepped through the window and dropped down into the cockpit, almost with enthusiasm despite his tiredness. He brushed away the tiny pieces of shattered glass from the pilot's seat and sat down. Xzjytheous was much larger than him so he was forced to move the seat much closer to the console to be able to operate the controls.

'Looks like there's a fuel leak in the rooftop cells' announced Nathan as a red warning light began blinking in front of him. 'Can you see anything up there Ethan?' he asked through his collar's built-in microphone.

'There's a massive rupture down the Starboard side' replied Ethan as he followed the long, jagged tear caused by scraping against the opening to the cave on collision, moving towards the back of the ship.

'How massive?' asked Nathan, praying for an easy fix.

'It's big enough to need some serious repairs. We will need some metal plating to patch it up. Those pieces of metal that we found inside the chamber with the Reptilian should do it' Ethan responded.

'It's daytime now and that cave is completely exposed to the outside from above. We'll make any other necessary repairs for now and finish up with that at the end. The days aren't too long on Zonju so we should be good' said Nathan as he checked the ship's other systems. 'Are you seeing anything else up there?' he asked.

'No, everything else seems intact' replied Ethan, examining the remainder of the ship's hull.

'Do you have anything to say to Colin at all? Anything you would like to say to us?' Corey asked Xzjytheous as the group gathered around the hatch that led down to the deployment bay.

'Corey' snapped Isaac, reminding him once again of Colin's presence.

Corey backed down and the group fell silent once again as they descended down the ladder.

'Nathan, can you divert some of the ship's power down to the deployment bay and run a recalibration on the auto-turrets down here?' requested Isaac.

'Affirmative, standby' replied Nathan's voice through the speaker in Isaac's collar.

'We need to re-activate these' announced Isaac, turning to Gala-Thius who held out his hand and redistributed the ball of energy back into the turrets on the floor.

The room turned pitch black, except for the glow of their suits, with the absence of their light source and Xzjytheous seized his opportunity. The Operatives heard the repeated slashing sounds of something striking their cy-bionic suits as sparks flashed in the air, lighting up the room for a fleeting moment before the darkness swallowed it up once more.

Although the Operatives couldn't see without their helmets on, Xzjytheous was slashing at them aggressively through the darkness with his improvised knife from the cockpit, each slash failing to be critical, striking against their cy-bionic exoskeletons as they buried their heads in their arms for protection.

Gala-Thius intercepted Xzjytheous and used his staff to repel the attacker away from the group. There was a sudden sound of smashing glass as Nathan re-routed the power and the deployment bay lights illuminated the room.

Xzjytheous was now on the floor with Gala-Thius standing over him. There was a quiet, humming sound building up, moving across the room from the control panel. On the floor beneath it was a scattering of broken, shattered glass shards. Isaac noticed a flicker of sparks as they spurted from the control panel next to the controls on the wall, having been struck.

'Back up the hatch, now' ordered Gala-Thius urgently.

The Operatives, still in shock from the fierce attack and amazed that they were all still alive, raced for the ladder while Gala-Thius kept Xzjytheous from pursuing them. Both Corey and Isaac successfully scrambled up the ladder and out of the hatch but, as bolts of fiercely-surging electricity darted around the deployment bay, Colin could feel himself losing control of his muscles, which turned numb, as the voltage exceeded the levels that his suit could withstand while only half way up the ladder.

The rubberised feet of the ladder were designed to prevent it from conducting the electricity but the voltage was surging so high now that it jumped past the rubberised feet and straight to the frame of the ladder.

Colin froze in place and his legs gave way beneath him. As he fell, a powerful bolt of electricity struck the chest of his armoured suit and he slammed, hard, against one of the electrified walls before another bolt hit him, slamming him back down into the floor of the electrified deployment bay.

'COLIN!' shouted Isaac.

The young Operative had seconds before his cy-bionic suit would give up under the dangerously high voltage levels.

Before the Assistant Patrol Leader could do anything and without giving it a second thought, Corey dropped down through the hole as a fierce flurry of sparks snapped around his boots. He grabbed Colin and threw him over his shoulder in an impressive display of strength. Corey then began to climb the ladder once more while feeling all of the effects of the ever-increasing electrical current surging through his suit, digging deep with determination and finding the resolve to resist them. Isaac reached down and helped to pull them both up.

Seeing that all three Operatives were clear of the deployment bay, Gala-Thius vanished on the spot and instantly reappeared next to them. They slammed the hatch shut and locked it as Xzjytheous leapt right at them with stunning power. They were only just able to heave the tremendously heavy door over the hole before the enraged Reptilian reached it.

'How did you do that?' asked Colin, amazed by Gala-Thius' abilities as Xzjytheous now began pounding furiously and with brute force against the hatch, which Isaac and Corey used all of their strength on, locking it as tight as possible.

As the three Operatives staggered backwards, looking down at the silver slashes all over their armoured suits, Isaac overruled Colin's question as he shouted through to the cockpit. 'Re-engage the auto-turrets Nathan' he instructed, trembling and slightly out of breath.

There was the audible sound of a volley of blaster bolts striking the hatch and then a loud thud as Xzjytheous crashed to the floor of the deployment bay.

'Keep him covered while he works on dislodging the debris. He can't escape the mountain because of the light outside but I want to make sure he doesn't make matters worse for us. If he doesn't work, give him an incentive' instructed Isaac as they moved back into the cockpit and stepped back out through the window.

'How are we looking?' asked Isaac as he approached Ethan.

'He's still unconscious and there's a rupture in the Starboard fuel tank but we have a plan for that. We can't do anything about it until it turns dark again though' replied Ethan.

'Meanwhile, you should get some rest until Anthony returns with some food' said Gala-Thius.

'Who's going to take the first watch?' asked Colin.

'I'll do it' replied Corey almost immediately. Isaac turned to look at him, studied him for a moment, and then nodded in silent agreement.

'Is the ship's heating operational?' asked Colin, turning to Nathan who remained at the ship's console.

'Yep' replied Nathan as he adjusted some of the settings.

At last, things were starting to go their way. They were finally able to get some rest, soon they would have food and they now had warmth as well. Thankful for small mercies, they stepped back inside the ship with Isaac and Corey carrying Tino and opened a door in the back wall, having walked beyond the round hatch in the cargo-hold and stepped through to the sleeping quarters. It wasn't the most comfortable of rooms and they would have to sleep on the floor but they didn't care.

'So...where do we go from here?' asked Corey as he observed the almost-hypnotic, floating, spiralling Beconium in the containment field of the grenade customisation generator in the cargo-hold.

'I'm sure everyone will forgive you. Isaac just has a lot to deal with and none of us have been in a situation as bad as this before' replied Nathan's voice.

'I know...but I meant the Reptilian. We have a ruthless, terrifying beast in the deployment bay of his own ship...as our prisoner. He would know exactly how to sabotage the ship in order to escape and, even if he didn't, we're on our own now, we have nobody to turn him over to' Corey went on. He was listing a whole array of dangers they were faced with but chose, for now at least, to keep his thoughts of a solution to himself as the others surely wouldn't approve.

'Get some sleep for a few hours if you want' sighed Corey as he moved back into the cockpit and joined Nathan, brushing the shattered glass off one of the other seats and placing his blaster on top of the console.

As a pilot, Nathan was used to sleeping in the pilot's seat rather than the floor or sleeping platforms while on missions so he slid the seat back away from the console to avoid accidentally hitting the controls while asleep and reclined it into an almost-lying-down position. Almost immediately, with his thoughts on Tamatha, the terrified family and the other rescued prisoners, hoping that they make it to safety, Nathan fell fast asleep.

Corey activated a screen on the console and watched Xzjytheous working in the deployment bay to ensure he wasn't engineering a means of escape or of overpowering them.

Several hours went by as Corey sat, staring at the screen, feeling an anger building up inside him as he contemplated everything that they had been through at the hands of the Reptilian.

Letting out a heavy sigh through his nose, his eyes shifted from the screen to his blaster and back to the screen again. After a few minutes of fighting the urge to reach for his blaster, he gave in and picked it up. Grabbing it by the barrel, he smacked the handle into the palm of his hand repeatedly, continuing to watch the prisoner on the screen. Agitated he leaned back and forth pushing against the back of his seat as he started to bang the back of his head against the headrest as if trying to shake the troubling thoughts from his mind.

Despite being an I.S.S. Operative, Corey couldn't deny that he was just a scared child beneath that emerald suit. He had been the same on Crystalosis when trying to escape the Deathstalker Squadron but he was powerless to do anything back then. He had been able to hide his fear behind his anger, so much so that he was even starting to fool himself into thinking he was genuinely angry with everything and everyone, consumed by the front he had been putting on. He wasn't powerless to face his fear this time though.

Corey threw himself to his feet and, with his blaster clutched tight in his hand, he strode right past Nathan, who remained fast asleep in his seat. He approached one of the weapon customisation consoles that had the separate components of a grenade hovering above one another in the machine's projected containment field. Cycling through the different options of shells, contents, attachments and triggers, the machine generated the type of grenade he wanted. The upper and lower halves of the casing closed together, sealing the required contents inside and Nathan retrieved the floating weapon from the containment field. Clutching it tightly in his hand, he continued on, further into the cargo-hold.

Reaching down to open the hatch, Corey suddenly paused as if he had heard something calling out to him. He looked back over his shoulder at the various weapons mounted on the wall in the cockpit.

With the grenade still in his hand, he slotted his blaster into its holster and picked up the weighted plasma blaster rifle, with the bayonet currently retracted beneath the barrel, the same weapon that had intrigued him when they first reached the wreckage.

He slung the weapon's attached strap over his shoulder and unlocked the hatch; pulling the heavy, round door open. With the electrical current since powered down by Nathan in the cockpit during the repairs, Corey jumped down through the hole in the floor, just as he had done earlier to rescue Colin. As he landed, knees bent, he straightened up and directed the blaster rifle at the Reptilian that stared back at him.

There was a moment of contemplation which Corey read in the prisoner's eyes. Suddenly, Xzjytheous leapt through the air, straight at the open hatch with the same power he had done before. The auto-turrets all fired simultaneously but the Reptilian moved with such speed that every blast missed him.

Corey had anticipated this scenario though and rather than depending on the turrets doing what they had been programmed to do by Nathan, he threw the grenade at the ceiling, near the edge of the door as he had been trained to do.

A powerful blast in the form of a bright, blue ring erupted from the casing and hit Xzjytheous in the torso, knocking him away from the hatch. The energy ring also generated an electro-magnetic field which caused the door to slam shut above them as the Reptilian fell back to the floor. Corey slowly trained the plasma blaster rifle back on the prisoner as the loud ringing sound indicated it charging up.

'We need to talk' he said, deploying the bayonet with a loud, sharp ring.

CHAPTER 20
THE GRAVEYARD OF FULGON

As she continued to explore the Rhinonoid, Parathax picked up a peculiar, beige stone that lay on one of the workbenches. Holding it up to the light, it glinted from within the tiny, narrow funnels that ran into the stone.

Parathax knew that what she held in her hand was a piece of fulgurite, a rare phenomenon that occurs when sand is heated to temperatures even hotter than a sun by a lightning strike. This particular piece of fulgurite, however, wasn't so innocent. It was a sample that had been acquired by the I.S.S. mere days ago following the Deathstalker Squadron's strike on a peaceful, inhabited world which had resulted in the total encrustation of the entire planet, along with all that lived upon it.

Parathax set to work on forging a weapon of immense power and volatility from the resources around the room, filing down and embedding the now-glinting piece of fulgurite into the top of the weapon's hilt, the funnels that ran through it now much more visible.

The filing and sanding of the fulgurite had created a molecular excitation within the stone and, gradually an electric-purple glow began to radiate from within the funnels. In order for the weapon to be truly feared more than any other, Parathax would need to hyper-charge the fulgurite with radiation and remnant plasma of the Deathstalker blaster bolts the only place she could, the graveyard of the newly-renamed planet, Fulgon.

Beneath the furious lightning storms and falling acid rain, on the fulgurite-encrusted surface of Fulgon, teams of researchers and scientists from all across the galaxy had descended on the world after rescue attempts had responded, far too late, to distress signals sent out during the Deathstalker Squadron's strike. The teams were curious as to what could have possibly transformed the atmosphere, melted and encrusted an entire planet so completely in such a short space of time. There had been no anomalies created by the sun before it had been permanently blocked out by the darkness of the clouds and, based on the dramatic and horrifying positions that the humanoid and airborne animal husks were found in, it was clear that the transition had been very sudden.

Many of the beings that had lived on the world appeared to have been fleeing with a look of terror as teardrops of the falling acid now ran down their encrusted faces. Some were still embracing one another, just as they had done as they had awaited their imminent fate.

A small group of scientists and researchers, dressed in white radiation suits to shield them against the hostile environment and wearing various pieces of technology including a Geiger counter to measure the levels of radiation coming from the terrain and the victims of the strike, were carefully using intricate tools to gather samples for testing and analysis. When it came to gathering a biological sample from one of the victims, they wanted to obtain the specimen while continuing to show respect to them but the tools they were currently using such as laser scalpels etc. could damage the body of the victim so one of the scientists broke away from the team to gather the necessary equipment from their landing zone, beyond a raised area of terrain that had bulged up with trapped, hot air when the Deathstalker strike took place.

Unbeknownst to any of them at first, the Geiger counters that the scientists and researchers were wearing were beginning to show increasing levels of radiation beyond that which was already present in the fulgurite. As the lone scientist disappeared behind the rise, he heard the sound that he and surely everyone on the planet feared. His Geiger counter spiked, crackling at first until a sudden screech from it made him instinctively look up.

A volley of huge, scarlet blaster bolts rained down from above the dense clouds which now also had an ominous red glow to them. The blaster bolts exploded with sheer ferocity as they struck the shuttles at the landing zone. The scientist threw himself to the ground to avoid the debris from the mass explosion.

As the sound of chunks of metal hitting the ground quickly gave way to the flaring and crackling of flames from their wreckages, the scientist raised his head inside his helmet and looked up. Beyond the scuffs and scratches that now covered the visor, he could see a large vehicle descending from the clouds. It had eight legs with thrusters in each of the feet and striking, curved, scarlet laser disks and spikes blazed from the hull.

The man watched as the Rhinonoid slowly descended towards the ground until it settled amongst the wreckage. Squinting, the scientist edged closer, leaning in towards the inferno as a slow but loud, rhythmic stamping shook the ground beneath his feet, growing louder and louder. Suddenly, a fierce volley of debris shot out from the flames, straight at him. The Rhinonoid was advancing through the destroyed landing zone with its scarlet laser disks and horns still active meaning anything that they touched would be cast out as a fierce projectile.

The stamping sound stopped and, as the scientist slowly lowered his arm away from his helmet, having staggered backwards several paces, he saw a black, cloaked shape standing amongst the flames. Seemingly undeterred by the fire, the figure continued to slowly advance as bolts of energy jolted up from the funnels in the new terrain, sometimes exploding through the fulgurite where it was thin, creating clouds of dust. The energy appeared to be getting drawn into an object that was clutched in the dark figure's hand.

With the other members of the various research teams rushing to the landing zone to investigate the unprovoked and violent attack, they were quickly stopped in their tracks as Parathax emerged from behind the rise clutching a sword, the scientist walking before her as her prisoner. Bolts of electric-purple energy continued to jolt out of the ground and into the hilt beneath the shiny, silver blade of Parathax's sword.

After the horrors of the recent Deathstalker strikes across the galaxy, some taking place on their home worlds such as Polarious, each and every one of the scientists and researchers had an idea of who was standing in front of them and what she was capable of... they were all wrong.

With Parathax slowly raising her sword and holding it out at the unarmed men and women, each of them grew pale as the blood drained from their faces in terror. Slowly backing away, they begged Parathax for mercy as she slowly continued her advances, toying with them.

Suddenly, Parathax stopped. Everything fell still. Even the wind that had whistled through the funnels in the surrounding fulgurite had ceased as the entire world held its breath. The sword's blade, made up of two separate narrow blades, separated and shot off the hilt like a missile, embedding itself in the chest of one of the humanoid husks and revealing a long, extended, metal spear in its place.

Yelling in terror to one another, the scientists and researchers attempted to flee but, one by one, Parathax struck at them with her spear, yelling with a mixture of passion and fury, a powerful surge of energy launching each victim a hundred feet through the air. With every strike the piece of fulgurite in the hilt grew more volatile and unpredictable, causing plasma to jolt out with unprecedented ferocity as it exploded chunks of the previously-victimised husks away, in clouds of dust.

Parathax strode forward in pursuit of the fleeing scientists and researchers, driven with malicious intent. As she finished striking down the group, the sound of static could be heard from behind a large rock. Parathax held her spear high into the air to hyper-charge it further, explosions erupting from the fulgurite all around her until the rock that the last scientist, the one she had originally taken prisoner, was hiding behind, was blasted away.

Weak at the knees, the scientist scrambled to his feet. He was trying desperately to transmit a distress signal to any Interstellar Scout forces in the area but the only reply that came back was static.

'You...you murdered these people...An entire world' the scientist stammered as he stumbled backwards.

He looked down at his communicator to check the channels for any response from the I.S.S. but still nothing came. Parathax continued to move towards him, fuelled by his obvious fear.

‘Along with so many others’ replied Parathax, with an evil grin as she looked deep into the man’s eyes.

The scientist swallowed hard and got his fear under control. Understanding and accepting that he was about to share the same fate as Parathax's many other victims, he closed his eyes and awaited the inevitable.

Moments later, the surge of plasma from the piece of fulgurite embedded in the hilt, blasted him through the air with explosive power. Parathax unleashed her full power through the black energy that enshrouded her, levelling the entire area, terrain and husks alike.

The resulting electric-purple plasma energy that had been released was drawn into the piece of fulgurite in the hilt of her weapon from every direction, giving the glinting funnels in the stone a blinding glow. She then tore the blade of her sword from the husk with the black energy that spiralled around it, placed it back over the spearhead and locked the two halves of the blade back together again as she returned to the Rhinonoid.

CHAPTER 21
BECON FORTIFIED

The Beconium Storms of Becon raged furiously outside as the Rhinonoid began its descent, piloting itself through the extreme turbulence, in search of a suitable landing zone. Parathax, clad in her stolen Beconium-coated cy-bionics, now stood in the deployment bay at the top of the ramp, awaiting the Rhinonoid's landing and the ramp's descent.

The sound of the Rhinonoid's sub-thrusters began to roar beneath her as the huge tank slowly lowered itself down, towards the planet's surface. Finally the feet of the tank sank into the radioactive sand, cutting power to its sub-thrusters as its body settled over its legs. Moments later, the deployment bay ramp began to descend. Parathax didn't wait for the ramp to rest at the bottom, striding down during its descent as soon as the barricade hatch had risen up enough.

The bright, scarlet blaze of the horns and spikes, emitted from the Rhinonoid, could be seen from a great distance, even amongst the raging storm. Parathax stepped off the ramp and moved across the sandy surface of the planet without leaving a footprint. She moved around to the side of the Rhinonoid to inspect the damage to the hull from smashing Oli through the wall.

Beconium, that had been caught up in the wind, drifted into the room containing the customised armoured suits, sweeping across the floor and gathering up against the far wall.

Parathax had already had two encounters with the Interstellar Scouts and narrowly missed a third in the chamber on Zonju. There was no doubt that they were now coming for her. If she had received the distress signal from Crystalosis, it was highly likely that others had too. Before she could advance her conquest with the Deathstalker Squadron and eradicate the I.S.S. to take her revenge on Sol, their Founder, she would first need to make her stand here, on Becon.

Stepping forward, to the foot of the enormous, towering dunes, she stretched out her arms above her head and then threw them down, with force, letting out a deafening, primal howl as streams of black energy exploded out of the blackness that enshrouded her, shooting off in all directions. All around her, huge structures erupted from the ground. Towers, spires and walls exploded from the ground, forming an immense, imposing fortress, shaped by the Beconium and contained by the black streams of energy that swirled around and wove through them.

Parathax returned to the room in the Rhinonoid where Oli kept his customised suits and studied the long, illuminated, scarlet 'S' shape that ran diagonally across the floor of the room as she moved over it. She moved to the far end of the room where the door led to the Quarantine Wing. She looked down and charged up a powerful blast of black energy which she then blasted down at the end of the 'S' on the floor. The end of the illuminated path slammed down, revealing itself to be a disguised ramp that led down to another level in the Rhinonoid.

The illuminated, white walls of the room containing Oli's custom suits revealed a glowing, scarlet panel between each of the suits. The holographic panels appeared to display schematics for the suits' capabilities along with diagrams of experimental modifications and enhancements for each suit.

Parathax descended the illuminated, scarlet walkway into the hidden room. It was very dark at first but, as she crossed the room, various lights began to turn on above the workbenches that were scattered around in response to her armoured components triggering the sensors. At the far end of the room, standing in an empty space in the wall and illuminated by a series of lights built into the cavity, was a shiny, sapphire I.S.S. Initiate cy-bionic exoskeleton.

The suit was shorter than Parathax thought it would be and it appeared to be badly damaged with scratches, scuffs, burn marks and the calf on one of the legs was dented out of shape; distorting the light. It was also filled with holes that had been pierced in it, as if the leg part of the armour had once been crushed in the jaws of a fierce predator.

Conjuring one of her Polarian Beconi', Parathax set to work on enhancing the abomination's capabilities, utilising the stolen Interstellar Scout technology so that they could be experimented on further and the modifications could then be applied to her entire strike force.

Having achieved her fiercest adaption of her Polarian Beconi' yet, modified a variety of Oli's customised suits to serve her in the coming battle and used a wide selection of Beconium-contaminated weapons and pieces of gold cy-bionic armour from the Quarantine Wing to create a suit of her own, more enhanced than any used by the I.S.S, Parathax returned to the Rhinonoid's cockpit and activated its Expansion Matrix.

The various hatches opened up all around the tank and, just as they had on Zonju, roads, passageways, tunnels and walls, constructed entirely of metal and circuitry, extended from it and began intuitively creating an impenetrable layer of armour around every Beconium structure both outside the fortress and the intricately-constructed insides of it as well.

An enormous, imposing shadow began to emerge from the Beconium storm that raged outside, dwarfing everything below and swallowing it up in darkness as it cut through the shroud, drawing in explosive bolts of lightning from all around as it descended. As it moved over the fortress, the tank's expansions reached high up into the sky and began to encase it in the same armoured plating that covered the Rhinonoid and the fortress, forming a formidably large and threatening star cruiser, Parathax's infamous flagship, The Stealthy Intoxicator.

During her previous assaults, the cruiser had been constructed entirely of Beconium and encased in salvaged machinery from shipyards, space stations and the surface of Polarious 5. Much of it had been scavenged in the wake of Xzjytheous' rampage across the galaxy as he had sought to avenge his family's deaths. The entire cruiser had been held together and animated by the black, twisted energy that formed Parathax's body but, now that Parathax also had the Rhinonoid, she now had additional armour, weapons, crew and soldiers to man her cruiser and, soon, her fleet.

The Rhinonoid's thrusters fired up once more and the tank began to rise up into the air, detaching from its extensions. Its ascension was slow and calculated as Parathax stood in the cockpit, looking out over her stronghold as she guided the tank towards the cruiser above. Carefully, the Rhinonoid moved into the hanger bay and docked inside.

Parathax moved down the deployment bay ramp and into the hanger bay where large, fuzzy shapes, made up entirely of Beconium with black energy spiralling through and around them, formed ships, aerial fighters and shuttles. They were gradually encased in armour plating which continued to spread throughout The Stealthy Intoxicator like a virus, building more intricate structures and electrical systems throughout the cruiser, renewing it entirely.

As Parathax drifted down the long, well-lit corridors towards the bridge, strings of black energy twisted around everything that had been built. She passed doorway after doorway, hanger bay after hanger bay, stairwell after stairwell and elevation platform after elevation platform which led to the many, many upper and lower decks.

On reaching the bridge, humanoid shapes formed of Beconium moved around the enormous room, going about their various tasks as they too became encased in silver armoured plating from the Rhinonoid. Parathax drifted right by them, towards the ballistic glass observation deck at the front, also generated by the Expansion Matrix.

'Prepare to launch for Polarious Five' spoke the spectral voice as a crew member stepped up beside her. A launch alarm sounded throughout The Stealthy Intoxicator and pilots emerged from rooms on every deck of the ship. Linguistic Emulators meant that, even though none of the humanoids could physically speak themselves, they had an alternative method of communication.

Looking out from the window of the observation deck, Parathax observed thousands of her ships launching from the cruiser's many hanger bays and flying out, beyond the planet's atmosphere, to start gathering resources from Polarious 5 for her to build more Polarian Beconi'. She would await her enemy's vain onslaught and then begin with the dead of Becon as they fell.

CHAPTER 22
WRESTLING WITH DEMONS

Corey felt like he was merely watching himself from across the room, powerless to intervene. As a member of the Interstellar Scouts he too had a duty, a responsibility, to care for all living creatures and he knew it but, in this moment, while reason tried to restrain him, all he could do was grow more angry and shout louder to block it out.

'I was interrupted earlier but we're alone now. So, I'll ask again. Do you have anything to say? Do you feel any remorse? Any guilt?' he asked, slowly advancing a couple of paces closer, towards the Reptilian, tightening his grip on the plasma blaster rifle tighter still, his hands trembling with rage as he felt himself succumbing to his emotions against his better judgement. Corey wrestled with himself to pull the weapon away as he awaited Xzjytheous' response.

He could now see for himself, what the rest of the Patrol had seen from him. While Nathan had tended to the Reptilian's wounds to help it, Corey had drawn a weapon on the same creature and was threatening to kill it in anger. Even Isaac had done this but had then been able to remove himself from the situation in a much shorter amount of time than Corey was proving himself able to do.

Although distracted by his internal struggle and while Xzjytheous continued to remain silent, Corey briefly noticed the Reptilian's eyes flick to the side.

In his anger, he hadn't noticed the round hatch slowly, silently, opening in the ceiling. He frowned as he turned to look over his shoulder to find two Polarian Beconi' hovering, menacingly, behind him. Before Corey could react and with a powerful kick, Xzjytheous knocked the blaster rifle right out of Corey's hands; breaking the strap that hung on his shoulder. Both the weapon and Corey were sent tumbling, across the floor, to the other side of the deployment bay.

Having been stunned by the attack, Corey quickly snapped out of it, scrambled across the floor to retrieve the blaster rifle and barrel rolled to the side, regaining his feet and deploying his respirator mask over his nose and mouth as the two hunters separated their dishes, flooding the entire room with toxic clouds of Beconium.

Amongst the pandemonium, Corey strained to see through the fog, firing a volley of blaster bolts in the Reptilian's direction but Xzjytheous was too fast. The escaping creature scrambled up the ladder and slammed the hatch shut behind him, locking it, before fleeing The Knightfall.

In his hasty retreat, Xzjytheous awoke Nathan who sat bolt upright and fired multiple shots at the fleeing prisoner, all of which missed.

'Corey?' asked Nathan, looking about himself as he heard a muffled sound nearby. Having looked down at the screen that Corey had left on, showing the deployment bay, he rushed over to the hatch and began unlocking it as fast as he could, heaving it open.

The Beconium smog came gushing up through the hole in the floor and began flooding the cargo-hold and cockpit. Nathan threw himself backwards and crawled away, reversing as fast as he could to escape the toxic fumes.

At the other end of the room, the door to the sleeping quarters opened up and a weary Tino stepped out, holding his sore head in his hand.

'CLOSE THE DOOR!' yelled Nathan, frantically, as the smog engulfed him. Isaac appeared behind Tino, peering through the doorway to investigate the commotion.

Although Polarian Beconi' had the ability to fit through small spaces by manipulating how wide or narrow their metal dishes were in similar motions to jellyfish, even to become as narrow as a squid head, one of the dishes now furiously tore its way straight through the floor, using its scarlet laser-bladed edges, hurtling right towards the doorway. Isaac grabbed Tino and threw him to the floor, out of the way of the dish. The other Operatives reached for their blasters and began firing at the rapidly-moving, airborne assailant. While they were distracted, the clouds of smog flooded the sleeping quarters, enshrouding every single one of them, suffocating them.

Suddenly, from beyond the clouds of thick, toxic fumes, came a long, shining blade, hurtling through the air and narrowly missing several of the Operatives' faces as it brushed by them and thrust straight into the dish, pinning it into the wall at the end of the room. The others already lay, lifelessly, on the floor of the deployment bay, that is, if they were ever alive at all.

In an instant, the toxic clouds dissipated and all that remained were the scraps of metal, the rusty-coloured Beconium dust that covered the floor and the Operatives, Tino and Gala-Thius, all of whom, curiously, survived the ordeal unscathed. Fortunately, none of them were exhibiting any of the immediate onset symptoms of Beconium Poisoning either.

Everyone turned to look at Corey, accusingly, as he wearily emerged from the hole in the floor.

'FISH!' grunted Anthony with glee as he stepped up, standing next to Corey. The man was soaking wet from the waves and grinning at them all with his teeth once more, his eyes bulging with excitement. He was covered in new cuts, bruises and what appeared to be giant sucker marks, as if produced by some sort of huge octopus. His ferocity and insanity, that had set them all on edge, had clearly paid off in his hunt for their meal.

'How...how...did we all survive that?' stammered Ethan as they all stepped out of the broken cockpit window.

'I don't know but I want everyone to monitor their vitals continuously until we know more' Isaac instructed, turning to the rest of the group to ensure that everyone heard him.

'At least we can finally have some food though. I'm starving' announced Colin who was instantly taken aback, as were the others, by the few tiny fish that lay on the floor amongst the toxic Beconium dust at Anthony's feet, hardly enough to feed one person, let alone eight and now inedible regardless.

They all looked up at Anthony, who appeared to be very proud of himself, their fury evident. Despite his large size and remarkable strength, any one of the Operatives could have quite easily and gladly killed him in that moment had it not occurred to Ethan to check if The Knightfall had supplies onboard which, fortuitously, it did.

'These things again? What even are they?' asked Nathan, gently kicking at one of the dishes with his foot.

'Polarian Beconi'' replied Gala-Thius.

'What's a Polarian Beconi'?' asked Isaac.

'Plural' smiled Gala-Thius. 'The singular is Polarious Beconus' he continued.

'Sounds Earth Latin for a really lethal insect' said Nathan, frowning.

'You're not far off. Polarian Beconi' are swarming plagues formed up of Beconium Storms originating from the planet Becon and the tormented souls of their victims contained within polarised energy fields. These energy fields are generated by scrap metal salvaged from Polarious Five. I hadn't anticipated Parathax leaving some of them behind' replied Gala-Thius.

'We saw loads of them a few hours ago. Four Con-Haarian shuttles landed with prisoners who had survived the Deathstalker Squadron's strike on Polarious. When we saw them, we put a stop to them before the situation escalated' explained Isaac.

'Who's Parathax?' asked Nathan, turning to Gala-Thius.

'She was the one responsible for the strike against your fleet above Polarious Five' Gala-Thius replied.

There was an intense pause as every member of Biker Delta Squadron 5-6-5 stopped gathering food and looked up at him.

'How did you know about the battle above Polarious Five?' asked Isaac. His question was never answered when he drew his blaster on Gala-Thius on first arriving on Zonju.

Ashamedly, with his eyes diverted away from the group of Operatives and his eyebrows raised, he confessed everything he had been doing on Zonju with Parathax since he and Anthony left the I.S.S.

'We've heard of you ever since we were Initiates - Captain Tony and Captain Thius. you were with the I.S.S?' asked Nathan.

'Yes, but not as you know it' replied Gala-Thius.

The group wanted him to elaborate on this and discuss his origins so, warily, Gala-Thius told them everything he had told Tino before they had arrived. He chose not to go into too much detail though until he knew the group better. They were, after all, technically his enemy since he and Anthony had fled the I.S.S. all those years ago and it seemed that the hunt for them was still ongoing, a revelation that set Gala-Thius on edge.

'Why now though? Why would Parathax wait all this time before striking at the I.S.S. and putting her plan of conquest into action?' asked Nathan.

'It has always been about timing. I fear that Parathax set about corrupting Xzjytheous long ago. When he finally renounced his life on Biolum after killing his military Commander and set off rampaging across the galaxy, Parathax had him brought here to be tortured, relentlessly, augmenting his capabilities and transforming him into a raging beast to lead her Deathstalker Squadron' Gala-Thius explained before pausing as the Operatives looked to one another.

'Stay here and regain your strength' instructed Gala-Thius, casting his eyes out into the cave.

'Where are you going?' asked Isaac, still not fully trusting of the old man, especially as this was now the third time he had given this instruction and, in doing so, implied that he was going elsewhere.

'The Reptilian mustn't be allowed to escape to re-group with Parathax and there is at least one other crashed shuttle within these tunnels' replied Gala-Thius with a sense of urgency and responsibility.

'Nathan and Corey will accompany you and assist if you encounter any hostility' insisted Isaac, much to the displeasure of the two Operatives who had finally had their first opportunity to rest and eat.

'No. Anthony alone will accompany me. It's already daytime and any exposure to the sunlight here can be fatal if concentrated by the crystals. We move swiftly, in the shadows of the mountain and small in numbers' countered Gala-Thius.

'What about those things?' asked Tino, indicating at the rack of inactive bionics that was still extended from the side of The Knightfall, recalling how they had helped him earlier.

‘No. No way. They belong to the Reptilian and if he ambushes them, he could easily override them and send them back out to hunt us and we would never even know it’ replied Isaac.

‘To be honest though, he probably could have done that any time he wanted, remotely, while we’ve been here’ Nathan pointed out.

Isaac thought for a moment as he glanced back over at the rack of inactive bionics. ‘Fine’ he replied, climbing to his feet and approaching the ship.

‘You will be under armed guard the whole time. You go out there, you locate the Reptilian and you bring him back’ he instructed as he activated two of the armed bionics from The Knightfall Guard.

Isaac was still reluctant as Gala-Thius, Anthony and the two bionics crossed the enormous cave, heading towards the tunnels beyond and he viewed it as potentially foolish even, to trust the two of them so freely but he had seen that Nathan and Corey were both exhausted. He would have been putting them at risk if he made them go and, although there wasn’t much to go on, there was logic in the old man’s argument, they did need to find Xzjytheous before he could regroup with Parathax.

Resigned, as he sat back down, Isaac cast his eyes back to his food and allowed, arguably the group’s only source of information and a potential traitor, based on the stories, to venture off into the tunnels in search of Xzjytheous. He just hoped he had made the right decision.

As the Operatives and Tino ate with ravenous hunger, having raided the supplies again and taken as much as they could carry out into the cave, Isaac drew the thin piece of steel that was slotted into the wrist-guard of his armoured suit, causing a piece of flint, roughly the thickness and half the length of a pencil, to spring up and lock into place from behind the slot. He approached a small, wooden pyramid structure that Nathan had constructed from the fire-making supplies they had brought up from their destroyed shuttle and, with several strikes of the steel along the piece of flint, the erupting sparks ignited the kindling that consisted mostly of Silver Birch bark gathered from Earth and Felaloris. The sparks quickly took to the dry twigs, bark and natural, flammable oils before igniting the rest of the wood, starting as a flickering flame but quickly turning into a roaring fire.

The flames illuminated a significant portion of the cave with a warm glow, the crackling sound from the flammable oils, a comfort to them all as they gathered around.

As the group continued to eat, a cooling breeze drifted through The Knightfall, blowing the Beconium out of the window and across the floor towards the oblivious group.

'So, are you one of us?' asked Nathan who was monitoring a holographic projection from one of his badges to observe the planet and its rotation to gauge how much longer was left for them to wait before nightfall. Following up his question, he looked away from the hologram and turned to Tino who sat slightly separate from the rest of the group, eating in silence as the rest of them were conversing. Tino looked up from his food, awkward and unsure of how to respond.

'We're elite Operatives with the I.S.S. which stands for the Interstellar Scouts. That's one of our uniforms that you're wearing, albeit a VERY badly damaged one' explained Isaac with a friendly smile, hoping to make Tino feel more at ease. Tino let out a short, quiet laugh with a mixture of amusement, confusion and embarrassment after the ordeal he had endured.

'Our Patrol is Biker Delta Squadron Five-Six-Five. That's actually our Patrol Leader's suit you're wearing...my brother's' said Colin as he tailed off and looked away again.

Corey was relieved that the group's attention was now on Tino rather than him. He too had deliberately sat himself slightly separate from the other Operatives to avoid drawing further attention to himself. He had, after all, just stranded them on Zonju and allowed Xzjytheous to escape which, when combined with his other, admittedly-poor judgement calls since leaving The Scout Hut, really didn't portray him as a member of the team that the others valued.

He followed the conversation, waiting for a pause, because he really wanted to apologise to the others and had wanted to for some time. He finally found his opportunity after listening to the others for, what felt like, forever. He went to open his mouth but then, believing that it was much too soon, he bit his tongue and chose to remain silent, trapped in his own torment instead as he just stared back down at his food.

'So what do we do now?' asked Ethan, turning to the rest of the group.

'Well, we have the metal plating that we need here now. We should have enough to make the necessary repairs to the systems in the deployment bay and the ruptured fuel cell. Flight systems were relatively intact and I have already restored the ones that weren't so once we've patched up those components, we can get out of here' replied Nathan.

'Go get some rest. We'll finish up with the repairs, sleep the remaining time that we have to spend here and then wake you when we're ready to launch' instructed Isaac, turning to Corey.

Although starting to keep his thoughts and feelings to himself to aid the group's productivity, Isaac believed Corey's judgement, hazard perception and risk assessment had all been way off and his course of action had been very poorly calculated, allowing the prisoner to escape and endangering the lives of the rest of the group.

While there was no excuse for his actions, all of these things, Isaac put down to him being overtired as Corey, while often impulsive, didn't normally behave so irrationally.

Corey nodded and, because the floor of the sleeping quarters was now covered in Beconium, he simply brushed off one of the seats in the cockpit with his gloved hand and used it as a bed, just as Nathan had.

'Colin and Ethan, you guys go down to the deployment bay and continue repairing the wiring for the deployment bay hatch's systems. Nathan and I will get started with welding the metal plates onto the fuel cell' said Isaac. Tino remained where he was, unsure of what to do.

'Do you want to help us out?' asked Colin, turning to the quiet boy. It was a comfort to Colin that Tino was wearing his brother's armoured suit. It was like a piece of Oli was still there with them.

'Sure' replied Tino as he followed Colin and Ethan inside.

'Throw those metal dishes up when you get down there' said Nathan, waiting at the open hatch.

But when the three of them reached the bottom of the ladder, Colin found the dishes to be extremely heavy and near impossible to move, not to mention the edges of them were razor-sharp. Not even the combined strength of all 3 of them could budge it.

'It's too heavy!' Colin called up to Nathan.

Slowly, the Beconium-covered dish began to move, seemingly of its own accord. Colin, Ethan and Tino slowly and cautiously backed away as Colin rested his hand on his blaster in its holster. The other two dishes in the deployment bay also began to reanimate, all of them spinning beneath a layer of Beconium as they rose up into the air, towards the hatch. The Operatives watched on, bewildered. Then with a loud, heavy clang, the three dishes dropped to the floor next to Nathan who stared down at them, entirely speechless.

CHAPTER 23
REPAIRS AND REVELATIONS

Isaac joined Nathan with some cutting and welding tools so that the dense metal could be sliced into manageable pieces. Nathan cut pieces out of the metal dishes with one of the plasma-bladed tools, deliberately making them larger than they needed to be so at least they wouldn't waste the metal by making them too small. Meanwhile, Isaac began gathering up the pieces of metal to take up to the roof of the ship.

'That should do it, we'll trim them down to size when we get up there if we need to' said Nathan as Isaac gathered up the remaining pieces.

As Nathan stepped out into the cave and climbed on top of the ship, he noticed that the Beconium had been swept up in the breeze and had landed on top of the ship.

'NO, NO, NO!' he panicked, unable to believe his eyes as he broke into a brief jog up to the roof.

'Isaac, are the others in the deployment bay finished up yet? We have some Beconium contamination up here and it's going to perish the hull if we don't remove it quickly' called Nathan as Isaac passed the replacement parts up to him.

'I'll check' replied Isaac, handing him the final piece of metal.

Down in the deployment bay, Colin, Ethan and Tino were stripping back pieces of the wire beneath the floor panels and soldering it back together to get the electrical systems back online so that they could seal the large sliding hatch in the floor.

'This isn't working, we need to keep the Beconium out of the wiring otherwise it will eat away at it and either short-circuit or shut down the ship's systems altogether while we are in flight' said Colin, frustrated, as he fought to keep the contaminant out of the holes in the floor.

'Tino, can you hand us a couple of those floor panels?' asked Ethan, indicating at the stack of mesh panels piled up next to him.

'Yeah sure, how many?' asked Tino.

'Just two' replied Ethan reaching out for them.

'What are you doing?' asked Colin as Ethan created a wedge shape out of the panels with the group positioned behind it.

'Making a windbreak' replied Ethan as he concentrated on balancing them against each other.

'It will only work partly though because the panels have gaps in them, the area needs to be entirely clear of Beconium' said Colin.

'Won't that mean that all of the wires will get damaged?' asked Tino

'No, most of the wires are insulated and anything that has made it between the gaps in the floor, can be dragged out through the hatch in the floor as we launch' explained Colin. 'It's just these exposed wires that we need to protect from corrosion for now' he continued, slamming the tiny-flamed tool to the floor, irritated.

'Do we really need all of the floor panels to be able to fly the ship?' asked Tino after a moment of contemplation as he watched on.

'Not really. As long as nobody touches anything while we are in flight, the ones that are intact should be fine' replied Colin. 'Why? What are you thinking?' he continued.

'Well, if we can cut all of these small strips of metal out of one of the panels...' he started, indicating at the small pieces of metal that made up the thin rectangular holes in the floor panel. '...And then weld them together to make a solid barrier...' Ethan finished, looking to Colin.

'Yeah, that might work actually' replied Colin a hint of enthusiasm in his voice. He handed various cutting and welding tools to Ethan and Tino and they each grabbed a floor panel.

Eventually, they had cut and welded together enough of the panels to form a more suitable sheet of metal to cover up most of the hole in the floor and only leave the stripped lengths of wire exposed so they could work on them until, finally, the open deployment bay hatch in the floor slid shut.

'Nice work' said Colin after they insulated the repaired wires and climbed to their feet.

'We've got Beconium on the ship's hull, can you guys come and clean it off before it starts corroding the metal while we repair the fuel cell?' asked Isaac, peering down through the round hole in the ceiling.

'You're kidding me. How did it get on top of the ship?' asked Colin, pained by what he was hearing.

'It probably got caught up in the wind. It has picked up a bit over the past twenty minutes or so' replied Isaac as he straightened his back and moved back towards the cockpit.

'If I never see any Beconium again after today, it will be too soon' said Colin as he led the other two towards the ladder.

'It's made its way into the fuel itself' Nathan announced as he peered down at the sediments floating in the liquid through the ruptured metal.

'How much?' asked Isaac as he climbed back up to the roof of the ship.

'Not enough to be a problem if we seal it up RIGHT NOW. Whatever is in there at the moment will burn up in the ship's thrusters but we really can't afford to let any more get in there' replied Nathan, weighing up the situation carefully.

Beconium was a volatile substance and he knew that any grit or sediment in the ship's machinery could cause a blockage, which would be fatal if they were already airborne and something went wrong. He just hoped that he wasn't being too careless in his assessment but he didn't voice these feelings as he didn't want to set everyone on edge any more than they already were.

Nathan was quickly learning a lot about being both an independent pilot and Operative with the I.S.S. after the past few days. He had already understood the chemical reactions involved with mixing the substances together and knew what opportunities could be stretched and where to draw the line but this had always been theoretical. His confidence, however, had grown immensely since the assault on the I.S.S. fleet so he knew he could rely on his own judgement and intuition to get them all off Zonju safely.

They all quickly set about scraping and scrubbing the Beconium off the hull and welding the metal plates to the fuel cell, covering the fuel up with some of the remaining panels to prevent any sparks from igniting it.

'Once we're done with this, we just need to repair the cockpit window and then we can leave this place' said Colin as he frantically scraped the contaminant off the metal.

'Where will we go though?' asked Tino as he helped scrub the blotches and pitting specs that were starting to eat away at the ship's silver hull.

'We need to track down an I.S.S. fleet and warn them about Parathax, radio silence is no longer an option' replied Colin.

'Gala-Thius said Parathax attacked our fleet right?' asked Isaac, turning to the others. 'And we already know that Xzjytheous was aiding in the destruction of The Scout Hut from the inside during his escape...I wonder if the Reptilian is connected to Parathax in more ways than just to lead the Deathstalker strikes' he continued, thoughtfully.

'When I was stuck on his ship, he did say that he was taking me to Parathax on Zonju' Tino interjected.

'Why? I mean what would Parathax want with you?' Nathan asked.

'He said that I was a deserter to the I.S.S. and...'

'And what?' pressed Isaac.

'...And that I was an accessory to their demise' Tino recalled.

He could feel the rest of the group growing wary of him as they looked to one another and he could tell something very bad had already happened that confirmed what the Reptilian had said.

Keeping any further details of The Polarious Sector Assault on his Patrol's fleet quiet for now, Isaac decided that he needed to gather more information about Tino, immediately.

'Where did all of this start for you?' asked Isaac, suspiciously.

'I don't know. I mean I can't remember anything other than I woke up in some old abandoned house. Something big and burning with silver flames fell from the sky and crashed into the sea but when I went to look, all I could see were huge rocks in the water.

A red light came from one of the rocks and destroyed the part of the hill that the house was sat on and I fell from it, down to the sea. Then I woke up onboard this ship' explained Tino, a look of fright on his face as he recalled the terrifying experience. 'Gala-Thius said I was in a battle on Earth where I got hit by one of the enemy ships...a Deathstalker. He said that's how I ended up in the house, covered in weird, black scars and that the Interstellar Scouts that I was with in the battle didn't remember me anymore' he continued.

Nathan suddenly pieced it all together. Everything Sarah and Tamatha had said about an Operative that had been left on Earth after falling from a Deathstalker and crashing through the roof of an I.S.S. safe house. It appeared that, if what Tino was saying was true, the two girls held some sort of residual memory of him. Still, Nathan remained quiet until he could mention it to Isaac in private later.

'Assimilation Matrix technology' Isaac concluded, based on Tino's description of the giant rocks.

'What were these...black scars, you got from the battle?' asked Isaac, his curiosity growing.

'I have them in different parts of my body and they do look like I've been stabbed by something like Gala-Thius said but I can't remember it happening...except...' Tino paused as he recalled the effects of the black substance in his body, realising the amnesia effect it had been having on him.

'Except what?' Isaac pressed.

'Except when I touch the injuries, they hurt really badly and I see things. I see how I got the injuries but it isn't me in the visions... it can't be' Tino explained, growing less and less convinced by his own beliefs as he went on.

'Sound familiar?' asked Isaac, turning to Nathan who nodded in response.

'What do you mean?' asked Tino.

'Don't worry about it' replied Isaac, who, like Nathan, decided not to discuss the extra details they had been told, in front of Tino for the time being. Isaac then walked across the roof of the ship, towards him.

Isaac, however, was worried about it. Tamatha had told him and Nathan that she had seen an Operative impaled by a Deathstalker's bladed blaster canon during the battle on Earth that preceded the Polarious Sector Assault on the I.S.S. fleet. Tino appeared to be another significant piece of the puzzle alongside Parathax, Xzjytheous and the Deathstalker Squadron. However, he wasn't sure how to fit them all together yet.

Corey was unable to sleep with all of the noise so he rejoined the group, offering an extra pair of hands wherever they were needed.

'Nathan, secure that final panel. Corey, help him and you two finish cleaning the hull' Isaac continued as he walked past Colin, Ethan and Tino.

'What about me?' Tino asked.

'Come with me and give me your suit' replied Isaac, turning his head slightly, but not looking at him.

Tino looked to Colin and Ethan nervously in response to the sudden change in everyone's behaviour but the only thing the two of them could do was smile reassuringly at him but, despite their efforts, there was no hiding their true thoughts.

Tino slowly climbed to his feet and followed, nervously. The two of them dropped down to the cave floor and Isaac led him to the other side of the huge chamber. He then sat down on a rock as he gestured for Tino to join him on another one next to it.

CHAPTER 24
AN OPERATIVE'S RE-INVESTITURE

'It's been a very long and trying few days for us' said Isaac, wearily rubbing his face in his hands and then running his fingers through his fiery orange hair, looking Tino in the eye.

Tino felt like Isaac was about to drop a bombshell on him and wanted to point out that he too had had a difficult few days but he remained silent and let Isaac say what he had to say, struggling to maintain eye-contact with him.

'I don't know how you tie into the I.S.S. if, indeed, you do at all, despite what Gala-Thius says' Isaac lied before pausing for several seconds. He now knew who Tino was based on Tamatha's story but he wanted to figure out whether he could trust Tino before involving him in the group. Then came the predicted bombshell.

'But you do tie in with multiple enemies who have tried to kill us numerous times over the past few days' he said, reaching for his blaster in its holster. Tino's eyes widened with dread as he stared at the weapon. His rescuers, and those who he believed were becoming his friends, were now going to kill him.

'Your revelation just now, in front of us all, has told me everything that I need to know. Stand up and step out of the suit' Isaac instructed.

'I...I don't know how to' replied Tino, trembling with fear as he slowly rose to his feet, looking from the blaster to Isaac and back to the blaster again.

Isaac used his own suit to initiate an Assistant Patrol Leader Override on all of the systems in the suit Tino was wearing. The armour extended on all of its built-in bionic components, pivoting in various parts until it had opened up and revealed the torn, smelly flight suit that the boy was wearing. Tino remained standing inside the open suit of armour.

'Get out then' said Isaac, impatiently and with a nudge of his head. Tino forced himself to be brave and stepped out onto the cold, sharp rocks of the cave floor, in his bare feet.

'Show me your injuries?' Isaac instructed, standing up and moving towards him. Tino didn't move. He just stared at Isaac nervously, wishing for it all to be over quickly.

Isaac looked down and adjusted the setting of his blaster using a small twistable wheel on the butt of it and a loud, high-pitched ringing sound was emitted from it as it charged up. Waiting to see if any hostile reaction would be provoked from Tino, he squeezed the trigger and a welding flame flared up from the end of it.

Still, Tino didn't attempt to defend himself. Isaac walked straight towards Tino as the terrified boy closed his eyes but Isaac just walked straight past him. It wasn't in Isaac's nature to intimidate others like this but he had to step up to the mark and ensure that, if there was any hostile intent, the situation was controlled, for the safety of both himself and his Patrol.

It took a couple of seconds for Tino to dare to open his eyes again but, when he finally did, he slowly turned around to see Isaac welding and soldering the damaged components of the free-standing emerald suit from behind it, repairing its jet propulsion unit as well as the functions of each of the round, diamond and uniquely-shaped badges on the arms and torso which, gradually, began to flicker with light as the glass began to repair itself on each of them. Finally, the bright, blue interior tracking dots began darting, in different directions, around the grey lines within the padding.

'Wherever we go when we leave here, it's going to be dangerous. These enemies – Parathax, the Reptilian, the Deathstalker Squadron as well as those that serve them, such as the Con-Haarians, all want to tear down the Interstellar Scouts by taking you hostage and using you to bait us here as well as any other I.S.S. rescue units in the vicinity. We've seen others captured and brought here to await some horrendous fate with those Polarian Beconi' but they failed to capture any of us. You're safe now. We'll stand strong against them and give you a family to be a valued member of' said Isaac as he recalled the way Oli had treated Colin when they had first met.

Turning off the flame and slotting his blaster back into its holster, he stepped away from the suit which was now illuminated with brilliant light.

'Show me' Isaac instructed, directing his eyes towards the torn fabric in Tino's clothing. Tino was still reluctant but slowly complied. He pulled the torn fabric slightly apart to reveal his blackened injuries.

'They look painful' Isaac said sympathetically as he inspected the wounds. Tino just hoped that he wouldn't trigger any more of the visions. 'We have medical supplies with us from our ship. We can help you' Isaac continued.

'Why? Don't you have enough problems to deal with without helping me as well? I'm sure I can learn to live with it' replied Tino.

'We're Interstellar Scouts. Helping people is what we are all about. I'm just sorry we couldn't get to you sooner' replied Isaac quietly, shaking his head. As the one in command of the patrol, he felt responsible for everything Tino had been through even though he knew the rescue was put into action as soon as it possibly could have been. He at least had to give Corey credit for saving Tino, even if he did lose the Rhinonoid in the process.

Tino noticed that he was about to say something else but Isaac hesitated.

'...I can't be certain...but I think I know a way to help you get your memory back as well...if you trust us' replied Isaac. Isaac's wording mixed with his initial hesitation had Tino on edge but the group of Operatives seemed like genuine, kind, caring people. Finally Tino nodded.

He climbed back into the repaired cy-bionic exoskeleton and Isaac led him back across the cave to The Knightfall, questioning his own judgement the whole way. His plan was inspired by Oli's plan to disable and capture the Deathstalker Squadron just days before the assault on the I.S.S. fleet but those were powerful, hulking and practically-indestructible machines of global destruction...Tino was a kid.

'Nathan, Corey, I'll need your help with this' Isaac announced, putting aside any negative thoughts and feelings he held towards

Corey as well as any concerns he had about what he was about to attempt. The three of them then led Tino into the inside of The Knightfall, down to the cargo-hold.

'So what's happening?' asked Tino, growing extremely nervous. Isaac thought his plan through one last time to make sure he was absolutely certain of what he was doing.

'This ship's deployment bay is designed to stun and even incapacitate prisoners with powerful electrical currents but we can use that to our advantage' Isaac explained. Nathan and Corey both developed nervous expressions on their faces, of which Tino caught a glimpse.

'Tino's injuries were caused by contact with one of the Deathstalkers and I think that some kind of...neurotoxin, was transferred into his body which explains the loss of memory and why your body goes into spasm when you touch the wounds and have the visions' explained Isaac, looking from Nathan and Corey, back to Tino.

'Wait...What are you saying?' asked Tino, growing more and more fearful.

'Tino, injuries like those should have killed you...immediately. Don't get me wrong, you would have fallen with honour. Your sacrifice was a noble one that, without a doubt, saved countless lives. You are being kept alive by your injuries though. Those visions you've had are an adverse reaction to them. I think the black stuff that surrounds the injuries is engineered to numb your nervous system and block your memory. I think you have already realised that. When you touch the injuries, it stimulates them and your body shoots the pain through your nervous system and up to your brain which counteracts the numbing and amnesia effects of the neurotoxin. That is you in those visions' Isaac explained.

'You're cy-bionic suit will protect you during the process and we'll be monitoring and controlling everything from here' Isaac went on, in a bid to reassure Tino.

'But what are you going to do? What process?' asked Tino, still very scared and now feeling more like a stranger in his own body than ever.

'We need to burn up everything that the Deathstalker put into your body and, at the same time, hopefully, jump start your nervous system so you can remember everything that happened and work your body for yourself rather than being driven by whatever has been put inside you' replied Isaac. 'Don't worry. Just trust me, your suit will keep you safe' Isaac reassured again.

Tino knew that his suit would keep him alive, just as it had when he had fallen unconscious during his last episode in The Knightfall's electrified deployment bay however, he was still extremely reluctant. Before he could protest or ask any more questions, Corey rolled his eyes and hit Tino in the back of his suit with a stun bolt from his blaster. Tino fell through the hole in the floor and slammed down onto the loose panels in the deployment bay.

'WHAT DID YOU DO THAT FOR!?' yelled Isaac, reeling around, angrily, to face Corey.

'He broke my nose earlier' replied Corey, half joking.

'Unbelievable' said Isaac, appalled by Corey's actions.

'It was all taking too long, we've been here forever' Corey argued, already leading the way back to the cockpit and adjusting the settings on the console.

'I need him to trust us' Isaac insisted. 'Look, just activate the systems with a steady incline of voltage and direct the current so he is off the floor in the centre of the room. I'll feed his suit's readings through to my visor and we can adjust everything as we go' he continued, closing his helmet over his head and sealing the deployment bay hatch shut.

'How do you know this will work and won't just end up killing him?' asked Nathan, worriedly, as he followed Isaac into the cockpit.

'He's wearing Oli's suit, it's got added compensators that other suits don't' Isaac replied as he tried not to think about the risks that were involved.

On the screen, the three Operatives watched as bolts of white, blue and purple electricity jolted across the room and struck Tino's suit.

'Steady. Readings are stabilised. Bring up the levels gradually. I'll tell you when to stop' Isaac watched the readings being transmitted from the suit Tino was wearing, to his visor. 'Slower Corey, nice and steady' Isaac instructed, concentrating hard and holding out his own hand as if he was the one controlling the levels.

The bolts of electricity were now streaming continuously into Tino's suit as they continued to suspend him in mid-air. An alert flashed up inside Isaac's visor which read

'BIO-SYSTEMS CRITICAL

NEURAL OVERLOAD IMMINENT'.

'OK, CUT! CUT! CUT HIM OFF!' Isaac shouted, throwing himself forward to check that all of the levels were immediately powered down. Nathan and Corey quickly decreased the voltage levels, slowing down only just before they reached zero to gently place Tino back on the floor of the deployment bay. The last few flashes of sparks flared and snapped from the floor panels around Tino's body as Isaac rushed back into the cargo-hold and heaved the hatch open.

He descended down the ladder, put Tino over his shoulder and climbed back up with Nathan and Corey helping them through the hatch.

Isaac then took Tino straight into the sleeping quarters and, making sure there was no Beconium around, placed the boy down on the sleeping platform, retracting his helmet.

'Welcome back to the Interstellar Scouts Tino' he said, smiling with relief that his plan hadn't killed the boy. Although Isaac, nor any of the other Operatives, really knew him, Nathan, Corey, Colin and Ethan had also gathered outside the room, watching curiously. There was a definite intrigue that they all shared in Tino's story.

'Where are we up to on repairs? The sun is almost set' said Isaac as he left the room, closing the door behind him.

Nathan, Corey, Colin and Ethan accompanied him through the ship as they moved back out, into the cave.

'The starboard fuel cell has been patched up and the deployment bay hatch is operational' replied Nathan.

'Colin, Ethan, did you get all of the Beconium off the hull?' asked Isaac.

'We did but that breeze is still here so it's only a matter of time before it ends up back on there' replied Colin.

'We really need to launch before it gets blown all over the ship again' continued Corey.

'Agreed' replied Isaac.

It was the first thing that Corey had said in a long time that Isaac actually agreed with. Was he finally becoming an equal member of the team or was Isaac and the rest of the group just too distracted to let him annoy them anymore? Either way, Corey was committed to the idea that it was time he discretely set aside his self-importance and his desire to be better than Isaac and actually be helpful. He still couldn't bring himself to apologise to the group for fear that they wouldn't accept it so he decided to show them how sorry he was instead through his hard work. He'd wanted his friends back ever since he was alone on the shuttle with his thoughts.

'Let's get this window repaired and we'll be ready' Isaac continued, leading them back around to the cockpit.

'We don't have any glass to fill it in though' said Corey.

'I have an idea for that' replied Isaac. 'Grab these two Polarious Beconus dishes' he instructed.

'What for?' asked Nathan as he crouched down and started heaving one of them across the floor, with all of his strength, towards them.

'If there is one thing that I learnt from Oli as our Patrol Leader, it's to make use of whatever your environment gives you and be innovative with it. We're going to create a modification of the scarlet laser technology that Oli adapted for the Rhinonoid' explained Isaac enthusiastically.

'When the Polarian Beconi' attacked us before, the dishes had scarlet laser-bladed edges' said Corey, as he realised what Isaac was talking about.

'Remove the centre and stretch out the edges into one long length. Watch your hands, they may be inactive now but those edges are still razor-sharp' warned Isaac.

Nathan and Corey quickly set about the final reparation task.

'Fit one to the top of the window frame and one directly opposite it on the bottom frame. Make sure the angles are exact' said Corey. 'The emitters themselves MUST be perfectly parallel' he continued, catching himself being bossy again. He quickly stopped himself from proceeding any further. 'With a bit of re-wiring, theoretically, they'll power up when we engage the ship's flight systems' he continued, trying to add an explanation onto the end of the instruction so he didn't seem so controlling.

'Theoretically?' asked Nathan, nervously, pausing to look Corey in the eye. 'You do realise that if this goes wrong, there are plenty of different places on this ship where you lot will be safe and, as the pilot, I'm going to be the one with or without a big wall of death in my face whenever I fly us anywhere. Neither of these options is ideal for me. And you're throwing 'theoretically' into the mix as well?' he said.

'Sorry. Yeah, don't worry; your wall of death will definitely be there the whole time. Just...don't crash...and maybe double-check the ship's safety restraints' joked Corey with a playful smack on Nathan's shoulder.

The mood seemed a little lighter for everyone, for now at least, as they were finally leaving but, at the back of everyone's mind was the question, where were they going next?

CHAPTER 25
LAST LIGHT OF A DYING ZONJU SUN

The wind did not veil the spectral howls that echoed down the passageways. With a keen focus in his eyes, Gala-Thius appeared to slowly turn his head back and forth in acknowledgement of what remained unseen to the single working eye of his grunting companion. He was silently interacting with it without speaking a word, not so much as a gesture while completely ignoring the two armed bionics that escorted the two of them.

Anthony had spent long enough with Gala-Thius during his mystical practices to identify when the old man was communicating unconventionally but he rarely acknowledged the seriousness of these interactions and negotiations. Instead, he smiled a huge grin with his blackened teeth, his eyes wide with enthusiasm and intrigue as he followed behind Gala-Thius, waving at the walls and darkness like an inquisitive child, hoping that whatever was there could see him and would be smiling and waving back at him.

As they walked, Gala-Thius also contemplated what the Operatives had told him about the stories they had heard of him and Anthony. He had assumed that, after all of this time, the I.S.S. surely would have given up their pursuit of intelligence on them but they clearly hadn't. Not only that but they were now compromised by a group of Operatives that would surely report their location to their superiors upon debrief when they eventually rendezvous with their fleet. Action needed to be taken to ensure that didn't happen.

Gala-Thius and Anthony turned to enter the chamber where Parathax had co-ordinated her hunt from but, upon stepping into the archway, Gala-Thius came to a sudden halt, eyeing the black crystal throne upon which Parathax had sat.

Cunning, as he waited above the archway, Xzjytheous allowed the pair to enter the chamber a few steps before pouncing from behind. His attack, swift and precise, meant that it was all over before the Reptilian's victims knew what had happened.

From the grasp of an unconscious Gala-Thius, tumbled an I.S.S. Distress Signal Badge. As the two bionics watched their true owner, Xzjytheous retrieved the badge from the floor of the cave, pinching it between his stained claws, admiring the device. Then, accompanied by the two bionics, he climbed the wall of the round chamber, all the way up to the top, emerging through the opening where he put his plan into action on escaping Zonju.

Soon after, Gala-Thius began to slowly open his eyes, pained by the crushing weight of the huge Reptilian coming down on top of him. He gradually rose to his feet and staggered across the chamber to retrieve his black, crystal staff from the bottom of the steps that led up to the throne. It seemed odd that it had travelled so far across the floor from where he fell. Surely their attacker would have taken it to ensure he remained disarmed rather than simply moving it. It was also strange that the staff appeared to be perfectly parallel to the steps as well, just like it was when he had bowed down before Parathax earlier.

As he began to reach down to the floor, the old man paused. Something was very much amiss. He exhaled slowly in acknowledgement and preparation as he cast his eyes up, looking about the chamber in observation of all that still remained unseen to Anthony, who was now also returning to his feet and looking for a fight.

In a single, rapid motion, Gala-Thius crouched down, grasped his staff and swiftly angled the crystal tip at the end of it with such precision that it captured and diverted the blazing beam of toxic light from the fiery, setting sun. It had shot out, straight towards Anthony from the crystal throne, marking last light of a dying Zonju sun.

'RETREAT! TO THE KNIGHTFALL!' yelled Gala-Thius as he wrestled with the powerful beam of light that grew evermore concentrated. The blast of photons was so powerful that it had the strength to reposition the staff as Gala-Thius used all of his might, resisting against it.

More beams of toxic sunlight darted across the chamber in all directions, forming a web, a three-dimensional maze of deadly lasers. Anthony stumbled about carelessly, resisting the urge to cower in submission in the helpless, hopeless situation he found himself in. Or so he believed.

Gala-Thius thrust his staff into the ground, causing a network of black Beconium-core crystals to erupt, fiercely from the ground, obstructing the beams of light around the chamber. Then, unhindered by his advanced age, he bolted towards the archway that Anthony was already trying to retreat to.

'FLY!' the old man yelled as he grabbed Anthony and pushed him out through the archway, to the cover of the tunnel beyond as he repelled the beams of light from behind which now breached the barrier that exploded across the chamber in a shower of crystal shards, hurtling through the Beconium shroud.

The rays of amber light began to burn through the tunnel walls and bleed through the cracks that ruptured through the mountain.

Anthony raced ahead while Gala-Thius repeatedly fended off the threats for both of them. Anthony was formidable in a fight but, being unable to defend himself against this particular foe, gave Gala-Thius a sense of responsibility for him.

He diverted one of the solar beams away from them and swept it across the wall, like a powerful laser, causing an old cave-in, that he had made when they first arrived on Zonju, to be blown away, into a scattering of boulders, covering the floor of a smaller cave, the cave where Gala-Thius and Anthony had left their shuttle wreckage after they crash-landed it there. There was no time to contemplate the uncovered ship though as their situation worsened.

As they continued to race back to the cave where the I.S.S. Operatives had based themselves, they were cut off from in front. Gala-Thius had to think fast if he was going to save them both now.

Then, in an unexpected display of power, Anthony let out a fierce cry of rage as he charged, with all of his might, directly at the wall of the tunnel next to where Gala-Thius happened to be diverting one of the light beams to.

Using brute force, Anthony charged straight through the thin crust of the weakened wall and exploded into another tunnel, deeper in the mountain and free of any cracks that the toxic sunlight could filter through.

Impressed, though slightly out of breath, Gala-Thius led Anthony down the tunnel, towards the sound of voices; the exploding crystals still audible from behind. The tunnel brought them out into the cave where the group of I.S.S. Operatives were almost ready to leave.

With Nathan and Corey already onboard, Isaac, Colin, Ethan and Tino climbed inside through the currently-inactive cockpit window, followed by Gala-Thius and Anthony.

'Where's the Reptilian and the bionics?' asked Isaac.

'Made a tactical retreat' replied Gala-Thius calmly, entirely disregarding the deadly ordeal that he and Anthony had just endured.

'Where you are all going now, Parathax and Xzjytheous will be waiting for you. You're about to need all of the help you can get. Our allegiance to the I.S.S. was severed long ago but there is no denying, its downfall would be devastating for this galaxy and those beyond. We will aid you in this battle' announced Gala-Thius to the other Operatives, all of whom were confused as to why the two of them were also boarding the ship. Isaac nodded in agreement.

'You guys might want to go into the sleeping quarters for a moment. This launch is going to be unpredictable' announced Nathan as he sat in the pilot's seat and moved it closer to the console.

The rest of the group made their way through the doorway to the sleeping quarters and, no sooner had they closed the door behind them and Nathan started up the ship's flight systems, they heard Nathan scream at the top of his lungs in terror. They all rushed back out to investigate as showers of sparks exploded all around the newly-installed laser wall emitters, now in place of the window, while Nathan took cover behind his seat.

The scarlet laser wall flickered several times causing multiple small explosions of shattered glass from the remainder of the window and then it finally stabilised.

Nathan fired an aggravated stare in Corey's direction before standing back up and returning to the pilot's seat. Isaac moved up to the cockpit to aid Nathan in getting The Knightfall safely airborne and understanding that, as the pilot, Nathan was the one giving the orders, Isaac did as instructed.

Corey, Colin, Ethan and Tino decided to also join Nathan and Isaac in the cockpit for the launch while Gala-Thius and Anthony remained in the sleeping quarters. Isaac finished adjusting the settings on his side of the console for the launch sequence and Nathan confidently, enthusiastically even, adjusted his posture in his seat and reached for the thrusters' controls.

'Hold onto something. Engaging reverse thrusters' announced Nathan as the ship's engines vamped up, the hull creaking and juddering, scraping against the opening to the cave as everyone's eyes, nervously, followed the sounds across the ceiling.

'Steady, we don't want any more damage to the ship' Isaac reminded Nathan moments before the last hint of the sunset gradually lit up the edges of the cave, indicating that they had safely pulled away.

For the briefest of moments, Nathan felt a wave of anxiety hit him as he was about to activate the ship's forward thrusters to turn The Knightfall around and, hopefully, burn up the Beconium Particulates that had mixed with the fuel. If something went wrong though, it could block up the fuel feed to the thrusters and send the ship plummeting down the side of the mountain, carrying them all to their deaths.

'Leave the deployment bay hatch open until we reach full thrust, we need to jettison any remaining Beconium from the room' Colin reminded Nathan.

'What's that?' asked Ethan as he noticed something coming right at them.

'The Polarian Beconi' are reanimating without the dishes. I didn't know that was possible' replied Gala-Thius as he too, now emerged from the sleeping quarters.

'Is that a face?' asked Isaac, squinting close to the laser wall.

'Probably one of its victims' Gala-Thius reminded them.

‘It’s gaining on us and moving fast’ warned Colin. ‘We need to turn and fire the thrusters now’ he continued urgently.

‘We’re still in the wrong position to fire the thrusters’ replied Nathan, concentrating hard on navigating The Knightfall away from the mountainside and into the correct angle to fly away from it.

‘It’s going to get inside the deployment bay’ warned Ethan.

At that moment, Colin lunged forward and pulled the large handle leaver that activated the ship’s thrusters. As they began to fire up, they sputtered as, due to the angle the ship was at, all of the Beconium particulates had been swept up against the filter and there was just too much of a blockage for it to handle.

The blockage restricted the flow of fuel to the thrusters entirely. Loud alarms started to sound throughout the ship as The Knightfall tumbled through the air, hurtling towards the bottom of the mountain while the entire group shouted and screamed, trying desperately to brace themselves on the swivelling seats.

Nathan, while equally terrified, focussed his mind to remain as calm and collected as possible. With a series of smacks from his hand, he adjusted a couple of settings on the ship’s console and, just as they were about to strike the rocks and black crystals which pierced through the crashing waves at the foot of the mountain, the fuel gushed to the opposite end of the tank, sweeping the particulates away from the filter.

In one huge, powerful explosion, the fuel surged into the thrusters and they soared into the sky. It was fortunate that they were pointing upwards at that moment otherwise they would have smashed into the rocks and crystal formations below at extremely high speed.

The loud echo of a distressed cry for help howled on the wind from the cave with a single outstretched arm amongst the jettisoned Beconium and then nothing.

The remaining Beconium Particulates that made up, unbeknownst to them, what was left of Oli, were dragged out of The Knightfall’s deployment bay hatch, which then closed, locking shut as the ship left the atmosphere. The terrified boy drifted back down towards the cave below, abandoned.

He had been trying to get the group's attention since he fell through the planet's atmosphere from the Rhinonoid, since he found them, since he protected them against the Polarian Beconi' attack and since he helped them move the heavy equipment they needed to repair the ship. But they never saw him, not even when he had shouted at the top of his voice when he joined them on the roof of The Knightfall's wreckage. They never heard him.

CHAPTER 26
THE BECONIUM BEINGS

Although Oli still saw himself as just as human as he had always been, to anybody else standing there, all they would see would be a dusting of rusty-coloured Beconium which swept across the floor in the breeze, like the surface layer of sand on a beach being caught up in the wind, a wisp upon the rocks. Nothing, to his eyes, was as it should have been. Everything he looked at now appeared fuzzy, in a spectrum of rusty shades. Since sneaking around onboard the Rhinonoid, Oli was quickly discovering that his body had been undergoing a major transformation...and it still was. He was mutating.

As night fell on Zonju once more, Oli hopelessly made his way into the mountain's tunnel systems, abandoned, helpless and alone.

As he walked, he saw others moving through the caves and tunnels but they didn't appear as human as he did. They reminded him of how he saw himself moments before being punched through the Rhinonoid's hull. They were humanoid but, like his surroundings, they were fuzzy and appeared to be made entirely of Beconium. They didn't appear to notice him as they moved around, sluggish and without intent. It was as if they were only half alive.

Oli frowned to himself as he watched one of them moving down the tunnel ahead of him. He didn't know what the creature was. There had been no record of such an entity in the I.S.S. archives while he was studying as an Initiate. He could only describe them as Beconium Beings. Observing it closely, the humanoid appeared to drag its feet over the rocks and tiny, black crystal clusters that stuck up from the ground, making no effort to move around them and, any Beconium that fell from its body, simply followed behind, trailing across the floor until it was absorbed back up into the culmination again.

There was something very eerie about watching the bald-headed creature just stroll down the tunnel, entirely oblivious to Oli's presence.

As Oli continued to follow the mysterious entity, his attention was drawn to a small opening in the wall on his right-hand side. He could hear the distant crashing of the waves at the foot of the mountain as he looked through the opening, into the small cave beyond. The ruins of another shuttle caught his eye. He identified it as a dated I.S.S. shuttle, the sort he had only learned about through study of the I.S.S. archives. It was very badly damaged and appeared to have long been in a state of decay.

Oli was just about to continue on down the tunnel, turning his gaze away, when he also spotted his customised Pyrotech armoured suit on top of the shuttle. Above it, in the curved ceiling, was a large hole that had been smashed by the suit as it had collided with the mountainside.

Realising that it must have fallen from the Rhinonoid along with him and homed in on the nearest piece of I.S.S. technology it could find, he tried to retrieve it but, in the state in which he now found himself, he was unable to even touch it, let alone retrieve it and put it on.

Crestfallen, he lowered his hands, his fingers still flexed as if he was holding the suit within them. Oli hung his head, broken and defeated, surrendering as he accepted the reality with which he was faced.

As he proceeded on and the tunnel curved round a bend, Oli peered around and came to a slow halt. He called out to the entity that had apparently been waiting for him to catch up. Had it seen him following after all? He was hoping to gain some sort of understanding of what was going on.

Although Oli heard his own voice calling out, the only sound that truly echoed through those tunnels and out, to the chambers beyond, was the wailing and howling of the wind. The wind howled back down the tunnel in response - the tortured cries of the distressed, tormented souls, eternal in their turmoil, now encircling the Beconium boy that lay upon the floor. The moans and cries grasped at the boy, his arms, his legs, his neck. In cruel conviction upon the foul breath of their icy whisper, they took him up and away, away, down the passageway.

Silence fell. A heavy cloak, weighing, burdened upon the pulsing of his flaring ears became further-burdened still. The walls of the tunnel felt as though they were hemming in, growing dark as they consumed all, light sound, space and time.

Oli shivered, feeling a sharp chill run from his neck, down his spine as he opened his eyes. He looked about himself in confusion as he raised his head up off the cold and damp of the stone tunnel floor, an uneasy feeling brewing from deep within. The fog, illuminated by the silver, lunar glow, bled through the cracks in the wall of the tunnel. What had just happened? How much time had just passed? Is this what he had become? Was he like that other entity now? Doomed to wander these tunnels forever with no intent? No purpose? Trapped in the eternal haunt of a nightmare? The idea was much too frightening for Oli to dwell upon.

As he returned to his feet, it occurred to Oli that, as he had undergone...whatever he had just undergone, he had also moved... or been moved. He was now standing where the strange entity had previously been. Extremely unsettled as he finished moving around the bend, he could see an archway opening up to his left.

The dusting of rusty Beconium on the floor, that he had been reduced to, drifted through the archway which opened up into a large chamber. The top of the cave was missing and it was aglow with luminous fog which spilled down from above, bathing the cave in the glow from the enormous moon above.

In the centre of the floor, he could see some of the same metal dishes that the group had taken from the Polarian Beconi' to repair the ship.

Wondering if he could make use of the scrap metal, Oli made his way across the room towards them. As he moved through the chamber, he could see huge, black crystal pillars that encircled the room. There were cavities carved out, high up in the walls of the cave and, beyond the pieces of metal on the floor, a set of steps led up to a platform with a huge throne upon it, carved entirely of enormous, black crystals. Oli looked about himself in search of whoever the throne was intended for but he was entirely alone.

Returning his attention to the round pieces of metal on the floor, he reached out but then paused as he suddenly felt like there were eyes fixed on him from behind. He withdrew his hand and slowly turned around. Several feet behind him, stood the bald humanoid but it didn't do anything to him, nor did it speak. It was just standing there, studying him, its head tilted to the side slightly. Oli believed it was trying to understand who he was and what he was doing.

'I'm sorry, I don't understand what is going on here' Oli's voice echoed in his own ears. 'I'm Oli. I'm with the Interstellar Scouts. Those people that left in the ship' he explained.

Still, the only sound that reverberated around the huge cave was not his voice, but a howling wind. The humanoid didn't respond, it just remained where it was, staring at Oli.

'I'm lost' said Oli, frowning as he walked over towards the creature that stood in front of him. 'Can you help me?' he called out. 'Can you hear me?' he continued, now slightly more wary as he approached. 'Hello!?' he shouted. This was so surreal. He circled the entity but it didn't observe his movements. It remained staring at the throne, not at all phased by him.

Oli diverted his attention back to the pieces of metal that lay on the ground but, as he turned, he saw thousands of the Beconium Beings standing right in front of him. Oli jumped back with fright. The bald headed entity grabbed hold of him from behind, restraining him, as streams of Beconium were leeched out of the surrounding black crystals that Gala-Thius had generated during his time on the planet and the toxic streams were drawn into the entity's form, strengthening and enlarging it.

As the others began to attack him, viciously, Oli cried out in terror, screaming helplessly. He couldn't control his arms or his legs as he was being held in place. Not only that but he was also unarmed. There was absolutely nothing he could do to defend himself.

As the onslaught came at him, the gusts of wind intensified in the chamber, howling loudly as clouds of Beconium dust were swept up into the air before falling back to the ground again, repeatedly.

Oli spotted one of the Beconium Beings making their way over towards the metal dishes that lay on the floor as he struggled desperately to break free of the restraint, the whole time enduring punch after punch.

The dishes began to rise up off the ground, capturing the attention of all of his attackers. The two dishes then began hurtling around the room, spinning in opposite directions as if an invisible rod joined them together at the centre. The attackers chased the metallic objects through the air in their hundreds, being absorbed into the Polarian gravitational field the dishes generated, as they fought for possession of the only remaining sets of Polarious Beconus devices.

Oli collapsed to the floor as the other two sets of dishes rose into the air and the entity that had restrained him went in pursuit of them also. The Beconium Beings engaged one another in a fierce battle, hurtling around the cave as they collided into the towering, black crystal pillars, clashing against one another with their scarlet, laser-bladed edges as sparks rained down to the ground from the collisions. Oli was now positive that he had suffered the same fate as the rest of these tormented souls, all of them victims of Beconium Poisoning from various attacks by the Polarian Beconi'.

The only difference for him was that he was poisoned on Becon but the outcome had ended up the same after he was seemingly only partially restored on Crystalosis. Oli knew that, if he was going to stabilise himself, he would need to fight to acquire a pair of those dishes to make use of their containment field. He would then, hopefully, be able to attempt a more permanent fix later.

The Beconium Beings must have previously been contained within the Polarian energy fields as Polarian Beconi' before the dishes were destroyed, releasing them and turning them into this new form.

While they were all distracted, Oli made a tactical retreat out of the chamber and returned to the cave where his Pyrotech armour had crash-landed. Having witnessed the entity drawing the Beconium out of the crystals to enable it to interact with him, he wondered if he had the same abilities that would allow him to interact with the armoured suit. If this plan was going to work, he would need to be extremely careful as the suit was covered in volatile, replenishing nano-explosives.

The purpose of the suit was to cover distance rapidly or to get from A to B without the need to navigate around obstacles such as walls while also being heavily armed. Instead, he could just explode through the Beconium Beings while remaining safe. One wrong move now though and the armour would detonate and take that whole portion of the mountain with it.

Having arrived back in the small cave to retrieve his Pyrotech suit, Oli questioned how he was supposed to go about absorbing the Beconium from the crystal structures as he weaved his way between the enormous rocks that Gala-Thius had littered the floor with during his and Anthony's escape. He approached one of the larger crystals and placed his hands upon it, hoping that it would respond to his touch, but nothing happened.

Oli felt a burning rage erupting from within him. Forgetting that he was now merely a conglomeration, he slapped his hands, repeatedly, against the crystal. He punched at it and hammered his fists against it, shouting and screaming out in frustration. Still, the Beconium remained.

Having spent all of the energy he had, the boy looked up into the crystal and saw the reflection of the cave around him but he couldn't see himself. For the first time, he realised that, despite his consciousness being intact, he had no reflection; he had no form. Right now, he wasn't even formed like one of the Beconium Beings. He was merely a culmination of neurons, mobilised by his intent.

All that he had seen of himself since being thrown from the Rhinonoid was a memory contained within the Beconium that coated the floor.

Was that even true? Or did it go back further than that? His sickness, the battle onboard The Scout Hut, talking to Corey on the shuttle...seeing the group in the cave before they had left him there...Had it all just been a twisted and distorted memory from a long-lost life that he'd been clinging to, lost within this nightmare?

He sat down on the wing of the wrecked shuttle and placed his head in his hands as he started to break down and cry. Suddenly, he felt a bizarre sensation in the fingertips of his left hand. Looking up at the large crystal across from him, he could see his hand in the reflection but nothing else. Slowly it faded away again. Oli closed his eyes and concentrated as hard as he could, trying not to be distracted by the collisions that echoed down the tunnel from the large chamber, the howl of the wind, nor the crashing of the waves.

After several seconds, the feeling came back again, now in both hands. He quickly opened his eyes and, once again, saw his reflection starting to appear in the blackness of the large crystal. Looking about himself, streams of Beconium were flowing through the air towards him from the crystals around the cave.

Maintaining his concentration, Oli, slowly turned to look back at his reflection. He could now see his entire body. His I.S.S. suit that had formed around him was blotched and speckled with Beconium and, as he rose to his feet, approaching the crystal to look more closely at his reflection, he raised his hand up to his face which was burnt on one side but he couldn't feel it. He suspected that it was due to part of him being inside The Knightfall's ruptured fuel cell which then got fed through into the ship's thrusters when it launched.

He approached the Pyrotech armoured suit which still identified him, opening up for him to enter as he neared it. The wind blew particulates away from his body only for it to immediately restore once again from the streams of Beconium bleeding out of the crystals, into him.

Oli lay down inside the armoured suit, which now kept him contained, as it closed back up around him, the augmented cy-bionics moulding to his emerald suit's shape. This wasn't a permanent fix but it would be enough to get him the resources that he did need to keep himself stabilised.

Using his visor to scan the flight capabilities of the crashed I.S.S. shuttle, Oli determined that, despite the damage and the crystals that had been thrust through certain parts of the vessel with the intent to disable it permanently, it could, potentially, still fly well enough to achieve escape velocity and breach Zonju's atmosphere.

Oli exited the cave as the streams of Beconium tailed off and he moved back into the tunnel, arming the nano-explosives on his

Pyrotech suit as he went. He stepped back into the large chamber where a fierce Beconium storm had erupted to the point that the wind had become a severe gale and visibility was extremely low in the fierce, rusty shroud. The Polarian Beconi' swarmed around fiercely, their scarlet-bladed rims cutting through the storm, ferocious in their attacks as they narrowly missed Oli, grazing by the walls as they clashed against one another, deflecting away, only to come about once again. Huge chunks of rock and crystal were sliced away and came crashing down around him.

Keeping his head as low down as possible, Oli ran from cover to cover, behind pillars, rocks and crystal clusters as he made his way across the chamber, towards the throne. Looking up, he could see that the barrels of the Polarian Beconi' blaster cannons had now deployed from the rotating dishes as they tore, increasingly more aggressive, through the air, blasting at one another through the swarms of Beconium particulates that trailed behind them like a plague of ravenous locusts. The burning-scarlet blaze of the fight moved out, through the missing ceiling, beyond the cave and into the night sky above.

While the Pyrotech armour was weaponised, its arsenal was intended for relatively close combat. Oli needed to arm himself against the powerful blaster bolts and other weapons that ignited the sky above him from a distance.

Remembering the potential dangers of using energy weapons, vehicle thrusters and jet propulsion units on Crystalosis, he knew the only way he would be able to deal with these opponents would be to charge up the black crystals on the throne.

Although Oli enjoyed customising a wide assortment of high-tech gadgets for his armoured suits and the Rhinonoid, ever since he was an Initiate with the I.S.S, he liked to keep some things simple and low-tech to make his use of these tools more meaningful, he didn't become lazy in his problem-solving abilities and so he could take control when situations like this arose.

He pulled a thin piece of steel, attached to a small beaded chain ring, from his sleeve which armed a small, compact missile on his forearm, much like arming a hand grenade by pulling out the pin. The missile sprung up from his arm and locked into position. A spring-loaded grip trigger flipped into position in the palm of his hand. He had been inspired for the device when he was still only an Initiate with the I.S.S. in a sapphire, armoured suit during his mission training.

Watching and concentrating hard on the airborne Polarian Beconi' Oli waited for the right moment when one of them would dive back down into the cave. This is where his knowledge of energy conversion from his studies with the I.S.S. would become really useful.

As soon as his opportunity came along, he seized it. He raced up the steps towards the throne as fast as he could, ran past the crystal structure and jumped straight off the ledge behind it, squeezing the trigger in the palm of his hand as he leapt into the air.

A chain reaction of detonations was triggered from the bottom of the suit, progressing upwards, which catapulted Oli high off the ground, towards the top of the chamber. As the series of detonations depleted, he used the momentum of the blasts to run up the side of one of the pillars to gain more height as the explosives replenished. He then back flipped away from the crystal pillar and squeezed the handle again, triggering the next series of detonations which threw him through the air, across to the opposite side of the chamber.

He was now at a high enough altitude to be level with the walls with the holes carved into them. Once again, using the momentum that he had gathered, he ran across the side of the wall.

Dishes from the Polarian Beconi' sliced into the wall in quick succession, narrowly missing him. With the containment field thinned, the Beconium storms flooded out from between the dishes in an attempt to suffocate the Operative. Oli kicked away from the wall, twisting through the air towards the nearest of the dishes. He landed in a back handspring on the first one, launched himself onto the next and then back flipped through the air, aiming the missile on his forearm directly at one of the, now-once-again, airborne Polarian Beconi'.

He struck the steel in his hand across the piece of flint, protruding from his suit behind the missile. A flash of blinding sparks erupted from the strike, triggering the missile and launching it at the target.

Oli then thrust the piece of steel back into its slot in his wrist-guard and triggered the explosives one more time which sent him hurtling over the huge crystal throne below, just as the missile struck one of the Polarian Beconi', drawing its attention. It began firing volleys of blaster bolts at Oli who opened the Pyrotech suit while still airborne.

The shots narrowly missed the suit and struck the throne below, hyper-charging the crystals with the energy from the blasts and causing the structure to erupt in a spectacular display of lethal, perpetual laser beams that streamed out in all directions from the crystals, cutting through anything they touched, including the walls, as crystal shards and huge boulders fell to the ground, now much more rapidly and with much more volatility. Oli allowed his malleable form to pour out of the armoured suit in a stream of Beconium particulates, to be swept up in the wind.

The missile strike had damaged one of the metal dishes, compromising the polarised containment field and forcing the battling occupants to bail out before one of the concentrated laser beams struck them.

The now-unoccupied dishes were sent spiralling out of control, towards one of the pillars in Oli's direction. The stream of rusty particulates, that was Oli, dived down for the dishes as the Beconium bled out of the crystals all around the chamber, streaming through the air towards him and restoring his physical body as he reached both hands out towards the containment field between the dishes, tearing through the air at immense speed.

The containment field was drawn towards his outstretched hands and drew him in, just in time, before smashing into the ground. Oli tucked his arms in to protect his body as he and the dishes crashed to the floor. He rolled across the ground, hugging the dishes close, and eventually used the momentum to throw himself back to his feet.

He lowered the dishes that floated in mid-air, pivoting slowly next to his arms which came down to his sides, revealing his restored body in the glow of the scarlet laser rims that now blazed, bright, around the edges of the dishes. Although he suspected that his mutation remained on a sub-atomic level, he was no longer formed of a culmination of Beconium. There were no burns on his face and his vision was entirely restored.

Relieved to have survived the ordeal and seeing that his emerald suit of armour was uncompromised, Oli turned around to see the Beconium beings standing around him, enraged by his attack. Streams of energy were pouring fiercely into them from all around the room.

Suddenly, there was a loud whooshing sound from behind as the automated Pyrotech armour landed on the floor, scraping the piece of flint on its arm against a rock as the suit tumbled against it. The resulting deployed missile, from the armour, narrowly missed Oli's face as he turned just in time to see it soar past him. It rocketed across the chamber and struck the wall above the archway, causing the rocks and crystals that formed the wall to crack and rupture until its integrity failed and the archway caved in.

Oli was now trapped inside the chamber, with the infuriated Beconium Beings now charging at him. He raced over to the throne, sliding under, jumping over, ducking and dodging the moving laser beams from the crystals as the streams of light moved around the chamber. With one final slide across the floor, the dishes detected the incoming obstacle that Oli was heading directly for and their edges began to burn more fiercely with scarlet laser energy as he reached out with one of them, slicing a thin piece of crystal clean off from a much larger cluster at the foot of the throne.

Oli swept the crystal up in his hand as the laser beam continued to fire the stream of lethal energy from its point. He needed a diversion to get past the Beconium Beings, to retrieve the Pyrotech armour and to flee the cave. He reached out with the crystal, directing the laser beam straight at one of the Polarian Beconi' as he leapt high into the air, rolling over before landing and allowing the dishes to hurtle beneath him, missing narrowly. The beam of energy sliced straight through the metal dishes as their momentum carried them across the chamber until they stopped dead, having embedded themselves in the wall, their laser-bladed edges dimming until they had faded entirely.

Amazed that his improvised strategy had worked, Oli quickly turned the laser beam on the Beconium Beings as they appeared to cautiously back away.

What Oli hadn't realised, however, was that a final remaining Polarious Beconus was now drawing in the shards of metal from the floor as they collectively swirled around, rapidly, in its containment field.

Realising what it was preparing to do, Oli urgently backed away with a rapid toe-to-heel action as he moved towards the Pyrotech suit, never once taking his eyes off the hostiles as he held out the crystal, directing the laser beam in their direction as they tried to edge towards him, only to once again back away from his ferocity, bearing his teeth and lunging fiercely at them before quickly resuming his retreat.

Then, from behind the distraction of the Beconium beings, came a blaster bolt, straight at Oli which, just by blind chance, struck one of the dishes that floated just inches away from his arm, almost shield-like. This was Oli's exact thought as it had blocked the perfectly aimed blaster bolt from hitting him.

He directed the laser beam from the crystal shard he was holding, through the crowd of Beconium Beings and sliced straight through the two dishes which sent one of the metal shards that had been swirling around in the containment field, tearing through the air, right at him.

The metal shard slashed across his armoured suit, leaving a long, silver gash across the chest-plate between two of the deep slash marks that came from his encounter with Xzjytheous onboard The Scout Hut.

Oli looked down at the damage and then back up at the approaching Polarious Beconus which had somehow managed to remain airborne despite Oli's clean-cut attack. He turned back to it just in time for another shard to cut through the air, straight at him again, like a throwing knife. Oli blocked the incoming projectile with one of the floating dishes which followed as he raised up his hand to cover his face.

The Polarious Beconus continued to advance, slow and malevolent, as Oli directed the laser beam from the crystal through the dishes once more. Still, the hostile remained. His attack that had completely destroyed the other Polarian Beconi' didn't seem to even deter this one. It appeared that it had adapted to his tactics and was utilising its containment field to maintain its overall structure, regardless of the damage it sustained.

With a swift glance over his shoulder, Oli finished shuffling backwards and stopped next to the Pyrotech suit. He dropped the crystal to the floor, jumped inside the armour while the dishes remained in place on the outside of the wrist-guards and then retrieved the crystal once again.

He triggered the suit's explosive chain reaction which launched him through the air, straight towards the caved-in archway. He needed to escape the chamber and, while he could quite easily have used the Pyrotech suit to get out through the open top of the cave, he also needed to get to the crashed I.S.S. shuttle in the cave back down the tunnel.

As he landed back on the ground, he opened the suit up and barrel rolled out of it, taking it with him by grabbing its wrist. He tore out the thin piece of steel and, stretching the suit's arm out from the outside, he recovered from the roll, arriving in a crouched position and struck at the embedded piece of flint, launching a newly locked-in missile at the obstructed passageway. The Polarious Beconus continued to volley shards of metal through the air at Oli, now combined with blaster bolts, as he returned to the Pyrotech suit and deflected the attacks away with one hand controlling the dish while his other hand slashed at the approaching hostile using the laser beam from the crystal.

Still unable to cut down his assailant, Oli turned and raced, as fast as he could, across the final stretch of the cave, clambering through the hole he had made in the fallen debris.

As he tumbled to the floor on the other side, scrambled to his feet and hurried down the tunnel, Oli heard an explosive sound, the volley of loud, powerful blaster bolts chasing him from behind. The bright flare of blinding blaster bolts illuminated the tunnel from around the bend he had just passed as the barricade of rocks and crystals was blown out, into the tunnel, a cloud of dust erupting behind the fleeing Operative.

It seemed that nothing could stop the Polarious Beconus and the Beconium Beings from pursuing him. All he could hope to do now was run and run fast, faster than he ever knew he could, because there was no doubt now, they were coming. Not for the dishes, not anymore. They were coming for him.

Oli wasn't used to fleeing. Normally he stood his ground but now all he could feel was anxiety, anticipation and huge amounts of adrenaline surging through his body, making him weak at his trembling knees.

Suddenly, Oli tripped and fell to the floor, the crystal rolling away from him. Terrified, he quickly looked back over his shoulder to see the staggering, fuzzy shadows of the Beconium Beings against the bend in the moonlit wall, rushing down the passageway, coming for him.

Desperately, Oli scrambled across the floor and retrieved the black crystal shard. He tried to slow the Polarious Beconus and the Beconium Beings down while he made his escape by sweeping the laser beam back and forth across the tunnel ceiling between them and him, causing another cave in.

He then emerged from the cloud of dust and ran through the archway, clambering over the boulders that littered the floor, to reach the ship's crash site as he heard another explosive volley of blaster bolts obliterating the obstruction from behind, a mere few seconds later. They were closing in on him...very, very fast. The chase was almost over.

There was nowhere left to go now and his terrifying pursuers would be there in moments. Oli climbed up onto the roof of the ship, turned the laser beam on the archway, renewing the cave-in as a final attempt at delaying the Polarious Beconus and the Beconium Beings.

He then dropped down, through the shuttle's escape hatch, throwing away the crystal as it would tear apart the ship's interior if he took it with him.

He rushed into the cockpit and, on seeing the mess that had been made of the controls; he set about hotwiring the ship. As he frantically worked, he once again heard the loud, muffled, sound of blaster bolts explosively tearing through the debris that separated him from his fate. He could see the glow of the explosive plasma energy from behind the rocks as it grew brighter and brighter.

As the ships systems came online, Oli rose to his feet and stepped out of the bulky Pyrotech suit that encased his standard emerald I.S.S. suit so that he could pilot the ship more comfortably. The area around the caved-in entrance was now completely ablaze with light from the fierce, rapid blasts of the Polarious Beconus to the point where some of the rock was starting to fizz and liquidise.

Oli began to pull the ship away from the cave just as his enraged pursuers made it through the barricade. Rocks and crystal shards struck the outside of the ship from the blast causing it to judder.

While still unsure of how much the ship had to offer and hoping that the thrusters and life support hadn't just taken a critical hit from the explosion of debris, Oli turned the shuttle away from the mountainside and fired up the forward thrusters, hoping and praying to achieve and maintain escape velocity.

Oli suddenly felt his face turning pale with terror as he heard the projectile shards of metal, hurtled through the air from the containment field, piercing the ship's hull all over. He ducked and dodged, covering his head with his arm as the debris breached the ship entirely and thrust, like knives and raining bullets, through the roof of the cockpit. Powerful, pressurised jets of hot, white smoke flooded the cockpit and blasted out through the holes made by the projectiles. A single blast from the Polarious Beconus hit the crystal that Oli had left on the floor as the abomination entered the cave, causing the crystal to spin around on impact and the laser beam swept across the underbelly of the ship, tearing away the landing gear. The ship could no longer leave the planet due to the hull-breach and, with the landing gear now gone as well, Oli couldn't even set the ship down elsewhere on the planet's surface.

The Polarious Beconus unleashed the Beconium storm from within its containment field and it washed over the entire ship in a thick wave of particulates and toxic gas, bleeding through the holes in the hull and creating blockages throughout.

The ship's thrusters cut out as the particulates clogged up the fuel lines and Oli began choking as the toxic gas flooded the cockpit, suffocating him as the white smoke turned to rusty-orange.

There was no escape. The ship met its final fate as it went into a freefall nosedive to the foot of the mountain, taking Oli with it.

CHAPTER 27
THE AUGMENTATION INTERLINK

Xzjytheous had been to Zonju previously when he had first been delivered to Parathax by a bounty hunter who had betrayed him after they'd formed an alliance back when Biker Delta Squadron 5-6-5 were all just Initiates in their sapphire, armoured suits. It was, for this reason that Xzjytheous knew of the Black-Burn Fighter launch chambers that were blown in the outer walls of the Zonju mountains, much like the one used by the Con-Haarians to land their shuttles that had been laden with prisoners before Isaac, Nathan and Tamatha liberated them.

With the I.S.S. Distress Signal Badge now in his possession and having escaped from Gala-Thius and Anthony, Xzjytheous had taken shelter from the sunlight in one of the passageways that had been left by the Rhinonoid's Expansion Matrix, used by Corey when rescuing Tino.

Now as a silhouette in the moonlight, the Reptilian raced, on all-fours, across the rocky expanse and up the near-vertical exterior of one of the nearby mountains until he reached the nearest launch chamber. He climbed into the docked Black-Burn Fighter and set a flight course for Becon into the ship's Galacta-Nav. As soon as the fighter was clear of any obstacles, Xzjytheous fired up its augmented burn thrusters and, in a split second, the ship was gone.

Moments later, the cockpit of the Black-Burn Fighter was aglow with amber light, reflected from the slow-turning, deadly planet of Becon. As the Reptilian waited, an orbital space station came into view, drifting above the planet.

Long before Xzjytheous was in servitude to Parathax, he had rampaged across the galaxy in his own fierce vendetta to avenge the death of his family at the hands of the small Biolum Military. This rampage had led him to a Beconium-mining and research facility, used for military purposes, and it was where he had first encountered the Interstellar Scouts in person on one of their infiltration and intelligence gathering missions while he was in pursuit of a target - Jason Campbell, the man who would eventually be assigned as Biker Delta Squadron 5-6-5's first Troop Leader.

Later betrayed by the very people who he had helped to track Jason and with the I.S.S. long since gone, Xzjytheous had severed his ties and returned to the facility, killing everyone onboard and began using it for himself as one of several outposts that he had raided and taken control of across the galaxy.

These bases were connected by an augmentation interlink, allowing Xzjytheous to move between mobile outposts in an instant. This particular outpost now served as storage for a bionic army that the Reptilian had built, an army he now intended to unleash to redeem himself.

The Black-Burn Fighter docked in the hanger bay, capturing the attention of the bionics that patrolled the area with weapons that had been stolen from the soldiers and miners that once occupied the station.

Xzjytheous climbed out of the fighter, strode across the hanger bay and leapt high into the air, landing on the walkway that overlooked the landing zone. He moved under an archway and continued along the walkway which then ran above a neighbouring room, the walls and floor still covered in black blaster-bolt burn marks from the fire fight he was locked into with the I.S.S. while pursuing Jason.

Moving through the doors at the end of the walkway, Xzjytheous entered the station's primary control deck and used the various consoles to activate the Contingency Protocol.

Huge squads of invisible, powered-down bionics rose up on platforms throughout the station from the lower, Beconium-contaminated storage levels. It was only when the Reptilian flooded the station with Ultraviolet light that their power cores began to absorb and store the light as energy, allowing them to be seen and power up after being stored down on the lower decks for so long. Xzjytheous also activated the augmentation interlink, leaving it on a perpetual cycle which allowed for armed patrol ships, stolen from the other outposts and pre-automated, to travel across the galaxy on a repeated cycle in search of hostiles while the station guarded the planet below.

Before leaving, Xzjytheous activated the station's external weapon systems. Anyone who was fortunate enough to make it past those defences would immediately be dealt with by the bionics but he didn't want to risk the station being exposed to a long range attack if a fleet assault was attempted.

With the station's external defences on standby, Xzjytheous then returned to the hanger bay. He didn't, however, board the Black-Burn Fighter he had arrived in. Instead, he boarded a larger, more heavily-armoured and weaponised ship that had been docked in the hanger bay and hidden by a stealth field generator.

The Spyglass had been stolen by Xzjytheous when he had fled Biolum and gone on his rampage so it too was dependent on the light as a power source, like most vehicles and facilities on Biolum, as it was such an abundant resource in that part of the galaxy.

Once onboard The Spyglass, Xzjytheous activated the stations remaining internal defences in the form of pivoting laser walls and explosives that emitted trip-beams, invisible to both the naked eye and most technology, certainly that of the Interstellar Scouts. The patrolling bionics, however, had specialised sensors which allowed them to both see and evade the lasers.

With the station fully armed and its defences raised, Xzjytheous exited the hanger bay onboard The Spyglass and headed down to the planet below.

CHAPTER 28
THE ALLEGIANCE

From The Stealthy Intoxicator's observation deck on Becon, Parathax, smiling an evil grin to herself, oversaw the return of hundreds of shuttles bearing enormous hauls of salvaged scrap metal from Polarious 5 trailing in their wake. There was enough to create an entire fleet of cruisers and a Polarian Beconi' invasion force of immeasurable size.

As the ships set their cargo down on the planet's surface, Parathax made her way back to the hanger bay where the Rhinonoid was docked. Anticipating an attack from the I.S.S, she chose to take several stealth field generators from the stolen tank but leave it safe and secure on board the cruiser as it was of strategic value, providing a huge tactical advantage to whoever controlled it. She, instead, decided that she would take her own Augmented Black-Burn Fighter down to the ground below so she could set about creating her invasion force of Polarian Beconi'.

Parathax unleashed a powerful blast of dark, thorny energy which darted out to various consoles and control panels around the hanger bay and began interfacing with them. A huge hatch opened up in the ceiling, high above, as jets of white smoke on either side of the hatch surged outwards, hissing loudly. A huge fighter descended from the blackness beyond the hatch, secured to a powerful, mechanical arm with a vast array of articulation capabilities. Slowly, the arm lowered the fighter towards the floor of the hanger bay, a blazing red glow radiating from its cockpit window as its flight and weapon systems automatically began their initialisation. From the four corners of the Augmented Black-Burn Fighter's docking zone, rose four heavily-armoured interceptor drones with enhanced weapon capabilities.

Parathax's Augmented Black-Burn was much more imposing than other Black-Burns. It was almost twice the size, its thrusters were known to leave a slashing trail of blazing, scarlet light across the sky in the fighter's wake and the blacker than black colouration of the fighter showed the sharp, clean-cut, angled lines of radioactive-green light that ran through various parts of its wings while a blinding, almost-white spotlight ran, repeatedly, along the illuminated, green, bladed edges of the wings, that vaguely resembled a Deathstalker Fighter, in rapid, teardrop pulses.

The beauty of having such a huge haul from Polarious 5 and an entire planet of a once-prosperous civilisation was that both swarmed with the tormented souls of the dead, those who's ships had been struck within the debris field above or on Polarious 5 and those who had died instantly of Beconium Poisoning on Becon during a Beconium-ore meteor strike. Three resources were needed to create Polarian Beconi' and the polarised scrap metal and the Beconium alone weren't enough.

Emerging from her fighter, having returned to the ground, Parathax drifted through the growing Beconium storm, towards the enormous, tangled clusters of metal. As she glided over the Beconium that made up the planet's surface, levitated above the ground by her own dark aura, the black shroud within the modified gold cy-bionic suit that she now wore began to seep and flare out of the cracks in it which were caused by the Beconium contamination. Streams of black energy poured out, towards the huge chunks of metal.

Seemingly weightless, the metal levitated into the air under the influence of the black energy which then proceeded to tear it apart again and again and again into smaller and smaller chunks.

Some of the larger pieces of metal were left intact and levitated high above the ground with stealth field generators from the Rhinonoid attached to them. Once the stealth field generators were activated, any attack force that came after her wouldn't even make it through the invisible barricade, to the planet's surface.

Once thousands upon thousands of pieces of scrap metal had been torn apart and moulded into containment field dishes for her new Augmented Polarian Beconi', Parathax looked out to the Beconium dunes on the horizon and poured her black energy out into them also. The storm quickly intensified, raging fiercely as the planet's atmospheric radiation spiked higher and higher, converting into more fierce, explosive bolts of lightning in the dense shroud.

The world trembled beneath her, a loud, harsh whisper of an ancient, long-lost language echoing on the wind as long streams of Beconium were pulled, through the air, from the immense mounds. They swept by the rows of dishes that levitated, inches of the ground, awaiting their new occupants and, as they streamed through, the spirits of Becon's long-dead were filtered out, their screaming faces swirling around between each of the pairs of dishes, trapped within their containment fields which flooded with shrouds of toxic gas and Beconium particulates.

Parathax had intended the same fate for the prisoners brought to Zonju by the Con-Haarians. They had failed her but it was of little consequence. Once the Interstellar Scouts were no more, the inhabitants of Con-Haar, the survivors of Polarious and every other civilisation out there would share the same fate as they fell to her dominion.

Eventually the entire expanse of Beconium dunes for miles around had been levelled to the ground, the remnants of which, simply being carried away in the storm as it calmed, the echo of the ancient language fading to a whisper and then silence. Parathax's invasion force was now ready for interplanetary conquest.

As she turned away, something caught her eye, a tiny black spot against the burnt-orange sky. Parathax grinned as it tore through the air towards the ground. Her grin, however, quickly gave way to a look of surprise and intrigue as she realised that, rather than an entire strike against her, the I.S.S. sent just a single, small ship to Becon. Nevertheless she would begin with them and the rest would surely follow.

Moving closer to the ground, the ship began to slow down and alter its course. Rather than attempting to land on the planet's surface, as she had anticipated, it moved into position to dock in one of The Stealthy Intoxicator's many hanger bays as Parathax watched on, her curiosity deepening. She returned to her Augmented Black-Burn Fighter and took it back up to the hanger bay where the intruder had docked.

Having landed back on the cruiser, Parathax emerged from her fighter to find Xzjytheous and his two bionics standing in front of her, surrounded by the armoured Beconium beings stationed onboard her ship.

'Reptilian' she laughed.

He must have had a very serious reason for being there as, the last time he stood before her, he was mere seconds from being executed at the hands of her Polarian Beconi'. Parathax awaited his explanation but none came.

'Kill him' she said simply as she turned her gaze away and slowly moved past him, making her way towards the corridor beyond the hanger bay and leaving the soldiers to advance on the creature.

Xzjytheous threw a rectangular object in Parathax's direction which drew her attention, stopping her in her tracks as it clattered across the floor. Retrieving it, she could see that it was an Interstellar Scouts Distress Signal Badge from one of their cy-bionic suits.

'STAND DOWN!' she commanded her soldiers as she quickly moved back across the hanger bay, towards Xzjytheous, the badge clutched tightly in her grasp.

'You know what this is?' she asked Xzjytheous, levitating the object above her hand as it rotated in front of him, the reflection of the lights above sweeping across the words behind the thick glass of the badge.

Satisfied that he had regained the fascination of the soon-to-be dominant force in the galaxy; Xzjytheous set about also regaining her favour.

'I stole it from the chamber on Zonju, the only proof of their leader's survival. They will come to you and you will kill them all' hissed Xzjytheous, faithfully as he took to his knee before Parathax, bowing his large, ridged head.

'No' she replied in a loud whisper as she moved closer to the Reptilian, towering over him. Her black shroud reached out through the cracks in her armour, wrapping its ice-cold tentacles around him and feeding off his fear. 'You shall bring them. They will be reduced to Beconium like those that fell before them and will join my conquest as Generals in my Polarian Beconi' invasion force. Their ghostly cries will bellow across the cosmos as they choke on their failure, eternally, in their bespoke raging storms.'

Xzjytheous slowly glanced around as the hanger bay appeared to gradually darken. 'A shadow shall be cast, so dark that even the blaze of your home world, Biolum, will be smothered. Fail me again and Biolum will fall beneath a darker shadow, the Deathstalker Squadron – No mercy, no survivors' she elaborated, extending a pale, icy finger from beyond the armoured glove which retracted away from her hand and back, over the wrist-guard, hooking it slightly as her long finger nail dug into the flesh beneath the Reptilian's chin, forcing him to look back up at her.

'Rise Reptilian, my loyal disciple, and follow my path to war and conquest' Parathax commanded, scratching her nail under his chin with a single slash as she turned away.

Xzjytheous hung his head slightly, hiding his face as he cast the piercing black pupils of his amber eyes back up at Parathax, the darkness of the hanger bay receding. He then returned to his feet and followed her across the hanger bay, past rows of ships, and into the Rhinonoid where she activated and hid the Distress Signal Badge in the jet propulsion unit refuelling station. Meanwhile, Xzjytheous left his two bionics to guard the room containing Oli's customised suits.

CHAPTER 29
ON OUR HONOUR!

Biker Delta Squadron 5-6-5 and their new companions, having finally found the opportunity to get the rest that they had so desperately needed, were suddenly awoken by an alert that sounded throughout The Knightfall, which had remained in orbit above Zonju while everyone recovered from the shear fatigue they were all experiencing.

'There's a distress signal coming in. On an I.S.S. signature' announced Nathan as he opened his eyes and sat forward in the pilot's seat, acknowledging the beeping sound coming from the console.

'Where from?' asked Isaac, as he joined Nathan in looking down at the screen. The two Operatives then gazed up at each other with dread.

'Ethan, when did you lose your Distress Signal Badge?' asked Isaac, warily, as the signal's signature was confirmed by the empty slot on Ethan's armoured suit.

Ethan slowly looked about the cockpit at the other Operatives staring at him as he entered from the cargo-hold. Gala-Thius remained silent as, being a former I.S.S. Troop Leader, it was one of the first things he had noticed when he originally met the group.

'ETHAN!' repeated Isaac urgently, causing the young Operative to jump with fright.

'Crystalosis' he said, quietly and ashamed as he hung his head. He knew that he was in trouble with the group and that his Distress Signal Badge might be baiting them into a trap especially now that both Xzjytheous and Parathax were out there, hell-bent on taking down the I.S.S.

'Where?' asked Isaac, barely catching Ethan's reply.

'How?' asked Colin, standing next to him.

Ethan felt like crying through the guilt and discomfort of everyone staring him down in silent accusation but he had really wanted to help Colin in that moment when Oli fell during the Deathstalkers' attack. This was the price that he now had to pay for doing, what he believed, was the right thing.

This resonated with Corey as it was the same lesson that he'd had to learn while arguing with Isaac as they had left Oli behind. Ethan had made his decision and now he had to face the consequences, consequences that might just be too intense for him to handle.

Colin picked up on how Ethan was feeling and walked him out of the cockpit, placing his arm reassuringly over his friend's shoulder.

'Becon' announced Isaac, as soon as the door closed behind Ethan and Colin. He knew the rest of the group were waiting to ask what was displayed on the screen.

'What's Becon?' asked Tino, now awake, although still regaining his memories. He had suddenly felt the mood become much heavier in the cockpit.

'It's where Anthony and I went when we fled Parathax all those years ago' Gala-Thius reminded Tino.

'Becon is an inhospitable world where all life has been wiped away. We don't know the exact details but I.S.S. intelligence suggests it was caused by a radioactive meteor strike. We believe the meteor contained a sort of rusty, toxic metal as a sandy substance called Beconium, the same stuff you saw inside those dishes that attacked us back on Zonju' explained Isaac.

'It's a desolate world now. The entire planet resembles just one big desert' continued Nathan.

'It's where our friend was killed' finished a brooding Corey, believing that nothing could have been done to prevent the loss of Oli, however indirect, from the moment that blaster bolt from Xzjytheous had hit his suit's respiratory filter.

'Do you think it's a trap?' asked Nathan, turning back to Isaac, although he was almost certain that everyone knew the answer.

'Ethan's here with us so he's not triggering the signal, it's under his signature and it's coming from Becon, one of the most hostile planets in the system. I don't know anyone that could survive being there for very long at all' replied Isaac as he went through a process of elimination to reach the most likely scenario.

'I do' interjected Gala-Thius after a long, drawn-out silence. The other Operatives collectively turned to look at him.

'Parathax could survive on Becon for as long as it chooses. It's not alive enough to be affected by the environment' he explained.

'You told me Parathax was an ancient being like you and that she experimented with dark conjurations' Tino recalled, turning to Gala-Thius.

'What IS Parathax?' asked Corey who, unlike Tino, picked up on Gala-Thius' use of the word 'it' rather than 'he' or 'she'.

'It's an Astral Alias' replied Gala-Thius, trying to hold back the horrifying memories that Tino had prompted of Parathax's origins long ago.

'As in that's not its true name and form?' asked Corey, remembering back to his attacker who took control of the Rhinonoid on Zonju and guessing that it might have been the same entity.

'As in refined, perfected evil. You young Operatives are now wading into very dangerous waters. No amount of awarded badge upgrades on your uniforms can protect you against an entity like this. A lack of name or form is insignificant. You're right. Parathax did experiment with dark conjurations long ago, until it found Becon, raised it to the ground with that meteor and so were born, its Polarian Beconi'. If Parathax and its creations have moved to a war footing and established a base of operations on Becon, as I suspect it has with your stolen vehicle, there is no hope' replied Gala-Thius bluntly, turning to look each of the Operatives straight in the eye. 'If it sees you coming, it won't even bother to adopt an alias, it'll just kill you without giving it a second thought.

Isaac, Nathan, Corey and Tino all stared at Gala-Thius, their mouths all hanging slightly agape.

The silence filled the cockpit as Gala-Thius composed himself. 'I urge you all, retreat now' he warned.

The stunned silence continued as Isaac contemplated the 'lose / don't win' scenario he now found himself leading. He could either order a retreat, let Parathax win effortlessly and wait for the fall of the Interstellar Scouts, them included followed by intergalactic conquest or they could confront Parathax, make a noble stand and fall with honour in protection of the intergalactic communities that they had pledged, on their honour, to defend. If they made a stand, they would at least know that they had upheld their morals as Interstellar Scouts. One way or another, it was the end. They were the only ones who knew what and where Parathax was to be able to make a stand. Parathax had won.

'Set a course for Becon' instructed Isaac, exhaling hard after a moment of contemplation.

Gala-Thius frowned hard at Isaac's foolish decision.

'BUT IT'S A TRAP!' argued Corey, jumping to his feet and extending his arm at the display to accentuate his statement, just as he had when they followed the distress signal coming from Zonju, demonstrating how stupidly reckless Isaac was being.

'Exactly. An I.S.S. Distress Signal Badge has been activated by one of the most deadly beings, on one of the most deadly planets out there. Any survivors of the I.S.S. brave enough to come out of hiding to answer a distress call will also be out there, en-route to Becon right now. They're completely unaware of the massacre they will be walking into. We must get there first and take out that distress signal. Maybe some survivors will be able to scramble to the furthest reaches of the galaxy or seek refuge on other worlds and then rendezvous safely elsewhere to mount some sort of offensive... eventually' replied Isaac who was done fighting with Corey.

'Course set for Becon. Standby for augmented burn' announced Nathan as he put the co-ordinates into the Galacta-Nav and adjusted the ship's settings.

In the blink of an eye, The Knightfall arrived in orbit at their destination. The rusty glow of Becon flooded through to the cockpit despite the scarlet laser barriers in place of the window as Colin and Ethan rejoined the group.

Tino rose to his feet and slowly approached the window as a tear crept out from the corner of his eye, rolling down his cheek.

'This is where it happened? Where the Deathstalkers were captured and Oli died?' he asked.

'You knew Oli?' asked Colin.

Tino nodded slowly. 'He was my closest friend' he replied.

The Operatives all frowned; slightly confused as they had all spent a lot of time with Oli, especially Isaac, Nathan and Colin but they had no prior memory of Tino.

'Oli didn't actually die here, he was just attacked. There were a lot of complications that followed but we lost him on Crystalosis' replied Isaac, sorrowfully.

The group approached the weapon-customisers that ran along the wall of the cargo-hold and began working at the station that had the broken down sections of the knife floating above one another in the containment field.

One by one, the Operatives customised a sword with a shiny, colour-stained, steel blade and a high-voltage electrical current flowing through the middle of it that they intended to use in combat against Parathax and Xzjytheous.

They each customised the sword hilt differently to suit their preferred method of gripping their weapon and added different attachments to them. Some hilts had a tiny blaster angled down at the blade to channel a plasma bolt towards an enemy if their sword was blocked, some had detachable blade sections that could propel four separate sections of the blade through the air at multiple assailants but all had a thin piece of flint and a clear coating just above the blade's edge which, possibly, served the most important purpose of all, something they had learnt from the last time they were stranded in the radiation storms of Becon - Visual communication.

The cockpit had an extremely atmospheric feel to it as the group returned to the front and watched the slow turn of the burnt-orange planet below. Being back here made the Operatives of Biker Delta Squadron 5-6-5 vividly relive the last time they were on Becon, the horror of waiting out the radiation storms and Oli's uncertain fate, closing in on him as they had all fought hard to protect him until they were evacuated.

As it turned out, it had all been for nothing and now they were back to do it all again, only this time there was no extraction coming for them and this mission was much more dangerous with much higher stakes.

'No inbound ships on the scanners. Standing-by to begin landing approach' announced Nathan as he flicked several switches on the console, unaware of Xzjytheous' heavily armed battle station in orbit and starting to move around the crest of the planet as, it too, searched for intruders.

Isaac stood up and turned to the group as they gathered around him, his voice projecting through the cockpit for everyone to hear. Although he spoke to everyone collectively, he included a lot of comforting sub-text for Colin's sake.

'There's no denying the toll Becon took on us the last time we were here. When we were shot down and had to survive until extraction, we were I.S.S. Operatives but we were inexperienced at working as a Patrol. These past few days, each of you have proven yourselves in carrying out your duties, working together to survive and putting the safety of others first. I thought Oli was very privileged to be assigned the position of our Patrol Leader and I couldn't see why he would never just take the lead without speaking to the rest of us and the Troop Leaders first and why he would always have us make decisions collectively instead but these past few days I have come to understand why he did that. There is real danger out there and each of us has an important role to play in our Patrol to ensure the mission is a success. The enemy is waiting for us, mocking us, down there. They have taken the tank that Oli built, the suits that Oli wore. Whether the I.S.S. drowns in the toxic sands of Becon today or we live to venture on, we will fight in Oli's honour! Oli sacrificed himself to save us and we will follow him to the end to save the Interstellar Scouts and all those it protects. There may be refined, perfected evil awaiting you and me down there but the galaxy was like that long before Parathax ever came along and, as Interstellar Scouts, it is our job to become the imperfections. Every selfless act we choose to help others, however small, creates an imperfection in that evil. Remember that. Do your best. Do your duty' Isaac finished, holding back tears and unable to project his voice any longer, for the emotion he was feeling. The other Operatives watched on, inspired by his words, improvised though they were, smiling in memory of Oli.

'ON OUR HONOUR!' replied the Operatives' passionate, collective voice.

They activated their 'Master at Arms' Badge on the sleeve of their armoured suits, causing their blasters to hyper-charge.

'Ok Nathan, take us down' Isaac instructed.

An air of tension and anxiety flooded the ship as they felt it descending.

'Respiratory filters active and helmets sealed for arrival. Have your respirator masks on standby' instructed Isaac as he and the others interacted with their First Aid Badges so that, at the touch of it at any given time, their respirator masks would deploy to help them breathe in the hostile environment. 'Our Primary Objective is to stop that distress signal from transmitting, by any means necessary before any I.S.S. forces are baited into the trap. Defeating Parathax and Xzjytheous, while equally important, is the Secondary Objective' he continued.

Isaac then activated his suit's Meteorology Badge to assess the environmental conditions at the co-ordinates that the distress signal was being transmitted from.

'I don't suppose Oli ever completed his research and experimentation with the effects of Beconium did he?' asked Isaac.

Colin shook his head. 'He came close with a few trials which he was trying to refine in his room to cure his own condition but he never saw it through' he explained.

'In that case, our main environmental concern is skin contamination. Do not let the Beconium touch your skin. That being said; only use your helmets if you absolutely have to. None of us need to be reminded of how severe the radiation storms are down there and they WILL demand use of our helmets but, even without the storms, the atmospheric radiation is enough to interfere with our visor systems and we'll be blinded so don't rely on them' Isaac instructed.

The Operatives, including Tino, followed the orders and prepared themselves for deployment as Nathan fired up the forward thrusters, directing them towards the signal as the ship shook violently around them, tearing through the planet's atmosphere.

CHAPTER 30
THE RETURN TO BECON

From the observation deck of The Stealthy Intoxicator, Parathax and Xzjytheous watched through the window as the black speck of The Knightfall came into view, high above the planet's surface.

'Ever the heroes' Parathax mocked. 'Remain onboard and guard the bridge. It's a key strategic target for them' it instructed as it activated the stealth field generators on the huge chunks of metal that were floating level with the cruiser. It then deployed the gold helmet of its modified cy-bionic suit and returned to the hanger bay to take its ship down to the planet's surface.

As it approached its Augmented Black-Burn Fighter, it passed one of Oli's customised armoured suits, standing guard at the foot of the Rhinonoid's deployment bay ramp and looking about at its surroundings, as if occupied.

Each of Oli's suits were enhanced with an Expansion Matrix, similar to that used by the Rhinonoid which, with Parathax putting it to use on all of the suits it had positioned around the battlefield, made them enormous as well as much more powerful than they would otherwise be.

The staircases in the sides of the Rhinonoid were retracted up, into its hull, so that only one entrance was available with the hole smashed in the side being guarded by Xzjytheous' two bionics, from inside.

The suit's original purpose was to rescue people from burning environments or counter the effects of the Inferno suit through the use of powerful, pressurised CO2 jets designed to smother out the Oxygen from a fire using Carbon Dioxide but its new purpose was to seal any intruder inside the Rhinonoid's deployment bay with all other hatches secured shut and then flood it with CO2 to suffocate anyone that tried to either take the tank back or disable the Distress Signal Badge that was transmitting from the refuelling station.

Parathax departed the hanger bay and landed its fighter on the ground below, accompanied by the four interceptor drones. They set down in front of the enormous fortress which was now occupied along the battlements and on the towers by the Polarian Beconi' as well as twin armoured suits positioned at the two extreme ends at the front of the fortress. These suits were more specifically designed using the same expansion technology as the Rhinonoid for creating armoured shelters and defences on the spot when the safety of the Rhinonoid wasn't an option.

As The Knightfall descended, Corey identified the enormous Stealthy Intoxicator as the huge, imposing war cruiser that they had seen within the Polarian Nebula while evacuating The Scout Hut.

Having been fortunate enough to avoid the enormous clusters of invisible Polarian scrap metal that floated above, Nathan noticed that the ship's various systems and instruments were being affected by an external force as he deployed The Knightfall's landing gear and, slowly, settled the ship down to the ground, sinking slightly into the rusty, orange sand.

Parathax, floating weightlessly alongside its Augmented Black-Burn Fighter, waited patiently in front of the descended ship, a long, Beconium-stained, steel sword, also forged from the contaminated I.S.S. armour and weaponry it had found in the Rhinonoid's Quarantine Wing, clutched in its hand.

The Knightfall's loading ramp lowered to reveal the six I.S.S. Operatives, clad in their emerald, armoured suits, standing at the top. Gala-Thius and Anthony remained behind to defend the ship and operate its weapon systems if it became necessary.

The group made their way down the loading ramp, led by Isaac, and stopped once they reached the bottom. The closer they moved to the bottom of the ramp, the more the group felt strangely disorientated, like their minds couldn't focus properly, their thoughts distorted. This was caused by an extremely low-pitched, inaudible frequency that reverberated from Parathax's Augmented

Black-Burn Fighter. While inaudible, however, its effects were visible to the naked eye as it radiated as a transparent, rippling sphere around the ship. This same frequency was what was causing The Knightfall's systems to malfunction as it landed.

There was absolute silence except for the wind that swept across the vast expanse, sweeping a dusting of Beconium over the feet of each of the Operatives and the gentle scraping and clattering of small armoured plates that formed Parathax's helmet rattling around their opponent as the mechanical bionics constantly adjusted their positions to accommodate its lack of physical form.

Nathan looked upwards at the huge, imposing warship overhead as Colin looked to the armoured suits overlooking them from the fortress walls.

Retracting its helmet, Parathax grinned, menacingly, at the group as it waited for them to make their move.

Each of the Operatives removed their Distress Signal Badge from their armoured suit. They threw them down in front of their opponent and fired a single blast at their own badge, destroying them all as Parathax remained entirely unthreatened by their weapons.

'Your objective was to draw the surviving members of the I.S.S. out to finish us off but that's not going to happen. If we fail to stop you, we'll make sure they don't come looking for us' announced Isaac stepping forwards from the group.

'The trap is set. They're already coming, blinded by the same compassion that betrays you. You cannot stop me before your fleet arrives' taunted Parathax's ghastly voice, an ice-blue mist seeping out from between the constantly-adjusting armoured panels in the helmet where its mouth was.

Isaac took a few more paces, slowly but confidently, towards it as he tried to resist the growing effects of the low-pitched frequency being emitted from Parathax's Augmnted Black-Burn.

'You failed to destroy us in the Polarious Sector assault and you WILL fail now. It's our duty and we are honour-bound to it' he replied, grasping the hilt of his customised sword from his utility belt. Triggering a powerful spring mechanism, the doubled up hilt that served as a cover for the blade, released and arced downwards; locking into position on the bottom to double the hilt's size. This allowed the four spring-loaded sections of the blade to flick out in sequence and lock into their position also in a fierce flurry of sparks.

Isaac and Parathax locked eyes fiercely as the other Operatives deployed their swords too, in the same way. Parathax raised its sword into a defensive position, adopting a combat-ready stance.

'Lower your blade, boy, and submit to your fate, the first to fall in the Polarian Beconi' Conquest!' it ordered.

Suddenly, a buried Polarian Beconi' dish magnetised Isaac's suit holding him in place while a second one descended from within the range of the stealth field generators, hiding the huge chunks of debris, overhead. As the dish descended towards him, the polarised containment field grew stronger between them and began to excite the Beconium within it. Without giving it a second thought, both Nathan and Corey ran to Isaac's aid.

As Nathan thrust his sword through the dish buried in the Beconium to disrupt the containment field, Corey raised his sword above his head, charging at Parathax with a fierce yell.

'Go! Find the distress beacon!' Nathan shouted back to Colin, Ethan and Tino as he and Isaac followed Corey in the attack.

'Where do we start?' yelled Tino as Colin raced towards the towering fortress, closely followed by Ethan.

'We need to get up there!' replied Colin, looking up at the battlements.

'We'll use the jet propulsion units!' announced Ethan as he went to activate the illuminated red button in the middle of his collar.

'No, save the fuel, we might need it' replied Colin, holding out his arm to stop him.

'How do we get up there then?' asked Tino looking up at the huge wall.

Colin looked around urgently for something they could use to their advantage. 'Ethan, the suit up there; get its attention' instructed Colin as he pointed out the huge, silver customised suit at the far end of the wall. 'Come with me' he continued, grabbing Tino's arm and pulling him close to the wall, out of sight of the armoured suit.

'And then what?' asked Ethan, calling back to Colin as he eyed Oli's customised, armoured suit but Colin had already rushed off with Tino. Ethan drew his blaster from its holster and hesitantly fired several shots in the direction of the armoured suit which, on spotting its attacker, leapt from the wall and landed, heavily, on the ground, the impact launching a shroud of Beconium into the air around it.

Ethan returned his blaster to its holster and, looking over his shoulder and then back to the suit repeatedly, he quickly retreated. With a nervous weakness in his knees and almost falling over in the resistance of the Beconium as he pushed through it with his heels, he backed away towards the corner of the wall that Colin and Tino were waiting behind, as the huge armoured suit strode furiously towards him, speeding up gradually as it gained on the young Operative with every stride.

Under the intense circumstances, it took a moment for Ethan to realise that he could now stop squinting against the bright shine of the Beconium that caught the sunlight as he backed into the shade of a large, ominous shadow.

Frowning as he lowered his sword, he turned around to find Colin and Tino with their backs to him, holding up their own swords against the second of the twin customised suits that had landed behind them, both of which had come charging at the Operatives simultaneously.

Dodging to the side, out of the way of a powerful punch, Colin grabbed hold of a stunned Tino so that wherever Colin went, he went too.

'Are these suits weaponised?' shouted Ethan, turning back to see the other suit finally catch up with him.

'No!' replied Colin, dodging another attack from his adoptive brother's creation. 'They are heavily armoured though!' he continued as he struck the suit with several slashes from his sword.

As the sword slashed against the metal of the suit, blinding, green sparks erupted from Colin's blade, caused by the thin piece of flint running along the slightly-angled edge of the blade, combined with the rough, transparent coating that covered the rest of it. The coloration of the sparks was produced by the coating on the blade that allowed different Operatives to be identified from a distance when radio communication wasn't possible. The sparks also served as a secondary weapon by dazzling an opponent in battle, a technique that had been adapted and taught to the entire Patrol by Oli.

As Colin, Ethan and Tino fought to get control of Oli's animated suits, Isaac, Corey and Ethan were locked in a fierce duel with Parathax. Sparks of orange came from the Beconium on Parathax's sword while sparks of blue erupted from Nathan's, sparks of yellow flared from Isaac's and flashes of purple exploded from Corey's, coinciding with the colour of their shiny, steel blades with every clash.

Due to the volatile and flammable nature of Beconium, every time the steel blades clashed against each other, creating the sparks, slashed away and then swept through the Beconium on the ground, an arc of blinding, colourful fire would trail behind the blades before immediately fizzling out.

'FLANK!' shouted Corey as he kicked his foot out at Parathax while Nathan followed his instruction, however, Parathax was too fast. It blocked Nathan's attack as the energy, that bled from the cracks in its suit, wrapped around Corey's leg and sent him hurtling through the air, across the battlefield.

Having just about managed to deploy his helmet before impact, Corey tumbled, at speed, through the Beconium until he eventually came to a stop, digging his toes and gloved fingers into the toxic sand.

He quickly regained his feet, blinded by static interference on his visor, caused by the radiation. He retracted his helmet again and raced back towards the flashes of blue, yellow and orange, an exhausting endeavour as it was exactly like running through sand. This was made more difficult by the weight of the emerald suit that he wore.

'Do these things have any kind of weakness?' asked Tino, through gritted teeth, as he struggled to block the powerful attacks from the suit that he and Colin were facing.

'My brother built these!' replied Colin as he continued to repeatedly strike at the suit and evade its attacks with a mixture of agility and impressive flips.

'SO NO WEAKNESS THEN!?' shouted a frustrated Ethan conclusively as he dodged around the other suit.

'We need to use them to our advantage' replied Colin.

'How? What do we do?' asked Tino as he too struck the suit in a shower of blue sparks from his blade.

Colin had learned from the one I.S.S. Operative that lived and breathed its principles and survival skills of using only what was available in the situation - His brother. Noticing a speckled area of metal on its back from Beconium contamination, he knew that the metal would be weakened there by now from the impurities in the rusty substance.

In one fluid motion, Colin slashed across the weakened spot and jet propulsion unit fuel began spilling out. Following through from his first slash, he swept the sparking sword through the Beconium on the ground and sliced as hard as he could, right down the centre of its back with a blazing green arc following his blade, igniting the fuel and sending the suit soaring into the air as he grabbed hold of its arm.

He let go of the suit as it rocketed over the fortress and landed in a roll on the walkway along the top of the wall, the destroyed suit crashing down next to him and taking several of the guarding Polarian Beconi' with it.

As Colin recovered from the roll, he drew his blaster from its holster and began firing at the now-advancing Beconium humanoids that were armoured in metal from the Rhinonoid's Expansion Matrix. Charging up the steps to the battlements, these soldiers had no visible weakness, no jet propulsion units and nothing exposed to take them out in a single hit.

As they came at him, Colin raced backwards, slashing to meet attack after heavy attack from their own Beconium-coated blades. He knew that distance was going to be the key here. As he parried away their advances in repeated flashes of green and orange sparks, Colin took a few rapid steps back, in a toe-to-heel motion as he drew his hyper-charged blaster from its holster, built into the side of his leg.

He fired his blaster rapidly at his opponents as well as the tiny one attached to the hilt of his sword every time he parried away an attack, increasing the temperature of the metal and igniting the Beconium within. As there were multiple targets coming at him, he had to deflect every attack and repeatedly fire between each of them to prevent them from cooling back down. It took a lot of firepower before the first soldier glowed, permanently red, the surface metal fizzing before it finally erupted over Colin's armoured suit.

Colin had to work fast to get the cooling silver metal off his suit otherwise it would restrict his movement if it solidified over his suit's cy-bionics. He now knew that he needed to factor in a lot more distance than he had initially planned when taking out his assailants.

'Grab its arm!' instructed Ethan as he and Tino continued to block the other customised suit's attacks.

Tino did as instructed and restrained the suit's left arm as Ethan did the same with its right.

'Colin!' Ethan shouted through the radio in his helmet.

Although Ethan's voice was distorted by the radiation, Colin knew what was required of him. He leaned over the side of the wall and fired a rapid volley of blasts down at the suit's weakened back, igniting its jet propulsion unit and carrying both Operatives up to the top of the fortress wall, where they joined Colin in fending off the Beconium Beings.

'THE DISTRESS SIGNAL IS COMING FROM INSIDE! WE NEED TO FIGHT OUR WAY THROUGH!' shouted Colin.

'COVER EACH OTHER!' shouted Ethan, over the noise of clashing steel and blasters being fired. The three Operatives positioned themselves back to back and fired in the directions they were facing as they proceeded along the wall, down the steps and into the now-deserted main courtyard.

Making sure they had taken out every enemy soldier, they turned to face the huge reinforced door in front of them, retracting their blades into their hilts, closing the bottom half of the hilts up over the small amount of the blades that remained protruding to meet the top half and returning them to their utility belts.

'How do we get inside?' asked Ethan, breathlessly, as the three Operatives cautiously broke their formation.

'This has all been constructed from the Rhinonoid's Expansion Matrix. Oli built the Rhinonoid to resist the effects of hostile terrain so while Beconium will weaken the metal, it will take a long time before we can breach it by force' said Colin, examining the metal.

'We could...' Ethan started but he was immediately interrupted as the enormous doors in front of him began to open outwards. Hundreds of Polarian Beconi' spilled out, into the courtyard, hovering just above the ground in a militaristic display.

Colin dragged Tino, aggressively, behind one door while Ethan rushed, in a side-stepping motion, behind the other.

'Ethan, trigger your grappling hook and scale the door. We need to be quick before they see us' instructed Colin through his helmet's radio as he holstered his blaster and activated one of the illuminated badges on his suit, swiping through a range of holographic tools that were suspended in mid-air, as a projection, from the badge while Tino did the same.

Tino found that the process felt very natural as it was embedded deep in his muscle-memory. There was no time to utilise the tools on their utility belts, they had to use their back-up, a mindset that every member of the Interstellar Scouts is trained to adopt.

'Line up your shot' instructed Colin, grabbing Tino's arm and extending it outwards, directed towards the top of the door. There was a three second countdown as the grappling hook harpoon sprung up and locked into firing position from his suit's forearm. It fired at the same time as Colin's. The hooks sprung out of the harpoon and caught the edge, over the top of the door.

'Try and keep up' Colin said, quietly, as he began quickly and silently walking up the side of the door, followed by Tino, reeling in the cables as they went.

'I'm almost at the top' announced Ethan.

'Good, as soon as you get there rappel down the other side and get straight to cover' replied Colin, looking over his shoulder at the huge gathering of Polarian Beconi' below.

On reaching the top, the Operatives repeatedly kicked away from the other side of the doors, unhooking their grappling hooks as they neared the bottom, before dropping down to the floor and rushing inside as the doors closed behind them.

The Operatives looked back over their shoulders in acknowledgement of the closed doors. Nothing could interrupt them now.

'Sweep the area to make sure we're alone' instructed Colin, retracting his helmet as they were now protected from the Beconium by the metal from the Rhinonoid.

Glancing around the large entrance hall, the armoured walls appeared to be draped in a fluid, black substance with bright, radioactive-green lines cutting through the wall at various angles.

'We probably shouldn't touch that' announced Colin, glancing from wall to wall, feeling strangely hemmed in by the energy that covered them.

He and the others, once again, drew their blasters as Ethan and Tino searched the area, retracting their helmets also.

'Isaac, be advised, the enemy has reinforcements on standby behind the fortress wall' announced Colin through his collar's built-in radio on Isaac's channel but all he could hear in response was a lot of static as the thick, metal walls and radiation from outside blocked the signal. Both groups were now on their own.

Back outside, Parathax had created some distance between itself and Isaac, Corey and Nathan. It unleashed a powerful blast of the black energy that bled from the cracks in its suit and several humanoid creatures, made entirely of Beconium, shaped and animated by the energy, rose up from the ground. The three Operatives turned their attention to Parathax's diversion, moving into a more defensive stance as Parathax rushed for its Augmented Black-Burn Fighter.

The attacks that the Operatives came at the Beconium Beings with were completely useless as their blades just went right through them like a stick through sand. Suddenly, huge, black crystals erupted from the ground, smashing into the enemies as Gala-Thius stood at the foot of The Knightfall's loading ramp, his staff thrust into the ground. The Operatives staggered backwards, dodging the powerful crystals shooting up from the ground.

'PARATHAX IS FLEEING, RETURN TO THE SHIP! NOW!!' shouted the old man's voice through the speaker in the Operatives' suits. Isaac looked over his shoulder to see the thrusters on Parathax's Augmented Black-Burn Fighter beginning to glow. He drew his blaster and fired several shots but all they did was create a rippling effect on the ship's invisible, protective shielding.

'GET BACK TO THE KNIGHTFALL NOW! LET'S GO!' Isaac ordered as he raced back towards the ship, closely followed by Corey and Nathan.

CHAPTER 31
AMBUSH ON THE BRIDGE

'Can we shoot it down?' asked Corey as they ran up the loading ramp and into the deployment bay.

'It's out of range but I think I know where it's going' replied Nathan as they quickly climbed up the ladder, rushed into the cockpit and Nathan jumped into the pilot's seat.

Confidently initiating The Knightfall's launch sequence, the ship rose up off the ground and Nathan guided it up towards The Stealthy Intoxicator above the battlefield but, as they increased in altitude, swarms of Black-Burn Fighters launched out of the ship's multiple hanger bays and began firing on them.

'HOLD ON! EVASIVE ACTION!' shouted Nathan as he aggressively manoeuvred The Knightfall away from the blaster bolts that rained down over them.

Suddenly, the entire group collectively yelled out with fright as one of the huge, upgraded Polarian Beconi' hurtled towards the ship from the side, its scarlet laser-bladed rims ablaze. It clashed, aggressively and with immense force, against the wall of laser energy in place of the cockpit window, jolting the ship and throwing the group forwards, over the controls. The Polarious Beconus was immediately deflected in a violent eruption of sparks but, moments later, the ship was rammed by another, then another and another.

'WE WON'T SURVIVE THIS BATTERING! GO FULL THRUST, STRAIGHT TOWARDS THE NEAREST HANGER BAY!' instructed Isaac, throwing himself forward and using the back of Nathan's seat to hold himself up against the violent swaying of the ship.

'FULL THRUST!? WE'LL NEVER DOCK, THE SHIP WILL CRASH!' argued Nathan as the group was thrown left and right.

All they could do was hold onto something, anything nearby, to help them stay standing.

'THERE! THAT HANGER BAY, NOW!' instructed Corey pointing out a nearby opening in the cruiser.

'GET DOWN TO THE DEPLOYMENT BAY AND PREPARE FOR IMMEDIATE INSERTION!' Nathan instructed as he activated one of his badges to synchronise with and pilot the ship remotely, just as he had during the Viper Fighter attack on their way to Crystalosis.

Nathan increased The Knightfall's thrust, gradually, guiding it towards the hanger bay as he joined the others and continued to dodge the onslaught of Black-Burn Fighters that flew around The Knightfall in offensive formations.

'Almost there...We're nearly...' started Nathan but his concentration was broken as one of the huge Polarian Beconi' rammed the side of The Knightfall. 'WE'VE LOST THE SHIELDS!' he yelled over the blaring alarms. The ship had been knocked off-course by the impact and its repaired starboard fuel tank was suddenly torn clean off the side of the roof by an unseen obstacle floating in mid-air, a part of Parathax's barricade. The Knightfall spiralled out of control as it roared towards the ground.

'ABANDON SHIP! GO! GO! MOVE!' Isaac ordered frantically.

The ship threw the group all around the deployment bay before smashing, at speed, into the ground. The Operatives had only just had enough time, before impact, to vacate the deployment bay by climbing out through the hatch that slid open in the floor.

They activated their jet propulsion units, rocketing back up towards the cruiser. Gala-Thius and Anthony remained on board the ship having made it to the safety of the sleeping quarters.

'Activate your stealth field generators' instructed Isaac as they soared closer to the cruiser's nearest hanger bay.

Now completely invisible to the naked eye, the three Operatives landed beneath the ledge outside the hanger bay that Parathax had docked inside. As they often operated on the ground or in the Rhinonoid, they never quite got used to the sheer scale of a fighter when one was flying over their heads, almost within touching distance. They were enormous.

Isaac led the climb up and across the parts of the cruiser's hull that stuck out until they reached the inside of the hanger bay, completely undetected.

'Stay low' instructed Isaac, quietly, as they made their way across the hanger bay, the loud roar of Black-Burn Fighters launching, sweeping by overhead.

The Operatives could still see each other as their suits' signatures showed up and moved in their place on their visor displays.

'Ok, save your suits' power' instructed Isaac as they moved out into the corridor and dashed from cover to cover, retracting their helmets as they went.

'What hit us?' asked Corey as they drew their blasters and charged them up, a ringing sound increasing in both pitch and volume as the weapons vibrated in their grasp.

'I don't know. I didn't even see anything' replied Nathan, shaking his head.

'We need to find Parathax and end this now. Keep an eye out for the Rhinonoid as well, it must be onboard somewhere' instructed Isaac, turning back to the other two Operatives.

'Where are we going?' asked Nathan.

'Head for the bridge. We have two options. Take control of the ship or take it out of play' replied Isaac.

'There are three of us. How are we going to take the ship?' asked Corey doubtfully.

'I said there are two options. Be prepared' replied Isaac.

The sub-text was a serious wakeup call for Corey, which made him that much more determined to make sure that the ship did end up under I.S.S. control. The three Operatives rose up from their cover and extended their swords from their doubled-out hilts as they rushed down the corridor in search of the bridge.

Inside the fortress, Colin, Ethan and Tino were trying to home in on the distress signal.

'That was incredible the way you dodged that suit's attacks and used it to get onto the wall' said Ethan.

'Thanks, Oli taught me. He loves...loved...doing flips all the time' replied Colin. 'Hold on. I've lost the distress signal' he continued, pausing and pivoting on the spot as he, Ethan and Tino made their way across the vast entrance hall.

'Me too. It just stops dead here' replied Ethan, looking about himself.

'Even if it was here, right where we are, we'd still be detecting it until it was turned off' said Colin, confused.

'Didn't you lose radio contact with the others when we walked in here?' asked Ethan as he started to piece the situation together.

Colin looked to Tino and Ethan as the realisation dawned on him.

'This is a trap...IT'S AN AMBUSH!' announced Colin, urgently, as he and Ethan retreated back towards the doors only to find the black, fluid energy that had covered the walls, now creeping across the floor, ebbing towards them.

'What's happening?' asked Tino, struggling to reach the same conclusion but following what the other two were doing regardless.

'The signal isn't coming from in here, it's coming from the cruiser above the fortress' announced Ethan as he and Colin warily backed away from the approaching black energy that crawled after them.

'We've been baited. For them' said Colin, hopelessly, as he and the others slowly turned around to see two Polarian Beconi' slowly emerging from an archway behind them, followed by three sets of hovering dishes waiting to be flooded with Beconium and the three victims.

'HELMETS!' yelled Colin as he went to reactivate his own helmet but nothing happened. It was the same with the other two as they frantically tried to reactivate their own helmets.

Tino raised his blaster to the advancing Polarian Beconi' but Colin quickly pulled his arm back down.

'If you damage the containment field, the Beconium will spill out and we'll breathe it in. They need a fresh supply of Beconium before they kill us. Let them capture you while I figure something out' said Colin, putting away his weapons followed by the others doing the same.

The Polarian Beconi' came to a stop in front of them, backing them up against the doors.

Back on board The Stealthy Intoxicator, Isaac, Corey and Nathan fought their way through hoards of Parathax's soldiers to get to the ship's bridge.

Upon reaching the Command Deck, the group found themselves cut off from the bridge by a reinforced, armoured door.

'How do we get through?' asked Isaac looking for some means of overriding the door's controls.

Corey stepped forward and tried to force the door open but, even before attempting it, he was confident that it wouldn't budge and, sure enough, it didn't.

'Wait. Look' called Nathan as he leaned in close to one of the consoles on the doorframe.

'What have you found?' asked Isaac.

'Beconium. Just the tiniest amount. It looks like the metal is corroded by it' replied Nathan, observing it more closely.

'It's hardly surprising' Corey pointed out, frustrated. 'We're on Becon, we're surrounded by the stuff' he continued.

'I have an idea. Stand back and get ready' he said, thinking back to the duel on the planet's surface.

Nathan wiped his gloved hand over the control panel, scraping off any Beconium that was stuck to the padded palm from the planet's surface and positioning it at the edges of the panel, similar to the corrosion that was already there. He then pulled out his thin piece of steel from his sleeve, deploying his piece of flint and locking it into position. He lined up the flint with the tiny bit of visible corrosion and struck at it with the piece of steel. A flurry of sparks erupted over the control panel, igniting the Beconium and damaging the inner-workings, forcing the doors to unlock and slide open.

As they rushed through the doors, they were met by Xzjytheous who was waiting for them on the observation deck at the end of the walkway. In his clawed hands, he clutched two long, steel swords which he held out at his sides.

The three Operatives came to an abrupt halt, as if they had run into an invisible wall, as Isaac held out his arms to stop the other two from running past him.

'You fought well. But the Polarian Beconi' Conquest is upon us. The legions stand ready and await their Commanders' Xzjytheous hissed.

'Isn't Parathax their Commander?' asked Isaac, projecting his voice across the large room as he lowered his sword to his side.

'Parathax oversees. Your friends will lead the Polarian Beconi'' replied Xzjytheous as the huge window of the observation deck behind him showed a live feed of the captured Operatives below as they were escorted out, through the hoards of Polarian Beconi' that waited in the courtyard.

'THE REPTILIANS OF BIOLUM ARE A PEACEFUL SPECIES! WHAT DOES PARATHAX HAVE ON YOU THAT MAKES YOU WANT TO DO THIS? THEY'RE KIDS!' shouted Nathan, furiously, as he aggressively stepped a couple of paces forward, ahead of Isaac.

Corey used Nathan's shouting as an opportunity to discretely put his hands behind his back and pull out the piece of steel from his suit's wrist-guard, deploying the piece of flint that sprung up from the compartment in his sleeve. He then locked a separate, shorter, customised knife from the Knightfall onto a device that he wore behind the piece of flint.

'A peaceful species?' repeated Xzjytheous. 'AS PEACEFUL AS ALL OF YOU!' he yelled, implying that the I.S.S. was no more peaceful than the Biolum military that murdered his family. He started running at the group, down the walkway with immense speed, building his momentum.

Isaac, Corey and Nathan raised their swords and charged back at him but, on connecting blades, Isaac swept his sword upwards, from beneath one of Xzjytheous' blades, forcing it aside and clearing a part of the walkway for Corey to slide across the floor, straight past the Reptilian.

As Corey slid, he triggered the device on his arm that the knife was locked onto, causing it to spin rapidly and repeatedly scrape over the flint in passing, dazzling the Reptilian with flurries of sparks and slashing the blade over its legs in the same motion.

'GO! GET THEM OUT OF THERE!' shouted Isaac as Corey regained his feet and sprinted towards the observation deck window as fast as he could, activating his helmet as he fired several shots of his blaster at the glass.

He fired up his jet propulsion unit, launching himself straight through the window and skydived, all the way down to the fortress courtyard. As he rolled out of his landing, he used the momentum to return to his feet and, in one fluid movement, threw himself over the two Polarian Beconi', cutting through the tops of the dishes, along with the three vacant ones, with a single slash of his sword.

'GET BACK INSIDE!' Corey shouted to Colin, Ethan and Tino on seeing how many Polarian Beconi' were in the courtyard. Corey turned to follow the group back inside the fortress but he was met by a long, Beconium-covered blade, held across his throat as a volley of blasts from the Polarian Beconi' struck around the doorway to the entrance hall, causing it to weld shut, cutting off their escape.

On The Stealthy Intoxicator's bridge, a fierce duel raged along the walkway, towards the cruiser's observation deck. Sparks of red erupted from Xzjytheous' two swords as he slashed and parried away Isaac and Nathan's strikes.

Eventually, the two Operatives had Xzjytheous backed all the way to the observation deck at the far end of the bridge. Although he did counter attack his two opponents, there also appeared to be restraint as most of his movements were defensive.

'LOOK! LOOK DOWN THERE! LOOK WHAT THATMONSTER HAS MADE YOU A PART OF!' shouted Isaac, furiously, stepping away from the duel to point out the scene down below while Nathan covered their opponent with an outstretched sword.

Xzjytheous, knowing that the Operatives didn't want to fight him, as evidenced by the distance they had created between him and them, lowered his two swords to his sides as he turned to look out of the window.

Despite what the creature may or may not have felt, the two Operatives both knew there was no turning back. Xzjytheous realised he had been defeated and was now a prisoner of the

Interstellar Scouts. The best he could hope for now was to go out on his own terms. He raised up one of his swords and went to turn on Nathan but deliberately left himself open to be struck down.

Isaac raised up his own sword, leapt forward and blocked the attack from above Xzjytheous' head then, with one powerful side kick to the chest, Nathan kicked Xzjytheous through the hole that Corey had made in the observation deck window. The two Operatives then re-activated their helmets and followed the Reptilian, activating their jet propulsion units to take them back down to the ground.

CHAPTER 32
PARATHAX VICTORIOUS

'It's over. Escort the prisoners to the battlements and commence conversion' Parathax instructed as it lowered its sword away from Corey's throat, forcing him to retract his helmet into his suit's collar.

Colin, Ethan, Tino and Corey were escorted across the courtyard and up the steps to the front wall of the fortress, beyond which, lay the vast expanse of Beconium awaiting them.

Outside the fortress, the sun gleamed off Gala-Thius' golden armoured suit as he ventured out from the wreckage of The Knightfall to retrieve Xzjytheous' body that had landed on the ground nearby.

On returning Xzjytheous to the ship, he removed the armoured suit and put it on the Reptilian, activating the respirator mask function to help bring him back to consciousness before retracting the helmet.

Slowly, the wounded creature began to open its eyes and look about at its surroundings. Gala-Thius gently placed his hand on Xzjytheous shoulder, kneeling down next to him.

'The battle is almost over and Parathax has almost won. If the Astral-Alias leaves Becon with an invasion force, there will be no stopping it. I am not the biggest ally to the I.S.S. but that small group of Operatives out there genuinely cares. They have minutes before their souls are torn from their bodies and they spend eternity in torment, drowning in a containment field of Beconium. Please. Help them' Gala-Thius pleaded in a quiet, calming voice.

Xzjytheous began coughing behind the mask as he struggled to sit up, falling back to the loading ramp.

'I'm sorry. The effects of the Beconium have already started to set in but there's still time to redeem yourself before the end. What happened to your family on Biolum was unforgivable. What

Parathax made you do to all of those people on Polarious, on Fulgon and so many other worlds, alongside the Deathstalker Squadron, has brought you nothing but more pain and suffering.

Please, my old friend, don't die in vain' Gala-Thius continued as he helped Xzjytheous to sit up.

Xzjytheous couldn't speak for the Beconium that had reached his lungs, but Gala-Thius could see in the Reptilian's eyes that he wanted to be able to die in the right way – The way Xzjytheous had always claimed he would fall, ever since they met and befriended one another before the Interstellar Scouts or even the Inter-Solar Scouts was founded, many lifetimes ago.

Frowning curiously, Gala-Thius leaned down, over Xzjytheous, and removed a small, black dart that he found embedded in the Reptilian's neck – a Deathstalker Sting. He then drew on his mystical abilities and quickly drew out the toxins that had been used to corrupt Xzjytheous into serving Parathax before they could dissipate into his system.

Standing, defeated upon the battlements, Corey, Colin, Ethan and Tino awaited their imminent fate.

'I can't breathe' gasped Tino, as he inhaled the particles of Beconium being carried on the wind.

His knees started to give way beneath him and his eyes began to water as Colin and Ethan grabbed him to help keep him up. The entire group was feeling the effects but their training had made them disciplined enough to fight through it, training that Tino was still unable to recall.

'What are they waiting for?' Corey mumbled to himself as he looked about at the Polarian Beconi' that surrounded them.

The Operatives discretely activated their respirator masks which assisted their breathing. Tino, however, was now also exhibiting symptoms that weren't typical of Beconium Contamination, nor the later-onset Beconium Poisoning. Black lines began branching and crawling out from his wounds, up his neck and over his face as he began shaking uncontrollably.

'WHAT'S HAPPENING!?' yelled Ethan. His question was quickly answered by the deafening, thunderous explosion that shook the entire fortress, throwing them to the floor.

'No' whispered Colin's shaky voice as he realised.

The five enormous, jet-black, bladed fighters of the Deathstalker Squadron roared through the sky, towards the battle, trailing a towering tsunami of Beconium in their wake as the sheer power of the five ships stirred up the ground below.

Parathax spotted Isaac and Nathan who had rocketed to the ground on their jet propulsion units and were advancing from outside the fortress. However, both Operatives were quickly buried in the giant wave of Beconium that swept over them in the wake of the Deathstalker Squadron and they only just had enough time to close up their helmets as they prayed their respiratory filters would hold up.

Parathax moved, across the top of the wall, towards the five hulking fighters, grinning menacingly. Uncharacteristically, the Deathstalker Squadron suddenly came to a standstill, hovering over the fortress. The wind began to pick up at a sinister pace and bolts of electricity from the radiation began darting across the walls, towers and floor of the fortress.

Parathax descended the steps to the courtyard behind the fortress wall and came to a stop beneath the Deathstalker that was positioned directly in the middle of the large square, formed by the other four. The Astral-Alias raised its hands, high into the air and the radiation bolts grew much more fierce, striking the gold, Beconium-contaminated suit that it wore.

Slowly, Parathax rose into the air as the fortress vanished in the shroud of the fierce Beconium storm that raged across the battlefield. Enormous bolts of lightning exploded through the storm, striking at The Stealthy Intoxicator as well as the five Deathstalkers, hyper-charging them.

Isaac and Nathan burrowed their way through the Beconium with fierce determination, blinded through their visors by the radiation interference. They breached the top of the mound but found themselves still unable to remove their helmets due to the storm that now raged around them.

The distorted image flickered on the inside of their visors as they looked about themselves. Communication through their radios was also blocked by the intensified radiation so the only way Nathan could get Isaac's attention to show him the horrifying sight he had just caught a glimpse of, was to shake his shoulder aggressively and indicate at Tino who was now suspended high in the air, above the fortress wall, with streams of black energy being bled from his wounds and absorbed by the four outer Deathstalkers. The energy was then channelled from them, into the central fighter and streamed down into Parathax's body in the courtyard below. Isaac and Nathan watched on helplessly, as too did Corey Colin and Ethan, powerless to help.

Once the last of the black energy had been bled from Tino's wounds, he fell through the air and slammed down, heavily, in front of Parathax on the metal floor of the fortress courtyard, quivering uncontrollably as vivid memories of both his last encounter with the Deathstalker Squadron and of being an I.S.S. Operative, flooded his mind all at once.

Parathax moved past the Operative and returned to the battlements as everyone watched on in horror, unsure of what they had just witnessed. It rose up into the air, higher and higher above the fortress until it was level with The Stealthy Intoxicator. As everyone observed, entirely helpless, the Astral-Alias unleashed a powerful blast of black energy with a deafening, ghastly wail, disabling the stealth field generators around the enormous chunks of debris that it had positioned above the battlefield.

Parathax raised its arms above its head and, with all of its might, threw them back down, hurtling the enormous chunks of tangled metal right at Isaac and Nathan in a bid to finish them off.

The two Operatives froze and watched in dread as the shadows that were cast over them grew bigger and darker. There was nothing to be done. They couldn't run from, dodge, hide from or destroy these gigantic chunks of debris that dwarfed them.

They both instinctively looked away and threw themselves to the ground.

CHAPTER 33
THE TURN OF THE TIDE

Silence fell. The raging storm subsided immediately. It was as if it was never there in the first place. Isaac opened his eyes slowly and rolled over onto his back. For the briefest of moments, he thought he was dead, squinting to try and see beyond the blindingly-white, shimmering light that flooded through his helmet's flickering visor. Then, a loud roar shook the ground, the sea of Beconium trembling around him.

'Initiating thrust. Maintain formation' announced a disjointed but unmistakable female voice through the speaker inside his helmet.

Isaac frowned as he held his hand in front of his visor, shielding his eyes against the light. Gradually, the light began to move further away from him as he slowly began to sit up.

'Re-attain altitude and standby to break formation' the crackling female voice continued.

'The fleet is in orbit and all deployment units on standby and awaiting your signal' announced an adult male voice over the speaker.

As his eyes adjusted, Isaac could now see the enormous chunks of debris rising, back up, into the sky with bright streaks of light coming out of them from all directions. Isaac turned to look at Nathan, helping him, as the two of them slowly returned to their feet.

'This is Interstellar Scouts Polarious Sector Patrol. Altitude attained, standing by to break formation' announced the female voice.

'Copy that Polarious Sector Patrol. You are clear to break formation. I.S.S. Scout Hut, commence your descent' announced a separate, younger male voice over the speaker.

'I know that voice' Isaac said to himself quietly, slightly out of breath.

Then, looking out to the horizon, he could see the tiny black dot, a single Interstellar Scout Viper Fighter, tearing through the sky towards them at extreme speed. A silver tri-trail slashed across the sky behind the Viper from the two fins and tail as the pilot fired up the forward thrusters to full burn, a fiery explosion erupting from the back of the fighter.

The roar of the thrusters was almost deafening as the Viper came screaming by overhead, first over Isaac and Nathan and then over the rest of the group standing on the wall of the fortress. The Viper Fighter fired a rapid burst of blaster bolts at the Deathstalkers, causing them to break formation in pursuit of the intruder.

'Is that...' started Ethan as he and the others deactivated their respirator masks.

'You're kidding me...I think it is' replied Corey.

'OLI!' Colin cried out jumping up and punching at the sky, ecstatically, as his brother soared over the fortress a second time, firing multiple shots at the Polarian Beconi' that guarded the group and taking them out, affording the Operatives the opportunity to get the upper-hand on the battle, now driven by an enormous morale boost.

Oli's arrival was immediately followed by a blaze of amber and turquoise plasma bolts that swept across the sky above the entire battlefield from the super-charged Stealthy Intoxicator and The Scout Hut above, blinding, as bright as a sun.

Squadrons of I.S.S. Funnel-Web Fighters began launching huge chunks of tangled metal, still charged with the blaster bolt energy they had conducted during the Polarious Sector Assault. The blazing debris soared off in all directions, striking The Stealthy Intoxicator, the fortress and Parathax's forces as the Funnel-Webs increased the velocity of the projectiles.

'ALL STRIKE TEAMS, SCRAMBLE! SCRAMBLE!' ordered the female voice that both Isaac and Nathan had both known belonged to Sarah from the moment she had saved them.

Swarms of I.S.S. Viper Fighters broke away from the chunks of debris that remained, having been hidden as parts of them, disguised as scrap metal the entire time. Meanwhile, inside The Scout Hut's various hanger bays, the cruiser using its huge internal hydraulics to spread out its various components, hundreds of Viper Fighters had locked themselves into position at a downward angle, each facing diagonally into a narrow chute that ran through the inner-hull of the cruiser. Carried on a deployment mechanism, they were launched along the tracks in the chutes followed by a long row of white lights at the sides and soared out, through open hatches in the cruiser's underbelly. This allowed the Vipers to disembark while shielded by The Scout Hut and descend through the cloud cover without being immediately shot down.

The fighters scrambled into flight as they moved into attack formations, erupting into a fierce dogfight with the dark shroud of enemy Black-Burn Fighters that spilled out of The Stealthy Intoxicator's hanger bays, in pursuit of the I.S.S. reinforcements.

'Five-Six-Five Viper Escort, on me' instructed Sarah as she soared through the sky and moved towards the incoming Black-Burn Fighters.

'Lock onto my fighter signature and fall into interceptor formation' she continued as she saw the other four fighters from her squadron moving into position.

'Five-Six-Five Viper Bravo, locked on' responded Emma.

'Five-Six-Five Viper Charlie, locked on' came Timothy's voice.

'Five-Six-Five Viper Delta, locked on' announced Pete.

'Five-Six-Five Viper Echo, locked on' followed Jess' voice, all coming through the speaker in Sarah's cockpit.

'UGH! BLACK-BURNS, SO NEGATIVE!' came the unmistakable exaggeration and vocal emphasis of Timothy and his flamboyant personality.

'They made it' Nathan said to himself, unable to believe his eyes. 'They all survived' he continued as he looked up at the huge I.S.S. Scout Hut descending below the orange-grey clouds.

Both he and Isaac were slightly teary-eyed. While they couldn't have been more happy to know that they had survived the Polarious

Sector Assault, they had been unable to put a stop to the distress signal before any further I.S.S. forces arrived. If The Scout Hut was here, other I.S.S. forces would surely be en-route by now, heading straight into Parathax's trap.

'Scout Hut, I'm moving in to dock with the enemy cruiser. Dispatch a shuttle to the ground for Biker Delta Squadron Five-Six-Five. Isaac, have the pilot lock onto the hanger bay where the distress signal is most prominent and rendezvous with me there' instructed Oli.

'Standby to escort Five-Six-Five, up to the enemy cruiser' instructed Sarah, eyeing the descending shuttles and searching for the one that was heading towards the group of Operatives on the ground.

'Standing by' replied Pete's voice, more serious than the others as, teary-eyed, Isaac listened to the conversation over his built-in speaker, watching as the shuttle came down to pick them up.

On realising that Parathax had vanished and with their heart and passion for their mission revitalised, Corey, Colin and Ethan, while aiding a weakened Tino, used their jet propulsion units to get down to the ground outside the fortress so they could board the incoming shuttle. As they looked up, they could see the other shuttles pouring out of the multiple hanger bays of The Scout Hut, carrying I.S.S. Operatives and Troop Leaders down to the ground to engage Parathax's invasion force of Polarian Beconi' and Beconium Beings.

'Ok, get in! Get on board!' shouted Isaac, turning to the others as a shuttle landed nearby to take them up to The Stealthy Intoxicator.

The group was, however, completely oblivious to the fact that Xzjytheous had also boarded the shuttle with them, hidden by a stealth field generator.

As the shuttle slowly lifted off the ground and started flying up towards The Stealthy Intoxicator in pursuit of Parathax's Augmented Black-Burn Fighter, Isaac stood up and turned his back on the rest of the group to hide his emotion. It would do them no good to see their leader in the state he was in. Xzjytheous, cloaked by his personal stealth field generator however, could see how emotional Isaac was. From losing his parents on Polarious, to losing his sister onboard The Scout Hut. Xzjytheous had been responsible for both of those losses. Despite, now knowing that Sarah had survived, Xzjytheous could see on Isaac's face, in his eyes, the pain that he had caused, not just to him but to billions upon billions across the galaxy.

Remembering his conversation with Isaac on Zonju, on their way to investigate the Con-Haarian convoy, Nathan slowly approached Isaac and placed a reassuring hand on his shoulder. Isaac composed himself and sat back down opposite Tino.

'Are you ok?' asked Isaac, leaning across to Tino who was now conscious again and starting to breathe more easily now while, evidently, still in extreme pain from his wounds.

Tino nodded in response but he then looked down and saw the deep gouges and ruptures in his suit that the black energy had been leeched through and didn't dare think about the damage to the wounds themselves.

'I remember everything' he said.

'I'm so sorry. I thought we had burnt up the last of it with the electricity in the deployment bay but...' Isaac, abruptly, cut his apology short, frowning, as he suddenly found himself remembering everything about Tino as, so too, did the others.

Overcome with emotion and relieved that their close friend of so many years was ok and regretting that they had ever forgotten him, even if it was caused by the black substance left by the Deathstalker on Earth, all they could do was embrace Tino tightly and make sure he knew that they were there for him.

This, however, didn't change the fact that they had a job to do, a job that Tino was now much more driven to see completed, despite his injuries.

Outside the shuttle, a fierce shower of blaster bolts sprayed across the escorting Vipers from a ship that was unlike any of the others. Parathax's thorny, black energy, that engulfed its cruiser, had now also overridden all functions onboard The Spyglass, which Xzjytheous had left, docked in The Stealthy Intoxicator's hanger bay.

The Spyglass, now accompanied by Parathax's four interceptor drones, soared out of the opening in the cruiser and roared straight at the small, incoming convoy as Sarah, Emma, Jess, Pete and Timothy fired back in a bid to protect 5-6-5's shuttle during its approach. A few of the blasts from The Spyglass struck Sarah's leading Viper, causing her to bang her head, hard, against the inside of the cockpit as the ship jolted violently. Focussing hard against the pain and dizziness she was starting to feel, Sarah continued to do her job as the leader of Viper Strike Squadron but Jess was less fortunate.

'I'VE TAKEN SUBSTANTIAL DAMAGE...LOSING ALTITUDE!' shouted Jess as the group of Viper Fighters tried to keep the Black-Burns away from the shuttle. 'EJECTION COMPROMISED! DEPLOYING COUNTER-MEASURES, I'M GOING DOWN!' Jess continued frantically.

Emma broke away from the group of Vipers to assist Jess, leaving Sarah, Timothy and Pete to accompany the shuttle for the remainder of the landing approach.

Emma eyed the downed Viper as it tumbled across the ground, protected by its under-curled tail and trailing a cloud of Beconium in its wake. She could see that the port and starboard stabiliser fins had successfully jettisoned as well. The only problem was that the crash hadn't gone unnoticed and, as Jess emerged from her fighter, blinded by her sealed helmet, Emma could see a number of Parathax's ground forces making their way towards the wreckage to investigate. Emma brought her Viper Fighter about and went into a near-vertical nosedive.

The Viper struck the ground a split-second after Emma levelled it out, wedging the stabiliser fins into the ground and coming to an abrupt halt. Emma released her harness, deployed her helmet over her head and jumped onto the roof of her fighter, taking cover behind the ballistic glass window as she fired her blaster at the approaching enemies. Jess took cover behind one of the stabiliser fins and began firing also.

'Standby for docking' instructed the pilot from the shuttle's cockpit.

The Operatives were all excited to once again be reunited with Oli and none more so than Colin. Isaac smiled to the young Operative as the shuttle moved into the shade of The Stealthy Intoxicator's hanger bay.

As the shuttle docked and the loading ramp descended, the Operatives could see Oli had already exited his Viper and moved, swiftly, to crouch down behind a piece of machinery, dressed in his Pyrotech suit. He turned to acknowledge the rest of Biker Delta Squadron 5-6-5 as they joined him but there was no time for a big happy reunion just yet, although Oli couldn't help briefly putting a reassuring hand on Tino's shoulder, as he too now remembered him and their many missions together since they were Initiates.

The hanger bay appeared empty except for one of Oli's customised armoured suits which seemed oblivious to their presence. Nevertheless, the Operatives quickly and silently made their way across the hanger bay, keeping as close to the ground as possible to avoid detection.

'All clear, green light to disembark' announced Oli, into his suit's microphone and, on that update, the I.S.S. shuttle lifted up once again and flew back out of the hanger bay. Oli now had his own sword, retracted into its hilt, on his utility belt which he had retrieved from one of the rucksacks beneath his desk onboard The Scout Hut before arriving at the battle.

'The signal's coming from the Rhinonoid' Oli said, quietly, as he looked beyond a docking Black-Burn Fighter, to his customised tank. 'The most likely target is the Suit Storage Unit' he continued.

'We can't make it through the sides; it's all sealed up' whispered Nathan doubtfully as he peered around the other side of the machinery that they were hidden behind.

'What are that suit's capabilities?' asked Isaac.

'Pressurised CO2 for combustion damage-control' replied Oli. He looked down at the Polarian Beconi' dishes that floated next to his suit's forearms. 'Wait here and cover me' he continued as he cautiously emerged from the hiding place.

He carefully moved from cover to cover, making his way towards the Rhinonoid, as the other Operatives drew their blasters and trained them on Oli's customised armoured suit that stood guard at the foot of the tank's deployment bay ramp.

Unbeknownst to Oli though, the tank was already being infiltrated through the hole that was smashed in the other side of it. Xzjytheous had broken away from the shuttle and the rest of the group under the influence of the gold armoured suit's stealth field generator.

Noticing the Inferno suit at the far end of the room with its back to him, the Reptilian, quietly, climbed through the damaged hull and looked around the room at the remaining selection of customised armoured suits as he deactivated the device that had hidden him, conserving its power.

At the far end of the room, stood a matt-grey suit – Oli's Nanonoid armour. The microscopic, autonomous-response robots created the illusion that the suit was made more of a malleable liquid substance rather than solid armour.

As he approached, Xzjytheous stepped out of the gold suit and, using his clawed hand to make an incision down the middle of his body; shed a perfect full layer of skin from himself.

He returned to the gold, armoured suit and leaned in closely to the peculiar suit standing on its podium. As Xzjytheous leaned in closer to examine it, the substance began reaching out to him; taking hold of the gold armoured suit he was wearing and engulfing it entirely.

He approached one of the bionics that he had left to guard the room, placed it into the skin and remotely adjusted its build to fill it out. Extendable rods on hinges began to unfold inside it, increasing in density and reaching down every limb and every joint to make it move and behave exactly as he would.

He handed his two swords to the bionic in the animated skin, then, with one last look at the Inferno suit, that guarded the room from the corridor, Xzjytheous re-activated his stealth field generator and jumped back out, through the hole in the wall of the tank, taking the disguised bionic, the remaining, undisguised bionic and Oli's Nanonoid armour with him in his search for Parathax.

Back on the planet's surface, Emma and Jess of Viper Strike Squadron – 5-6-5's fighter escort, were finding that their blasters were having a minimal effect on their attackers so, seeing her chance, slim though it was, Emma jumped back into the cockpit and re-initiated her Viper's weapon systems. In a fiercely rapid spray of blaster bolts from the ship's canons, the advancing enemies were obliterated almost immediately.

'Thanks' said Jess with a sigh of relief through the speaker in Emma's helmet.

'Don't mention it. We're both grounded now though. We need to get back up there' replied Emma as she dropped back down to the ground, looking about for a means of getting airborne again.

'There was a larger downed ship, not too far back that way. I caught a glimpse of it as I came down' Jess mentioned, indicating at a nearby dune, renewed by the storm.

Jess was quite overweight for her age as she didn't see much in the way of ground combat with being a pilot and Emma knew that climbing the huge dune between them and the ship Jess had spotted would be no easy feat for her.

Emma's concentration was suddenly broken as The Spyglass, accompanied by Parathax's four interceptor drones, targeted them. The shower of rapid-fire blaster bolts rained down over the two Viper Fighters, destroying them in an inferno of flame and black, billowing smoke. The two Operatives were only just able to throw themselves clear of the explosion in time. Nevertheless, their armoured suits that were as undamaged as the day they received them, weren't spared the bombardment of shrapnel that erupted from the blast.

The Spyglass and interceptor drones soared past, overhead and rejoined the aerial battle.

Looking about, Emma could see the stabiliser fins that had jettisoned from Jess' Viper as she came down. Neither of them had enough power in their jet propulsion units to gain the necessary altitude to clear the dune but there was enough to cover some distance along the flat.

Applying some ingenuity, a key trait of any I.S.S. Operative, Emma used the light-weight triangular pieces of metal as platforms for them to stand on so they didn't have to battle the deep and formidable Beconium sand. Using the T-bar that originally held the fins onto the fighter and allowed them to quickly and safely detach, the two Operatives held on tight and fired up their jet propulsion units, allowing them to glide across the surface of the desert, around the dune, towards The Knightfall.

Across the battlefield, Parathax's forces were targeting the grounded Knightfall. Gala-Thius rushed out in front of the wreckage and thrust his staff into the deep Beconium sand causing enormous black crystals, filled with Beconium, to explode up, high into the air, creating an immense barrier, so high that it blocked out the sun and cast a shadow over the downed ship. Anthony fended off any hostile forces that made it past Gala-Thius' defences with an assortment of weapons that he had customised from the generators inside The Knightfall.

Their efforts, however, did not go unnoticed. As an endless, vicious bombardment of blaster bolts and laser-bladed edges from the Polarian Beconi' smashed away at the barrier, an Interstellar Scouts shuttle, escorted by a squadron of Viper Fighters, blasted through the crystalline structure, obliterating it and landed alongside The Knightfall.

Onboard The Stealthy Intoxicator, as Xzjytheous raced across the hanger bay en-route to the bridge where he was sure Parathax would be waiting for the Operatives, the disguised bionic wearing the Reptilian skin sprinted with extreme speed straight at the group that were covering Oli's movements towards the Rhinonoid.

'ISAAC!' shouted Colin as he spotted Xzjytheous' decoy running at them.

'OPEN FIRE!' Isaac ordered as he and the others turned their blasters towards the incoming target.

However, the group of Operatives were unable to land a single hit as the assailant dodged around the blasts with extreme speed and agility. It leapt high into the air and raised the two swords in its hands above its head. The Operatives drew their own blades and, as it landed behind them, began striking at their opponent which, effortlessly, parried away their attacks, backing away, across the hanger bay.

The Operatives were attacking their enemy with so much ferocity that they didn't even realise that it wasn't counter-attacking, although, admittedly, the Operatives' onslaught was so fierce that they left no opening for counter-attack, even if it intended to.

As the duel raged between the I.S.S. Operatives and the bionic in the Reptilian skin, Oli ran at his customised armoured suit that was guarding the Rhinonoid and activated the chain reaction of detonations on his Pyrotech suit, launching himself past the animated suit and enabling himself to land on one of the many bridges and walkways that were suspended from the ceiling of the hanger bay by long metal cables on pulley systems.

He took his sword from his utility belt, extending the blade from its hilt and also drew a shorter knife from its sheath as he slowly backed along the bridge watching cautiously for the suit pursuing him.

As he leaned down over the metal poles that acted as railings, he could see that the suit had indeed deserted its post of guarding the Rhinonoid's deployment bay ramp but it was nowhere else to be seen either.

Suddenly the walkway jolted, swinging on the cables and causing Oli to lose his footing, throwing both arms around the metal poles as the huge, animated suit grabbed at the railings and flipped itself over them, up onto the walkway. Oli took a single slash at the armoured suit creating a flash of green sparks as the suit raised its arms and flooded the entire walkway with a thick fog of CO2 gas.

Oli shielded his face behind the two Polarian Beconi' dishes suspended next to his forearms. He then activated his helmet to scan the environment, through the fog, for the suit as he raised up the two blades and adopted a defensive stance, bending slightly at the knees and moving slowly as he ventured through the thick shroud.

There was no sign of the suit on the bridge but, as he looked above himself, to the network of bridges and walkways overhead, he could see the suit's signature moving further and further away. Oli was certain that he was being baited and knew it would be much easier to take the opportunity to board the Rhinonoid right now while it was unguarded but the rest of the group would then be left open to attack from the armoured suit.

He went to, once again, trigger the explosive chain reaction of the Pyrotech suit he was wearing to gain some altitude and pursue the animated suit but, due to the high concentration of CO2 eliminating the Oxygen around him, the explosives wouldn't spark. Knowing that this automatically eliminated other tools such as his jet propulsion unit, he decided that he needed an alternative way to get up there.

Oli carefully climbed up the three metal poles that formed the safety railings at the sides of the bridge and, holding out his arm to keep his balance, he reached his sword hand up above him, searching in the fog with the blade for the next walkway. On making contact with a metal frame on the underside of the walkway, he collapsed his sword, returning it to his utility belt, but kept his knife drawn.

He then blindly jumped into the fog, reaching out with both hands. His arms went straight through the gaps in the frame and he used all of his upper-body strength to pull himself up onto the walkway as it swayed on the metal cables. Then, as he regained his feet and looked up, he could see, by the indicator on his visor, that the suit had stopped moving and was now waiting for him several levels above him.

Oli calmed his breathing through his helmet's built in respirator and focussed on nothing other than the obstacles in his way. Then, in an impressive display of agility, he made his way from bridge to walkway, moving higher and higher as he also climbed the cables, until he was just one level away from the suit that awaited him on the slightly swaying walkway above him.

He had mostly made it through the cloud of fog now and could both breathe and see the armoured suit above him without the use of his helmet. Retracting it, he looked about himself for a way to take out his opponent without actually getting up onto the next level as he knew the suit would just knock him back over the edge due to a lack of railings.

Knowing that the suit wouldn't be able to use its built-in jet propulsion unit either due to the amount of CO2 beneath them,

Oli drew his blaster and aimed for the two cables that the above walkway was attached to at the far end.

He fired several blasts at them, melting the metal on contact, until the cables snapped and the armoured suit slid down the walkway, disappearing into the shroud below and hitting the floor with a loud, heavy bang.

As the suit had fallen towards the floor of the hanger bay though, the black, thorny energy that twisted around it, lashed out at Oli, knocking him off his feet and sending him over the edge of the walkway.

It felt like everything was moving in slow motion for Oli as he fell. Everything around him turned to a rusty orange colour as his entire body dissolved into a swirling vortex of Beconium caught within the containment field of the two dishes at his arms.

The dishes began spinning rapidly in opposite directions as Oli began tearing through the air in his converted form. As he swept past the group of Operatives duelling with the animated Reptilian skin at the far end of the hanger bay, one of the dishes scraped across the floor, causing Oli to be thrown from the containment field in human form. Gliding through the air, he reached out with his sword and slashed over the hostile's body in a streak of blinding, green sparks which erupted from the blade before being dragged back into the containment field and reverting back into Beconium form, all in the blink of an eye, before his feet could even touch the floor.

The Reptilian skin burst into emerald flames, ignited by the sparks and fell to the floor at the Operatives' feet as the bionic metal device retracted the hinged metal rods back into itself, lying on the ground, entirely inactive and hidden by the fire.

Having arrived at the downed Knightfall, Emma and Jess deactivated their jet propulsion units and drew their blasters as they stepped off their Viper fin platforms. They recognised it as the hostile ship from The Scout Hut's hanger bay but were unsure of the nature and intentions of its current occupants.

As they ascended the loading ramp, they were met by a group of gold-armoured I.S.S. Troop Leaders from The Scout Hut. Standing amongst them were Gala-Thius and Anthony who had been taken prisoner by the I.S.S. and were being prepared for transportation to the cruiser, both for their history of desertion with the I.S.S. and for having been discovered onboard a known enemy ship.

'The battle is won' insisted Gala-Thius as he and Anthony wrestled with their captors. Suddenly, he stopped. He relaxed every muscle in his body and slowly turned his attention to Emma and Jess with a pained expression on his face. It was as if he had seen something that he couldn't describe but it horrified him. 'Too late' he said simply, after which, he surrendered to the guards.

CHAPTER 34
CONTINGENCY PLAN: INITIATED

As Oli hurtled around the hanger bay, a pilot climbed into a docked Black-Burn Fighter and activated its flight and targeting systems. The ship slowly rose up into the air and began firing on the metal dishes that propelled Oli around the hanger bay.

'GET DOWN! TAKE COVER!' shouted Isaac as Oli flew by. It took a moment for the Operatives to process everything as they made for the Rhinonoid's deployment bay ramp.

'Get to the cockpit' instructed Isaac, looking about the outside of the tank to make sure they weren't being followed as the rest of the group ran up the ramp, into the deployment bay.

'The doors are sealed' announced Colin as he climbed the ladder and tried to pry them open. Isaac ran up the ramp and quickly clambered to the top of the ladder to offer some assistance while the other Operatives tried the various alternative doors and hatches.

'Ok, head back outside, we'll get in through the top and take out the fighter with the rooftop blaster canon' instructed Isaac on finding that the doors wouldn't budge.

Suddenly there was a loud metallic bang from behind as the armoured suit that Oli had been facing, cut off their exit route, moving to the foot of the ramp. There was a brief moment where each of the Operatives simultaneously realised the trap they had inadvertently run into.

The suit raised up its bulky arms and began flooding the deployment bay with pressurised CO2. Coughing and spluttering, the Operatives blindly attempted to reactivate their helmets as the deployment bay ramp began to rise up. Unable to reactivate their helmets or respirator masks in time, the Operatives fell to the floor of the tank, one by one.

Back in the hanger bay, in his Beconium vortex form, Oli manoeuvred evasively between docking and launching fighters, weaving through the network of bridges and walkways that dangled from above as the airborne Black-Burn Fighter continued to track his movements and fire at him.

He made his way to the bridge that the hostile suit had fallen from as it was now only dangling from one end. As he moved past it, he angled the bottom dish to hit against it, straining the containment field as the momentum continued to carry the top dish and allowing him to reach out with his arm and grab the frame that was fitted to the underside of the walkway.

Having regained his physical form and with the dishes now floating like shields next to his forearms once again, Oli also placed his feet on the frame as he drew his blaster. The blaster fire from the enemy fighter ceased as its targeting system lost track of him but, at such close range, Oli could still hear, over the sound of the engines, the blaster canons' machinery moving into different positions, searching for him.

Maintaining his grip on the frame on the underside of the walkway, Oli reached out with his blaster and lined up his shot. He knew that what he was about to attempt was extremely risky and there was a good chance that not everything would go to plan but it was only a matter of time before another enemy fighter would move in to dock in the hanger bay and see where he was taking cover.

Blocking out any further doubt from his mind and confident that he recognised the sound of the engine that was dependent upon combustion, Oli aimed his blaster. He had learned from his time as an I.S.S. Initiate, lighting his campfire on the survival camp with his Troop Leader, Jason, that Oxygen was needed in order for combustion to occur. If he removed the Oxygen enough from inside the fuel lines, even briefly, the fighter's engine systems would fail.

He fired several shots from his blaster at the cables of one of the other walkways, causing the metal to melt. The bridge dropped into a vertical position and swung across the hanger bay, hitting the side of the enemy ship and knocking it towards him and rupturing the fuel lines in the process. He quickly activated the chain reaction of explosives on the Pyrotech suit which threw him through the air towards the remaining dangling cables that had been melted.

He reached out with his hand and grabbed the cable, using the momentum of the explosions to swing closer to the Black-Burn as the pilot attempted to regain control.

On seeing Oli swinging towards the fighter, the pilot began firing on him once more but Oli was too quick. He released his grip on the cable, somersaulted through the air and landed on the Black-Burn's blazing blaster canons with all of his weight, forcing them to point downwards while still firing. The blasts struck the armoured suit outside the Rhinonoid as well as the Rhinonoid itself.

As the smouldering remains of the suit fell to the floor of the hanger bay, the clouds of CO2 that rose up from the new opening that had been made in the tank, cut the Oxygen out of the fighter's engines, while also starving its intake vents and feed lines of further Oxygen, preventing fuel combustion and it fell to the floor of the hanger bay, exploding into a ball of flame that the CO2 simply wasn't enough to smother. The explosion triggered a chain-reaction across the hanger bay to the other docked and airborne fighters, destroying them all.

Oli glided down the cable and dropped down, through the hole in the roof of the Rhinonoid, falling straight through to the deployment bay which was now almost completely clear of the suffocating shroud.

He approached each of the unconscious Operatives, quickly activated their respirator masks and moved them into the recovery position. He then rose back to his feet, climbed the ladder at the far end and approached the sealed doorway at the top.

The tri-laser interface on the doorframe had been damaged from the blast so Oli initiated a Patrol Leader override on the door and it slid open. Cautiously, he stepped through the doorway, grasping at the grip of his sword's hilt but not releasing the four layered blades yet as he wanted to have the option to switch to his blaster quickly, should he need to, as he slowly proceeded into the Rhinonoid, heading towards the cockpit. Oli had a hunch that the distress signal would be transmitting from either there or the room where he kept his custom suits.

Meanwhile, on the main command bridge of The Stealthy Intoxicator, Parathax awaited the I.S.S. Operatives. In eager anticipation of their arrival the Astral-Alias looked out over the battlefield below where the Polarian Beconi' had now advanced beyond the walls of the fortress and also moved to various vantage points on the walkways and towers to fire on the I.S.S. from above. Fighters swarmed around the two gigantic cruisers in a fierce dogfight and it appeared that both sides were sustaining heavy casualties.

Parathax heard the door open behind it but didn't turn around to face its opponent. It was fully aware of his betrayal to assist the I.S.S.

'You're not as thick skinned as your scales would suggest... REPTILIAN' the Astral Alias said in its ghastly voice. It quickly turned and began firing a blaster on Xzjytheous, who came charging at it down the walkway, ducking, dodging and flipping over every single attack.

Parathax drew its sword as its opponent reached the observation deck. It started slashing at him as Xzjytheous, now unarmed from leaving his swords with his diversion in the hanger bay, used a variety of martial arts techniques to block and counter-attack with kicks and punches.

Eventually, Xzjytheous got the upper hand on Parathax and knocked it back, off the thick glass floor of the observation deck and onto the metal walkway. Live wires from the ship's electrical systems dropped down from the ceiling like long tentacles, making contact with the metal floor and electrifying it, along with Parathax's armoured suit as the bolts of electricity made the dangling wires jump and whip about.

Xzjytheous dissolved to the floor in a pile of black ash as the electricity reached him, at which point Parathax realised that it had been a decoy, a second animated Reptilian skin occupied by the other bionic that had previously been guarding Oli's suits onboard the Rhinonoid. The decoy had been intended to keep Parathax occupied and weaken it as the real Xzjytheous had crawled across the ceiling, sabotaging the bridge's electrical systems.

Xzjytheous dropped down behind Parathax in the Nanonoid suit that he had taken from Oli's customised collection onboard the Rhinonoid. Without skipping a beat, Parathax pointed its blaster to the side and took a single shot without even looking at the source of the sound. Xzjytheous fell to the floor wounded as the electrical current had, unexpectedly, inhibited the suit he was wearing. The blast was fired specifically to not be immediately fatal, to make him suffer as his life slowly ebbed away.

'Oli, it's Isaac, are you there?' Isaac asked through his suit's built-in radio as he and the other Operatives began to regain consciousness in the Rhinonoid's deployment bay.

'Yeah, I'm here' replied Oli, whispering as he crept through the Rhinonoid's refuelling station. 'I'm just making my way through the Rhinonoid to the cockpit now' he continued, warily looking about himself.

'We're on our way' replied Isaac, helping the other Operatives to their feet as they tried to overcome the feeling of wooziness from the Oxygen deprivation.

'No' replied Oli's voice as he came to a stop opposite the Quarantine Wing, having an idea.

'Repeat?' asked a confused Isaac.

'Negative, refuel your jet propulsion units and get to the cruiser's bridge. That Reptilian you fought was a decoy, a diversion. I could feel it through my blade as I struck it down. We need to find out what it was trying to divert us from' explained Oli.

'Do you think he's helping Parathax prepare for another attack?' asked Isaac, looking from the deployment bay ramp that was still sealed up, to the staircases that were still locked into the walls.

'I don't know. We have to stop it though before they have a chance to do whatever they are planning' Oli replied as he slowly made his way down the zig-zagging passageway of contaminated equipment, turning slightly sideways-on to avoid touching any of it.

He looked down at his hand that was, once again, turning to Beconium and falling apart slightly before reverting back to normal again. It appeared that the metal dishes had become damaged even further in that final confrontation with the Black-Burn Fighter.

A distant rumble became audible from back down the passageway but the distance was misleading due to the zig-zag shape of the corridor and, suddenly, the ceiling flaps shot open above him and immediately slammed back down in a wave as part of the rumbling sequence, fading away as the venting pressure continued on, down the corridor. Something else was making its way, slowly, down the passageway towards him from behind. He could tell because once the rumbling sequence had passed him it came up from behind again moments later as the repeatedly-darting chain of small, white lights at the sides of the floor set him on edge, casting moving shadows as they shot by him.

'We don't have much time' Oli announced, breathing in deeply and letting out a heavy sigh.

Although Oli knew they will have all seen his new abilities, he didn't want to tell the other Operatives about the true extent of his condition as it would distract them from the mission. He had to just push any worries to the back of his mind and stay focussed on moving forward while keeping plenty of distance between him and whatever was chasing him from behind.

As Oli moved around the corner and approached the room where he kept his customised suits, he could see that the Nanonoid armour, as well as numerous other suits, was gone and there was no sign of the transmitting Distress Signal Badge either.

'Isaac, be careful, they've taken the...' Oli started through his radio but he was quickly interrupted by a fierce, fiery blast as the animated Inferno suit blocked the doorway, preventing his attempt to leave the room.

Oli jumped backwards, stunned with fright. He quickly recomposed himself and retreated towards the still-descended scarlet 'S' shaped walkway that led to his experimentation lab below. With the Inferno suit following him, he jumped straight down rather than following the walkway as he didn't want to trigger the motion-sensors for the lights.

Hiding in the shadows, Oli climbed out of his heavy Pyrotech suit and deployed the rectangular sonar device in the side of his emerald helmet, just like he had on Crystalosis. He waited until the

Inferno suit had made its way past him, being careful to stay out of the lights that it was starting to trigger and then began firing sonar pings at his old, sapphire Initiate suit that was displayed in a space in the wall, at the end of the room.

The Inferno suit took the bait, mistaking the Initiate armour for Oli as the pings rebounded from it drawing the enemy closer to investigate.

Oli climbed back into the Pyrotech suit and clambered back up onto the walkway but, with the Inferno suit no longer having the sonar pings to investigate, it turned around and spotted Oli as he fled.

Oli tried to raise the walkway back up but it had been damaged by Parathax's aggression earlier. With the Inferno suit now quickly striding back up the scarlet walkway after him, Oli turned and ran, frantically, back down the zig-zag corridor of the Quarantine Wing, sidestepping as fast as possible while tripping over and stepping on the contaminated pieces of armour that littered the floor, nearly twisting his ankle, as the Inferno suit flooded the passageway with flames, engulfing everything in its path including the corridor's electrical systems that led to the door at the end. Oli's escape route was sealed off as the hatch closed ahead of him.

Oli frantically tried to force the door open but it had locked in place. He looked about himself, desperately, in search of another means of escape.

Quickly raising a ceiling panel, he jumped up, as high as he could, with his outstretched arms and used all of his upper-body strength to pull himself up before the flames caught up with him, the Inferno suit still in pursuit.

Oli allowed the ceiling panel to drop back down on its hinges and removed the Pyrotech suit, activating it to follow him at a distance as he army-crawled, as quietly as possible, through the enclosed metal tunnel. The Pyrotech suit was basically a massive collection of explosives that he neither wanted to be wearing or be next to while the Inferno suit was hunting him.

CHAPTER 35
RETURN TO THE BRIDGE

'Hold up. I'm reading extremely high voltage levels up ahead. Activate your jet propulsion units. Minimal thrust' instructed Isaac.

As Isaac, Nathan, Corey, Colin, Ethan and Tino slowly rose up into the air, using their fully-refuelled jet propulsion units and moved through the doorway to the bridge, they were met by Parathax who had taken the Nanonoid suit from a wounded Xzjytheous and animated it using its own black energy, just as it had with the others.

'Parathax isn't affected by the electricity. How do we stop it?' asked Colin as the group retracted their helmets and used one of their badges to keep their thrusters burning while directing themselves using their suits' interior sensory tracking lights. They also returned the bars into their chest plates to avoid them getting in the way.

Isaac looked about the room, assessing the situation. It would be impossible to launch a full frontal assault against the Astral-Alias due to the dangling live wires which occasionally struck each other with a jolt of electricity, whipping each other into the air as sparks rained down from the ceiling.

'There's Oli's Nanonoid suit' said Ethan.

'Looks like it's not damaged by the electricity either' replied Nathan.

'We need to get the Reptilian to safety. Colin, Ethan and Tino, we'll take Parathax, you three get him to The Scout Hut' instructed Isaac as he began to realise the true reason for the decoy keeping them busy in the hanger bay.

The Nanonoid suit began slowly striding along the walkway, towards the group as the dangling wires brushed over its shoulders, bolts of electricity buzzing through the air, being drawn into it as it approached.

'How do we get to him?' asked Ethan.

'We'll go outside and then fly in through the window of the observation deck' replied Colin, quickly weighing up their options. As the three of them turned to leave the bridge, however, a powerful blast shook the entire ship, causing the group to nearly fly into the electrified wall as bolts of electricity snapped out at them.

'The Scout Hut has breached the shields' announced Tino as the bridge levelled back out.

'We don't have time to navigate the ship while it's under fire. I'll stay here and keep the Nanonoid suit occupied. You and Ethan navigate the bridge and complete the objective' instructed Tino, turning back to the deadly obstacle course in front of them.

'When the ship tilts from the next blast, turbo-charge your thrusters and fly beneath the wires as they sway with the ship's list' instructed Isaac as he, Nathan and Corey deployed their swords and drew their shorter knives from their sheaths, preparing to charge at Parathax.

Tino drew his blaster and aimed at the Nanonoid suit as it approached the group.

'Watch for stray wires and prepare for evasive manoeuvres' said Colin, turning to look at Ethan as they focussed hard, calming their breathing in anticipation.

The next powerful blast from The Scout Hut struck The Stealthy Intoxicator's hull and the entire ship leaned to the side once again, causing the live wires to sway away from them.

The Operatives turbo charged their jet propulsion units and they rocketed over the walkway of the bridge, dodging the occasional wire that spontaneously got flung back in their direction from a jolt of electricity as they touched. Isaac, Nathan and Corey all threw their knives at the electrified floor where Parathax stood as they soared towards the Astral-Alias, creating a conductive triangle around it and using the metal blades to enclose it in an electrical prison that linked the blades together, concentrating the energy to overpower its armour.

Now that it couldn't retreat, as the electricity was conducted to the contaminated suit it was wearing, the three Operatives could concentrate on finishing it off before any more I.S.S. forces could be baited into its trap.

Colin and Ethan grabbed Xzjytheous from the floor as they hovered above him, his scaled body acting as an insulator against the electrified walkway.

'Let's get him up to The Scout Hut' said Colin as he struggled to lift up the wounded Reptilian while extremely aware of how close his metal boots were to the floor. This was worsened by the weight of Xzjytheous dragging him down further.

The sound of clashing blades could be heard as the other three Operatives faced off against a captured Parathax, blaster fire echoing around the bridge as Tino fired repeatedly at the advancing Nanonoid suit while trying to maintain some distance from his target.

Colin, trying to remain focussed and to keep the frustratingly high level of noise and tension at bay, bent his knees and tucked in his heels while being careful to not touch the flames from his jet propulsion unit as his toes moved closer to the electrified metal floor under the weight. This was where all of those flips that he had done with Oli, strengthening his legs and core muscles in the process, would actually pay off as he used all of his strength to keep himself from touching the floor.

Dropping lower and lower until he was a mere couple of centimetres away from the electrified floor, he had to make sure that, whatever happened, his toes and knees DID NOT TOUCH IT. However, pulling his toes away now only made his knees more prominent. Although he didn't realise it, he had almost completely stopped breathing as his chest grew tight under the prevailing stress.

His legs had grown tired, his knees aching. He couldn't pull his feet away any longer as the muscles began to tremble and fail.

'We need to go full thrust. RIGHT NOW!' shouted Colin, barely able to see the gap between his suit and the floor anymore, trying to not panic or make a wrong move with his legs as he and Ethan activated their helmets.

'I'M READY! LET'S GO!' replied Ethan and, now just an inch or so away from the floor, the two Operatives' jet propulsion unit thrusters blazed with blinding light and they exploded through the already smashed window of the observation deck, carrying Xzjytheous, still unconscious, between them.

Once outside, Colin immediately retracted his helmet to let the wind cool him down as sweat poured down his face from the tension.

Onboard the Rhinonoid, Oli, very carefully, made his way through the ceiling of the tank's bottom deck, being very, very gentle as he placed one armoured wrist-guard in front of the next, pulling himself along as he headed for the jet propulsion unit refuelling station. Through the repeatedly-rising and closing ceiling panels on which he crawled, he could hear the slow, heavy footsteps of the Inferno suit as it patrolled the area, hunting him. To avoid giving away his location, he had to repeatedly roll to the side or move part of his body out of the way as he heard the waves approaching so the panels could rise and fall without his weight holding them down.

On figuring out where about the Inferno suit was, he crawled his way through the remainder of the ceiling as fast as possible. The timing was absolutely crucial for his plan to work.

When he reached the refuelling station, Oli spotted the transmitting Distress Signal Badge amongst a gathering of pipes that fed to the huge fuel tanks, about two-thirds of the way up. He couldn't just blast the badge though because the fuel tanks would explode with him right above them.

Oli dropped down from the ceiling and landed in the large, freezing cold room, followed by the Pyrotech suit seconds later. He moved through a doorway at the end of the room and took his customised suit down to the tank's deployment bay, setting its parameters to stand guard and wait for him.

He then returned to the refuelling station to bait the Inferno suit into his trap. He couldn't just make it ignite the fuel; its exterior was impervious to combustion and temperature damage. He needed something much more drastic. Having sped up, the loud, rhythmic boom of each of the suits footsteps got louder and louder as it locked on and closed in on its target, the pounding in concert with the frantic beat of the boy's heart.

Oli drew his blaster and activated one of the badges on the arm of his emerald cy-bionic suit. A holographic display was projected from it which, he cycled through rapidly, using the emerald laser dots on the fingertips of his gloves. He selected the Rhinonoid icon, immediately followed by several frantic swipes through a variety of sub-options which triggered a loud clanging and depressurisation sound from the tank.

Repeatedly adjusting his focus to see through the hologram, checking for his pursuing attacker, Oli swiftly swiped left, right up and down, casting away the variety of options being projected from the badge until only a holographic control panel remained.

The Inferno suit suddenly emerged from behind the huge fuel tanks as Oli raised his blaster, setting his sights on it.

Seemingly undeterred, the Inferno suit continued to advance. Oli fired several blasts of harmless energy at strategic points on the refuelling tanks, causing pressurised fuel to spill out, which the Inferno suit mistook for water, intended to extinguish its fires. It aimed at the streams of fluid and triggered the flamethrowers in its arms, igniting the fuel.

Oli jumped backwards, allowing the two of them to become separated by a continuous stream of fire as it ignited the floor of the refuelling station. It was now just a matter of time before the enormous fuel tanks exploded.

Oli selected an option on the holographic control panel, causing the section of the Rhinonoid behind him to jettison and lift away from the refuelling station, as the opposite end containing the tank's cockpit and front blasters did the same, splitting the tank into three sections.

With the explosions becoming more volatile around him, he quickly turned, sprinted and leapt across, through the open doorway of the jettisoned middle section, to the rear section. He landed in a roll which he used to throw himself back onto his feet and immediately raced down to the deployment bay with all of the speed he could gather.

Exiting the corridor and nearing the top of the ladder that led down to the deployment bay, Oli heard the sound he had been dreading. Four incendiary grenades, launched by the Inferno suit, made it across to his section of the tank and clattered down the corridor towards him, detonating halfway along. Using his built-up momentum, Oli back flipped, landed on his hands and performed a fiercely ambitious sequence of rapid back handsprings to avoid the shrapnel from the casings.

Retreating towards the ledge, he committed to a double back flip, throwing himself over the edge, landing on his feet and immediately throwing his body up against the wall to allow any further debris to shoot past him.

Amazed that he had actually made it, Oli straightened his legs, moving away from the wall and quickly returned to the holographic projection. He activated another option on the display to pilot all portions of the Rhinonoid out of The Stealthy Intoxicator's hanger bay, the still-deployed scarlet spikes of laser energy cutting through all they passed as Oli then proceeded to remotely operate the rooftop blaster canon above the refuelling station as the sections circled one another, high above the battlefield.

He aimed it at the roof of its own section and, while firing at it repeatedly along with additional blaster fire from the blasters on the detached front section of the tank, Oli also remotely piloted the rear section that he was standing in, out of the hanger bay as the entire central part of the tank, where the Inferno suit was standing, erupted in a ball of flame and white-hot metal, obliterating the suit, the refuelling station and the transmitting Distress Signal Badge in the process.

Once the rear portion of the Rhinonoid was safely away from The Stealthy Intoxicator, Oli triggered the control panel on the wall to deploy the row of motorbikes out of the side of the airborne tank.

As he went to pull his hand away, he began to deteriorate into the rusty orange substance again before, once more, reverting back to his full human form. He wasn't sure how much longer the containment field generated by the dishes would last.

Leaving the Pyrotech suit in the deployment bay, he made his way, along the expansion and climbed onto his motorbike, his blonde hair blowing fiercely in the wind as he squinted his eyes and clenched his jaw tight. He used the holographic projection from his badge to bring up the same controls that Corey had activated on Zonju, triggering the Rhinonoid's Expansion Matrix under the category of its Restoration Protocol.

From the small portion of the Rhinonoid that remained, came a series of long passageways, chunks of armoured plating, legs, thrusters and blasters until the entire Rhinonoid was completely restored alongside him in its original colouration of dark green and brown which matched their flagship, The Scout Hut. Oli smiled and just took a moment to look at and admire his beloved tank that he had built with the rest of Biker Delta Squadron 5-6-5.

He then triggered another setting and the tank began to fully initiate its Expansion Matrix Protocol, opening up all of the hatches in the hull and deploying the vast array of passageways, roads and platforms from it as it came to a stationary position over The Stealthy Intoxicator. Looking back down, Oli activated a function to make all of the vacant motorbikes lock onto and follow his.

It was time to end this.

'Five-Six-Five Viper escort, lock onto me and provide some aerial cover' he instructed.

'On our way Oli' replied Sarah's voice.

Oli looked up to see the three Viper Fighters being piloted by Sarah, Timothy and Pete, flying in formation towards him. Oli revved up the engine of his motorbike, deployed his helmet over his head and tore away from the deployment rack, followed by the other bikes in an arrow formation.

Like a missile, he rocketed down one of the silver, metal roads that had been deployed from the Rhinonoid, straight towards The Stealthy Intoxicator, gripping the handlebars tighter and revving the engine harder as he tore down the track, faster and faster.

Back on the bridge of The Stealthy Intoxicator, Isaac, Ethan and Corey had almost used up their entire supply of fuel in their jet propulsion units and the glow of the blue triangle with the yellow 'V' at the edges on the backs of their cy-bionic suits had almost entirely faded.

If the fuel reserves depleted entirely, they would drop to the electrified metal floor and be killed instantly by the extremely high voltage surging through it.

Parathax blocked one of the strikes made at it and Corey seized the opportunity to land a crippling blow to its suit as he repeatedly hacked and slashed across its visor in a fierce combination of attacks, smashing and rupturing it in various places, causing its dark energy to bleed out of its containment. Parathax furiously used one of the contaminated wrist-guards it was wearing to hit Corey in the face, the electricity surging through its suit, hitting his and throwing the Operative back against the window with immense force, damaging his jet propulsion unit. This forced Corey to drop onto the glass platform of the observation deck as the same alarm began sounding from it as it had for Tino onboard The Knightfall, the royal-blue and gold lights on his back and chest now flashing on and off with scarlet. Corey ducked and dodged as he tried to see beyond the live wires that swung inches away from him as he drew his blaster but he couldn't fire on either Parathax or the Nanonoid suit that Tino was facing as the environment was just far too unpredictable.

CHAPTER 36
OUT OF TIME

Having arrived onboard The Scout Hut and refuelled their jet propulsion units, Colin and Ethan hauled Xzjytheous, still unconscious, towards the medical wing to assess his condition. Along the way, they passed the entrance to the command bridge from where the Commissioner and his Advisors were observing the devastation of the battle.

The gold-armoured Advisors caught sight of Colin, Ethan and Xzjytheous in the entrance behind them.

'HOSTILE TARGET ON THE BRIDGE!' one of them yelled as he and all of the others drew their blasters on Xzjytheous. 'SECURE HIM!' he continued as the swarm of gold-armoured suits charged towards the three of them, causing Colin and Ethan to back away slightly for fear that they weren't going to stop.

Xzjytheous was dragged onto the bridge with Colin and Ethan following behind, protesting against the aggression and explaining that the Reptilian had been aiding them. Regardless, their words fell on deaf ears.

'Sir, we have received a report from the surface. The Knightfall has been secured along with two high-value prisoners' announced one of the Troop Leaders across the room at a communications station.

'They're allies too. They assisted us on Zonju' insisted Colin.

'There's more' continued the Leader. 'The prisoners claim the battle is won but it's too late. What does he mean?' he relayed the message, somewhat bewildered.

The Commissioner turned to look out of the large window once again. 'Turn all canons on the enemy cruiser's bridge' he ordered.

'YOU CAN'T! WE STILL HAVE OPERATIVES ON THERE!' protested Ethan.

'Boy, you're naive as an I.S.S. Operative. You clearly didn't gain enough experience during your partial term as an Initiate, your remarkable feats aside. Those Operatives are outmatched and will fall sooner or later regardless. At least, this way, their sacrifice will be meaningful. This will all soon be over and, when it is, you will be demoted back to an Initiate until you learn both your place and the true cost of ensuring victory' insisted the Commissioner.

'Ensuring victory?' Colin muttered to himself, dumbfounded. The Commissioner's behaviour as well as his choice of words were extremely out of character for him. Something had to be done. He couldn't just stand there and watch.

The Scout Hut's enormous primary blaster canons pivoted and locked onto The Stealthy Intoxicator as Colin and Ethan desperately looked about themselves, helpless.

'We do our best. We do our duty...On our honour' announced the Commissioner.

Suddenly all of the cruisers targeting systems went offline. The Commissioner and his Advisors looked down to see that Xzjytheous, now awake, had disabled the ships blaster canons.

'GET HIM ON HIS FEET!' roared Commissioner Hanson.

Two of his Advisors gripped Xzjytheous by the arms and dragged him until he was standing, hunched over, in front of the Commissioner. The old man looked the Reptilian in the eyes.

'SECURE HIM IN CONTAINMENT!' the furious man commanded before turning to the Troop Leaders at their stations. 'Repair the weapon systems and, in the meantime, order the fleet above the planet to initiate an orbital strike over the battlefield' he ordered as Xzjytheous was led off the bridge. Equally furious, Colin and Ethan both drew their blasters on the Commissioner.

'You have no honour' insisted Colin bluntly.

'Sir, we've lost contact with the fleet in orbit. It's not the radiation either, there is no signature to transmit to' announced one of the other Troop Leaders sat at the Communications Console.

High above the planet, where a fleet of I.S.S. cruisers had taken up their positions after Tamatha had located them, having dropped the civilian survivors off at Felaloris, huge chunks of debris now drifted away from one another as Xzjytheous' space station drifted by. The Reptilian's heavily armed cruiser, that had discovered the fleet during its passage along the augmentation interlink, had obliterated it entirely before immediately vanishing once again, en-route to its next defensive position on the interlink.

Onboard The Stealthy Intoxicator's bridge, Nathan's thrusters now also began to sputter as his remaining fuel ran out. He bobbed up and down above the electrified floor, the alarm sounding from his suit and scarlet lights flashing to alert him of his depleted fuel reserves as he tried to remain airborne long enough to get to safety.

Corey fired the harpoon of his grappling hook into the dropped-down ceiling panels, next to Nathan, who was now bending his knees to pull his legs up and keep his feet from touching the floor just as Colin had.

On seeing the escape route that Corey had created for him, Nathan hit the red button at the centre of his collar. The flashing scarlet, ballistic glass bars sprung out from their flush position in his emerald armoured suit and the ends locked into their vertical position. Nathan quickly leaned forward and hooked the thick, armoured, glass bars over the insulated cable of Corey's harpoon and used it to zip-line down, to the glass platform.

By the time he landed, the fuel on his jet propulsion unit had run out entirely but for the occasional wisp of a flame but nothing strong enough to create any lift.

Both Operatives were now grounded and unable to help which left Isaac, alone, to fight Parathax and Tino to fight the Nanonoid suit.

From the glass observation deck, Nathan spotted something moving above him, on the edge of one of the metal-mesh ceiling panels. It was one of Xzjytheous' grenades and it was rolling straight towards a ceiling panel that was dropped downwards. If it rolled down and landed on the floor it would detonate and take them all with it.

Nathan rushed to the edge of the glass floor and reached out as far as he could to catch the grenade before it touched the electrified floor. It dropped down and landed right in the palm of his gloved hand but he was leaning so far forward on one leg that he lost his balance and fell. Corey was only just able to grab Nathan by the arm and leg in time and drag him back to safety.

'ISAAC!' yelled Nathan as he armed the grenade.

Suddenly, as Isaac looked to Nathan, Parathax struck one of the blades from the Operatives' three short knives on the floor, breaking the electrical circuit that it was contained within. Isaac quickly kicked at Parathax's armoured suit, with all of his strength, electrifying his own suit which threw him back, towards the deadly, dangling wires. As Parathax fell backwards towards the wall, Nathan threw the grenade. The four electrodes deployed from it, captured Parathax in its containment field of electric-blue energy and pinned the furious Astral-Alias up against the side of the bridge.

Before the wires could touch him, Isaac launched himself forward with all of the thrust his jet propulsion unit could generate and struck out at Parathax with the intent of a fatal blow from his sword but, before the blade could make contact, Parathax faded away on the spot and the sword went straight through the suit that had contained it.

Isaac yelled out in frustration. It had escaped again.

Drenched in sweat, he landed on the glass platform alongside Nathan and Corey, just as he depleted the last of his jet propulsion unit's fuel also, the same alarm and flashing scarlet lights coming from his suit as had done from the rest of the group.

The three Operatives, now sick of being led on a constant chase, rose up their blasters and fired a single shot simultaneously, taking out the Nanonoid suit effortlessly.

Tino carefully made his way towards the observation deck, weaving between the lethal, dangling wires. The jet propulsion unit on Tino's suit burned out also, inches away from the glass platform. The three Operatives grabbed hold of him and dragged him through the air to the glass they were standing on, a split-second before he landed on the electrified walkway.

At last, the alarms faded. The bridge fell still and silent.

'It caught you didn't it' said Isaac, observing the cut on the side of Corey's face from being hit by Parathax's wrist-guard.

'It had Beconium on' continued Nathan as he tried to catch his breath, referring to the armour that Parathax had been wearing and somewhat pained by the idea of reliving the same scenario they had done when they thought they had lost Oli.

'No, no, it's fine' replied Corey with a wave of his hand as he turned away from the group.

'You would fire on your own Operatives after all they do in service of the I.S.S?' asked Colin, keeping his blaster trained on the Commissioner on The Scout Hut's bridge.

'THE SACRIFICES THEY MAKE!? THE RISKS THEY TAKE!?...and you call this honourable?' he continued.

Colin was pained to see the I.S.S. in this light as he had always viewed them as the heroic, never leave a man behind type. This was the way it had always been, so what had changed since the attack above Polarious 5?

With everyone's focus turned away from the window that overlooked the battlefield though, nobody saw the blaster bolt that was fired on The Stealthy Intoxicator's bridge regardless...by its own blaster canon.

'INCOMING! GET DOWN!' yelled Corey as the explosive impact overpowered his voice.

The group of Operatives threw themselves down, onto the thick glass of The Stealthy Intoxicator's observation deck and deployed their helmets from their suits. It was far too late though. The powerful blaster bolt had already struck the bridge, along with a bombardment of repeated, heavy blasts from the other blaster canons positioned around The Stealthy Intoxicator, completely obliterating that portion of their own ship. Parathax watched on from the top of a tower on the fortress below, grinning wickedly, having ordered the bombardment.

As the group of Operatives fell amongst the debris towards the outside of the ship's hull, Oli revved the engine of his motorbike until he and the other Operatives' motorbikes were moving so fast that the Rhinonoid's Expansion Protocol couldn't keep up with the speed of the vehicles.

The ferocity of the aerial combat had intensified drastically and the Polarian Beconi' were becoming increasingly more aggressive. Groups of them hurtled through the sky in formation and, as they locked onto an I.S.S. fighter, they each narrowed themselves out into an elongated bullet shape and used themselves as missiles, intercepting their targets and smashing straight through them.

These new Polarian Beconi' were heavily enhanced which enabled them to, occasionally, when the impact had been successful, deploy their tentacles which trailed from behind, catch the falling pilot in mid-air and channel the plasma from their containment fields, through the tentacles and into the pilot's suit, encrusting them in fulgurite. As the encrusted pilots fell, they would be blasted and the mixtures of fulgurite and Beconium would be drawn into the containment fields where the victims would be sustained in agony by the jolts of plasma contained inside with them.

Oli shot off the end of the metal road that had been unfolding in front of him and landed on the main hull of The Stealthy Intoxicator, lining up with the falling Operatives as they spread out their arms and legs to create as much wind resistance as possible, slowing their descent.

Everyone on the bridge of The Scout Hut looked on, stunned, at the obliteration of The Stealthy Intoxicator's bridge. There was nothing left for Colin and Ethan to bargain over. Colin quickly turned around and began blasting at the already-weakened window as he and Ethan both ran at it. They fired up their jet propulsion units as The Troop Leaders attempted to detain them both.

The two Operatives exploded through the glass, leaving the cruiser's safety features to take over, separating them with a scarlet laser wall, similar to the makeshift one used on The Knightfall.

'I WANT THE NAMES OF THOSE OPERATIVES AND WHAT PATROL THEY BELONG TO! WHO IS THEIR TROOP LEADER!?' shouted the furious Commissioner.

'Colin Anderton and Ethan Stanley of Biker Delta Squadron Five-Six-Five, Sir. Records indicate that their Troop Leader is... was...Jason Campbell' replied one of the Advisors.

'I should have known. The one that led an enemy straight to us while in pursuit of him?' asked the old man.

'Yes Sir. Reports also indicate that there was a second mercenary present when Jason was captured...A Reptilian with the same class of ship as the hostile one that was broken out of impoundment, The Knightfall' the Advisor replied.

The Commissioner approached the wall of scarlet energy and looked out over the battlefield, seemingly lost in a moment of contemplation.

The Commissioner then, silently, turned around and began walking across the bridge to the doors at the end. As he walked away, a tiny, black, three-pronged metal dart fell to the floor of the bridge behind him – a second Deathstalker Sting. Colin and Ethan hadn't spotted the tiny object embedded in the side of Commissioner Hanson's neck as it was hidden behind his collar but there was one ally to Biker Delta Squadron 5-6-5 who was also working on the bridge.

Tamatha N'Ocea had been watching everything happening on the bridge from behind her closed helmet and had spotted the Deathstalker Sting as it had dropped to the floor.

While she discretely watched on, one of the Commissioner's Advisors retrieved the dart as it rolled to his feet. He held it up to the light, studying it, as it also caught the scarlet light of the embedded bars on the fronts of his shoulders. The Advisor gave a final glance at the Commissioner as the doors to the bridge closed behind him.

'UGH! SISTER, YOU NEED SOME SPARKLES!' announced Timothy, one of Viper Strike Squadron's pilots as he flew by in his Viper and sprayed an incoming Black-Burn Fighter with turquoise blaster bolts. The Black-Burn began spiralling through the air in a shower of sparks, like a pin-wheel, straight towards him.

'OH DARLING, STOP IT WITH THE DRAMA! YOU DON'T NEED TO TWIRL TO LOOK FABULOUS!' he continued before the fighter exploded in a fiery explosion.

Timothy's helmet was immediately flooded with the sound of hysterical laughter from the Operatives of Biker Delta Squadron 5-6-5 who were struggling to concentrate on timing their landing right. Their eyes were watering with laughing so hard, as were the rest of the pilots in Viper Strike Squadron.

The group of Operatives successfully landed on the seats of their motorbikes as Isaac dragged Tino onto the back of his. Colin and Ethan soared by overhead with their jet propulsion units, having left Xzjytheous on The Scout Hut. They matched the speed of the bikes as they moved in closer to them until they grabbed the handlebars and deactivated the thrusters on their jet propulsion units.

After a few seconds, the laughter subsided and a new heavier feeling came down over the battlefield as Oli eyed Parathax, still standing on one of the fortress towers, now without its gold armoured suit.

'Five-Six-Five, standby to break formation. Head down to assist Polarious Sector Patrol. I'll face Parathax alone' instructed Oli's voice, through their helmets' speakers.

'Negative. It's too strong for just one person' argued Isaac who knew that Oli would be no match for the Astral Alias.

Several more Black-Burn Fighters began pursuing the group of Operatives, firing on them as the motorbikes weaved evasively to avoid them.

'THAT'S AN ORDER, ISAAC! GO!' Oli commanded urgently, the pressure mounting as he deactivated the setting that was making the other motorbikes follow him.

As the other bikes peeled away from Oli's and he began drifting away from between the parallel green lights that darted along the middle road and over the amber lights, a blaster bolt from one of the Black-Burn Fighters struck the road, right next to him. Had it impacted just moments earlier it would have hit the Patrol collectively.

The power of the explosion threw Oli from his motorbike, launching him and the vehicle high into the air as the Operative hurtled over the edge of the road. With his eyes squeezed tight-shut, he felt a sudden jolt of his entire body as one of the Polarian Beconi' caught him in its tentacles while falling. A split second later the Polarious Beconus exploded in a ball of flame as a blaster bolt from Pete's Viper Fighter struck it, just as Oli felt a second jolt, now yanking on his arm.

He slowly opened his eyes to see Sarah grasping his wrist as she dangled from a cable that was secured to one of the eyelets of her customised Viper Fighter, now operating on remote-pilot from Timothy's cockpit as both Timothy and Pete continued to fire on the surrounding Black-Burn Fighters.

The two Leaders of their respective Patrols soared through the air, under the protection of Timothy and Pete's Viper Fighters until, finally, they were back over The Stealthy Intoxicator.

This harrowing series of events occurred in extremely rapid succession. As a result, Sarah launched Oli through the air and he barrel-rolled across the hull of the immense cruiser just as his motorbike came crashing down from above, exploding in a ball of flame as it smashed into a raised part of the cruiser.

As Oli regained his feet, he found that the tentacle that had been clinging to his leg had briefly started encrusting his suit in fulgurite before the Polarious Beconus was shot down. The shards had shattered on his landing and now littered the hull of the cruiser at his feet, still bridging the gap between one another with an occasional, weak, flicker of plasma. Oli used his foot to flick the shards over the edge of the cruiser, down to the ground below.

Meanwhile the leader of Viper Strike Squadron had reeled the cable back in, climbed across the textured surface of her Viper Fighter using the tiny, raised dots for added grip and climbed back into the cockpit to rejoin the battle.

An eerie silence surrounded Oli, who now retracted his helmet into his suit, the cold wind sweeping over his sweat-covered face and hair as the dogfight and surface combat raged, far below. He felt extremely isolated but had a feeling that he wasn't alone as he glanced around at the surface of the enormous warship.

He took a few steps forwards, his eyes darting back and forth, wide and alert. Suddenly a loud whistling sound came from high above which gradually turned into a deafening, screeching roar.

A series of six Viper Fighter stabiliser fins rained down from above and thrust, like enormous amber blades, into the hull of The Stealthy Intoxicator. Oli stumbled, ducked and dodged as the huge, deadly projectiles surrounded him. He desperately tried to run for cover but, inevitably, what followed immediately cut off his escape;

the Viper Fighters from which the fins had been jettisoned, or, rather, torn.

The flaming, tangled wreckages of three Viper Fighters littered the hull of the cruiser in front of him, black, billowing smoke flooding the sky around him as Oli immediately rushed to aid the pilots and drag them out of the wreckages. Although unsure whether any of them had survived the crash, one by one he dragged them out of their cockpits, deployed their parachutes and tossed them over the edge to descend, down to the ground. It seemed odd to Oli that these Vipers were flying so high above the battlefield as there weren't even any Black-Burn Fighters that high up.

Suddenly, another Viper crashed down, beyond the first three wreckages. Debris flew through the air, raining down over Oli as he held up his arms to cover his face. It wasn't enough though, tiny pieces of metal slipped by him and slashed across his face. Pained, Oli placed his gloved hand over his face only to find the black, padded palm of his glove covered in blood caused by the shrapnel that had hit him. Unsteady on his feet, Oli looked up, just as a huge mechanical monstrosity exploded through the shroud of black smoke, launching itself right at him with immense power.

Oli fell backwards and frantically reversed away from the hulking, armoured contrivance. It was mostly black with blue lights that darted around in various directions around it and it walked on four huge legs with a long, gold spike on the end of each one. Five scorpion tail-like anchors from the destroyed Vipers arched high above the machine with their three-piece orange casings retracted and wielding the curved, purple spikes with glowing emerald laser emitters contained within. Repeatedly, it stabbed and thrust its legs and tails at Oli as he struggled to regain his feet under the relentless onslaught.

Looking behind himself as he scrambled away, he could see that his escape was, once again, cut off by a dense, black shroud, from which, a furious storm of electric-purple plasma bolts struck out in all directions from Parathax's hypercharged Fulgurite-infused sword, forcing Oli to flee back towards the mechanical monstrosity.

While the bolts of plasma were uncontrollable and viciously rapid, they could not be directed. Nevertheless, the tiring Operative repeatedly dodged out of the way of the furious attacks from both directions until he finally grabbed one of the tails and it launched him high into the air, over the attacking machine and, as he tumbled across the hull behind it, he fled, back towards the crashed Vipers.

On reaching the scattering of fins that were thrust into the top of the cruiser, the spikes of the scorpion tails elongated and struck out around him, forcing him to take cover behind the fins, the bolts of plasma from the other side of the fin surging by and striking out at anything they came close to. The tails continued to strike out, the emerald laser tips cutting, slashing and gashing over the amber paintwork of the fighters' remnants as they left luminous green slash marks all over them, flickering with sparks, before, eventually, fading to silver where the orange paint had been cut away.

Suddenly, just as Oli drew his knife and sword to make his stand, his arms were pulled down to their sides as streams of black energy poured into two of the Viper fins that he was standing between, that then redistributed to the Patrol Leader, restraining him. His hair blew fiercely in the wind as he gritted his teeth, his bloodied face contorted as he wrestled to break free but it was no use.

'You have fought well and still you fail. Your friends, the Reptilian, all have failed. All will inevitably fall' Parathax's voice echoed on the wind, mocking Oli, taunting him loudly to be heard over his furious grunts as he completely exhausted himself.

As Parathax's sword materialised at his throat, the blade suddenly shot off, through the air, revealing a double ended spear as the Astral-Alias also cast aside its sword's hilt. The enormous monstrosity that had attacked Oli, collapsed in on itself repeatedly as it approached Parathax, revealing itself to be the gold cy-bionic suit that it had been wearing previously as it, once again, encased the ghostly entity.

Little did Oli and Parathax know, the rest of Biker Delta Squadron 5-6-5 had made their way back to the cruiser after Isaac had taken over control of the Rhinonoid's expansion and created a road back up to The Stealthy Intoxicator. The group of Operatives watched on in horror as, in a demonstration of pure rage, Parathax struck Oli, relentlessly with the top end of its spear and then the main body of it, crippling him further as, with each strike, a powerful explosion of purple lighting erupted from the weapon, surging across the sky, the hull of the ship and Oli's shredded suit.

Isaac didn't know how much more Oli could take so, eyeing the huge pivoting blaster canons that were positioned alongside Oli and Parathax, he hurtled his knife, as hard as he could, at the dome of one of them, damaging the crystal within.

Beams of lethal laser energy exploded in every direction from the dome beneath the turret's barrel, striking fighters, indiscriminately, as they soared by as well as the fins that were feeding the black energy out at Oli.

Oli, released by the destruction of the fins, collapsed but there was no time for the self-pity born of his pain and exhaustion. He rose back to his feet, trembling and raised up his sword.

He and Parathax ducked and dodged around the energy beams with every blast of the cruiser's powerful blaster canon as they engaged in a fiercely fast-paced duel of green spark flashes and purple lighting explosions with every clash.

'Accept the fate of all you love. The I.S.S. and all that your filth pitifully protects will fall under my dominion' seethed Parathax, leaning in close to Oli's bloodied face as the two of them locked blades.

They then slashed their weapons away from each other, striking them against the metal hull of the ship which, due to the friction, ignited both like striking a match. Their weapons, Oli's ablaze with green and Parathax's with orange from the Beconium, now remained alight with fierce, blinding flame.

From the ground, Emma and Jess, who remained with the now-vacated Knightfall, were fending off an advance of Beconium Beings that were unlike the others on the battlefield. These particular Beconium Beings had come from one of the Polarian Beconi' that had been shot down. They had emerged from the damaged containment field but had become armoured in fulgurite by the plasma that had also been contained in the force field. As they advanced, bolts of plasma, struck out from the narrow funnels that ran through their bodies and, despite the many blasts that hit them from Emma and Jess' weapons, while penetrating the fulgurite armour, it simply got replenished as a bolt of plasma from elsewhere on their own bodies or one of the others struck out at the exposed Beconium and encrusted it once again, with new funnels and various other imperfections in it each time.

As they retreated towards the ship, they could see an I.S.S. Operative moving through the air, towards them, beneath a scarlet parachute with a gold trim that matched their jet propulsion unit indicator across their chest and back. Simply from these colours, this Operative could be identified as a survivor from the I.S.S. Libera, one of the other I.S.S. cruisers that came under fire above Polarious 5 during the assault on the fleet.

The Operative fired a volley of blaster bolts from above while making sure to fire at the back of the group first, taking out the Beconium Beings in such a way that they couldn't replenish their fulgurite armour.

The Operative landed on the Beconium sand with bent knees. As she rose up, she detached her parachute from her emerald suit of armour, grabbed Emma and Jess by the arms and hurried them onboard The Knightfall, retracting her helmet into her collar.

The dark-skinned girl with her dark hair tied up at the back appeared extremely distressed as she took one last look about herself before briefly explaining her behaviour in a very strong Earth-Zimbabwean accent. 'My name is Tamatha N'Ocea. I was amongst the fleet at Polarious Five!' she explained as she began to sweat and hyperventilate, looking about herself once more.

'Emily Longfield and Jessica Brophy of Viper Strike Squadron. We're stationed onboard The Scout Hut' replied Emma, slightly bewildered about how distressed Tamatha appeared to be.

'I know who you both are!' Tamatha bulldozed through the formality. 'You must tell Isaac of Biker Delta Squadron Five-Six-Five...It's the Commissioner...HE CAN'T BE TRUSTED!' she cried.

Emma and Jess both looked at her confused.

'What do you mean? Of course he can be trusted' replied Jess but Emma remained silent, remembering something that Sarah, the Leader of Viper Strike Squadron, had said to her following the strike on the fleet after the pilots had re-grouped.

'We need to alert a Troop Leader' Emma finally announced as she pieced everything together.

'NO! IT'S TOO DANGEROUS! ONLY TELL ISAAC!' Tamatha ordered. The two grounded pilots tried to get more information from Tamatha but were unable to get a word in.

'There's no time. I have your Operative signature designations now. I'll make contact soon' she said, looking at the updated records being projected into a hologram from one of the badges on her suit before quickly deactivating it.

'Be safe' Tamatha finished, with a final, frightened look at both of the girls. She then closed her helmet back up, raced back down The Knightfall's loading ramp and rocketed away with her jet propulsion unit, leaving Emma and Jess to watch on, speechless.

The duel between Oli and Parathax was rapidly becoming extremely volatile as they made their way around the surface of The Stealthy Intoxicator, striking and slashing at one another until, finally, Parathax landed a particularly fierce blow against one of the Polarian Beconi' dishes that Oli was using as a shield, followed by a series of immensely powerful strikes and hacks at his cy-bionic suit, rupturing it further and smashing entire chunks of it away, its rage apparent as it yelled out furiously, purple lightning fiercely exploding out in all directions with every strike of its weapon. Parathax then flipped a trigger on the hilt of its weapon, allowing the hyper-charged piece of fulgurite to spring up. A furious storm of purple plasma bolts struck out at Oli's sword from the glinting funnels in the stone, powerfully launching the weapon out of his grasp and casting it far across the hull of the cruiser, out of reach.

Parathax extended its weapon towards Oli, forcing him to back away, towards the cruiser's damaged blaster canon.

'Calling all Interstellar Scout forces. This is the I.S.S. Roe Lea, I.S.S. Libera, I.S.S. High Bank and escort cruisers. We're coming into orbit above Becon and we have contingency reinforcements en-route in response to your distress signal. You've stopped transmitting but we have your location locked in. Standby for extraction' announced a voice through the speaker built into Oli's collar, much to his horror.

'AND SO FALL THE INTERSTELLAR SCOUTS!' Parathax taunted in acknowledgement of its victory.

It was hopeless. Oli couldn't radio back to warn them due to the radiation. He looked up at the sky, horrified, as the Deathstalker Squadron broke away from the battle and ascended, with immense speed, through the atmosphere in preparation to ambush the inbound fleet.

'NO!' Oli yelled out with a squeak of despair in his voice as his eyes flooded with tears.

His fears were quickly confirmed as the yells and cries for immediate assistance and orders to abandon ship came over the radio before being quickly drowned out by the sound of blaster fire, explosions and static as the ships were totally obliterated, the entire fleet wiped out in just a few seconds. Silence fell as Oli looked to Parathax, broken-hearted.

For Oli, there was nothing more to be done, except, perhaps, sacrifice himself one last time for the people he cared about. Fighting his own reluctance, he regrettably closed his eyes and tried to find the courage to perform his final act of bravery.

With a slight stammer, he uttered the command into his suit's microphone. 'Override Rhinonoid Expansion Matrix Protocol.' There was a brief pause and then he completed the command. 'Jettison' he said bravely, his voice cracking as a tear rolled down his cheek.

'OLI! NO!' yelled a voice from behind. Oli quickly reeled around to see Colin racing towards him with the rest of Biker Delta Squadron 5-6-5 close behind. It was too late though.

The metal panels broke away from the cruiser as well as the fighters, infantry and the fortress below. Colin began to sink into the cruiser that was now reverting to its Beconium form.

'COLIN!' yelled Oli, horrified at the fate that awaited his adopted brother.

The damage to the Polarious Beconus dishes that had been sustaining Oli had become so extensive that they were now failing entirely. Oli felt himself turning back into his Beconium form as the stolen Rhinonoid armour, covering The Stealthy Intoxicator, jettisoned away, around him.

Parathax, blinded by its Deathstalker strike on the fleet in orbit, laughed wickedly as it raised up its weapon once more and rapidly cast out a furious storm of purple plasma bolts at the rest of Biker Delta Squadron 5-6-5 but Oli stepped in front of the attack, absorbing the energy as he slowly advanced towards Parathax, unhindered in his Beconium form.

Corey quickly sprinted forwards, past Isaac, Nathan and the others and launched himself at Colin, tackling him at the waist and throwing both Colin and himself over the edge of The Stealthy Intoxicator.

Parathax was momentarily stunned by its inability to stop Oli. The Astral-Alias unleashed the black energy that enshrouded it, pouring it into the piece of fulgurite to enhance its power further as the Astral-Alias retreated. It hadn't however, realised that the armour was also breaking away from the cruiser behind it as well. The suit it was wearing suddenly became trapped, sinking into the Beconium that now formed The Stealthy Intoxicator.

Moments later, Oli's blazing, emerald sword made contact with the remnants of the cruiser, it too sinking into the Beconium. The entire ship suddenly ignited, ablaze with blinding, emerald light until finally, the metal panelling came away from the damaged turret, erupting the laser beams in rapid, volatile spontaneity which struck Oli's Beconium body.

Crying out with rage and excruciating pain, Oli charged forwards in his blazing Beconium form and threw himself at Parathax, wrapping his arms around its armoured shroud and completely disintegrating it as it let out a deafening, ghastly wail.

Oli's ignited Beconium form was immediately encased, entirely, in fulgurite as he fell.

'THIS IS ISAAC, ASSISTANT PATROL LEADER OF BIKER DELTA SQUADRON FIVE-SIX-FIVE. ALL I.S.S.

FORCES DEPLOY YOUR HELMETS AND CLEAR THE AREA IMMEDIATELY. AIRBORNE PROJECTILES INCOMING!' Isaac radioed through to everyone below as the group went into freefall having leapt off the cruiser. The group dodged the enormous pieces of falling debris, while many of their jet propulsion units were still deprived of fuel.

Colin and Ethan, however, anticipating the need for additional fuel reserves had refuelled their own jet propulsion units when they had taken Xzjytheous to The Scout Hut. They deployed their bars from their chest plates and fired up the thrusters, grabbing hold of Isaac, Nathan, Corey and Tino, slowing their descent.

Chapter 37

In The Emerald Snow

The Polarian Beconi', Beconium Beings and Black-Burn fighters, all of which Parathax had conjured and created for the battle, were all instantly reduced back to shapeless mounds of Beconium and inanimate scrap metal as they all fell to the ground, the wind casting it across the battlefield before instantaneously stopping as the last of Parathax's influence over the planet's atmosphere wore off.

As the Operatives of Biker Delta Squadron 5-6-5 and Tino looked about themselves, they could see the blazing green Beconium from the destroyed Stealthy Intoxicator which fell softly around them, like twinkling snowflakes, sparkling against the orange sky.

The shape of an emerald Interstellar Scout suit could be made out, lying in the Beconium near The Knightfall's wreckage as Emma and Jess knelt down over it. Colin wasted no time in collapsing his sword and racing across the sand to the fallen Operative as the rest of the group followed close behind.

The I.S.S. Viper and Funnel-Web Fighters slowly descended, towards the ground, landing nearby.

The Operatives rolled the armoured suit over to reveal Oli, now back in his physical form again as he started to awaken, his face dirtied with Beconium. Sparks of plasma from Parathax's sword still occasionally flickered throughout his suit, disabling it and the fulgurite that he had been encased in had been smashed away as it appeared he had hit The Knightfall before rolling down to the ground.

'Help me sit him up' instructed Isaac over the sounds of the nearby fighters powering down their engines.

The group, insulated against the weak plasma remnants by the padding on the palms of their gloves, gently sat Oli up as he slowly opened his eyes. They collectively held their hands out to support him as he wearily looked around at them all. He seemed only half-conscious and not entirely able to comprehend what was happening.

'It's ok, we won' said Nathan, looking over his shoulder at the I.S.S. Operatives gathering nearby as the pilots climbed out of their ships. 'It's gone' he continued in a heavy breath, trembling, as he tried to contain his emotions.

Oli weakly tried to stand up while the Operatives grabbed his arms to assist him. He had no strength left in him though. His legs gave way beneath him, crumbling into a heap of Beconium as he fell back to the ground, lying on his front with the toxic substance filling his nose and mouth as his body struggled to stabilise in the failing containment field.

He strained himself to look up at the metal dishes near his hands. Sparks gently flickered out of them, confirming his fears as he tried to sit back up, the rest of the group watching on both confused and extremely concerned. Something was very wrong.

Sarah stepped forward from the gathering of pilots and other I.S.S. Operatives to join the group gathered around Oli, her long, fiery-red hair blowing in the wind as it swept across the back of her shiny, emerald suit.

'Sarah? What's happening?' asked Colin as Oli weakly tried to move his arms and legs.

'When you took him to Crystalosis to cure his Beconium Poisoning, he was successfully revived but an underlying symbiotic metamorphosis of some sort was also triggered. His cells mutated under the effects of the concentrated solar beam mixed with the Beconium in his body. Oli could only stabilise himself using these metal dishes on his arms but it appears they were badly damaged in the battle and now they are incapable of aiding him' announced

Sarah, walking by the group and kneeling down next to Oli, placing her gloved hand on his cheek reassuringly.

The group looked to her as they backed away a couple of steps, understanding what she was implying but not wanting to accept it.

'He doesn't have long now' she said quietly, trying to keep herself composed as Oli looked up at her, helpless and unable to speak. Still, his eyes spoke his pain and fear for him.

The other Operatives watched on, crying silently, tears rolling down their cheeks. Oli cast his eyes, past Sarah, to Colin, as if calling out to his younger brother.

Isaac placed his hand on Colin's shoulder.

'You can be with him this time' he said quietly as Colin looked up at the Operative, teary-eyed.

Colin then looked back to his older brother but couldn't bring himself to walk over to him so Isaac, keeping his hand on Colin's shoulder, began to walk over to Oli, encouraging Colin to come with him.

The resistance of wading through the Beconium was more prominent now than ever, the silence only broken by the swishing sound of their metal boots dragging through the metallic, sand-like substance as the light wisps drifted across the surface of the ground in the fading wind.

Isaac bravely smiled down at Oli as the dying Operative thanked him with his weary eyes. Sarah placed her hand on Colin's shoulder, comforting him, as he knelt down next to his brother. She then returned to her feet and walked away to join the rest of the group next to Isaac, leaving the two brothers alone in Oli's final moments.

A shuttle set down on the ground behind them but nobody even noticed at first until Sarah looked over her shoulder and spotted a pair of Troop Leaders descending the loading ramp. Sarah walked over to meet with them so she could help with clearing up the battlefield and recovering vital technology, as well as those who had fallen in the battle.

'Oli?' said Colin quietly, trying to be as brave as he could be for his brother. 'Oli?' he repeated again, shaking his brother gently and feeling like he was right on the brink of crying uncontrollably.

Oli let out a tired sigh as his eyes opened slightly, searching for the voice that called out to him.

'Colin...' he whispered, barely moving his lips as his heavy eyes closed again, reassured that his brother was with him.

'I tried...we all tried...' Colin stammered, unable to get the words out as he lost control of his emotions and began sobbing.

'I know...I know...I'm proud...' Oli whispered, now almost inaudibly as his words tailed off.

Colin looked up to the others, desperately, his lips quivering as Oli reached his fingers out to Colin, forcing his eyes to just open slightly to look at his younger brother.

Colin reluctantly took his brother's hand to comfort him unaware of the fact that Oli was actually holding Colin's hand as a reassurance to his younger brother.

'...I'm sorry...' Oli whispered with his final breath as his eyes closed for the final time and his face settled into the Beconium.

Colin rested his head against his brother's armoured suit, crying, as the other Operatives turned away and left him to grieve in private as the sun began to set on the horizon.

Just as the group turned their backs, Sarah came charging towards them as fast as she could.

'STAND ASIDE! EVERYONE CLEAR A PATH! ISAAC, NATHAN, COREY OVER HERE, NOW!' yelled Sarah as she and the two Troop Leaders rushed through the crowd, towards Oli.

'What's happening?' asked Colin.

'Here, hold this' instructed Sarah, handing a device to Isaac with a needle protruding from it. 'Down here, give me your hand' she instructed Corey, grabbing his wrist and dragging him down to his knees as she pulled off his glove and tossed it aside. 'Put your fingers here, under his chin and let us know as soon as you feel his pulse' she instructed.

The two Troop Leaders lifted Oli up and lay him down on a platform which then levitated roughly two feet off the ground.

'Nathan, access his First Aid Badge and activate his respirator mask as fast as you can' Sarah called back to Nathan. 'Give me that' she instructed, taking the device from Isaac and immediately injecting its contents into Oli.

'Move him into The Knightfall's deployment bay, now! MOVE IT!' ordered one of the gold-armoured Troop Leaders as the group, continuing their jobs, rushed Oli to the nearby wreckage.

Isaac, once again, eyeing the plasma energy flickering around Oli's suit and realising what they were doing, raced on ahead, climbed up to the cockpit and initiated the systems to electrify the deployment bay, just as they had done to help Tino.

'I just felt a weak pulse! HE'S COMING BACK!' shouted Corey.

'Get out of there, NOW!' Sarah yelled in response from the top of the ladder, next to the hatch.

As soon as Corey was clear of the deployment bay and the hatch was sealed, a powerful blast of electricity struck Oli's cy-bionic suit. His eyes shot wide-open and he gasped deeply behind his respirator mask with a sudden jolt.

CHAPTER 38
THE NEXT VENTURE

Later that evening, with Oli safely in recovery onboard The Scout Hut and Tino having his wounds tended to while debriefing the Commissioner's Advisors on what had happened between him and the Deathstalker Fighter during the battle on Earth that caused him to lose his memory, the cruiser's entire array of transport and cargo shuttles was sent out to retrieve all of the scrap metal from the planet's surface and also recover the Viper Fighters that had been stolen during the Polarious Sector assault and crashed down to the ground after Parathax's hold over them was broken.

Biker Delta Squadron 5-6-5 had remained at The Knightfall's wreckage to assist several Troop Leaders in its repairs to at least be able to move it up to The Scout Hut's hanger bay.

Meanwhile, Isaac and his sister were discussing their experiences from the past few days while Sarah held a cold compress to the head injury she had suffered during the battle at the hands of The Spyglass, in a bid to keep the swelling down.

'How is it that you were already here before we arrived?' asked Isaac as he turned to Sarah, both of whom were sat at the top of The Knightfall's loading ramp with their legs dangling over the edge.

'When The Scout Hut was attacked, it was too much of a risk to evacuate and fly out into the conflict only to land on Polarious Five so everyone camouflaged themselves amongst the debris that was already drifting around out there. We went through so many nightmare scenarios before we were finally brought here by the enemy without them realising' Sarah replied.

'How bad could it have been compared to what we've been through?' asked Isaac, indicating to the rest of Biker Delta Squadron 5-6-5.

‘A Con-Haarian boarding party infiltrated The Scout Hut and took the bridge, I was almost set adrift in the debris field when I was thrown from part of a destroyed ship while investigating The Knightfall landing on Polarious Five and, to save Oli, I had to abandon my fighter and face off against a squadron of stolen Vipers with my blaster and a grappling hook’ Sarah recalled.

‘Which reminds me, I tried to save you in the hanger bay. How did you even survive?’ asked Isaac.

‘Before I left my Viper, I used my grappling hook as an umbilical cord, securing it to one of my Viper eyelets. The wreckage that I hid inside started to fall towards some fuel canisters that were about to explode so, before it crashed, I reeled the cable back in. It dragged me out of the wreckage and took me all the way back to the safety of my Viper. The stolen Vipers then left the hanger bay’ Sarah explained.

‘Yeah, we ran into them again shortly after’ replied Isaac.

‘As crazy as all of that was though, my absolute highlight was that I was there to witness something very, VERY special – I got to hear Timothy call Pete ‘Twinkle Toes’’ she continued, unable to hold back her laughter any longer as Isaac also broke down in uncontrollable, hysterical laughter while imagining the big, strong, macho Pete’s reaction to being referred to by such a mocking name and especially by Timothy.

‘Tim’s a total legend. Remind me to congratulate him on that when I see him’ Isaac laughed, desperately trying to get his breath back and wiping a tear from his eye.

‘So, what else did you go through to get here?’ asked Sarah, brushing her long hair back behind her ear.

‘Oh, Corey shared with us how his feelings were hurt that I wanted Nathan to take my place when I thought I was going to die’ Isaac replied bluntly, knowing that no further explanation was needed.

Sarah placed a sympathetic hand on Isaac’s shoulder. ‘You need this more than I do’ she joked, offering him the cold compress in her hand.

'We'll be escorting The Knightfall back up to the cruiser once the repairs are done. How close are you?' asked Emma, Viper Strike Squadron's Assistant Patrol Leader.

'We're just waiting for the recalibration of the flight systems to complete and then we'll be ready!' announced Nathan's voice from the cockpit, overhearing Emma.

'Is something wrong?' asked Isaac, noticing a concerned expression briefly flash over Emma's face.

Emma paused for a moment in deep thought, trying to decide whether there was any substance to what was troubling her.

'It's just something you said when the rest of our squadron returned to the cruiser after the assault had passed' replied Emma, turning to Sarah.

Sarah gave her a questioning look, unsure of what she was getting at.

'You mentioned that Commissioner Hanson had remained onboard when everyone else had evacuated the cruiser and that he was behaving very strangely' Emma started.

'Oh, he was; it was really creepy' replied Sarah, turning to Isaac.

'During the battle, Jess and I were grounded and we took cover here but then we met another Operative who lost her fighter and was forced to parachute in. She was terrified and told us to tell you that something has gone very wrong with the Commissioner and... He can't be trusted' Emma explained.

'How did this Operative know me? Did she give a name?' asked Isaac, taken aback.

'She said her name was Tamatha...Tamatha N'Ocea' replied Emma.

Isaac smiled briefly, relieved that she had made it off Zonju and back to The Scout Hut.

'What does this mean?' asked Emma.

'I don't know but the other Troop Leaders should probably be informed to be on the safe side' replied Isaac, who didn't want another burden to carry.

Emma looked past Isaac's shoulder as one of the Troop Leaders moved by behind him to retrieve some equipment for recalibrating the ship's flight systems. Warily, she waited for him to return to the console before continuing.

'Tamatha was inconsolable. She insisted that no seniority should be told, only you and that she will reach out to us when it's safe to do so' insisted Emma in a forced, hushed tone, overruling Isaac's reluctance.

'In that case, I'll need to speak to Oli when he's up and about but, for now, take these for surveillance' instructed Isaac, removing the folded, collapsible bionics of The Knightfall Guard from their mounts on the rack that extended out from the normally-hidden compartment in the side of the ship.

'Station them on the bridge in Operative suits to carry out rudimentary tasks. Have Tamatha oversee them and contact us as soon as she reaches out to you so she can explain everything' instructed Isaac, stacking the folded bionics in Emma's arms.

Emma gave a worried nod and then turned to carry the bionics to her Viper Fighter.

'I couldn't help overhearing' announced a voice from behind.

Isaac and Sarah nervously turned to see Corey standing behind them inside the shuttle.

'While everyone is talking about Operatives jumping ship, I've decided that, once we have regrouped with another fleet, I'm going to transfer to a more combat-ready Patrol' he continued.

'What are you talking about?' asked Isaac, frowning up at the Operative as he climbed to his feet.

'I'm not suited to Biker Delta Squadron Five-Six-Five. I think I need to be doing more than just rescues and extractions. I need to be out there, holding off the enemy and covering you while you do your part' Corey explained as he picked up Parathax's spear from the floor of the ship and walked across the cockpit to mount it on the wall along with the other assortment of weapons.

'Ever the hero' replied Isaac with a smile.

Corey, with his back to Isaac and Sarah, nodded quietly and then went to return to his repairs.

'But you're not jumping ship and you're certainly not leaving this Patrol' Isaac continued.

Corey turned back to Isaac, frowning with confusion as the Assistant Patrol Leader joined Corey and took him to the side to speak with him in private.

'You made a lot of mistakes over the past few days but so have I and so have the rest of the Patrol. We weren't prepared to be on our own, being hunted without the guidance of a Troop Leader and Patrol Leader and there were times when I would have happily told you to transfer when we regroup but I think you have discovered a few things about yourself over the past few days as well. I think we all have to some extent but you rescued Tino, you co-ordinated the Patrol while those Black-Burns were firing on us on Crystalosis. I said before the battle that each member of our Patrol has an important role to play and your role is to fill in for the jobs that the rest of us are unable to do or are incapable of doing. You get the job done. All you need is the rest of us to draw the line, to stop you from bouncing too far in a direction that will endanger the mission. This Patrol needs you' Isaac explained.

'But...What about Oli?' asked Corey, slightly taken aback by Isaac's forgiveness.

'Oli will be fine now. I don't know the exact details of what's happening to heal him, I'll get Sarah to fill me in but listen...Thanks for helping me, I really do appreciate you doing your best and I am truly sorry for some of the things I said, I didn't mean them. I was just lost in the stress of the moment' replied Isaac, placing his hand on Corey's shoulder.

'Thanks for saving me when I fell off the platform' said Corey as he started to cry. He had wanted to restore his friendship with Isaac since he was alone on the shuttle on Zonju but the moment hadn't presented itself until now and, the acknowledgement of Isaac's friendship and sacrifices caught him off-guard.

After taking a few moments to compose himself, Corey returned to helping with The Knightfall's repairs.

'Only my brother could be stupid enough to remove his distress signal and destroy it right in front of the enemy' Sarah teased as Isaac rejoined her at the top of the loading ramp and sat back down.

'Actually, it wasn't only me. We all did it' replied Isaac in a smug tone. His sister exhaustedly looked at him, as if to ask why that would be better than just him alone doing something so stupid.

As the two siblings continued to talk, a gold-armoured Troop Leader approached The Knightfall's loading ramp from outside, capturing the attention of both Operatives.

'At the request of Commissioner Hanson, the Reptilian is being detained onboard The Scout Hut but we are making sure that his injuries and Beconium Poisoning are being tended to using a successful cure created by your Patrol Leader, Oliver. It's the same cure we used to bring him back and both are responding well to it. They will both make a speedy recovery. Also, we believe that a few Interstellar Scout cruisers may have been fortunate enough to escape the Deathstalkers' onslaught during the battle and we are currently attempting to establish contact with them. The only ones we are aware of right now are the I.S.S. Roe Lea, the I.S.S. Libera and the I.S.S. High Bank. The cruisers each serve very different purposes, as you know and locating them will allow us to rebuild the fleet' the Troop Leader announced.

The Operatives were relieved to hear that perhaps some ships had survived the fierce strikes over the past few days but their relief was quickly cut short.

'...There's more...' the Troop Leader went on, his concern and hesitation evident.

'Based on the account given by Oliver when he rendezvoused with the rest of us before the battle...' the Troop Leader stumbled over his words once again.

'Oliver reported a period of time that was unaccounted for, during which, he underwent some sort of...displacement'.

'He was exploring the tunnel systems on Zonju, passed out and then, when he woke up, he had moved further down the passageway' Sarah clarified for Isaac.

The one consistency, based on our tests and the debrief, is that the symbiotic properties of the Beconium can override the synapses in the brain and, for lack of a better word, temporarily zombify the victim' the Troop Leader went on.

'You mean...like...mind control?' asked Isaac, looking from the Troop Leader to Sarah and back to the Troop Leader again, his facial expression becoming that of increasing bewilderment at how fanciful the whole idea sounded.

'We don't understand the extent of it yet though. We do have experiments up and running and are using the research of both your Patrol Leader and your former Troop Leader, Jason Campbell, to help us understand why some Beconium causes poisoning and some zombifies. Your Patrol Leader has come into direct contact with this substance in varying circumstances in recent days. It is for that reason that the decision has been made that Oliver will be confined to quarantine under armed guard, pending further testing' explained the Troop Leader.

The Operatives' mouths hung slightly agape. Although nobody spoke in response, they both felt the same gut-punch, triggered by this announcement, their stunned eyes falling to the Beconium beneath them.

Joining the Troop Leader, a few moments later, were two other Troop Leaders, also in gold, armoured suits, along with a further two familiar faces. Gala-Thius and Anthony both stood at the foot of the ramp with their restraints now removed.

Gala-Thius, who now looked totally different to the way he did earlier, now had a trimmed beard and moustache and his hair was tidily tied into a ponytail at the back. As the only one who had put forward a potential way to save Oli after overhearing Isaac and Colin discussing Oli's experiments before the battle and by jumpstarting the bio-chemical reaction of the symbiotic relationship between Oli and the Beconium using The Knightfall's electrified deployment bay, he had earned a pardon but both he and Anthony were stripped of all formal high ranks that they had once held.

Gala-Thius was now nothing more than a standard Troop Leader, operating with a Patrol. Following the capture of their very first Troop Leader when they were just Initiates and the death of their second one during the Polarious Sector Assault, Gala-Thius was assigned to Biker Delta Squadron 5-6-5 as their new Troop Leader. Meanwhile, Anthony was to undergo extensive assessment.

'Xzjytheous has informed us that, while it's highly unlikely Parathax will return now, there is much that we don't know about Astral-Aliases and I agree. We can't rule out the possibility of Parathax resurfacing. Either way, many of its forces are still out there, including the Con-Haarians, the Polarian Beconi' and, of course, the Deathstalker Squadron. Xzjytheous fears that they will target peaceful civilisations without much in the way of a military defence first, to try and rebuild a powerful strike force. One of the most likely worlds they will target is Biolum' announced Gala-Thius.

'As soon as we establish contact with The Roe Lea, The Libera and The High Bank, Viper Strike Squadron, along with a number of other fighter escorts, will be dispatched to assist the three cruisers in rendezvousing with The Scout Hut at Biolum. Meanwhile, you should all return to the cruiser and get your own doses of Oliver's cure for Beconium Poisoning as a precaution as it will combat contamination to your skin as well. Once you have the all-clear we are launching a mission to take control of an orbital outpost above the planet which is believed to be run by the Reptilian. Once we have taken it, it will become an I.S.S. medical facility for the purpose of curing, primarily, Beconium-induced sicknesses but will also provide medical aid in other areas as well. It will be a very straight-forward mission with no enemy resistance as scanners indicate that it's unoccupied. Once The Roe Lea, The Libera and The High Bank have been located, we will move on to Biolum ahead of them, that way we will be harder to spot if there are any threats down there. We may have survived the Battle of Becon but countless civilisations are now in extreme, imminent danger as a result and they will look to us to help them. We MUST be prepared, YOU must be prepared' announced one of the Troop Leaders.

'We'll do our best. We'll do our duty. On our honour' replied Isaac, relieved to hear that Oli would be able to return to leading the Patrol following a brief recovery and assessment of his condition but also confident that he could now comfortably fill Oli's role in the meantime with the Patrol now working as a team.

'ON OUR HONOUR!' repeated the rest of Biker Delta Squadron 5-6-5, collectively.

'Flight systems restored, we're ready to disembark and dock with the cruiser' announced Nathan as he studied the console in the cockpit and began initiating The Knightfall's launch sequence.

Gala-Thius and Anthony made their way up the loading ramp as it began to close, joining Isaac, Nathan, Corey, Colin and Ethan in the cockpit while the other Troop Leaders made their way back to their own Kestrel Shuttle and Sarah climbed into her Viper which was landed nearby with the rest of Viper Strike Squadron.

Moments later, The Knightfall rose up off the ground, retracted its landing gear and soared, high into the air, followed by the five Viper Fighters of their escort, en-route to dock with The Scout Hut as the immense cruiser ascended above the clouds, into a burnt-orange sky.

Hey!

I hope you have enjoyed the first story in the Interstellar Scouts book series.

If you want to leave reviews, keep up to date with future releases and follow everything that I am getting up to behind the scenes, the Max Anderson-Hopkins social media pages are listed below.

Facebook
https://m.facebook.com/people/Max-Anderson-Hopkins-Author/100085538948346/

Twitter
@max_a_h_author

Instagram
max_anderson_hopkins

Printed in Great Britain
by Amazon

24155977R00229